THIRD EDITION

ESSENTIALS OF HEALTH CARE FINANCE

William O. Cleverley, PhD
Professor
Hospital and Health Services
Administration Division
Ohio State University
Columbus, Ohio

AN ASPEN PUBLICATION®
Aspen Publishers, Inc.
Gaithersburg, Maryland
1992

This publication is designed to provide accurate and authoritative information in regard to
the Subject Matter covered. It is sold with the understanding that the publisher is not engaged
in rendering legal, accounting, or other professional service. If legal advice or other expert
assistance is required, the service of a competent professional person should be sought.
*(From a Declaration of Principles jointly adopted by a Committee of the American Bar
Association and a Committee of Publishers and Associations.)*

Library of Congress Cataloging-in-Publication Data

Cleverley, William O.
Essentials of health care finance / William O. Cleverley. —3rd ed.
p. cm.
Includes bibliographical references and index.
ISBN: 0-8342-0341-3
1. Hospitals—Finance. 2. Hospitals—Accounting. 3. Health facilities—Finance.
4. Health facilities—Accounting. I. Title. [DNLM: 1. Costs and Cost Analysis.
2. Financial Management. 3. Health Services—economics. W 74 C635e]
RA971.3.C528 1992
362.1'068'1—dc20
DNLM/DLC
for Library of Congress
92-7533
CIP

Editorial Services: Barbara Priest

Library of Congress Catalog Card Number: 92-7533
ISBN: 0-8342-0341-3

Printed in the United States of America

2 3 4 5

*To my children
Michelle, Meredith, and Jamie*

Table of Contents

Preface

This book represents the third edition of a book published in 1978, entitled *Essentials of Hospital Finance*. The second edition, entitled *Essentials of Healthcare Finance*, was published in 1986; and now the third edition, published in 1992, retains that same title.

Throughout all three editions there has been one constant objective. I have tried to create a finance text that makes the jargon and techniques of finance understandable to health care executives and students of health care management. Response to the first two editions has been very good. Sales have been unusually high, which makes both my publisher and my family very happy. Letters and phone calls from purchasers have also been very supportive and also instrumental in the revisions that have been made. I believe that continuing improvements and enhancements have been added in each edition that have increased the overall utility of the book.

The first edition contained seven chapters that, for the most part, dealt with interpreting financial statements in the hospital industry. Between 1978 and 1986, the date of the second edition, major changes in the health care industry took place. The industry became much more diverse and included major organizations other than hospitals. Payment for hospitals shifted from a largely cost-based system to an increasingly competitive, prospectively based one. The second edition was double the size of the first, comprising 14 chapters. Additional examples and illustrations were added that included a variety of health care organizations. Almost all of the material was revised to reflect the new payment environment. Problems and solutions were also added to the end of each chapter in the second edition. This was a revision that resulted from a large number of requests from both health care management students and executives for some way to apply the material in the chapters to specific situations in order to test their understanding and comprehension.

Since 1986, there has been continuing evolution in the health care industry. Changes in payment systems for hospitals, physicians, and others have taken place. Hospitals now have their capital costs paid for on a prospective basis by Medicare. Physicians must now deal with RBRVS (resource-based relative value scales). These changes—along with others —are discussed in Chapter 2 and are reflected throughout the book.

Greater emphasis has been placed on working capital management and short-term cash planning. This trend may be reflective of the increasingly difficult financial position that many health care organizations are experiencing. Two new chapters were added that deal with these topics, which brings the total number of chapters to 16 in the third edition.

Illustrations, problems, and discussion were revised throughout the entire book to be reflective of the current conditions in the health care industry. Although the quantity of material in the book has increased significantly over time, its focus has not changed. The major objective still is to remove some of the mystery that surrounds finance, to make it more easily understood and useful to those present and future health care executives who must manage financially solvent organizations in an increasingly difficult and oftentimes hostile financial environment.

Acknowledgments

I have received the support and assistance of many individuals in the preparation of this book. Without the encouragement and support of these people this book would not have been possible.

One of the greatest sources of satisfaction that a teacher can receive is the expressed gratitude of his or her students. I have been extremely fortunate to have taught finance to a large number of very bright and positive students both at Ohio State University and in countless adult education seminars around the country. Much of the material that is presented in this book is a direct result of my teaching experiences.

Peggy Shields has spent countless hours trying to make sense out of illegible handwriting and sometimes illogical prose. Through it all she maintained her composure and caught numerous errors that hopefully are not part of this book. I want to thank her for her generous expenditure of time and dedication to excellence.

Finally, I want to thank my wife and three children for their understanding, love, and support. They have always helped to make my days brighter and to put life into proper perspective.

Chapter 1

Financial Information and the Decision-Making Process

This book is intended to improve decision makers' understanding and use of financial information in the health care industry. It is not an advanced treatise in accounting or finance but an elementary discussion of how financial information in general and health care industry financial information in particular are interpreted and used. It is written for individuals who are not experienced health care financial executives. Its aim is to make the language of health care finance readable and relevant for general decision makers in the health care industry.

Three interdependent factors have created the need for this book:

1. rapid expansion of the health care industry
2. health care decision makers' general lack of business and financial background
3. financial and cost criteria's increasing importance in health care decisions

The health care industry's expansion is a trend visible even to individuals outside the health care system. The hospital industry, the major component of the health care industry, consumes about 4.5 percent of the gross national product; other types of health care systems, although smaller than the hospital industry, are expanding at even faster rates. Table 1–1 lists the types of major health care institutions and indexes their relative size.

The rapid growth of health care facilities providing direct medical services has substantially increased the numbers of decision makers who need to be familiar with financial information; even greater expansion in the numbers of decision makers indirectly involved in health care has

1

Table 1-1 Health Care Expenditures 1974-1989 (Billions)

	1989	1974	Annual Growth Rate (%)
Total health expenditures	$604.1	$116.3	11.6
Percentage of gross national product	11.6	8.1	2.4
Health services and supplies	$583.5	$108.9	11.8
Personal health care	530.7	101.5	11.7
Hospital care	232.8	45.1	11.6
Physicians' services	117.6	21.2	12.1
Dentists' services	31.4	7.4	10.1
Other professional services	27.0	2.2	18.2
Drugs and medical supplies	44.6	11.0	9.8
Eyeglasses and appliances	13.5	2.8	11.1
Nursing home care	47.9	8.5	12.2
Other health services	15.9	3.3	11.1
Expenses for prepayment and administration	35.3	4.7	14.4
Government public health	17.5	2.7	13.3
Research and construction	20.6	7.5	7.0

Source: Health Care Financing Administration, Office of Financial and Actuarial Analysis, Division of National Cost Estimates.

compounded the need. Most of these decision makers work with health care regulations. Effective decision making in their jobs depends on an accurate interpretation of financial information. Many health care decision makers involved directly in health care delivery—doctors, nurses, dietitians, pharmacists, radiation technologists, physical therapists, inhalation therapists—are medically or scientifically trained but lack education and experience in business and finance. Their specialized education, in most cases, did not include such courses as accounting. However, advancement and promotion within health care organizations increasingly entails assumption of administrative duties, requiring almost instant, knowledgeable reading of financial information. Communication with the organization's financial executives is not always helpful. As a result, nonfinancial executives often end up ignoring financial information.

Governing boards, significant users of financial information, are expanding in size in many health care facilities, in some cases to accommodate demands for more consumer representation. This trend can be healthy for both the community and the facilities. However, many board members, even those with backgrounds in business, are being overwhelmed by financial reports and statements. There are important distinctions between the financial statements of business organizations (with which some board members are familiar) and those of health care facilities that governing board members must recognize if they are to carry out their governing missions satisfactorily.

Decision makers involved in regulation have also multiplied. These decision makers work primarily with quantitative information provided by the facilities they regulate; much of this information is financial, especially that from rate regulatory commissions. Many of these important and influential decision makers have some background in accounting and finance, but it may not be sufficient for their assigned tasks. In most situations, the agency staff serve only as a source of input for decisions that are made by a governing board. These boards usually represent a public constituency and may have little or no understanding of or experience with financial data. It is highly important for these individuals to have some minimum level of financial awareness if effective regulatory decisions are to be made.

The increasing importance of financial and cost criteria in health care decision making is the third factor creating a need for more knowledge of financial information. For many years, accountants and others involved with financial matters have been caricatured as individuals with narrow vision, incapable of seeing the forest for the trees. In many respects, this may have been an accurate portrayal. However, few individuals in the health care industry today would deny the importance of financial concerns, especially cost. Careful attention to these concerns requires *knowledgeable* consumption of financial information by a variety of decision makers. It is not an overstatement to say that inattention to financial criteria can lead to excessive costs and eventually to insolvency.

INFORMATION AND DECISION MAKING

The major function of information in general and financial information in particular is to oil the decision-making process. Decision making is basically the selection of a course of action from a defined list of possible or feasible actions. In many cases, the actual course of action followed may be essentially no action; decision makers may decide to make no change from their present policies. It should be recognized, however, that both action and inaction represent policy decisions.

Figure 1-1 shows how information is related to the decision-making process and gives an example to illustrate the sequence. Generating information is the key to decision making. The quality and effectiveness of decision making depend on accurate, timely, relevant information. The difference between data and information is more than semantic: data

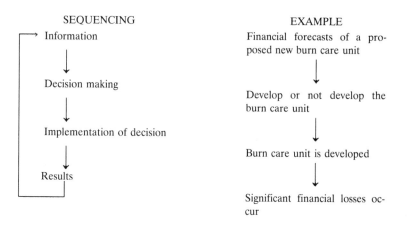

SEQUENCING

Information

Decision making

Implementation of decision

Results

EXAMPLE

Financial forecasts of a proposed new burn care unit

Develop or not develop the burn care unit

Burn care unit is developed

Significant financial losses occur

Figure 1-1 Information in the Decision-Making Process

become information *only* when they are useful and appropriate to the decision. Many financial data never become information because they are not viewed as relevant or are unavailable in an intelligible form.

For the illustrative purposes of the burn care unit example in Figure 1-1, only two possible courses of action are assumed: to build or not to build a burn care unit. In most situations, there may be a continuum of alternative courses of action. For example, a burn care unit might be varied by bed size or facilities included in the unit. In this case, prior decision making seems to have reduced the feasible set of alternatives to a more manageable and limited number of analysis.

Once a course of action has been selected in the decision-making phase, it must be accomplished. Implementing a decision may be extremely complex. In the burn care unit example, carrying out the decision to build the unit would require enormous management effort to ensure that the projected results are actually obtained. Periodic measurement of results in a feedback loop, as in Figure 1-1, is a method commonly used to make sure that decisions are actually implemented according to plan.

As previously stated, results that are forecast are not always guaranteed. Controllable factors, such as failure to adhere to prescribed plans, and uncontrollable circumstances, such as a change in reimbursement, may obstruct planned results.

Decision making is usually surrounded by uncertainty. No anticipated result of a decision is guaranteed. Events may occur that have been analyzed but not anticipated. A results matrix concisely portrays the possible results of various courses of action, given the occurrence of possible events. Table 1-2 provides a results matrix for the sample burn care unit; it shows that approximately 50 percent utilization will enable this

Table 1–2 Results Matrix for the Burn Care Example

	Event		
Alternative Actions	25% Utilization	50% Utilization	75% Utilization
Build unit	$400,000 Loss	$10,000 Profit	$200,000 Profit
Do not build unit	0	0	0

unit to operate in the black and not drain resources from other areas. If forecasting shows that utilization below 50 percent is unlikely, decision makers may very well elect to build.

A good information system should enable decision makers to choose those courses of action that have the highest expectation of favorable results. Based on the results matrix of Table 1–2, a good information system should specifically

- list possible courses of action
- list events that might affect the expected results
- indicate the probability that those events will occur
- estimate the results accurately, given an action/event combination (e.g., profit in Table 1–2)

One thing an information system does not do is evaluate the desirability of results. Decision makers must evaluate results in terms of their organizations' or their own preferences. For example, construction of a burn care unit may be expected to lose $200,000 a year, but it could save a significant number of lives. Weighing these results, or criteria, is purely a decision maker's responsibility—not an easy task, but one that can be improved with accurate and relevant information.

USES AND USERS OF FINANCIAL INFORMATION

As a subset of information in general, financial information is important in the decision-making process. In some areas of decision making, financial information is especially relevant. For our purposes, we identify five uses of financial information that may be important in decision making:

1. evaluating the *financial condition* of an entity
2. evaluating *stewardship* within an entity
3. assessing the *efficiency* of operations
4. assessing the *effectiveness* of operations
5. determining the *compliance* of operations with directives

Financial Condition

Evaluation of an entity's financial condition is probably the most common use of financial information. Usually, an organization's financial condition is equated with its viability or capacity to continue pursuing its stated goals at a consistent level of activity. *Viability* is a far more restrictive term than *solvency*; some health care organizations may be solvent but not viable. For example, a hospital may have its level of funds restricted so that it must reduce its scope of activity but still remain solvent. A reduction in approved rates by a designated regulatory or rate-setting agency may be the vehicle for this change in viability.

Assessment of the financial condition of business enterprises is essential to our economy's smooth and efficient operation. Most business decisions in our economy are directly or indirectly based on perceptions of financial condition. This includes the largely nonprofit health care industry. Although attention is usually directed at organizations as whole units, assessment of the financial condition of organizational divisions is equally important. In the burn care unit example, information on the future financial condition of the unit is valuable. If continued losses from this operation are projected, impairment of the financial condition of other divisions in the organization could be in the offing.

Assessment of financial condition also includes consideration of short-run versus long-run effects. The relevant time frame may change, depending on the decision under consideration. For example, suppliers typically are interested only in an organization's short-run financial condition because that is the period in which they must expect payment. However, investment bankers, as long-term creditors, are interested in the organization's financial condition over a much longer time period.

Stewardship

Historically, evaluation of stewardship was the most important use of accounting and financial information systems. These systems were originally designed to prevent the loss of assets or resources through employees' malfeasance. This use is still very important. In fact, the relatively infrequent occurrence of employee fraud and embezzlement may be due in part to the deterrence of well-designed accounting systems.

Efficiency

Efficiency in health care operations is becoming an increasingly important objective for many decision makers. Efficiency is simply the ratio of outputs to inputs, not the quality of outputs (good or not good) but the lowest possible cost of production. Adequate assessment of efficiency implies the availability of standards against which actual costs may be compared. In many health care organizations, these standards may be formally introduced into the budgetary process. Thus a given nursing unit may have an efficiency standard of 4.3 nursing hours per patient day of care delivered. This standard may then be used as a bench mark by which to evaluate the relative efficiency of the unit. For example, actual employment of 6.0 nursing hours per patient day may cause management to assess staffing patterns.

Effectiveness

Assessment of the effectiveness of operations is concerned with the attainment of objectives through production of outputs, not the relationship of outputs to cost. Measuring effectiveness is much more difficult than measuring efficiency because most organizations' objectives or goals are typically not stated quantitatively. Because measurement of effectiveness is difficult, there is a tendency to place less emphasis on effectiveness and more on efficiency. This may result in the delivery of un-needed services at an efficient cost. For example, development of outpatient surgical centers may reduce costs per surgical procedure and thus create an efficient means of delivery. However, the necessity of those surgical procedures may still be questionable.

Compliance

Finally, financial information may be used to determine whether compliance with directives has taken place. The best example of an organization's internal directives is its budget, an agreement between two management levels regarding use of resources for a defined time period. External parties may also impose directives, many of them financial in nature, for the organization's adherence. For example, rate-setting or regulatory agencies may set limits on rates determined within an organization. Financial reporting by the organization is required to ensure compliance.

Table 1-3 presents a matrix of users and uses of financial information in the health care industry. It identifies areas or uses that may

Table 1–3 Users and Uses of Financial Information

Users	Financial Condition	Stewardship	Efficiency	Effectiveness	Compliance
External					
Health care coalitions	X		X	X	
Unions	X		X		
Rate-setting organizations	X		X	X	X
Creditors	X		X	X	
Third-party payers			X		X
Suppliers	X				
Public	X		X	X	
Internal					
Governing board	X	X	X	X	X
Top management	X	X	X	X	X
Departmental management			X		X

interest particular decision-making groups. It does not consider relative importance.

Not every use of financial information is important in every decision. For example, in approving a health care organization's rates, a governing board may be interested in only two uses of financial information: (1) evaluation of financial condition and (2) assessment of operational efficiency. Other uses may be irrelevant. The board wants to ensure that services are being provided efficiently and that the rates being established are sufficient to guarantee a stable or improved financial condition. As Table 1–3 illustrates, most health care decision-making groups use financial information to assess financial condition and efficiency.

FINANCIAL ORGANIZATION

It is important to understand the management organizational structure of businesses in general and health care organizations in particular. Figure 1–2 outlines the financial management structure of a typical hospital.

The Financial Executives Institute has categorized financial management functions as either controllership or treasurership. Although few health care organizations have specifically identified treasurers and controllers at this time, the separation of duties is important to the

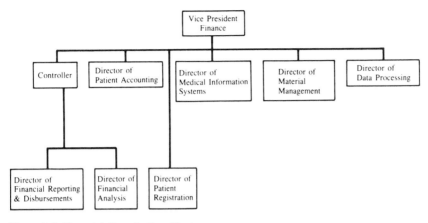

Figure 1–2 Financial Organization Chart

understanding of financial management. The following describes functions in the two categories of the Financial Executives Institute:

1. Controllership
   (a) planning for control
   (b) reporting and interpreting
   (c) evaluating and consulting
   (d) administrating taxes
   (e) reporting to government
   (f) protecting assets
   (g) appraising economic health
2. Treasurership
   (a) providing capital
   (b) maintaining investor relations
   (c) providing short-term financing
   (d) providing banking and custody
   (e) overseeing credits and collections
   (f) choosing investments
   (g) providing insurance

   The effectiveness of financial management in any business is the product of many factors, such as environmental conditions, personnel capabilities, and information quality. A major portion of the total financial management task is the provision of accurate, timely, and relevant information. Much of this activity is carried out through the accounting process.

An adequate understanding of the accounting process and the data generated by it are thus critical to successful decision making.

SUMMARY

The health care sector of our economy is growing rapidly in both size and complexity. Understanding the financial and economic implications of decision making has become one of the most critical areas encountered by health care decision makers. Successful decision making can lead to a viable operation capable of providing needed health care services. Unsuccessful decision making can and often does lead to financial failure. The role of financial information in the decision-making process cannot be overstated. It is incumbent on all health care decision makers to become accounting-literate in our financially changing health care environment.

ASSIGNMENTS

1. Only in recent years have hospitals begun to develop meaningful systems of cost accounting. Why did they not begin such development sooner?

2. Your hospital has been approached by a major employer in your market area to negotiate a preferred provider arrangement. The employer is seeking a 25 percent discount from your current charges. Describe a structure that you might use to summarize the financial implications of this decision. Describe the factors that would be critical in this decision.

3. What type of financial information should be routinely provided to board members?

SOLUTIONS AND ANSWERS

1. Prior to 1983, most hospitals were paid actual costs for delivering hospital services. With the introduction of Medicare's prospective payment system in 1983, hospitals now receive prices based on diagnosis-related groupings that are fixed in advance. Cost control and, therefore, cost accounting are critical in a fixed-price environment.

2. This problem could be set up in a results matrix (see Table 1-2). The two actions to be charted are to accept or to reject the preferred provider arrangement opportunity. Possible events would center on the magnitude of volume changes, for example, to lose 1,000 patient days or to gain 500 patient days. A key concern in estimating the financial impact would be the hospital's incremental revenue and incremental cost positions. In short, how large would the revenue reduction and cost reduction be if significant volume were lost? Actual gains or losses of business would be functions of the hospital's market position.

3. Board members do not need to see detailed financial statements on a routine basis. They need to see financial information that relates to their established plans to ensure that the plans are being met. If significant deviations have occurred, more details may be necessary to take corrective action or to modify established plans.

Chapter 2

Financial Environment of Health Care Organizations

Almost any measure of size would indicate that the health care industry is big business. Its proportion of the gross national product (GNP) has been steadily increasing for several decades and now represents 12 percent of GNP. Paralleling this growth, the pressures for cost control within the system have increased tremendously. Health care organizations that are not able to deal effectively with these pressures face an uncertain future. In short, as the expected demand for health services continues to rise over the next several decades as our population ages, successful health care organizations must become increasingly cost-efficient.

FINANCIAL VIABILITY

A health care organization (HCO) is a basic provider of health services, but it is also a business. The environment of an HCO viewed from a financial perspective could be schematically represented as follows:

In the long run, the HCO must receive dollar payments from the community in an amount at least equal to the dollar payments it makes to its suppliers. In very simple terms, this is the essence of financial viability.

The community in the previous schematic is the provider of funds to the HCO. The flow of funds is either directly or indirectly related to the delivery of services by the HCO. For our purposes, the community may be categorized as follows:

- Patients
    1. Self-payer
    2. Third-party payer
        (a) Blue Cross and Blue Shield
        (b) commercial insurance
        (c) Medicaid
        (d) Medicare
        (e) self-insured employer
        (f) other
- Nonpatients
    1. grants
    2. contributions
    3. tax support
    4. miscellaneous

In most HCOs, the great proportion of funds is derived from patients who receive services directly. The largest percentage of these payments usually comes from third-party sources, such as Blue Cross, Medicare, and Medicaid. In addition, some nonpatient funds are derived from government sources in the form of grants for research purposes or direct payments to subsidized HCOs, such as county facilities. Some HCOs also receive significant sums of money from individuals, foundations, or corporations in the form of contributions. While these sums may be small relative to the total amounts of money received from patients, their importance in overall viability should not be understated. In many HCOs, these contributed dollars mean the difference between net income and loss.

The suppliers in the above schematic provide the HCO with resources that are necessary in the delivery of quality health care. The major categories of suppliers are

- employees
- equipment suppliers
- service contractors
- vendors of consumable supplies
- lenders

Payments for employees usually represent the largest single category of expenditures. For example, in many hospitals, payments for employees represent about 60 percent of total expenditures. Table 2–1 is an actual income statement for a hospital that shows percentages of revenues and expenses. Payments for physicians' services also represent important financial requirements. In addition, lenders such as commercial banks or investment bankers supply dollars in the form of loans and receive from the HCO a promise to repay the loans with interest according to a defined repayment schedule. This financial requirement has grown steadily as HCOs have become more dependent on debt financing.

SOURCES OF OPERATING REVENUE

Table 2–2 provides a historical breakdown of the relative size of the health care industry and its individual industrial segments. The largest segment is the hospital industry, which absorbs about 40 percent of all health care expenditure dollars. This percentage has been declining over the last few years and is expected to decline further as other industry segments grow more quickly. The physician segment absorbs

---

Table 2–1 Statement of Revenues and Expenses for Memorial Hospital, Year Ended 1993 (000s Omitted)

	1993	%
Net patient service revenue	$48,306	96.99
Other operating revenue	1,499	3.01
Total operating revenue	49,805	100.00
Operating expenses		
Salaries and wages	24,189	48.57
Employee benefits	4,174	8.38
Professional fees	1,628	3.27
Supplies and other	15,307	30.73
Depreciation and amortization	3,586	7.20
Interest	819	1.64
Total operating expenses	49,703	99.79
Excess (deficiency) of revenues over expenses from operations	102	0.21
Nonoperating revenue	474	0.95
Excess of revenues over expenses	$ 576	1.16

Table 2-2 National Health Care Expenditures

	1980	1989	Annual Growth Rate (%)
National health care expenditures (billions)	$ 249	$ 604	10.34
Population (millions)	235	257	0.97
Per capita expenditures			
Personal health care			
Hospital care	$ 435	$ 907	8.50
Physicians' services	178	458	11.07
Dentists' services	61	122	8.00
Other professional services	37	105	12.32
Home health care	6	21	16.02
Drugs and other medical nondurables	85	174	8.21
Vision aids and other medical durables	21	53	10.59
Nursing home care	85	187	9.13
Other personal health care	20	41	8.55
Total personal health care	928	2,068	9.31
Program administration and insurance cost	52	138	11.45
Government public health	31	68	9.31
Research and construction	48	80	5.87
Total national health care expenditures	$1,059	$2,354	9.28

Source: Health Care Financing Administration, Office of Financial and Actuarial Analysis, Division of National Cost Estimates.

approximately 19 percent of total health care expenditures; this represents a modest increase over the last decade when expressed as a percentage of total health care expenditures. Nursing homes represent the third largest health care segment, constituting about 8 percent of all health care expenditures. Many individuals believe that future growth will be the fastest in this segment as the population ages.

Table 2-3 depicts the sources of operating funds for the three largest health care segments: hospitals, physicians, and nursing homes. Dramatic differences in financing among these three segments can be seen easily.

The hospital industry derives more than 50 percent of its total funding from public sources, largely Medicare and Medicaid. Of the two, Medicare is by far the larger, representing about 27 percent of all hospital revenue. This gives the federal government enormous control over hospitals and their financial positions. Few hospitals can choose to ignore the Medicare

Table 2-3 Sources of Health Services Funding, 1989

Source	Hospitals	Physicians	Nursing Homes
Private payments (%)			
Out of pocket	5.5	19.0	44.5
Private insurance	36.2	47.7	1.0
Other private	4.9	0.0	1.8
Total private payments	46.6	66.7	47.3
Government payments (%)			
Medicare	26.7	23.3	7.5
Medicaid	9.7	3.6	43.2
Other	17.0	6.4	2.0
Total government payments	53.4	33.3	52.7
Total payments (%)	100.0	100.0	100.0

Source: Health Care Financing Administration, Office of Financial and Actuarial Analysis, Division of National Cost Estimates.

program because of its sheer size. Another 38 percent of total hospital funding results from private insurance (largely Blue Cross), commercial insurance carriers, and self-insured employers. Direct payments by patients to hospitals represent approximately 7.5 percent of total revenue. The implication of this distribution for hospitals is the creation of an oligopsonistic marketplace. The buying power for hospital services is concentrated in relatively few third-party purchasers, namely the federal government, the state government, Blue Cross, a few commercial insurance carriers, and some large self-insured employers.

The physician marketplace is somewhat different from the marketplace for hospital services. A much larger percentage of physician funding is derived from direct payments by patients (approximately 28 percent). And, compared with hospital funding, a slightly larger percentage of physician funding results from private insurance sources, largely Blue Shield and commercial insurance carriers. Physicians derive approximately 44 percent of their total funds from this source, compared with 38 percent in the hospital segment. Public programs, while still significant, are the smallest source of physician funding, representing less than 28 percent of total funds. This situation results because more physician services, such as routine physical examinations and many deductible and copayment services, are excluded from Medicare payment.

The nursing home segment realizes almost no funding from private insurance sources. Its source of funding is split almost equally between public programs and direct payments by or on behalf of patients. The major public program for nursing homes is Medicaid, not Medicare. Medicare payments to nursing homes are largely restricted to skilled nursing care, whereas the majority of Medicaid payments to nursing homes are for intermediate-level care.

HOSPITAL PAYMENT SYSTEMS

One of the most important financial differences between hospitals and other businesses is the way in which their customers or patients make payment for the services they receive. Most businesses have only one basic type of payment: billed charges. Each customer is presented with a bill that represents the product of the quantity of goods or services received and their appropriate prices. Some selective discounting of the price may take place to move slow inventory during slack periods or to encourage large-volume orders. The basic payment system, however, remains the same: a fixed price per unit of service that is set by the business, not the customer.

In contrast, the typical hospital may have four or more different payment systems in effect at any given time. Each of these payment systems has a different effect on the hospital's financial position and might lead to different conclusions with respect to business strategy. It is thus extremely important to understand the financial implications of the various payment systems used by hospitals. The four major payment systems discussed here are

1. historical cost reimbursement
2. specific services (charge payment)
3. negotiated bids
4. diagnosis-related groups

Historical Cost Reimbursement

Until recently, historical cost reimbursement was the predominant form of payment for most hospitals. In addition to Medicare, most state Medicaid plans and a large number of Blue Cross plans paid hospitals on the basis of "reasonable" historical costs. Today, the major payers have abandoned historical cost reimbursement and substituted other payment systems.

Two key elements in historical cost reimbursement are reasonable cost and apportionment. Reasonable cost is simply a qualification introduced by the payer to limit its total payment. Examples of costs often defined as unreasonable and therefore not reimbursable are costs for charity care, patient telephones, and nursing education. Apportionment refers to the manner in which costs are assigned or allocated to a specific payer such as Medicaid. For example, assume that a hospital has total reasonable costs of $10 million, which represent the costs of servicing all patients. If Medicaid is a historical cost reimbursement payer, an allocation or apportionment of that $10 million is necessary to determine Medicaid's share of the total cost. Quite often, the apportionment is related to charges. For example, if charges for services to Medicaid patients were $3 million and total charges to all patients were $15 million, then $\frac{3}{15}$ or 20 percent of the $10 million cost would be apportioned to Medicaid.

Several important financial principles of cost reimbursement should be emphasized. First, cost reimbursement can insulate management somewhat from the financial results of poor financial planning. New clinical programs that do not achieve targeted volume or exceed projected costs may still be viable because of extensive cost reimbursement. This assumes that the payer does not regard the costs as unreasonable. Second, cost reimbursement can often be increased through careful planning, just as taxes can often be reduced through tax planning. The key objective is to maximize the amount of cost apportioned to cost payers subject to any tests for reasonableness.

Specific Services

Usually, a portion of a hospital's patients makes payment based on charges for the specific services provided, such as nursing, surgery, pharmacy, or laboratory. These charges may be regulated by external parties, such as state rate-setting commissions, or they may be completely unregulated and left to the discretion of hospital management. Commercial insurance carriers, self-insured employers, and self-pay patients are usually the largest sources of payment for specific services.

Payment for specific services has several important implications for financial management. First, revenue from specific services may represent the major source of profit to the hospital. In this case, pricing or rate setting becomes an important hospital policy (rate setting is addressed later in this chapter). Second, the hospital's rate structure should be based on projected volume and cost factors. Any unexpected deviation from the hospital's plan merits prompt attention.

Negotiated Bids

Negotiated bids represent a new type of payment for many hospitals. This type of payment results from a specific contractual arrangement between the hospital and a payer. A special contract with a health maintenance organization or a local employer is a common example of a negotiated bid arrangement. In some states, Medicaid might also be considered a source of negotiated-bid revenue. For example, in 1983, California hospitals bid for Medicaid contracts on the basis of rate per patient day. Hospitals that submitted low bids (e.g., a low rate per patient day) would often receive contracts to provide hospital services to Medicaid patients in a given area.

In a negotiated-bid payment environment, financial planning and control are critical—even more critical than in a specific services payment situation. The fee arrangement is usually contractually fixed for a period of time, usually a year. Unexpected increases in costs will not usually be a basis for contract renegotiation. Cost accounting and analysis are also important. It is imperative that management knows what it costs to provide a unit of service required in the contract. For example, if the negotiated bid is to provide all hospital services to subscribers of a health maintenance organization for a fixed fee per subscriber, the hospital must know both the volume and the cost of the required services. Ideally, the cost accounting system should define the incremental costs likely to be incurred in a given contract so that they can be compared to the incremental revenue likely to result from the contract.

Diagnosis-Related Groups

Payment by diagnosis-related groups (DRGs) became universal for hospitals in 1983 when Medicare initiated payment on this basis. Because of the sheer size of the Medicare program in most hospitals, hospital management was quickly forced to become familiar with the DRG payment system. In the Medicare DRG payment system, specific prices are established for 492 specific diagnostic categories. These prices are updated each year by Medicare to reflect inflationary changes.

From the hospital's perspective, the prices established by Medicare are fixed and not appealable. The hospital may decide not to continue providing a given DRG service because it loses money, but it cannot get Medicare to change prices in specific DRGs.

The financial implications of DRG payment are fairly clear. First, cost control becomes critical to long-term financial viability. Hospitals must produce a given DRG at a reasonable cost. There are four primary ways in which cost for a DRG can be reduced:

1. reduce the prices paid for resources
2. reduce the length of stay
3. reduce the intensity of service provided
4. improve production efficiency

Note that two of the four methods for DRG cost reduction involve medical staff decision making, namely reducing length of stay and reducing service intensity. It is thus necessary that hospital management focus more intensely on product lines. Ultimately, hospitals need to analyze the relative profitability of given DRGs comprising particular clinical services, such as psychiatry or surgery. Clearly, cost accounting by DRG is essential to any intelligent analysis of relative DRG profitability. Hospital cost accounting systems are usually structured around departments, such as dietary, laboratory, and physical therapy. However, DRGs require services from a number of departments, and therefore costs must be assigned from these departments to individual DRGs. This is no small problem, and accurate cost information is essential.

RATE SETTING

Stages in the Rate-Setting Process

Rate setting is an extremely complex and important management activity. The success or failure of the organization may ultimately depend on the quality of management decision making in this area. Assuming that reasonably accurate projections of both output and expense are available, there are at least three stages in the rate-setting process:

1. determining required net income
2. determining patient payment composition
3. determining bad debt and charity deductions

In most situations, net income is essential to the viability of the organization. The real issue is how much net income is acceptable. In this short discussion, it is not possible to answer this question in detail. However, in general, the rates must be established at levels that will meet budgeted financial requirements, that is:

Budgeted financial requirements = Total operating revenue

where

$$\text{Total operating revenue} = \text{Gross patient service revenue}$$
$$- \text{Allowances and uncollectables}$$
$$+ \text{Other operating revenue}$$

The required amount of income can now be defined as:

$$\text{Required net income} = \text{Budgeted financial requirements}$$
$$- \text{Budgeted operating expenses}$$

The above calculations ignore the existence of nonoperating revenue. If sizable and stable sums of nonoperating revenue are available, they may be used to subsidize operations. This is clearly an important policy determination and should be made by the board after a careful consideration of projected financial plans.

Budgeted financial requirements are cash requirements or expenditures that an entity must meet during the budget period. These requirements usually comprise four elements:

1. budgeted expenses, excluding depreciation
2. debt principal payments
3. increases in working capital
4. capital expenditures

Budgeted expenses at the departmental level should include both direct and indirect or allocated expenses. Depreciation charges are excluded because depreciation is an expense, not an expenditure; it does not require an actual cash outlay.

Debt principal payments include only the principal portion of debt service due. In some cases, additional reserve requirements may be established, and these may require additional funding. Interest expense is already included in budgeted expenses and should not be included in this category.

Working capital requirements include such things as necessary build-ups in inventory, accounts receivable, and precautionary cash balances. Planned financing of increases in working capital is a legitimate financial requirement.

Capital expenditure requirements may be of two types. First, actual capital expenditures may be made for approved projects. Those projects not financed with indebtedness require a cash investment. Second, prudent fiscal management requires that funds be set aside and invested to meet reasonable requirements for future capital expenditures. This amount should be related to the replacement cost depreciation of existing fixed assets. An HCO should fund some proportion of its replacement cost depreciation.

Determination of the patient payment composition is the next important stage in effective rate setting. It must be remembered that not all patients will actually pay the rates established. Many third-party payers—especially Blue Cross, Medicare, and Medicaid—do not pay billed charges. Therefore, the rate structure should incorporate the effect of these contractual allowances in the establishment of rates.

Finally, estimates of the expected write-off of charges for bad debts and charity care must be made. It is important to emphasize that these elements will be treated as deductions from gross patient service revenue, and not expenses. Although the correct financial reporting of bad-debt expense is to treat it as an expense, there is this option to treat bad debt as a deduction from revenue. Some hospitals may have especially large bad-debt and charity care loads if they serve a high percentage of medically indigent patients.

A Rate-Setting Model

It is possible to develop a very simple but realistic rate-setting model based on the above discussion. In algebraic form, revenue should be determined as follows:

$$\text{Revenue} = \frac{\text{Budgeted expenses} + \text{Desired net income} - \text{Noncharge-paying patient payments}}{\text{Proportion of charge-paying patients}}$$

The following example may help illustrate this formula. Let us assume that a hospital has 20 patients in the following payment categories:

DRG patients	10
Cost-paying patients	4
Charity care patients	1
Charge-paying patients	5
	20

Furthermore, assume that the hospital has budgeted operating expenses of $22,000, or $1,100 per patient, and the DRG payment rate is $1,000 per patient. If the hospital needs to earn a $3,000 net income, it must set its rates as follows:

$$\text{Revenue} = \frac{\$22,000 + 3,000 - 10,000 - 4,400}{.25}$$

$$= \$42,400 \text{ or } \$2,120 \text{ per patient}$$

The following income statement would result if the above expectations were realized:

Gross patient revenue

DRG patients (10 × $2,120)	$21,200
Cost patients (4 × $2,120)	8,480
Charity patients (1 × $2,120)	2,120
Charge patients (5 × $2,120)	10,600
Total	$42,400

Allowances and uncollectables

DRG patients [10 × ($2,120 − $1,000)]	$11,200
Cost patients [4 × ($2,120 − $1,100)]	4,080
Charity patients [1 × ($2,120 − 0)]	2,120
Charge patients [5 × ($2,120 − $2,120)]	0
Total	$17,400

Net patient revenue	$25,000
Operating expenses	$22,000
Net operating income	$ 3,000

A number of conclusions can be drawn from this example. First, rates often may be significantly above actual expenses. The hospital in this example had a rate structure that was almost 100 percent above its expenses, but it realized just $3,000 or 7 percent of its gross patient revenue as income. Health care executives and board members should not be surprised by the occurrence. Second, payer subsidies clearly exist. In this example, charge-paying patients paid almost twice the rate of cost-paying patients ($1,100) and more than twice the rate of DRG patients ($1,000). Third, the impact of charity care is directly related to the marginal cost of providing that care. In our example, removing the one charity care patient with no resulting reduction in expense would change required rates only marginally:

$$\text{Revenue} = \frac{\$22,000 + 3,000 - 10,000 - 4,632}{5/19}$$

$$= \$39,398 \text{ or } \$2,073.60 \text{ per patient}$$

However, removing $1,100 of cost (the average cost of treating one patient) would lead to a sizable reduction in rates:

$$\text{Revenue} = \frac{\$20,900 + 3,000 - 10,000 - 4,400}{5/19}$$

$$= \$36,100 \text{ or } \$1,900 \text{ per patient}$$

Finally, reductions in operating expenses can lead to sizable reductions in required rates if the percentage of cost-paying patients is relatively low. In our example, a 10 percent reduction in operating expense ($2,200) would yield a 17 percent reduction in rate per patient:

$$\text{Revenue} = \frac{\$19,800 + 3,000 - 10,000 - 3,960}{.25}$$

$$= \$35,360 \text{ or } \$1,768 \text{ per patient}$$

Cost reduction has in fact become a primary objective for many hospitals as their percentage of cost payment business declines.

MEDICARE PROSPECTIVE PAYMENT SYSTEM FOR HOSPITALS

It is somewhat risky to describe in detail the mechanics of Medicare's prospective payment system (PPS), given the fact that the system is still evolving. However, the enormous impact that this payment system has on the entire health care system dictates that some attempt be made here to examine its operation and implications. Still, readers are cautioned that the information provided here may not be accurate at the time of reading.

PPS was officially launched by Medicare on October 1, 1983. All hospitals participating in the Medicare program are required to participate in PPS, except

- psychiatric hospitals
- rehabilitation hospitals
- children's hospitals
- long-term care hospitals
- distinct psychiatric and rehabilitation units
- hospitals outside the 50 states
- hospitals in states with an approved waiver

PPS provides payment for all hospital nonphysician services provided to hospital inpatients. This payment also covers services provided by outside suppliers, such as laboratory or radiology units. Medicare makes one comprehensive payment to the hospital, which is then responsible for paying outside suppliers or nonphysician services.

The basis of PPS payment is the DRG system developed by Yale University. The DRG system takes all possible diagnoses from the International Classification of Diseases, 9th Revision, Clinical Modification (ICD-9-CM) system and classifies them into 25 major diagnostic categories based on organ systems. These 25 categories are further broken down into 492 distinct medically meaningful groupings or DRGs (Appendix 2–A contains a list of the 492 DRGs). Medicare contends that the resources required to treat a given DRG entity should be similar for all patients within a DRG category.

Total payments to a hospital under Medicare can be split into the following elements (see Figure 2–1):

- Prospective payments
  1. DRG operating payment
  2. DRG capital payment
- Reasonable cost payments

The DRG operating payment results from the multiplication of the hospital dollar rate and the specific case weight of the DRG. Appendix 2–A provides the most recent case weight for the 492 DRGs. The case weight for DRG #1, Craniotomy, Age > 17 Except for Trauma, is 3.3637. This measure indicates that in terms of expected cost, DRG #1 would cost about 3.3637 times more than the average case. A specific value is assigned to each of the 492 DRGs.

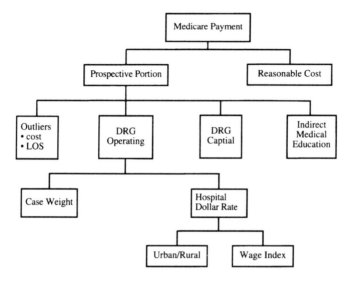

Note: LOS=Length of stay.

Figure 2-1 Breakdown of Medicare Payments to a Hospital

The dollar rate depends on the hospital's designated status as large urban, other urban, or rural. Large urban areas are metropolitan statistical areas with more than 1 million population. Rates for each of these categories are defined once a year by Medicare. Table 2–4 presents hypothetical rates as might be defined by Medicare.

Every hospital in the United States has a wage index value assigned to it. That wage index is multiplied by the labor component of the Medicare standardized payment to yield the DRG operating payment. If we assume that a large urban hospital has a wage index of 1.2509, its DRG operating payment for DRG #1 would be calculated as follows:

$$\$ = DRG\ weight \times [(Labor\ amount \times wage\ index) + Nonlabor\ amount]$$

$$\$ = 3.3637\,[(\$2,527 \times 1.2509) + \$1,041] = \$14,134$$

This dollar payment may be further increased by additional payments to cover the following areas:

- indirect medical education
- disproportionate share
- outlier payments

Table 2–4 Hypothetical Medicare Rates According to Hospital Status

	Rate	
Hospital Status	Labor	Nonlabor
Large urban	$2,527	$1,041
Other urban	2,486	1,025
Rural	2,534	817

An add-on to a teaching hospital is given and referred to as an indirect medical education adjustment. This allowance is related to the numbers of interns and residents at the hospital and the hospital's bed size. The allowance is over and above salaries paid to interns and residents, which are already covered as a reasonable cost. The additional payment is meant to cover the additional costs that the teaching hospital incurs in the treatment of patients.

A separate payment is also provided to a hospital that treats a large percentage of Medicare and Medicaid patients. This payment is referred to as a disproportionate share payment.

Outlier payments are additional payments for patients who use an unusually large amount of resources. There are two categories of outlier payments: (1) cost and (2) day. Cost outliers must be above $44,000, or two times the prospective payment rate for the DRG, whichever is greater. For the example shown above, the threshold would be $44,000, since two times the PPS rate would be $28,268. Day outliers represent cases in which the actual length of stay (LOS) is three standard deviations from the geometric mean LOS, or 32 days from the geometric mean LOS. Appendix 2–A provides the day outlier threshold in the last column. For DRG #1, a patient would need to have an LOS in excess of 44 days before any additional payment would be granted. After the 44th day, a per diem equal to 75 percent of the average cost would be paid. In our illustrative example, a patient who was in the hospital for 68 days would produce the following outlier payment:

$$(68 - 44) \times \frac{\$14,134 \times .75}{12.2} = \$20,853$$

The multiplication by 75 percent reflects the fact that only a portion of the hospital's cost is variable. Medicare assumes that the variable costs of outlier patients are 75 percent; alternatively, it assumes that the fixed costs are 25 percent.

Calculations for cost outliers are quite complex and beyond the scope of this book. As in the case of LOS outliers, only the cost beyond the cutoff point is reimbursed, and then only at 75 percent. For example, a cost outlier with a $84,000 total cost and a cutoff cost value of $44,000 would generate only $30,000 additional reimbursement (.75 × $40,000).

There is still a portion of the total Medicare payment that is related to reasonable cost (see Figure 2–1). Costs that are still paid for on this basis include

- direct medical education costs
- kidney acquisition costs
- bad debts for copayments and deductibles
- outpatient costs

Effective October 1, 1992, Medicare began to pay for capital costs on a prospective basis also. Prior to this date capital costs had been paid for on a reasonable cost basis. There is a ten-year phase-in for capital cost payment that is quite complicated and is not covered here. There is also a floor on capital cost payment that is set at 70 percent of inpatient capital costs. This means that the lowest payment for inpatient capital costs will at least equal 70 percent of the hospital's allocated inpatient capital costs. Capital costs include interest, depreciation, and lease rental costs. Taxes and insurance are also considered capital costs if they are related to capital assets.

There is a national standardized federal payment rate for capital costs that is similar to the national rates for labor and nonlabor costs discussed earlier. In 1992, the federal rate for capital costs was $415.59. This rate would be adjusted for the following factors:

- case mix, using the DRG relative weight
- indirect medical education
- outlier adjustments (the adjustment is much lower than before, to recognize the presumed fixed-cost nature of capital costs)
- disproportionate share adjustment
- geographic adjustment, using the wage index to impute higher costs to higher wage areas
- large urban adjustment of 3 percent, to reflect higher costs

As an illustration, assume that we wish to calculate capital payment for DRG #1 when the federal payment rate was $460.00. We will also assume that our hospital is in a large urban area with a wage index of 1.2509. No other adjustments are applicable. The amount of payment would be

$$\text{Capital payment} = \$460.00 \times 3.3637 \times 1.03 \times 1.2509 = \$1,994.00$$

MEDICARE PAYMENT FOR PHYSICIANS

Beginning in January 1992, Medicare began paying for physician services using a new resource-based relative value scale (RBRVS). This new payment system replaced the old reasonable charge method that had been the basis for physician payment since the inception of the Medicare program in the 1960s. Medicare pays the lesser of the actual billed charge or the fee schedule amount.

From Medicare's perspective, physicians are categorized as participating or nonparticipating physicians. A participating physician is a physician who agrees to accept Medicare's payment for a service as payment in full and will bill the patient for the copayment portion only. The copayment portion is usually 20 percent of the charge. As an example, assume that a patient received a service from a physician that had an approved fee schedule of $100.00. The participating physician would receive $80.00 directly from Medicare and would bill the patient for $20.00, which would represent the copayment portion of the bill. If the physician's bill for the service was only $80.00, Medicare would pay 80 percent, or $64.00, and the patient would be billed 20 percent, or $16.00. A participating physician agrees to accept assignment on each and every Medicare patient that he or she treats.

A nonparticipating physician can choose to accept assignment on a case-by-case basis. While this arrangement initially might seem advantageous, there are several major drawbacks. First, a nonparticipating physician has a lower fee schedule. The limiting charge is equal to 95 percent of the approved fee schedule. If the physician in the illustration just discussed were nonparticipating, the amount of the Medicare payment would be $95, not $100. This difference may not seem all that important if the physician can recover any of the difference from the patient. However, Medicare has placed some limits on the amount that a nonparticipating physician can recover from the patient. Medicare sets a maximum fee for a nonparticipating physician equal to 115 percent of the approved fee for a nonparticipating physician, which is already only 95 percent of the approved fee schedule for a participating physician.

A simple illustration may help to better explain this narrative. Assume that a nonparticipating physician provides services to a patient that have charges of $200, but Medicare's approved schedule for a participating physician is only $100. How much can the physician collect? The answer depends on whether the physician accepts or rejects Medicare assignment. First, assume that the physician rejects assignment. The maximum amount that can be collected from this service is

$$\$109.25 = [.95 \times \$100] \times 1.15$$

The entire amount will come from the patient directly. No check will be sent to the physician from Medicare. The final total payment could be allocated as follows:

Medicare payment to patient (.8 × $95.00)	$76.00
Patient's copayment (.2 × $95.00)	19.00
Additional patient payment	14.25
Total payment to physician	$109.25

The nonparticipating physician can also choose to accept assignment on a case-by-case basis. The advantage realized with assignment is that Medicare will now pay the physician directly for its portion of the bill. The disadvantage is that the physician must accept the fee schedule for nonparticipating physicians, which will only be 95 percent of the fee approved for participating physicians. In the example above, the nonparticipating physician who agreed to accept assignment on this patient would receive the following payments:

Medicare payment to physician (.8 × $95.00)	$76.00
Patient's copayment (.2 × $95.00)	19.00
Total payment to physician	$95.00

The participating physician would be able to receive $100.00 for this service because of the higher approved fee schedule. Of the total $100.00 in payment, $80.00 would come directly from Medicare and $20.00 from the patient as the copayment portion.

At the present time there are Medicare payment rates for almost all of the 7,000 current procedural terminology (CPT) codes. There are specific values for those codes that vary by region; presently there are distinct values for each of the 240 Medicare carrier localities. These payment rates result from the multiplication of three relative values and regional cost indexes. For every procedure there are three components that together reflect the cost of a particular procedure:

1. Work (RVUw)—This factor represents not only physician time involved, but also skill levels, stress, and other factors.
2. Practice expense (RVUpe)—This factor represents nonphysician costs, excluding malpractice costs.
3. Malpractice (RVUm)—This factor represents the cost of malpractice insurance.

Each of the individual relative values is then multiplied by a region-specific set of price indexes. To illustrate this adjustment, the weighted value for coronary artery bypass for Los Angeles is presented in Table 2–5. To determine the payment rate for this procedure in Los Angeles, the index-adjusted relative value would be multiplied by a conversion factor. If we assume that the conversion factor is 26.873, the approved charge for coronary artery bypass in Los Angeles would be $2,231 (83.02 × 26.873).

SUMMARY

Compared with most businesses, health care organizations are financially complex. Not only do they provide a large number of specific services, but their individual services often have different effective price structures. One customer may choose to pay on the basis of cost while

---

Table 2–5 Components of Price Adjustment for Coronary Artery Bypass in Los Angeles

	RVU	Cost Index for Los Angeles	Product
Work	25.63	1.060	27.17
Practice expense	38.90	1.196	46.52
Malpractice	6.81	1.370	9.33
Total			83.02

another may pay full charges. This variation in payment patterns creates problems in the establishment of prices for products and services. Indeed, the revenue function of a typical health care entity is usually much more complex than that of a comparably sized non-health care business.

Health care entities also depend quite heavily on a very limited number of key clients for most of their operating funding. Their largest client is often the federal government or the state government. Doing business with the government involves a significant amount of reporting to ensure compliance and adherence to government regulations. Moreover, since the federal government is such a large purchaser of services, a thorough understanding of the nature and implications of the Medicare payment system's rules and regulations is a must for effective management of a health care organization.

Yet, although health care organizations may be complex from a financial perspective, they are still businesses. Their financial viability requires the receipt of funds in amounts sufficient to meet their financial requirements.

ASSIGNMENTS

1. From the following data, determine the amount of revenue that needs to be generated to meet hospital financial requirements:

Volume	
Medicare cases	1,000
Cost-paying cases	400
Charity care and bad-debt cases	100
Charge-paying cases	500
Total cases	2,000

Financial data	
Budgeted expenses	$6,000,000
Debt principal payment	200,000
Working capital increase	250,000
Capital expenditures	400,000

Present payment structure
- Medicare pays only $2,800 per case, or a total of $2,800,000.
- All other cost payers pay their share of existing expenses.

2. Why is the accumulation of funded reserves for capital replacement more critical for nonprofit health care entities than for investor-owned health care facilities?

3. Rural hospitals receive less payment for specific DRGs than do urban hospitals. What might be the rationale to justify these differences?

4. Depreciation expense is recognized as a reimbursable cost by a number of payers who pay prospective rates for operating costs. Would you prefer accelerated depreciation (sum of the year's digits) or price-level depreciation for a five-year life asset with a $150,000 cost? Assume that inflation is projected to be 6 percent per year.

5. Nonprofit organizations should not make profits; instead, either their rates should be reduced or their services expanded. Evaluate the choices.

6. Using the data from problem 2 above, calculate the impact of a 10 percent reduction in operating expenses, that is, down to $5,400,000, on the required revenue and rate structure. Discuss the implications of your findings.

SOLUTIONS AND ANSWERS

1. The relevant calculation is as follows:

$$\text{Revenue} = \frac{\text{Budgeted expense} + \text{Desired net income} - \text{Noncharge-paying patient payments}}{\text{Proportion of charge-paying patients}}$$

$$\text{Revenue} = \frac{\$6,000,000 + \$850,000 - \$4,000,000}{.25}$$

$$= \$11,400,000 \text{ or } \$5,700 \text{ per case}$$

Desired net income

$$= \$850,000 = \$200,000 + \$250,000 + \$400,000$$

Noncharge-paying patient payments

$$= \text{Medicare payments} + \text{Cost-paying patient payments}$$

$$= \$2,800,000 + \frac{400}{2,000} \times \$6,000,000$$

$$= \$4,000,000$$

$$\text{Proportion of charge-paying patients} = \frac{500}{2,000} = .25$$

2. A nonprofit entity does not have the same opportunities for capital formation that an investor-owned organization does. Specifically, the nonprofit entity cannot sell new shares or ownership interests. It is, by and large, constrained in its ability to replace its assets and expand into new markets, to its accumulated funded reserves, and to new debt. In some special situations nonprofit organizations may receive contributions, but these amounts are usually not significant.

3. The major rationale for urban/rural hospital payment differences relates to severity-of-illness differences. Many individuals believe that urban hospitals are more likely to treat more severely ill patients. Rural hospitals contend that much of the variation is due to differences in the efficiency and effectiveness of care. At this time, it is not clear precisely what the causes of urban/rural hospital cost differences are, but such differences do exist.

4. The relevant comparative data might be as follows:

	Price Level Depreciation*	Sum-of-the-Years Digits Depreciation
Year 1	$ 31,800	$ 50,000
Year 2	33,708	40,000
Year 3	35,730	30,000
Year 4	37,874	20,000
Year 5	40,147	10,000
	$179,259	$150,000

*Depreciation in year $t = \frac{150,000}{5}(1.06)^t$. This term reflects compounding of straight line depreciation at 6 percent per year.

In most cases, price-level-adjusted depreciation would be better. However, for short-lived assets, accelerated depreciation may provide greater levels of reimbursement in earlier years to offset lower returns in later years. The lower the rate of asset inflation, the more desirable accelerated depreciation becomes.

5. Profit is essential to most business organizations because accounting expenses do not equal cash requirements. Additional funds or profit must be available to meet the financial requirements of debt principal payments, increases in working capital, and capital expenditures.

6. The relevant calculation would be as follows:

$$\text{Revenue} = \frac{\$5,400,000 + \$850,000 - \$3,880,000}{.25}$$

$$= \$9,480,000 \text{ or } \$4,740 \text{ per case}$$

A 10 percent reduction in operating expenses permitted a 17 percent reduction in rates ($5,700 to $4,740 per case). Cost control is critical in health care entities, especially in those with relatively low levels of cost payers. A reduction in rates is especially important when competing for major contracts in which price is a predominant determinant.

The Diagnosis-Related Group System of Service Classification

List of Diagnosis-Related Groups (DRGs), Relative Weighting Factors, Geometric Mean Length of Stay (LOS), and LOS Outlier Cutoff Points Used in the Prospective Payment System

DRG #	Major Diagnostic Category	Medical/ Surgical	Definition	Relative Weights	Geometric Mean LOS	Outlier Threshold
1	01	Surg	Craniotomy Age > 17 Except for Trauma	3.3637	12.2	44
2	01	Surg	Craniotomy for Trauma Age > 17	3.3233	11.3	43
3	01	Surg	*Craniotomy Age 0–17	2.8830	12.7	45
4	01	Surg	Spinal Procedures	2.4577	9.9	42
5	01	Surg	Extracranial Vascular Procedures	1.5241	5.5	35
6	01	Surg	Carpal Tunnel Release	.4868	1.9	17
7	01	Surg	Periph & Cranial Nerve & Other Nerv Syst Proc w CC	2.7185	11.6	44
8	01	Surg	Periph & Cranial Nerve & Other Nerv Syst Proc w/o CC	.7730	3.0	35
9	01	Med	Spinal Disorders & Injuries	1.2933	7.1	39
10	01	Med	Nervous System Neoplasms w CC	1.2834	7.7	40
11	01	Med	Nervous System Neoplasms w/o CC	.7545	4.4	36
12	01	Med	Degenerative Nervous System Disorders	.9372	6.9	39
13	01	Med	Multiple Sclerosis & Cerebellar Ataxia	.8524	6.7	39
14	01	Med	Specific Cerebrovascular Disorders Except TIA	1.2173	7.2	39
15	01	Med	Transient Ischemic Attack & Precerebral Occlusions	.6524	4.1	33
16	01	Med	Nonspecific Cerebrovascular Disorders w CC	1.0824	6.6	39
17	01	Med	Nonspecific Cerebrovascular Disorders w/o CC	.6331	4.4	36
18	01	Med	Cranial & Peripheral Nerve Disorders w CC	.8971	5.9	38
19	01	Med	Cranial & Peripheral Nerve Disorders w/o CC	.5735	3.9	36
20	01	Med	Nervous System Infection Except Viral Meningitis	1.9348	8.5	40

continues

List of Diagnosis-Related Groups (continued)

DRG #	Major Diagnostic Category	Medical/ Surgical	Definition	Relative Weights	Geometric Mean LOS	Outlier Threshold
21	01	Med	Viral Meningitis	1.4685	7.5	39
22	01	Med	Hypertensive Encephalopathy	.7190	4.4	35
23	01	Med	Nontraumatic Stupor & Coma	.8715	4.4	36
24	01	Med	Seizure & Headache Age > 17 w CC	.9792	5.3	37
25	01	Med	Seizure & Headache Age > 17 w/o CC	.5252	3.5	28
26	01	Med	Seizure & Headache Age 0–17	.8281	3.4	31
27	01	Med	Traumatic Stupor & Coma, Coma > 1 hr	1.3566	4.3	36
28	01	Med	Traumatic Stupor & Coma, Coma < 1 hr Age > 17 w CC	1.2371	5.9	38
29	01	Med	Traumatic Stupor & Coma, Coma < 1 hr Age > 17 w/o CC	.5525	3.2	35
30	01	Med	*Traumatic Stupor & Coma, Coma < 1 hr Age 0–17	.3496	2.0	17
31	01	Med	Concussion Age > 17 w CC	.7139	4.3	36
32	01	Med	Concussion Age > 17 w/o CC	.4145	2.6	25
33	01	Med	*Concussion Age 0–17	.2427	1.6	9
34	01	Med	Other Disorders of Nervous System w CC	1.1524	5.9	38
35	01	Med	Other Disorders of Nervous System w/o CC	.5648	3.7	36
36	02	Surg	Retinal Procedures	.6434	2.1	12
37	02	Surg	Orbital Procedures	.7951	2.9	35
38	02	Surg	Primary Iris Procedures	.3532	2.1	16
39	02	Surg	Lens Procedures w or w/o Vitrectomy	.4732	1.5	8
40	02	Surg	Extraocular Procedures Except Orbit Age > 17	.5101	2.0	23

41	02	Surg	*Extraocular Procedures Except Orbit Age 0–17	.3613	1.6	7
42	02	Surg	Intraocular Procedures Except Retina, Iris & Lens	.6162	2.1	15
43	02	Med	Hyphema	.3579	3.6	25
44	02	Med	Acute Major Eye Infections	.6119	5.5	36
45	02	Med	Neurological Eye Disorders	.5938	3.5	30
46	02	Med	Other Disorders of the Eye Age > 17 w CC	.6709	4.1	36
47	02	Med	Other Disorders of the Eye Age > 17 w/o CC	.3923	2.7	31
48	02	Med	*Other Disorders of the Eye Age 0–17	.3969	2.9	30
49	03	Surg	Major Head & Neck Procedures	2.2790	7.0	39
50	03	Surg	Sialoadenectomy	.6625	2.2	14
51	03	Surg	Salivary Gland Procedures Except Sialoadenectomy	.5871	2.0	18
52	03	Surg	Cleft Lip & Palate Repair	.7451	2.4	22
53	03	Surg	Sinus & Mastoid Procedures Age > 17	.6590	1.9	20
54	03	Surg	*Sinus & Mastoid Procedures Age 0–17	.6806	3.2	22
55	03	Surg	Miscellaneous Ear, Nose, Mouth, & Throat Procedures	.5134	1.6	14
56	03	Surg	Rhinoplasty	.5444	1.8	15
57	03	Surg	T&A Proc, Except Tonsillectomy &/or Adenoidectomy Only, Age > 17	.8501	3.4	35
58	03	Surg	*T&A Proc, Except Tonsillectomy &/or Adenoidectomy Only, Age 0–17	.3060	1.5	4
59	03	Surg	Tonsillectomy &/or Adenoidectomy Only, Age > 17	.4071	1.5	10
60	03	Surg	*Tonsillectomy &/or Adenoidectomy Only, Age 0–17	.2584	1.5	4
61	03	Surg	Myringotomy w Tube Insertion Age > 17	.8065	2.5	35
62	03	Surg	*Myringotomy w Tube Insertion Age 0–17	.3052	1.3	5
63	03	Surg	Other Ear, Nose, Mouth, & Throat O.R. Procedures	1.0595	3.8	36
64	03	Med	Ear, Nose, Mouth, & Throat Malignancy	1.1190	5.2	37
65	03	Med	Dysequilibrium	.4727	3.3	23
66	03	Med	Epistaxis	.4606	3.3	24
67	03	Med	Epiglottitis	.8708	4.2	32

continues

List of Diagnosis-Related Groups (continued)

DRG #	Major Diagnostic Category	Medical/ Surgical	Definition	Relative Weights	Geometric Mean LOS	Outlier Threshold
68	03	Med	Otitis Media & URI Age > 17 w CC	.7277	5.0	33
69	03	Med	Otitis Media & URI Age > 17 w/o CC	.5156	3.9	23
70	03	Med	Otitis Media & URI Age 0–17	.5295	3.2	32
71	03	Med	Laryngotracheitis	.8197	4.8	37
72	03	Med	Nasal Trauma & Deformity	.5741	3.4	35
73	03	Med	Other Ear, Nose, Mouth, & Throat Diagnoses Age > 17	.7500	4.1	36
74	03	Med	*Other Ear, Nose, Mouth, & Throat Diagnoses Age 0–17	.3386	2.1	20
75	04	Surg	Major Chest Procedures	3.0063	11.5	44
76	04	Surg	Other Resp System O.R. Procedures w CC	2.3804	10.6	43
77	04	Surg	Other Resp System O.R. Procedures w/o CC	1.0289	4.5	36
78	04	Med	Pulmonary Embolism	1.4273	8.7	41
79	04	Med	Respiratory Infections & Inflammations Age > 17 w CC	1.7813	9.2	41
80	04	Med	Respiratory Infections & Inflammations Age > 17 w/o CC	1.0066	6.7	39
81	04	Med	*Respiratory Infections & Inflammations Age 0–17	1.0899	6.1	38
82	04	Med	Respiratory Neoplasms	1.2453	6.7	39
83	04	Med	Major Chest Trauma w CC	.9606	6.2	38
84	04	Med	Major Chest Trauma w/o CC	.4920	3.7	32
85	04	Med	Pleural Effusion w CC	1.1643	6.8	39
86	04	Med	Pleural Effusion w/o CC	.6834	4.3	36
87	04	Med	Pulmonary Edema & Respiratory Failure	1.3851	6.0	38
88	04	Med	Chronic Obstructive Pulmonary Disease	.9942	5.9	38
89	04	Med	Simple Pneumonia & Pleurisy Age > 17 w CC	1.1658	7.1	39
90	04	Med	Simple Pneumonia & Pleurisy Age > 17 w/o CC	.7282	5.4	30

91	04	Med	Simple Pneumonia & Pleurisy Age 0–17	.7846	4.2	36
92	04	Med	Interstitial Lung Disease w CC	1.1997	6.9	39
93	04	Med	Interstitial Lung Disease w/o CC	.8028	5.2	37
94	04	Med	Pneumothorax w CC	1.2472	7.1	39
95	04	Med	Pneumothorax w/o CC	.6108	4.4	35
96	04	Med	Bronchitis & Asthma Age > 17 w CC	.9457	5.9	35
97	04	Med	Bronchitis & Asthma Age > 17 w/o CC	.6450	4.6	26
98	04	Med	Bronchitis & Asthma Age 0–17	.8262	5.5	37
99	04	Med	Respiratory Signs & Symptoms w CC	.7962	4.1	36
100	04	Med	Respiratory Signs & Symptoms w/o CC	.4983	2.6	18
101	04	Med	Other Respiratory System Diagnoses w CC	.9232	5.1	37
102	04	Med	Other Respiratory System Diagnoses w/o CC	.5272	3.3	30
103	05	Surg	Heart Transplant	14.0323	25.2	57
104	05	Surg	Cardiac Valve Procedures w Cardiac Cath	8.2575	18.1	50
105	05	Surg	Cardiac Valve Procedures w/o Cardiac Cath	6.1581	12.7	45
106	05	Surg	Coronary Bypass w Cardiac Cath	5.4470	13.6	46
107	05	Surg	Coronary Bypass w/o Cardiac Cath	4.9616	11.3	43
108	05	Surg	Other Cardiothoracic Procedures	5.9600	12.7	45
109	05		No Longer Valid	.0000	.0	0
110	05	Surg	Major Cardiovascular Procedures w CC	4.2703	10.3	42
111	05	Surg	Major Cardiovascular Procedures w/o CC	2.3980	7.5	40
112	05	Surg	Percutaneous Cardiovascular Procedures	2.0163	4.8	37
113	05	Surg	Amputation for Circ System Disorders Except Upper Limb & Toe	2.6925	14.3	46
114	05	Surg	Upper Limb & Toe Amputation for Circ System Disorders	3.5499	9.0	41
115	05	Surg	Perm Cardiac Pacemaker Implant w AMI, Heart Failure, or Shock	3.6795	11.9	44

continues

List of Diagnosis-Related Groups (continued)

DRG #	Major Diagnostic Category	Medical/ Surgical	Definition	Relative Weights	Geometric Mean LOS	Outlier Threshold
116	05	Surg	Perm Cardiac Pacemaker Implant w/o AMI, Heart Failure, or Shock	2.4973	5.7	38
117	05	Surg	Cardiac Pacemaker Revision Except Device Replacement	1.2743	3.7	36
118	05	Surg	Cardiac Pacemaker Device Replacement	1.6957	2.8	35
119	05	Surg	Vein Ligation & Stripping	.9379	3.5	36
120	05	Surg	Other Circulatory System O.R. Procedures	2.0736	7.4	39
121	05	Med	Circulatory Disorders w AMI & CV Comp Disch Alive	1.6210	8.2	40
122	05	Med	Circulatory Disorders w AMI w/o CV Comp Disch Alive	1.1667	6.0	38
123	05	Med	Circulatory Disorders w AMI, Expired	1.3920	3.0	35
124	05	Med	Circulatory Disorders Except AMI, w Card Cath & Complex Diag	1.1973	4.2	36
125	05	Med	Circulatory Disorders Except AMI, w Card Cath w/o Complex Diag	.7387	2.2	22
126	05	Med	Acute & Subacute Endocarditis	2.8874	16.3	48
127	05	Med	Heart Failure & Shock	1.0070	6.0	38
128	05	Med	Deep Vein Thrombophlebitis	.7906	7.4	33
129	05	Med	Cardiac Arrest, Unexplained	1.2551	2.4	34
130	05	Med	Peripheral Vascular Disorders w CC	.9118	6.1	38
131	05	Med	Peripheral Vascular Disorders w/o CC	.5882	4.5	37
132	05	Med	Atherosclerosis w CC	.7312	4.0	36
133	05	Med	Atherosclerosis w/o CC	.5342	3.0	26
134	05	Med	Hypertension	.5663	3.9	30
135	05	Med	Cardiac Congenital & Valvular Disorders Age > 17 w CC	.8770	4.9	37

136	05	Med	Cardiac Congenital & Valvular Disorders Age > 17 w/o CC	.5434	3.2	27
137	05	Med	*Cardiac Congenital & Valvular Disorders Age 0–17	.6239	3.3	35
138	05	Med	Cardiac Arrhythmia & Conduction Disorders w CC	.8211	4.5	36
139	05	Med	Cardiac Arrhythmia & Conduction Disorders w/o CC	.5149	3.1	23
140	05	Med	Angina Pectoris	.6226	3.7	25
141	05	Med	Syncope & Collapse w CC	.6950	4.3	35
142	05	Med	Syncope & Collapse w/o CC	.5006	3.1	22
143	05	Med	Chest Pain	.5118	2.7	18
144	05	Med	Other Circulatory System Diagnoses w CC	1.0888	5.2	37
145	05	Med	Other Circulatory System Diagnoses w/o CC	.6454	3.4	34
146	06	Surg	Rectal Resection w CC	2.5777	12.4	44
147	06	Surg	Rectal Resection w/o CC	1.6301	9.0	34
148	06	Surg	Major Small & Large Bowel Procedures w CC	3.1804	13.5	46
149	06	Surg	Major Small & Large Bowel Procedures w/o CC	1.5443	8.9	29
150	06	Surg	Peritoneal Adhesiolysis w CC	2.5069	11.4	43
151	06	Surg	Peritoneal Adhesiolysis w/o CC	1.2042	6.7	39
152	06	Surg	Minor Small & Large Bowel Procedures w CC	1.7255	8.7	41
153	06	Surg	Minor Small & Large Bowel Procedures w/o CC	1.0534	6.7	28
154	06	Surg	Stomach, Esophageal, & Duodenal Procedures Age > 17 w CC	4.1746	14.3	46
155	06	Surg	Stomach, Esophageal, & Duodenal Procedures Age > 17 w/o CC	1.5472	7.7	40
156	06	Surg	*Stomach, Esophageal, & Duodenal Procedures Age 0–17	.8281	6.0	38
157	06	Surg	Anal & Stomal Procedures w CC	.9372	4.6	37
158	06	Surg	Anal & Stomal Procedures w/o CC	.4909	2.5	18
159	06	Surg	Hernia Procedures Except Inguinal & Femoral Age > 17 w CC	1.0701	4.9	37

continues

List of Diagnosis-Related Groups (continued)

DRG #	Major Diagnostic Category	Medical/ Surgical	Definition	Relative Weights	Geometric Mean LOS	Outlier Threshold
160	06	Surg	Hernia Procedures Except Inguinal & Femoral Age > 17 w/o CC	.6156	2.9	20
161	06	Surg	Inguinal & Femoral Hernia Procedures Age > 17 w CC	.7382	3.2	34
162	06	Surg	Inguinal & Femoral Hernia Procedures Age > 17 w/o CC	.4476	1.8	11
163	06	Surg	Hernia Procedures Age 0–17	.6612	4.0	33
164	06	Surg	Appendectomy w Complicated Principal Diag w CC	2.1733	9.8	42
165	06	Surg	Appendectomy w Complicated Principal Diag w/o CC	1.2562	6.9	25
166	06	Surg	Appendectomy w/o Complicated Principal Diag w CC	1.2931	6.1	35
167	06	Surg	Appendectomy w/o Complicated Principal Diag w/o CC	.7597	4.0	15
168	03	Surg	Mouth Procedures w CC	1.0601	3.8	36
169	03	Surg	Mouth Procedures w/o CC	.5406	2.0	17
170	06	Surg	Other Digestive System O.R. Procedures w CC	2.7582	11.1	43
171	06	Surg	Other Digestive System O.R. Procedures w/o CC	1.1303	5.3	37
172	06	Med	Digestive Malignancy w CC	1.2549	7.0	39
173	06	Med	Digestive Malignancy w/o CC	.6218	3.6	36
174	06	Med	GI Hemorrhage w CC	.9735	5.5	37
175	06	Med	GI Hemorrhage w/o CC	.5723	3.8	23
176	06	Med	Complicated Peptic Ulcer	1.0235	5.9	38
177	06	Med	Uncomplicated Peptic Ulcer w CC	.7840	5.1	32
178	06	Med	Uncomplicated Peptic Ulcer w/o CC	.5656	3.8	22
179	06	Med	Inflammatory Bowel Disease	1.1141	7.1	39
180	06	Med	GI Obstruction w CC	.9216	5.8	38
181	06	Med	GI Obstruction w/o CC	.4988	3.8	26

182	06	Med	Esophagitis, Gastroent, & Misc Digest Disorders Age > 17 w CC	.7599	4.9	37
183	06	Med	Esophagitis, Gastroent, & Misc Digest Disorders Age > 17 w/o CC	.5198	3.5	25
184	06	Med	Esophagitis, Gastroent, & Misc Digest Disorders Age 0–17	.5125	2.7	18
185	03	Med	Dental & Oral Dis Except Extractions & Restorations, Age > 17	.7766	4.3	36
186	03	Med	*Dental & Oral Dis Except Extractions & Restorations, Age 0–17	.4062	2.9	23
187	03	Med	Dental Extractions & Restorations	.5094	2.3	26
188	06	Med	Other Digestive System Diagnoses Age > 17 w CC	.9846	5.2	37
189	06	Med	Other Digestive System Diagnoses Age > 17 w/o CC	.4697	2.8	30
190	06	Med	Other Digestive System Diagnoses Age 0–17	.7555	4.2	36
191	07	Surg	Pancreas, Liver, & Shunt Procedures w CC	4.4412	15.5	48
192	07	Surg	Pancreas, Liver, & Shunt Procedures w/o CC	1.7379	8.5	41
193	07	Surg	Biliary Tract Proc w CC Except Only Cholecyst w or w/o CDE	3.0275	14.0	46
194	07	Surg	Biliary Tract Proc w/o CC Except Only Cholecyst w or w/o CDE	1.6189	8.8	41
195	07	Surg	Cholecystectomy w CDE w CC	2.2099	10.6	43
196	07	Surg	Cholecystectomy w CDE w/o CC	1.3547	7.6	28
197	07	Surg	Cholecystectomy w/o CDE w CC	1.6872	7.8	40
198	07	Surg	Cholecystectomy w/o CDE w/o CC	.9076	4.5	25
199	07	Surg	Hepatobiliary Diagnostic Procedure for Malignancy	2.4049	11.9	44
200	07	Surg	Hepatobiliary Diagnostic Procedure for Nonmalignancy	2.7960	9.4	41
201	07	Surg	Other Hepatobiliary or Pancreas O.R. Procedures	2.3034	8.8	41
202	07	Med	Cirrhosis & Alcoholic Hepatitis	1.2231	7.2	39
203	07	Med	Malignancy of Hepatobiliary System or Pancreas	1.1784	6.8	39

continues

List of Diagnosis-Related Groups (continued)

DRG #	Major Diagnostic Category	Medical/ Surgical	Definition	Relative Weights	Geometric Mean LOS	Outlier Threshold
204	07	Med	Disorders of Pancreas Except Malignancy	1.0870	6.1	38
205	07	Med	Disorders of Liver Except Malig, Cirr, Alc Hepa w CC	1.2402	6.7	39
206	07	Med	Disorders of Liver Except Malig, Cirr, Alc Hepa w/o CC	.6029	3.7	36
207	07	Med	Disorder of the Biliary Tract w CC	.9732	5.5	37
208	07	Med	Disorder of the Biliary Tract w/o CC	.5532	3.3	26
209	08	Surg	Major Joint & Limb Reattachment Procedures—Lower Extremity	2.3795	10.1	36
210	08	Surg	Hip & Femur Procedures Except Major Joint Age > 17 w CC	1.9386	11.4	43
211	08	Surg	Hip & Femur Procedures Except Major Joint Age > 17 w/o CC	1.3747	9.0	36
212	08	Surg	Hip & Femur Procedures Except Major Joint Age 0–17	.9139	4.0	36
213	08	Surg	Amputation for Musculoskeletal System & Conn Tissue Disorders	1.7471	9.4	41
214	08	Surg	Back & Neck Procedures w CC	1.8748	8.9	41
215	08	Surg	Back & Neck Procedures w/o CC	1.1156	5.8	33
216	08	Surg	Biopsies of Musculoskeletal System & Connective Tissue	2.0321	10.1	42
217	08	Surg	Wound Debrid & Skin Graft Except Hand, for Musceskelet & Conn Tiss Dis	3.1641	14.1	46
218	08	Surg	Lower Extrem & Humer Proc Except Hip, Foot, Femur Age > 17 w CC	1.4112	7.2	39
219	08	Surg	Lower Extrem & Humer Proc Except Hip, Foot, Femur Age > 17 w/o CC	.8977	4.6	29

220	08	Surg	*Lower Extrem & Humer Proc Except Hip, Foot, Femur Age 0–17	.9130	5.3	37
221	08	Surg	Knee Procedures w CC	1.8350	7.7	40
222	08	Surg	Knee Procedures w/o CC	.9721	3.9	36
223	08	Surg	Major Shoulder/Elbow Proc, or Other Upper Extremity Proc w CC	.8044	3.3	25
224	08	Surg	Shoulder, Elbow or Forearm Proc, Exc Major Joint Proc, w/o CC	.6306	2.5	15
225	08	Surg	Foot Procedures	.7825	3.3	35
226	08	Surg	Soft Tissue Procedures w CC	1.3613	6.1	38
227	08	Surg	Soft Tissue Procedures w/o CC	.6791	2.9	25
228	08	Surg	Major Thumb or Joint Proc, or Other Hand or Wrist Proc w CC	.8015	2.6	28
229	08	Surg	Hand or Wrist Proc, Except Major Joint Proc, w/o CC	.5403	1.9	16
230	08	Surg	Local Excision & Removal of Int Fix Devices of Hip & Femur	.9278	4.1	36
231	08	Surg	Local Excision & Removal of Int Fix Devices Except Hip & Femur	1.0817	4.0	36
232	08	Surg	Arthroscopy	1.2448	4.0	36
233	08	Surg	Other Musculoskelet Sys & Conn Tiss O.R. Proc w CC	1.9873	9.0	41
234	08	Surg	Other Musculoskelet Sys & Conn Tiss O.R. Proc w/o CC	1.0365	4.6	37
235	08	Med	Fractures of Femur	1.0974	7.4	39
236	08	Med	Fractures of Hip & Pelvis	.8428	6.6	39
237	08	Med	Sprains, Strains, & Dislocations of Hip, Pelvis, & Thigh	.5583	4.4	36
238	08	Med	Osteomyelitis	1.5884	10.6	43
239	08	Med	Pathological Fractures & Musculoskeletal & Conn Tiss Malignancy	1.0269	7.5	40
240	08	Med	Connective Tissue Disorders w CC	1.1486	7.1	39

continues

List of Diagnosis-Related Groups (continued)

DRG #	Major Diagnostic Category	Medical/ Surgical	Definition	Relative Weights	Geometric Mean LOS	Outlier Threshold
241	08	Med	Connective Tissue Disorders w/o CC	.5704	4.5	36
242	08	Med	Septic Arthritis	1.2558	8.2	40
243	08	Med	Medical Back Problems	.6672	5.0	37
244	08	Med	Bone Diseases & Specific Arthropathies w CC	.7665	5.4	37
245	08	Med	Bone Diseases & Specific Arthropathies w/o CC	.5434	4.0	36
246	08	Med	Nonspecific Arthropathies	.5872	4.4	36
247	08	Med	Signs & Symptoms of Musculoskeletal System & Conn Tissue	.5445	3.6	36
248	08	Med	Tendonitis, Myositis, & Bursitis	.6673	4.6	37
249	08	Med	Aftercare, Musculoskeletal System & Connective Tissue	.7156	4.3	36
250	08	Med	Fx, Sprn, Strn, & Disl of Forearm, Hand, Foot Age > 17 w CC	.7021	4.5	37
251	08	Med	Fx, Sprn, Strn, & Disl of Forearm, Hand, Foot Age > 17 w/o CC	.4291	2.5	24
252	08	Med	*Fx, Sprn, Strn, & Disl of Forearm, Hand, Foot Age 0–17	.3454	1.8	15
253	08	Med	Fx, Sprn, Strn, & Disl of Upper Arm, Lower Leg, Exc Foot Age > 17 w CC	.7885	5.8	38
254	08	Med	Fx, Sprn, Strn, & Disl of Upper Arm, Lower Leg, Exc Foot Age > 17 w/o CC	.4238	3.5	35
255	08	Med	*Fx, Sprn, Strn, & Disl of Upper Arm, Lower Leg, Exc Foot Age 0–17	.4582	2.9	35
256	08	Med	Other Musculoskeletal System & Connective Tissue Diagnoses	.6409	3.8	36
257	09	Surg	Total Mastectomy for Malignancy w CC	.9024	4.6	24

258	09	Surg	Total Mastectomy for Malignancy w/o CC	.7057	3.6	15
259	09	Surg	Subtotal Mastectomy for Malignancy w CC	.9073	4.0	36
260	09	Surg	Subtotal Mastectomy for Malignancy w/o CC	.5720	2.4	14
261	09	Surg	Breast Proc for Nonmalignancy Except Biopsy & Local Excision	.6749	2.2	15
262	09	Surg	Breast Biopsy & Local Excision for Nonmalignancy	.4944	1.9	18
263	09	Surg	Skin Graft &/or Debrid for Skin Ulcer or Cellulitis w CC	2.6866	15.2	47
264	09	Surg	Skin Graft &/or Debrid for Skin Ulcer or Cellulitis w/o CC	1.2982	8.6	41
265	09	Surg	Skin Graft &/or Debrid Except for Skin Ulcer or Cellulitis w CC	1.3860	6.1	38
266	09	Surg	Skin Graft &/or Debrid for Skin Ulcer or Cellulitis w/o CC	.6814	3.0	35
267	09	Surg	Perianal & Pilonidal Procedures	.5922	2.7	35
268	09	Surg	Skin, Subcutaneous Tissue, & Breast Plastic Procedures	.7194	2.5	34
269	09	Surg	Other Skin, Subcut Tissue, & Breast Procedure w CC	1.6600	8.1	40
270	09	Surg	Other Skin, Subcut Tissue, & Breast Procedure w/o CC	.6551	2.9	35
271	09	Med	Skin Ulcers	1.2480	8.8	41
272	09	Med	Major Skin Disorders w CC	1.0789	7.4	39
273	09	Med	Major Skin Disorders w/o CC	.6575	5.4	37
274	09	Med	Malignant Breast Disorders w CC	1.1312	6.6	39
275	09	Med	Malignant Breast Disorders w/o CC	.5870	3.3	35
276	09	Med	Nonmalignant Breast Disorders	.5731	3.7	36
277	09	Med	Cellulitis Age > 17 w CC	.9198	7.0	39
278	09	Med	Cellulitis Age > 17 w/o CC	.6129	5.3	30
279	09	Med	*Cellulitis Age 0–17	.7278	4.2	24
280	09	Med	Trauma to the Skin, Subcut Tissue, & Breast Age > 17 w CC	.6639	4.6	37

continues

List of Diagnosis-Related Groups (continued)

DRG #	Major Diagnostic Category	Medical/ Surgical	Definition	Relative Weights	Geometric Mean LOS	Outlier Threshold
281	09	Med	Trauma to the Skin, Subcut Tissue, & Breast Age > 17 w/o CC	.4167	3.1	30
282	09	Med	*Trauma to the Skin, Subcut Tissue, & Breast Age 0–17	.3383	2.2	19
283	09	Med	Minor Skin Disorders w CC	.7350	5.2	37
284	09	Med	Minor Skin Disorders w/o CC	.4410	3.6	34
285	10	Surg	Amputat of Lower Limb for Endocrine, Nutrit, & Metabol Disorders	2.7210	15.1	47
286	10	Surg	Adrenal & Pituitary Procedures	2.4320	9.5	41
287	10	Surg	Skin Grafts & Wound Debrid for Endoc, Nutrit, & Metab Disorders	2.2533	13.4	45
288	10	Surg	O.R. Procedures for Obesity	1.8810	6.9	39
289	10	Surg	Parathyroid Procedures	1.0079	4.0	36
290	10	Surg	Thyroid Procedures	.7491	2.8	17
291	10	Surg	Thyroglossal Procedures	.4416	1.7	8
292	10	Surg	Other Endocrine, Nutrit & Metab O.R. Proc w CC	2.8387	12.1	44
293	10	Surg	Other Endocrine, Nutrit & Metab O.R. Proc w/o CC	1.1528	5.5	37
294	10	Med	Diabetes Age > 35	.7516	5.8	38
295	10	Med	Diabetes Age 0–35	.7400	4.4	36
296	10	Med	Nutritional & Misc Metabolic Disorders Age > 17 w CC	.9378	6.0	38
297	10	Med	Nutritional & Misc Metabolic Disorders Age > 17 w/o CC	.5303	4.0	31
298	10	Med	Nutritional & Misc Metabolic Disorders Age 0–17	.5396	2.7	30
299	10	Med	Inborn Errors of Metabolism	.8598	4.8	37
300	10	Med	Endocrine Disorders w CC	1.1191	6.9	39

301	10	Med	Endocrine Disorders w/o CC	.5923	4.1	36
302	11	Surg	Kidney Transplant	3.8891	13.9	46
303	11	Surg	Kidney, Ureter, & Major Bladder Procedures for Neoplasm	2.6645	11.5	43
304	11	Surg	Kidney, Ureter, & Major Bladder Proc for Non-Neopl w CC	2.3986	10.1	42
305	11	Surg	Kidney, Ureter, & Major Bladder Proc for Non-Neopl w/o CC	1.1821	5.3	37
306	11	Surg	Prostatectomy w CC	1.2922	6.9	39
307	11	Surg	Prostatectomy w/o CC	.7100	4.0	23
308	11	Surg	Minor Bladder Procedures w CC	1.4341	6.4	38
309	11	Surg	Minor Bladder Procedures w/o CC	.7375	3.2	31
310	11	Surg	Transurethral Procedures w CC	.8792	3.9	36
311	11	Surg	Transurethral Procedures w/o CC	.5182	2.3	16
312	11	Surg	Urethral Procedures Age > 17 w CC	.8174	3.8	36
313	11	Surg	Urethral Procedures Age > 17 w/o CC	.4607	2.1	17
314	11	Surg	*Urethral Procedures Age 0–17	.4271	2.3	26
315	11	Surg	Other Kidney & Urinary Tract O.R. Procedures	2.1027	7.0	39
316	11	Med	Renal Failure	1.2814	6.3	38
317	11	Med	Admit for Renal Dialysis	.4825	2.5	33
318	11	Med	Kidney & Urinary Tract Neoplasms w CC	1.0908	6.0	38
319	11	Med	Kidney & Urinary Tract Neoplasms w/o CC	.5455	2.6	32
320	11	Med	Kidney & Urinary Tract Infections Age > 17 w CC	1.0002	6.7	39
321	11	Med	Kidney & Urinary Tract Infections Age > 17 w/o CC	.6346	4.9	28
322	11	Med	Kidney & Urinary Tract Infections Age 0–17	.6334	4.6	35
323	11	Med	Urinary Stones w CC &/or ESW Lithotripsy	.7422	3.0	32
324	11	Med	Urinary Stones w/o CC	.3898	2.1	14
325	11	Med	Kidney & Urinary Tract Signs & Symptoms Age > 17 w CC	.6673	4.3	36

continues

List of Diagnosis-Related Groups (continued)

DRG #	Major Diagnostic Category	Medical/ Surgical	Definition	Relative Weights	Geometric Mean LOS	Outlier Threshold
326	11	Med	Kidney & Urinary Tract Signs & Symptoms Age > 17 w/o CC	.4219	2.9	25
327	11	Med	*Kidney & Urinary Tract Signs & Symptoms Age 0–17	.5444	3.1	32
328	11	Med	Urethral Stricture Age > 17 w CC	.6143	3.6	36
329	11	Med	Urethral Stricture Age > 17 w/o CC	.3978	2.0	18
330	11	Med	*Urethral Stricture Age 0–17	.2754	1.6	9
331	11	Med	Other Kidney & Urinary Tract Diagnoses Age > 17 w CC	.9566	5.3	37
332	11	Med	Other Kidney & Urinary Tract Diagnoses Age > 17 w/o CC	.5340	3.0	35
333	11	Med	Other Kidney & Urinary Tract Diagnoses Age 0–17	.9094	4.8	37
334	12	Surg	Major Male Pelvic Procedures w CC	1.7509	8.9	32
335	12	Surg	Major Male Pelvic Procedures w/o CC	1.3574	7.4	21
336	12	Surg	Transurethral Prostatectomy w CC	.9005	5.0	26
337	12	Surg	Transurethral Prostatectomy w/o CC	.6163	3.7	13
338	12	Surg	Testes Procedures, for Malignancy	.7776	2.9	35
339	12	Surg	Testes Procedures, Nonmalignancy Age > 17	.6382	2.5	35
340	12	Surg	Testes Procedures, Nonmalignancy Age 0–17	.4283	2.4	13
341	12	Surg	Penis Procedures	.9615	3.3	25
342	12	Surg	Circumcision Age > 17	.5955	2.5	35
343	12	Surg	Circumcision Age 0–17	.3742	1.7	6
344	12	Surg	Other Male Reproductive System O.R. Procedures for Malignancy	1.0492	4.4	36

345	12	Surg	Other Male Reproductive System O.R. Proc Except for Malignancy	.7263	3.3	35
346	12	Med	Malignancy, Male Reproductive System, w CC	.9609	5.8	38
347	12	Med	Malignancy, Male Reproductive System, w/o CC	.5016	2.7	35
348	12	Med	Benign Prostatic Hypertrophy w CC	.6709	3.9	36
349	12	Med	Benign Prostatic Hypertrophy w/o CC	.4049	2.3	20
350	12	Med	Inflammation, Male Reproductive System	.6731	4.9	28
351	12	Med	*Sterilization, Male	.3293	1.3	5
352	12	Med	Other Male Reproductive System Diagnoses	.5838	3.3	35
353	13	Surg	Pelvic Evisceration, Radical Hysterectomy, & Radical Vulvectomy	2.0590	10.1	42
354	13	Surg	Uterine, Adnexa Proc for Non-Ovarian/Adnexal Malig w CC	1.3909	7.2	33
355	13	Surg	Uterine, Adnexa Proc for Non-Ovarian/Adnexal Malig w/o CC	.8562	5.0	13
356	13	Surg	Female Reproductive System Reconstructive Procedures	.7076	4.1	17
357	13	Surg	Uterine & Adnexa Proc for Ovarian or Adnexal Malig	2.2167	10.2	42
358	13	Surg	Uterine & Adnexa Proc for Nonmalignancy w CC	1.1104	6.0	23
359	13	Surg	Uterine & Adnexa Proc for Nonmalignancy w/o CC	.7823	4.6	12
360	13	Surg	Vagina, Cervix & Vulva Procedures	.7757	4.1	30
361	13	Surg	Laparoscopy & Incisional Tubal Interruption	.8512	3.3	35
362	13	Surg	*Endoscopic Tubal Interruption	.4921	1.4	5
363	13	Surg	D&C, Conization, & Radio Implant, for Malignancy	.6440	3.1	28
364	13	Surg	D&C, Conization, Except for Malignancy	.5295	2.5	28
365	13	Surg	Other Female Reproductive System O.R. Procedures	1.6878	7.4	39
366	13	Med	Malignancy, Female Reproductive System w CC	1.1681	6.6	39

continues

List of Diagnosis-Related Groups (continued)

DRG #	Major Diagnostic Category	Medical/ Surgical	Definition	Relative Weights	Geometric Mean LOS	Outlier Threshold
367	13	Med	Malignancy, Female Reproductive System w/o CC	.4953	2.9	35
368	13	Med	Infections, Female Reproductive System	.9233	6.0	38
369	13	Med	Menstrual & Other Female Reproductive System Disorders	.5274	3.2	35
370	14	Surg	Cesarean Section w CC	1.0237	5.8	37
371	14	Surg	Cesarean Section w/o CC	.6456	4.1	11
372	14	Med	Vaginal Delivery w Complicating Diagnoses	.5235	3.3	30
373	14	Med	Vaginal Delivery w/o Complicating Diagnoses	.3169	2.1	8
374	14	Surg	Vaginal Delivery w Sterilization &/or D&C	.5045	2.5	9
375	14	Surg	*Vaginal Delivery w O.R. Proc Except Steril &/or D&C	.6735	4.4	29
376	14	Med	Postpartum & Post Abortion Diagnoses w/o O.R. Procedure	.3764	2.5	23
377	14	Surg	Postpartum & Post Abortion Diagnoses w O.R. Procedure	1.0278	3.1	35
378	14	Med	Ectopic Pregnancy	.7532	3.9	14
379	14	Med	Threatened Abortion	.2892	2.1	16
380	14	Med	Abortion w/o D&C	.2720	1.4	9
381	14	Surg	Abortion w D&C, Aspiration Curettage, or Hysterotomy	.3827	1.6	11
382	14	Med	False Labor	.1251	1.2	5
383	14	Med	Other Antepartum Diagnoses w Medical Complications	.3934	3.3	31
384	14	Med	Other Antepartum Diagnoses w/o Medical Complications	.3027	2.2	21
385	15	Med	*Neonates, Died or Transferred to Another Acute Care Facility	1.2084	1.8	34
386	15	Med	*Extreme Immaturity or Respiratory Distress Syndrome, Neonate	3.6039	17.9	50
387	15	Med	*Prematurity w Major Problems	1.8046	13.3	45

DRG	MDC	Type	Description			
388	15	Med	*Prematurity w/o Major Problems	1.1431	8.6	41
389	15	Med	Full Term Neonate w Major Problems	1.3846	6.1	38
390	15	Med	Neonate w Other Significant Problems	.8422	4.1	36
391	15	Med	*Normal Newborn	.2191	3.1	11
392	16	Surg	Splenectomy Age > 17	3.2912	11.6	44
393	16	Surg	*Splenectomy Age 0–17	1.5022	9.1	41
394	16	Surg	Other O.R. Procedures of Blood and Blood-Forming Organs	1.5719	5.7	38
395	16	Med	Red Blood Cell Disorders Age > 17	.7679	4.6	37
396	16	Med	Red Blood Cell Disorders Age 0–17	.5246	2.4	34
397	16	Med	Coagulation Disorders	1.2128	5.5	37
398	16	Med	Reticuloendothelial & Immunity Disorders w CC	1.2080	6.6	39
399	16	Med	Reticuloendothelial & Immunity Disorders w/o CC	.6661	4.0	36
400	17	Surg	Lymphoma & Leukemia w Major O.R. Procedure	2.5985	9.5	41
401	17	Surg	Lymphoma & Nonacute Leukemia w Other O.R. Proc w CC	2.2510	10.3	42
402	17	Surg	Lymphoma & Nonacute Leukemia w Other O.R. Proc w/o CC	.8701	3.6	36
403	17	Med	Lymphoma & Nonacute Leukemia w CC	1.6125	8.1	40
404	17	Med	Lymphoma & Nonacute Leukemia w/o CC	.7282	3.9	36
405	17	Med	*Acute Leukemia w/o Major O.R. Procedure Age 0–17	1.0281	4.9	37
406	17	Surg	Myeloprolif Disord or Poorly Diff Neopl w Maj O.R. Proc w CC	2.6566	10.9	43
407	17	Surg	Myeloprolif Disord or Poorly Diff Neopl w Maj O.R. Proc w/o CC	1.1519	5.3	37
408	17	Surg	Myeloprolif Disord or Poorly Diff Neopl w Other O.R. Proc	1.1046	4.3	36
409	17	Med	Radiotherapy	1.0094	6.4	38
410	17	Med	Chemotherapy w/o Acute Leukemia as Secondary Diagnosis	.5540	2.8	19
411	17	Med	History of Malignancy w/o Endoscopy	.4569	2.6	33

continues

List of Diagnosis-Related Groups (continued)

DRG #	Major Diagnostic Category	Medical/ Surgical	Definition	Relative Weights	Geometric Mean LOS	Outlier Threshold
412	17	Med	History of Malignancy w Endoscopy	.4216	2.1	21
413	17	Med	Other Myeloprolif Dis or Poorly Diff Neopl Diag w CC	1.3299	7.5	40
414	17	Med	Other Myeloprolif Dis or Poorly Diff Neopl Diag w/o CC	.7231	4.3	36
415	18	Surg	O.R. Procedure for Infectious & Parasitic Diseases	3.6042	14.9	47
416	18	Med	Septecemia Age > 17	1.5308	7.5	40
417	18	Med	Septecemia Age 0–17	1.0315	5.1	37
418	18	Med	Postoperative & Post-Traumatic Infections	.9585	6.5	39
419	18	Med	Fever of Unknown Origin Age > 17 w CC	.9548	5.8	38
420	18	Med	Fever of Unknown Origin Age > 17 w/o CC	.6484	4.5	30
421	18	Med	Viral Illness Age > 17	.6667	4.4	32
422	18	Med	Viral Illness & Fever of Unknown Origin Age 0–17	.5916	4.0	33
423	18	Med	Other Infectious & Parasitic Diseases Diagnoses	1.6240	8.2	40
424	19	Surg	O.R. Procedure w Principal Diagnoses of Mental Illness	2.3695	12.6	45
425	19	Med	Acute Adjust React & Disturbances of Psychosocial Dysfunction	.7113	4.7	37
426	19	Med	Depressive Neuroses	.6241	5.5	37
427	19	Med	Neuroses Except Depressive	.6028	5.2	37
428	19	Med	Disorders of Personality & Impulse Control	.7831	6.6	39
429	19	Med	Organic Disturbances & Mental Retardation	.9342	7.6	40
430	19	Med	Psychoses	.9074	8.8	41
431	19	Med	Childhood Mental Disorders	.7355	6.1	38
432	19	Med	Other Mental Disorder Diagnoses	.6960	4.3	36

433	20	Med	Alcohol/Drug Abuse or Dependence, Left AMA	.3754	3.1	35
434	20	Med	Alc/Drug Abuse or Dependence, Detox, or Other Sympt Trt w CC	.7689	5.6	38
435	20	Med	Alc/Drug Abuse or Dependence, Detox, or Other Sympt Trt w/o CC	.5141	4.7	37
436	20	Med	Alc/Drug Dependence w Rehabilitation Therapy	1.0782	16.4	48
437	20	Med	Alc/Drug Dependence, Combined Rehab & Detox Therapy	1.1775	15.1	47
438			No Longer Valid	.0000	.0	0
439	21	Surg	Skin Grafts for Injuries	1.5267	6.5	38
440	21	Surg	Wound Debridements for Injuries	1.8492	8.4	40
441	21	Surg	Hand Procedures for Injuries	.6872	2.4	27
442	21	Surg	Other O.R. Procedures for Injuries w CC	1.9377	6.2	38
443	21	Surg	Other O.R. Procedures for Injuries w/o CC	.7595	2.7	32
444	21	Med	Traumatic Injury Age > 17 w CC	.7566	5.2	37
445	21	Med	Traumatic Injury Age > 17 w/o CC	.4911	3.6	30
446	21	Med	*Traumatic Injury Age 0–17	.4738	2.4	22
447	21	Med	Allergic Reactions Age > 17	.4776	2.6	24
448	21	Med	*Allergic Reactions Age 0–17	.3428	2.9	17
449	21	Med	Poisoning & Toxic Effects of Drugs Age > 17 w CC	.7867	4.2	36
450	21	Med	Poisoning & Toxic Effects of Drugs Age > 17 w/o CC	.4428	2.5	25
451	21	Med	*Poisoning & Toxic Effects of Drugs Age 0–17	.5126	2.1	17
452	21	Med	Complications of Treatment w CC	.8184	4.2	36
453	21	Med	Complications of Treatment w/o CC	.4177	2.8	25
454	21	Med	Other Injury, Poisoning, & Toxic Eff Diag w CC	.9096	4.4	36
455	21	Med	Other Injury, Poisoning, & Toxic Eff Diag w/o CC	.4187	2.5	25
456	22	Med	Burns, Transferred to Another Acute Care Facility	2.0198	5.6	38
457	22	Med	Extensive Burns w/o O.R. Procedure	1.6731	3.0	35

continues

List of Diagnosis-Related Groups (continued)

DRG #	Major Diagnostic Category	Medical/ Surgical	Definition	Relative Weights	Geometric Mean LOS	Outlier Threshold
458	22	Surg	Nonextensive Burns w Skin Graft	3.9835	16.3	48
459	22	Surg	Nonextensive Burns w Wound Debridement or Other O.R. Proc	1.9637	10.5	43
460	22	Med	Nonextensive Burns w/o O.R. Procedure	1.0435	6.4	38
461	23	Surg	O.R. Proc w Diagnoses of Other Contact w Health Services	.8268	2.5	34
462	23	Med	Rehabilitation	1.8346	14.2	46
463	23	Med	Signs & Symptoms w CC	.7297	5.0	37
464	23	Med	Signs & Symptoms w/o CC	.4495	3.1	28
465	23	Med	Aftercare w History of Malignancy as Secondary Diagnosis	.3706	1.9	19
466	23	Med	Aftercare w/o History of Malignancy as Secondary Diagnosis	.5693	2.6	35
467	23	Med	Other Factors Influencing Health Status	.4303	2.5	35
468			Extensive O.R. Procedure Unrelated to Principal Diagnosis	3.4238	13.3	45
469			†Principal Diagnosis Invalid as Discharge Diagnosis	.0000	.0	0
470			†Ungroupable	.0000	.0	0
471	08	Surg	Bilateral or Multiple Major Joint Procs of Lower Extremity	3.9623	13.3	45
472	22	Surg	Extensive Burns w O.R. Procedure	13.9563	22.8	55
473	17	Med	Acute Leukemia w/o Major O.R. Procedure Age > 17	3.3381	9.8	42
474	04		No Longer Valid	.0000	.0	0
475	04	Med	Respiratory System Diagnosis w Ventilator Support	3.6094	9.8	42
476			Prostatic O.R. Procedure Unrelated to Principal Diagnosis	2.2175	14.3	46
477			Nonextensive O.R. Procedure Unrelated to Principal Diagnosis	1.4338	6.1	38

478	05	Surg	Other Vascular Procedures w CC	2.2177	7.2	39
479	05	Surg	Other Vascular Procedures w/o CC	1.3259	4.4	36
480		Surg	Liver Transplant	22.8213	36.6	69
481		Surg	Bone Marrow Transplant	15.2890	37.8	70
482		Surg	Tracheostomy w Mouth, Larynx, or Pharynx Disorder	3.1795	13.5	45
483		Surg	Tracheostomy Except for Mouth, Larynx, or Pharynx Disorder	14.1506	39.9	72
484	24	Surg	Craniotomy for Multiple Significant Trauma	6.2599	14.5	46
485	24	Surg	Limb Reattach, Hip and Femur Procs for Multiple Significant Trauma	3.0632	13.7	46
486	24	Surg	Other O.R. Procedures for Multiple Significant Trauma	5.2491	11.1	43
487	24	Med	Other Multiple Significant Trauma	1.8218	7.6	40
488	25	Surg	HIV w Extensive O.R. Procedure	4.3106	17.0	49
489	25	Med	HIV w Major Related Condition	1.9790	9.6	42
490	25	Med	HIV w or w/o Other Related Condition	1.1904	5.4	37
491	08	Surg	Major Joint & Limb Reattachment Procedures—Upper Extremity	1.5633	5.8	33
492	17	Med	Chemotherapy w Acute Leukemia as Secondary Diagnosis	2.5737	8.3	40

*Medicare data have been supplemented by data from Maryland and Michigan for Low-Volume DRGs.

†DRGs 469 and 470 contain cases that could not be assigned to valid DRGs.

Note: Geometric Mean is used only to determine payment for outlier and transfer cases.

Note: Relative weights are based on Medicare patient data and may not be appropriate for other patients.

Note: The abbreviations used (other than common terms shortened or collapsed for space purposes) are defined as follows: CC = complex complications; TIA = transient ischemic attack; T&A = tonsillectomy and adenoidectomy; O.R. = operating room; URI = upper respiratory infection; AMI = acute myocardial infarction; CV = cardiovascular; GI = gastrointestinal; CDE = common duct exploration; FX = fracture; ESW = extracorporeal shock wave; D&C = dilation and curettage; AMA = against medical advice; HIV = human immunodeficiency virus infection.

Chapter 3

General Principles of Accounting

Information does not happen by itself; it must be generated by an individual or a formally designed system. Financial information is no exception. The accounting system generates most financial information to provide quantitative data, primarily financial in nature, that are useful in making economic decisions about economic entities.

FINANCIAL VERSUS MANAGERIAL ACCOUNTING

Financial accounting is the branch of accounting that provides general purpose financial statements or reports to aid a large number of decision-making groups, internal and external to the organization, in a variety of decisions. The primary outputs of financial accounting are four financial statements that are discussed in Chapter 4 (see Tables 4–1, 4–2, 4–3, and 4–4 and Exhibit 4–1):

1. balance sheet
2. statement of revenues and expenses
3. statement of cash flows
4. statement of changes in fund balances

The field of financial accounting is restricted in many ways with regard to how certain events or business transactions may be accounted for. The term *generally accepted accounting principles* is often used to describe the body of rules and requirements that shape the preparation of the four primary financial statements. For example, an organization's financial statements that have been audited by an independent certified public accountant (CPA) would bear the following language in an unqualified opinion:

> In our opinion, the financial statements referred to above present fairly, in all material respects, the financial position of the XYZ Health Care Entity as of December 31, 19X2 and 19X1, and the results of its operations and its cash flows of general funds for the years then ended are in conformity with generally accepted accounting principles.

Financial accounting is not limited to preparation of the four statements. An increasing number of additional financial reports are being required, especially for external users for specific decision-making purposes. This is particularly important in the health care industry. For example, hospitals submit cost reports to a number of third-party payers, such as Blue Cross, Medicare, and Medicaid. They also submit financial reports to a large number of regulatory agencies, such as planning agencies, rate review agencies, service associations, and many others. In addition, CPAs often prepare financial projections that are used by investors in capital financing. These statements, although not usually audited by independent CPAs, are, for the most part, prepared in accordance with the same generally accepted accounting principles that govern the preparation of the four basic financial statements.

Managerial accounting is primarily concerned with the preparation of financial information for specific purposes, usually for internal users. Since this information is used within the organization, there is less need for a body of principles restricting its preparation. Presumably, the user and the preparer can meet to discuss questions of interpretation. Uniformity and comparability of information, which are desired goals for financial accountants, are clearly less important to management accountants.

PRINCIPLES OF ACCOUNTING

In addressing the principles of accounting we are concerned with both sets of accounting information, financial and managerial. Although managerial accounting has no formally adopted set of principles, it relies strongly on financial accounting principles. Understanding the principles and basics of financial accounting is therefore critical to understanding both financial and managerial accounting information.

The case example in our discussion of the principles of financial accounting is a newly formed, nonprofit community hospital, which we refer to as "Alpha Hospital."

Accounting Entity

Obviously, in any accounting there must be an entity for which the financial statements are being prepared. Specifying the entity on which the accounting will focus defines the information that is pertinent. Drawing these boundaries is the underlying concept behind the accounting entity principle.

Alpha Hospital is the entity for which we will account and prepare financial statements. We are not interested in the individuals who may have incorporated Alpha or other hospitals in the community, but solely in Alpha Hospital's financial transactions.

Defining the entity is not as clear-cut as one might expect. Significant problems arise, especially when the legal entity is different from the accounting entity. For example, if one physician owns a clinic through a sole proprietorship arrangement, the accounting entity may be the clinic operation, whereas the legal entity includes the physician and the physician's personal resources as well. A hospital may be part of a university or government agency, or it might be owned by a large corporation organized on a profit or nonprofit basis. Indeed, many hospitals have now become subsidiaries of a holding company as a result of corporate restructuring. Careful attention must be paid to the definition of the accounting entity in these situations. If the entity is not properly defined, evaluation of its financial information may be useless at best and misleading at worst.

The common practice of municipalities directly paying the fringe benefits of municipal employees employed in the hospital illustrates this situation. Such expenses may never show up in the hospital's accounts, resulting in an understatement of the expenses associated with running the hospital. In many cases, this may produce a bias in the rate-setting process.

Money Measurement

Accounting in general, but financial accounting in particular, is concerned with measuring economic resources and obligations and their changing levels for the accounting entity under consideration. The accountant's yardstick for measuring is not metered to size, color, weight, or other attributes; it is limited exclusively to money. However, there are significant problems in money measurement, which are discussed shortly.

Economic resources are defined as scarce means, limited in supply but essential to economic activity. They include supplies, buildings, equipment, money, claims to receive money, and ownership interests in other enterprises. The terms *economic resources* and *assets* may be interchanged for most practical purposes. Economic obligations are responsibilities to transfer economic resources or provide services to other entities in the future, usually in return for economic resources received from other entities in the past through the purchase of assets, the receipt of services, or the acceptance of loans. For most practical purposes, the terms *economic obligations* and *liabilities* may be used interchangeably.

In most normal situations, assets exceed liabilities in money-measured value. Liabilities represent the claim of one entity on another's assets; any excess, or remaining residual interest, may be claimed by the owner. In fact, for entities with ownership interest, this residual interest is called "owner's equity."

In most nonprofit entities, including health care organizations, there is no residual ownership claim. Any assets remaining in a liquidated not-for-profit entity, after all liabilities have been dissolved, legally become the property of the state. Residual interest is referred to as "fund balance" for most health care organizations.

In the Alpha Hospital example, assume that the community donated $1 million in cash to the hospital at its formation, hypothetically assumed to be December 31, 19X6. At that time, a listing of its assets, liabilities, and fund balance would be prepared in a balance sheet and read as below:

Alpha Hospital Balance Sheet
December 31, 19X6

Assets	*Liabilities and Fund Balance*
Cash $1,000,000	Fund balance $1,000,000

Duality

One of the fundamental premises of accounting is a very simple arithmetic requirement: the value of assets must always equal the combined value of liabilities and residual interest, which we have called fund balance. This basic accounting equation, the *duality principle*, may be stated as follows:

Assets = Liabilities + Fund balance

This requirement means that a balance sheet will always balance: the value of the assets will always equal the value of claims, whether liabilities or fund balance, on those assets.

Changes are always occurring in organizations that affect the value of assets, liabilities, and fund balance. These changes are called transactions and represent the items that interest accountants. Examples of transactions are borrowing money, purchasing supplies, and constructing buildings. The important thing to remember is that each transaction must be carefully analyzed under the duality principle to keep the basic accounting equation in balance.

To better understand how important this principle is, let us analyze several transactions in our Alpha Hospital example:

- *Transaction No. 1*. On January 2, 19X7, Alpha Hospital buys a piece of equipment for $100,000. The purchase is financed with a $100,000 note from the bank.
- *Transaction No. 2*. On January 3, 19X7, Alpha Hospital buys a building for $2,000,000, using $500,000 cash and issuing $1,500,000 worth of 20-year bonds.
- *Transaction No. 3*. On January 4, 19X7, Alpha Hospital purchases $200,000 worth of supplies from a supply firm on a credit basis.

If balance sheets were prepared after each of these three transactions, they would appear as follows:

- *Transaction No. 1*

Alpha Hospital Balance Sheet
January 2, 19X7

Assets		*Liabilities and Fund Balance*	
Cash	$1,000,000	Notes payable	$100,000
Equipment	100,000	Fund balance	1,000,000
Total	$1,100,000	Total	$1,100,000

Assets: Increase $100,000 (equipment increases by $100,000)
Liabilities: Increase $100,000 (notes payable increase by $100,000)

- *Transaction No. 2*

Alpha Hospital Balance Sheet
January 3, 19X7

Assets		*Liabilities and Fund Balance*	
Cash	$500,000	Notes payable	$100,000
Equipment	100,000	Bonds payable	1,500,000
Building	2,000,000	Fund balance	1,000,000
Total	$2,600,000	Total	$2,600,000

Assets: Increase $1,500,000 (cash decreases by $500,000 and building increases by $2,000,000)
Liabilities: Increase $1,500,000 (bonds payable increase by $1,500,000)

- *Transaction No. 3*

Alpha Hospital Balance Sheet
January 4, 19X7

Assets		*Liabilities and Fund Balance*	
Cash	$500,000	Accounts payable	$200,000
Supplies	200,000	Notes payable	100,000
Equipment	100,000	Bonds payable	1,500,000
Building	2,000,000	Fund balance	1,000,000
Total	$2,800,000	Total	$2,800,000

Assets: Increase $200,000 (supplies increase by $200,000)
Liabilities: Increase $200,000 (accounts payable increase by $200,000)

In each of these three transactions, the change in asset value is matched by an identical change in liability value. Thus, the basic accounting equation remains in balance.

It should be noted that, as the number of transactions increases, the number of individual asset and liability items also increases. In most organizations, there is a very large number of these individual items, which are referred to as accounts. The listing of these accounts is often called a chart of accounts; it is a useful device for categorizing transactions related to a given health care organization. There is already significant uniformity among hospitals and other health care facilities in the chart of accounts used; however, there is also pressure, especially from external users of financial information, to move toward even more uniformity.

Cost Valuation

Many readers of financial statements make the mistake of assuming that reported balance sheet values represent the real worth of individual assets or liabilities. Asset and liability values reported in a balance sheet are based on their historical or acquisition cost. In most situations, asset values do not equal the amount of money that could be realized if the assets were sold. However, in many cases the reported value of a liability in a balance sheet is a good approximation of the amount of money that would be required to extinguish the indebtedness.

Examining the alternatives to historical cost valuation helps clarify why the cost basis of valuation is used. The two primary alternatives to historical cost valuation of assets and liabilities are market value and replacement cost valuation.

Valuation of individual assets at their market value sounds simple enough and appeals to many users of financial statements. Creditors are often especially interested in what values assets would bring if liquidated. Current market values give decision makers an approximation of liquidation values.

The market value method's lack of objectivity, however, is a serious problem. In most normal situations, established markets dealing in second-hand merchandise do not exist. Decision makers must rely on individual appraisals. Given the current state of the art of appraisal, two appraisers are likely to produce different estimates of market value for identical assets. Accountants' insistence on objectivity in measurement thus eliminates market valuation of assets as a viable alternative.

Replacement cost valuation of assets measures assets by the money value required to replace them. This concept of valuation is extremely useful for many decision-making purposes. For example, management decisions to continue delivery of certain services should be affected by the replacement cost of resources, not their historical or acquisition cost—which is considered to be a sunken cost, irrelevant to future decisions. Planning agencies or other regulatory agencies should also consider incorporating estimates of replacement cost into their decisions to avoid bias. Considering only historical cost may improperly make old facilities appear more efficient than new or proposed facilities and projects.

Replacement cost may be a useful concept of valuation; however, it too suffers from lack of objectivity in measurement. Replacement cost valuation depends on *how* an item is replaced. For example, given the rate of technological change in the general economy, especially in the health care industry, few assets today would be replaced with like assets. Instead, more refined or capable assets would probably be substituted. What is the replacement cost in this situation? Is it the cost of the new, improved asset or the present cost of an identical asset that would most likely *not* be purchased? Compound this question by the large number of manufacturers selling roughly equivalent items and you have some idea of the inherent difficulty and subjectivity in replacement cost valuation.

Historical cost valuation, with all its faults, is thus the basis that the accounting profession has chosen to value assets and liabilities in most circumstances. Accountants use it rather than replacement cost largely because it is more objective. There is currently some fairly strong pressure from inside and outside the accounting profession to switch to replacement cost valuation, but it is still uncertain whether this pressure will be successful.

One final, important point should be noted: At the time of initial asset valuation, the values assigned by historical cost valuation and replacement cost valuation are identical. The historical cost value is most often criticized for assets that have long, useful lives, such as building and equipment. Over a period of many years, the historical cost and replacement cost values tend to diverge dramatically, in part because general inflation in our economy erodes the dollar's purchasing power. A dollar of today is simply not as valuable as a dollar of ten years ago. This problem could be remedied, without sacrificing the objectivity of historical cost measurement, by selecting a unit of purchasing power as the unit of measure: Transactions would then not be accounted in dollars but in dollars of purchasing power at a given point in time, usually the year for which the financial statements are being prepared. This issue is addressed later in this chapter, under "Stable Monetary Unit."

Accrual Accounting

Accrual accounting is a fundamental premise of accounting. It means that transactions of a business enterprise are recognized in the time period to which they relate, not necessarily in the time periods in which cash is received or paid.

It is quite common to hear people talk about an accrual versus a cash basis of accounting. Most of us think in cash basis terms. We measure our personal financial success during the year by how much cash we took in. Seldom do we consider such things as wear and tear on our cars and other personal items or the differences between earned and uncollected income. Perhaps if we accrued expenses for items such as depreciation on heating systems, air conditioning systems, automobiles, and furniture, we might see a different picture of our financial well-being.

The accrual basis of accounting significantly affects the preparation of financial statements in general; however, its major impact is on the preparation of the statement of revenues and expenses. The following additional transactions for Alpha Hospital illustrate the importance of the accrual principle:

- *Transaction No. 4.* Alpha Hospital bills patients $100,000 on January 16, 19X7, for services provided to them.

- *Transaction No. 5.* Alpha Hospital pays employees $60,000 for their wages and salaries on January 18, 19X7.
- *Transaction No. 6.* Alpha Hospital receives $80,000 in cash from patients who were billed earlier in Transaction No. 4 on January 23, 19X7.
- *Transaction No. 7.* Alpha Hospital pays the $200,000 of accounts payable on January 27, 19X7, for the purchase of supplies that took place on January 4, 19X7.

Balance sheets prepared after each of these transactions would appear as follows:

- *Transaction No. 4*

Alpha Hospital Balance Sheet
January 16, 19X7

Assets		Liabilities and Fund Balance	
Cash	$500,000	Accounts payable	$200,000
Accounts receivable	100,000	Notes payable	100,000
Supplies	200,000	Bonds payable	1,500,000
Equipment	100,000	Fund balance	1,100,000
Building	2,000,000		
Total	$2,900,000	Total	$2,900,000

Assets: Increase $100,000 (accounts receivable increase by $100,000)
Fund balance: Increases $100,000

- *Transaction No. 5*

Alpha Hospital Balance Sheet
January 18, 19X7

Assets		Liabilities and Fund Balance	
Cash	$440,000	Accounts payable	$200,000
Accounts receivable	100,000	Notes payable	100,000
Supplies	200,000	Bonds payable	1,500,000
Equipment	100,000	Fund balance	1,040,000
Building	2,000,000		
Total	$2,840,000	Total	$2,840,000

Assets: Decrease by $60,000 (cash decreases by $60,000)
Fund balance: Decreases by $60,000

- *Transaction No. 6*

Alpha Hospital Balance Sheet
January 23, 19X7

Assets		*Liabilities and Fund Balance*	
Cash	$520,000	Accounts payable	$200,000
Accounts receivable	20,000	Notes payable	100,000
Supplies	200,000	Bonds payable	1,500,000
Equipment	100,000	Fund balance	1,040,000
Building	2,000,000		
Total	$2,840,000	Total	$2,840,000

Assets: No change (cash increases by $80,000; accounts receivable decrease by $80,000)

- *Transaction No. 7*

Alpha Hospital Balance Sheet
January 27, 19X7

Assets		*Liabilities and Fund Balance*	
Cash	$320,000	Accounts payable	$0
Accounts receivable	20,000	Notes payable	100,000
Supplies	200,000	Bonds payable	1,500,000
Equipment	100,000	Fund balance	1,040,000
Building	2,000,000		
Total	$2,640,000	Total	$2,640,000

Assets: Decrease by $200,000 (cash decreases by $200,000)
Liabilities: Decrease by $200,000 (accounts payable decrease by $200,000)

In Transactions Nos. 4 and 5, there is an effect on Alpha Hospital's residual interest or its fund balance. In Transaction No. 4, an increase in fund balance occurred due to the billing of patients for services previously rendered. Increases in fund balance or owner's equity resulting from the sale of goods or delivery of services are called revenues. It should be noted that this increase occurred even though no cash was actually collected until January 23, 19X7, illustrating the accrual principle of accounting. Recognition of revenue occurs when the revenue is earned, not necessarily when it is collected.

In Transaction No. 5, a reduction in fund balance occurs. Costs incurred by a business enterprise to provide goods or services that reduce fund balance or owner's equity are called expenses. Under the accrual principle, expenses are recognized when assets are used up or liabilities are incurred in the production and delivery of goods or services, not necessarily when cash is paid.

The difference between revenue and expense is often referred to as *net income*. In the hospital and health care industry, this term may be used interchangeably with the term *excess of revenues over expenses* or *revenues and gains in excess of expenses*.

The income statement or statement of revenues and expenses summarizes the revenues and expenses of a business enterprise over a defined period of time. If an income statement is prepared for the total life of an entity, that is, from inception to dissolution, it happens that the value for net income would be the same under both an accrual and a cash basis of accounting.

In most situations, frequent measurements of revenue and expense are demanded, creating some important measurement problems. Ideally, under the accrual accounting principle, expenses should be matched to the revenue that they helped create. For example, wage, salary, and supply costs can usually be easily associated with revenues of a given period. However, in certain circumstances, the association between revenue and expense is impossible to discover, necessitating the accountant's use of a systematic, rational method of allocating costs to a benefiting time period. In the best example of this procedure, costs such as those associated with building and equipment are spread over the estimated useful life of the assets through the recording of depreciation.

To complete the Alpha Hospital example, assume that the financial statements must be prepared at the end of January. Before they are prepared, certain adjustments must be made to the accounts to adhere fully to the accrual principle of accounting. The following adjustments might be recorded:

- *Adjustment No. 1.* There are currently $100,000 of patient charges that have been incurred but not yet billed.
- *Adjustment No. 2.* There are currently $50,000 worth of unpaid wages and salaries for which employees have performed services.
- *Adjustment No. 3.* A physical inventory count indicates that $50,000 worth of initial supplies have been used.
- *Adjustment No. 4.* The equipment of Alpha Hospital has an estimated useful life of ten years, and the cost is being allocated over this time

period. On a monthly basis, this amounts to an allocation of $833 per month.

- *Adjustment No. 5.* The building has an estimated useful life of 40 years, and the cost of the building is being allocated equally over its estimated life. On a monthly basis, this amounts to $4,167.
- *Adjustment No. 6.* Although no payment has been made on either notes payable or bonds payable, there is an interest expense associated with using money for this one-month time period. This interest expense will be paid at a later date. Assume that the note payable carries an interest rate of 8 percent and the bond payable carries an interest rate of 6 percent. The actual amount of interest expense incurred for the month of January would be $8,167 ($667 on the note and $7,500 on the bond payable).

The effects of these adjustments on the balance sheet of Alpha Hospital, and on the ending balance sheet that would be prepared after all the adjustments were made, are presented below.

Adjustment	Amount of Change	Account(s) Increased	Account(s) Decreased
No. 1	$100,000	Fund balance	None
		Accounts receivable	None
No. 2	50,000	Wages and salaries payable	Fund balance
No. 3	50,000	None	Fund balance, supplies
No. 4	833	None	Fund balance, equipment
No. 5	4,167	None	Fund balance, building
No. 6	8,167	Interest payable	Fund balance

Alpha Hospital Balance Sheet
January 31, 19X7

Assets		Liabilities and Fund Balance	
Cash	$320,000	Wages and salaries payable	$50,000
Accounts receivable	120,000	Interest payable	8,167
Supplies	150,000	Notes payable	100,000
Equipment	99,167	Bonds payable	1,500,000
Building	1,995,833	Fund balance	1,026,833
Total	$2,685,000	Total	$2,685,000

It is also possible to prepare the following statement of revenues and expenses:

Alpha Hospital
Statement of Revenues and Expenses
For month ended January 31, 19X7

Revenues	$200,000
Less expenses	
Wages and salaries	$110,000
Supplies	50,000
Depreciation	5,000
Interest	8,167
Total	$173,167
Excess of revenues over expenses	$26,833

Note that the difference between revenue and expense during the month of January was $26,833, the exact amount by which the fund balance of Alpha Hospital changed during the month. Alpha Hospital began the month with $1,000,000 in its fund balance account and ended with $1,026,833. This illustrates an important point to remember in the reading of financial statements: *the individual financial statements are fundamentally related to one another.*

Stable Monetary Unit

The money measurement principle of accounting discussed earlier restricted accounting measures to money. In accounting in the United States, the unit of measure is the dollar. At the present time, no adjustment to changes in the general purchasing power of that unit is required in financial reports; a 1985 dollar is assumed to be equal in value to a 1993 dollar. This permits arithmetic operations, such as addition and subtraction. If this assumption were not made, addition of the unadjusted historical cost values of assets acquired in different time periods would be inappropriate, like adding apples and oranges. Current, generally accepted accounting principles incorporate the *stable monetary unit principle.*

The stable monetary unit principle may not seem to pose any great problems. In fact, when the inflation rate was less than 2 percent annually, it did not. However, given high rates of inflation, the effects of assuming a stable monetary unit can be quite dramatic. Imagine that the inflation rate in the economy is currently 100 percent, compounded monthly. The hypothetical entity under consideration is a neighborhood health care center that has all its expenses, except payroll, covered by grants from governmental agencies. Its employees have a contract that automatically adjusts their wages to changes in the general price level. (With a monthly inflation rate of 100 percent, it is no wonder.) Assume that revenues from patients are collected on the first day of the month following the one in which they were billed, but that the employees are paid at the beginning of each month. Rates to patients are set so that the excess of revenues over expenses will be zero. With the first month's wages set equal to $100,000, the following income and cash flow positions result for the first six months of the year:

	Income Flows			Cash Flows		
	Expense	Revenue	Net Income	Inflow	Outflow	Difference
January	$100,000	$100,000	0	$50,000*	$100,000	($50,000)
February	200,000	200,000	0	100,000	200,000	(100,000)
March	400,000	400,000	0	200,000	400,000	(200,000)
April	800,000	800,000	0	400,000	800,000	(400,000)
May	1,600,000	1,600,000	0	800,000	1,600,000	(800,000)
June	3,200,000	3,200,000	0	1,600,000	3,200,000	(1,600,000)
	$6,300,000	$6,300,000	0	$3,150,000	$6,300,000	($3,150,000)

*$50,000 is equal to the revenue billed in December.

Note the tremendous difference between income and cash flow. Although the income statement would indicate a break-even operation, the cash balance at the end of June would be a negative $3,150,000. Obviously, the health care center's operations cannot continue indefinitely in light of the extreme cash hardship position imposed.

Fortunately, the rate of inflation in our economy is not 100 percent. However, smaller rates of inflation compounded over long periods of time could create similar problems. For example, setting rates equal to historical cost depreciation of fixed assets leaves the entity with a significant cash deficit when it is time to replace the asset. Yet currently many third-party payers do in fact base payment on unadjusted historical cost depreciation, and few health care organizations actually set rates at levels necessary to recover replacement cost.

Fund Accounting

Fund accounting is a system in which an entity's assets and liabilities are segregated in the accounting records. Each fund may be thought of as an independent entity with its own self-balancing set of accounts. The basic accounting equation discussed under "duality" must be satisfied for each fund: assets must equal liabilities plus fund balance for the particular fund in question. This is, in fact, how the term *fund balance* developed; a fund balance originally represented the residual interest for a *particular fund*.

Fund accounting is widely employed by nonprofit, voluntary health care facilities, especially hospitals. It is not a basic concept or principle of accounting like those previously discussed, but it is a feature peculiar to accounting for many health care organizations. It evolved primarily for use in stewarding funds donated by external parties who imposed stipulations on the usage of those monies.

Two major categories of funds are presently used in the health care industry: donor restricted and general. A donor-restricted fund is one in which a third party, outside the entity, has imposed certain restrictions on the use of donated monies or resources. There are three common types of donor-restricted funds:

1. specific purpose funds
2. plant replacement and expansion funds
3. endowment funds

Specific purpose funds are donated by individuals or organizations and restricted for purposes other than plant replacement and expansion or endowment. Monies received from government agencies to perform specific research or other work are examples of specific purpose funds.

Plant replacement and expansion funds are restricted for use in plant replacement and expansion. Assets purchased with these monies are not recorded in the fund. When the monies are used for plant purposes, the amounts are transferred to the unrestricted fund. For example, if $200,000 in cash from the plant replacement fund were used to acquire a piece of equipment, the equipment and fund balance of the unrestricted fund would be increased.

Endowment funds are contributed to be held intact for generating income. The income may or may not be restricted for specific purposes. Some endowments are classified as "term" endowments. That is, after the expiration of some time period, the restriction on use of the principle is lifted. The balance is then transferred to the general fund.

General funds have no third-party donor restrictions imposed on them. In some cases, the governing board of the organization may restrict use, but, since this is not an external or third-party restriction, the funds are still classified as general.

CONVENTIONS OF ACCOUNTING

The accounting principles discussed up to this point are important in the preparation of financial statements. However, several widely accepted conventions modify the application of these principles in certain circumstances. Three of the more important conventions are discussed below:

1. conservatism
2. materiality
3. consistency

Conservatism affects the valuation of some assets. Specifically, accountants use a "lower of cost or market rule" for valuing inventories and marketable securities. The "lower of cost or market rule" means that the value of a stock of inventory or marketable securities would be its actual cost or market value, whichever is less. For these resources, there is a deviation from cost valuation to market valuation whenever market value is lower.

Materiality permits certain transactions to be treated out of accordance with generally accepted accounting principles. This might be permitted because the transaction does not materially affect the presentation of financial position. For example, theoretically, paper clips may have an estimated useful life greater than one year. However, the cost of capitalizing this item and systematically and rationally allocating it over its useful life is not justifiable; the difference in financial position that would be created by not using generally accepted accounting principles would be immaterial.

Consistency limits the accounting alternatives that can be used. In any given transaction, there is usually a variety of available, generally acceptable, accounting treatments. For example, generally accepted accounting principles permit the use of double-declining balance, sum-of-the-year digits, or straight-line methods for allocating the costs of depreciable assets over their estimated useful life; but the consistency convention limits an entity's ability to change from one acceptable method to another.

SUMMARY

In this chapter we discussed the importance of generally accepted accounting principles in deriving financial information. Although these principles are formally required only in the preparation of audited financial statements, they influence the derivation of most financial information. An understanding of some of the basic principles is critical to an understanding of financial information in general.

Six specific principles of accounting were discussed in some detail:

1. accounting entity
2. money measurement
3. duality
4. cost valuation
5. accrual accounting
6. stable monetary unit

In addition to these, the general importance of fund accounting, as it relates to the hospital and health care industry, was discussed. The chapter concluded with a discussion of three conventions that may modify the application of generally accepted accounting principles in specific situations.

ASSIGNMENTS

1. ABC Medical Center has undergone a recent corporate reorganization. The following structure resulted:

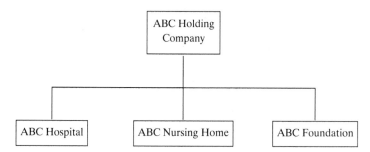

What difficulties might be experienced in preparing financial statements for the ABC Hospital?

2. Does the value of total assets represent the economic value of the entity?

3. What is the difference between stockholders' equity and fund balance?

4. A home health care firm has purchased five automobiles for use in treating its patients. Each automobile cost $12,000 and has an estimated useful life of three years. Each year, the replacement cost of the automobiles is expected to increase 10 percent. At the end of the third year, replacement cost would be $15,972. The firm anticipates that each automobile will be used to make 1,500 patient visits per year. If the firm prices each visit to recover just the historical cost of the automobiles, it will include a capital cost of $2.67 per visit ($12,000/4,500 total visits). Assuming the revenue generated from this capital charge is invested at 10 percent, will the firm have enough funds available to meet its replacement cost? How would this situation change if price level depreciation were used to establish the capital charge?

5. A health maintenance organization (HMO) has just been formed. During its first year of operations, the organization reported an accounting loss of $500,000. Cash flow during the same period was a positive $500,000. How might this situation exist, and which measure better describes financial performance?

6. What is the difference between restricted and unrestricted funds?

7. Why is consistency in financial reporting critical to fairness in financial representation?

SOLUTIONS AND ANSWERS

1. It may be difficult to associate specific assets and liabilities for the ABC Hospital. For example, debt may have been issued by the holding company to finance projects for both the hospital and the nursing home. In addition, commonly used assets may be involved, such as a dietary department providing meals for both hospital and nursing home patients. Some expenses may also be difficult to trace to either the hospital or the nursing home. For example, how should expenses that are common to the hospital, the nursing home, and the foundation (such as administrative expenses of the holding company) be allocated? Thus, many problems of jointness may make preparation of the financial statements for the hospital difficult, but such statements are still likely to be a necessity for adequate planning and control.

2. Only coincidentally would the value of total assets equal the economic value of the entity. Total assets, as reported in the balance sheet, represent the undepreciated historical cost of assets acquired by the entity. Economic value of an entity is related to the discounted value of future earnings or the market value of the entity if sold.

3. Both stockholders' equity and fund balance represent the difference between total assets and total liabilities. Stockholders' equity is used in investor-owned corporations to designate the residual owners' claims. Fund balance is used in not-for-profit corporations in which there is no residual ownership interest.

4. The following data are relevant to the pricing decision of the home health care firm with regard to the five automobiles:

Funds available with historical cost depreciation per automobile:

	Depreciation	Years Invested (10%)	Future Value (10%)
Year 1	$4,000	2	$4,840
Year 2	4,000	1	4,400
Year 3	4,000	0	4,000
	$12,000		$13,240

Shortage = $15,972 − $13,240 = $2,732/automobile

Funds available with price level depreciation per automobile:

	Depreciation	*Years Invested (10%)*	*Future Value (10%)*
Year 1	$4,400	2	$5,324
Year 2	4,840	1	5,324
Year 3	5,324	0	5,324
	$14,564		$15,972

Shortage = $15,972 − $15,972 = 0

Thus, the prices should be set equal to expected replacement cost. Clearly, pricing services to recover capital costs is critical to long-term financial survival.

5. The HMO could have received large payments in advance for providing health services to major employers. This would mean that a liability to provide future services exists. Both accounting loss and cash flow are important in assessing financial performance. The accounting loss is symbolic of a critical operational problem with regard to revenue and expense relationships. The positive cash flow may be temporary unless revenue exceeds expenses in future periods.

6. A restricted fund is one that has a third-party donor restriction placed on the utilization of the funds. An unrestricted fund has no such restriction.

7. Changes in financial reporting can impair the comparability of financial results between years for a given firm.

Chapter 4

Financial Statements

Understanding the principles of accounting is a critical first step in understanding financial statements. However, the format and language of financial statements may be unintelligible to the occasional reader. In this chapter we discuss in some detail the four major general purpose financial statements:

1. balance sheet
2. statement of revenues and expenses
3. statement of cash flows
4. statement of changes in fund balances

In addition, we examine the footnotes to the financial statements.

The balance sheet and statement of revenues and expenses are more widely published and used than the other two statements. Understanding them enables a reader to use the other two financial statements and financial information in general. Therefore, in the following discussion, we pay major attention to the balance sheet and statement of revenues and expenses.

The balance sheets examined in the following two sections illustrate the separation of funds into donor-restricted and general fund categories. Donor-restricted funds are not available for general operating purposes. The duality principle can also be seen operating in these balance sheets. Assets equal liabilities plus fund balance in both donor-restricted and general fund balance sheets. In both cases, the entity being accounted for is Omega Hospital (Table 4–1).

BALANCE SHEET: GENERAL FUNDS

Current Assets

Assets that are expected to be exchanged for cash or consumed during the operating cycle of the entity (or one year, whichever is longer) are classified as current assets on the balance sheet. The operating cycle is the length of time between acquisition of materials and services and collection of revenue generated by them. Since the operating cycle for most health care organizations is significantly less than one year (perhaps three months or less), current assets are predominantly those that may be expected to be converted into cash or used to reduce expenditures of cash within one year.

Cash and Cash Equivalents

Cash consists of coin, currency, and available funds on deposit at banks. Negotiable instruments such as money orders, certified checks, cashier's checks, personal checks, or bank drafts are also viewed as cash.

Cash equivalents include savings accounts, certificates of deposit, and other temporary marketable securities. Categorization as a cash equivalent requires that two criteria be met. First, management must intend to convert the investment into cash within one year or during the operating cycle, whichever is longer. Second, the investment must be readily marketable and capable of being transformed into cash very easily.

In Table 4–1, Omega Hospital has $1,304,403 in cash and cash equivalents at the end of 1992. Omega Hospital also has $157,803 in assets whose use is limited that are categorized as a current asset. These items are restricted for the payment of current liabilities and are most likely cash or cash equivalents. It is often useful to regard these items as an addition to cash and cash equivalents when assessing the adequacy of an organization's cash position because these funds will be used to satisfy maturing current liabilities. Omega's cash position might therefore be better stated by adding the two balances together and stating actual cash position as $1,462,206.

Accounts Receivable

Accounts receivable represent legally enforceable claims on customers for prior services or goods. In Omega Hospital, there are two categories of accounts receivable: patient and other. Other accounts receivable in a health care organization imply revenue derived from sources other than patient services. Common sources of other receivables would include rent from medical office buildings, revenues from educational programs, and sales of medical and pharmacy supplies to individuals other than patients.

Patient accounts receivable are usually the largest accounts receivable item, and, for that matter, the largest single current asset item in the balance sheet. Omega Hospital is no exception—it has an estimated $7,684,188 in accounts receivable that will eventually result in cash. The actual dollar amount of accounts receivable is higher but is reduced by estimated allowances.

A characteristic of hospitals and other health care organizations that makes their accounts receivable different from those of most other organizations is that the charges actually billed to patients are quite often settled for substantially less than the amounts charged. The differences are also known as allowances. Four major categories of allowances are used to

Table 4-1 Balance Sheet for Omega Hospital

	December 31	
	1992	*1991*
Assets		
Current assets		
Cash and cash equivalents (Note 1*)	$ 1,304,403	$ 966,485
Receivables		
Patient accounts, net of estimated uncollectable accounts and contractual adjustments (Notes 1 and 4)	7,684,188	6,075,295
Other	371,951	319,140
Medical supplies (Note 1)	780,358	680,514
Prepaid expenses	288,760	304,924
Assets whose use is limited and that are required for current liabilities	157,803	681,200
Total current assets	$10,587,463	$ 9,027,558
Assets whose use is limited (Notes 1, 6, and 7)		
By board for malpractice costs	233,369	215,585
By board for capital improvements	2,183,639	1,976,543
By agreement with third-party payer for funded depreciation	7,423,835	11,962,168
Under indenture agreement held by trustee, net of assets that are required for current liabilities	638,966	631,100
	$10,479,809	$14,785,396
Property and equipment, net (Notes 1, 5, and 7)	$29,974,266	$24,023,535

continues

Table 4–1 continued

	December 31	
	1992	1991
Other assets		
Land held for future expansion	480,981	896,511
Investment in partnership	256,070	116,769
Deferred financing costs (Note 1)	169,497	183,428
Cash value of life insurance	73,248	55,243
	$ 979,796	$ 1,251,951
	$52,021,334	$49,088,440
Liabilities and fund balance		
Current liabilities		
Accounts payable		
Trade	$ 1,464,426	$ 1,630,976
Accrued Liabilities		
Salaries and wages	1,097,192	898,376
Employee benefits	1,800,731	1,036,946
Interest	141,858	157,996
Other	151,919	310,963
Estimated third-party payer settlement		
(Notes 1 and 2)	30,000	397,991
Current portion of long-term debt	358,913	649,113
Total current liabilities	$ 5,045,039	$ 5,082,361
Estimated malpractice costs (Note 10)	$ 988,241	$ 1,087,000
Long-term debt, net of current portion (Note 7)	$ 5,475,000	$ 5,765,000
Contingent liabilities and commitments (Notes 5 and 10)		
Fund balance (Note 1)	$40,513,054	$37,154,079
	$52,021,334	$49,088,440
Specific purpose (Note 1)		
Cash and cash equivalents	$ 650,240	$ 498,549
Fund balance	$ 650,240	$ 498,549

*Note numbers refer to those in Exhibit 4–1.

restate accounts receivable to expected, realizable value:

1. charity allowances
2. courtesy allowances
3. doubtful account allowances
4. contractual allowances

A charity allowance is the difference between established service rates and amounts actually charged to indigent patients. Many health care facilities, especially clinics and other ambulatory care settings, have a policy of scaling the normal charge by some factor based on income. A courtesy allowance is the difference between established rates for services and rates billed special patients, such as employees, physicians, and clergy. A doubtful account allowance is the difference between rates billed and amounts expected to be recovered. For example, a medically indigent patient might actually receive services that have an established rate of $100, but be billed only $50. If it is anticipated that the patient will not pay even the $50, then that $50 will show up as a doubtful account allowance.

In most situations, contractual allowances represent the largest deduction from accounts receivable. A contractual allowance is the difference between rates billed to a third-party payer, such as Medicare, and the amount that will actually be paid by that third-party payer. For example, a Medicare patient may receive hospital services priced at $4,000 but actually pay the hospital only $3,000 for those services, based on the patient's diagnosis-related group classification. If this account is unpaid at the fiscal year end, the financial statements would include the net amount to be paid, $3,000, as an account receivable. Accounts receivable represent the amount of cash expected to be received, not the gross prices charged. Since most major payers—such as Medicare, Medicaid, and Blue Cross—have a contractual relationship that permits payment on a basis other than charges, contractual allowances can be, and usually are, very large.

The allowances are estimates and will, in all probability, differ from the actual value of accounts receivable that will eventually be written off. For example, Omega Hospital shows an expected value of accounts receivable to be collected as $7,684,188 in 1992, but it actually has $9,246,910 of outstanding accounts receivable.

Net accounts receivable	$7,684,188
Contractual allowances	531,885
Bad-debt and other allowance	1,030,837
Accounts receivable gross	$9,246,910

Since estimation of allowances is so critical to the reported value of accounts receivable, the methodology should be scrutinized. Just how was the estimate developed? Has the estimating method been used in the past with any degree of reliability? An external audit performed by an independent certified public accountant can usually provide the required degree of reliability and assurance.

Inventories / Supplies

Inventories in a health care facility represent items that are to be used in the delivery of health care services. They may range from normal business office supplies to highly specialized chemicals used in a laboratory.

Prepaid Expenses

Prepaid expenses represent expenditures already made for future service. In Omega Hospital, they may represent prepayment of insurance premiums for the year, rents on leased equipment, or other similar items. For example, an insurance premium for a professional liability insurance policy may be $600,000 per year, due one year in advance. If this amount were paid on January 1, then on June 30, $300,000 (one-half the total) would be shown as a prepaid expense.

Property and Equipment

Property and equipment are sometimes called fixed assets or shown more descriptively as plant property and equipment. Items in this category represent investment in tangible, permanent assets; they are sometimes referred to as the capital assets of the organization. These items are shown at the historical cost or acquisition cost, reduced by allowances for depreciation.

Land and Improvements

Land and improvements represent the historical cost of the earth's surface owned by the health care facility and the historical cost of any improvements erected on it. Such improvements might include water and sewer systems, roadways, fences, sidewalks, shrubbery, and parking lots. While land may not be depreciated, land improvements may. Land held for investment purposes is not shown in this category but appears as an investment in the other assets section.

Buildings and Equipment

Buildings and equipment represent all buildings and equipment owned by the entity and used in the normal course of its operations. These items are also stated at historical cost. Buildings and equipment not used in the normal course of operations should be reported separately. For example, real estate investments would not be shown in the fixed asset or plant property and equipment section but in the other assets section. Equipment in many situations is classified into three categories: (1) *fixed equipment*—affixed to the building in which it is located, including items such as elevators, boilers, and generators; (2) *major movable equipment*—usually stationary but capable of being moved, including reasonably expensive items such as automobiles, laboratory equipment, and x-ray apparatuses; and (3) *minor equipment*—usually low in cost with short estimated useful lives, including such items as wastebaskets, glassware, and sheets.

Construction in Progress

Construction in progress represents the amount of money that has been expended on projects that are still not complete at the date the financial statement is published. In Omega Hospital, there is currently $3,178,754 of construction in progress (Note 5 in Exhibit 4–1). When these projects are completed, the values will be charged to property and equipment.

Allowance for Depreciation

Allowance for depreciation represents the accumulated depreciation taken on the asset to the date of the financial statement. The concept of depreciation is important and useful in a wide variety of decisions. The following example illustrates the depreciation concept: A $500 desk is purchased and depreciated over a five-year life. The balance sheet values are presented below

	Year				
	1	*2*	*3*	*4*	*5*
Historical equipment cost	$500	$500	$500	$500	$500
Allowance for depreciation	100	200	300	400	500
Net	$400	$300	$200	$100	$ 0

In the case of Omega Hospital, there is $19,762,441 of accumulated depreciation at December 31, 1992. The historical cost base for this amount is $46,557,953 (Note 5 in Exhibit 4–1), the historical cost value of buildings and equipment. This means that 42.4 percent of the historical cost of present facilities has been depreciated in prior years. As the ratio of allowance for depreciation to building and equipment increases, it usually signifies that a physical plant will need replacement in the near future. Omega Hospital appears to be in such a situation, which may partially explain the current construction.

Assets Whose Use Is Limited

Most organizations will have some amounts listed under assets whose use is limited. In Table 4–1 Omega Hospital has $10,479,809 at the end of 1992. The nature of the asset limitation usually derives from one of two ways. First, the board may restrict certain funds to be used in only designated ways. For example, the board has restricted $233,369 for paying malpractice costs and $2,183,639 for capital improvements. These monies have been set aside and restricted by the board for these designated purposes. They could not be spent for any other purpose without the formal approval of the board.

Aside from a board restriction, funds may also be restricted by a third party. These restrictions are not from a third-party donor. If they were, they would be listed in the restricted funds section of the balance sheet. The most common third-party restriction is under indenture agreement. Omega Hospital has $638,966 of funds restricted under bond indenture. These are funds held by the bond trustee, usually for one or more purposes. Note 6 to Omega's financial statements (Exhibit 4–1) describes the nature of the restrictions under bond indenture.

Exhibit 4–1 Notes to Financial Statements

OMEGA HOSPITAL
December 31, 1992 and 1991

Note 1: Organization and Summary of Significant Accounting Policies

Organization—Omega Hospital (the Hospital) is accredited by the Joint Commission on Accreditation of Healthcare Organizations and operates a licensed 224-bed acute care hospital delivering health care services in Boise, California. The Hospital is a not-for-profit, nonsectarian institution, governed by a board of trustees elected from the community.

Omega Hospital Foundation (the Foundation) is a separate nonprofit corporation whose articles of incorporation identify the Hospital as the Foundation's primary beneficiary. Assets of the Foundation at the balance sheet dates and transactions with the Foundation during 1992 were not material to the Hospital's financial statements.

Exhibit 4–1 continued

Fund accounting—The Hospital accounts for and reports its financial position and results of operations within general and restricted funds. Only assets restricted by a donor or grantor are presented as restricted funds. All other assets are presented in the general fund. Assets whose use is limited by debt agreements, trust agreements, and the board of trustees are presented in a separate section of the general fund balance sheet.

Statement of revenues and expenses of general fund—For purposes of display, transactions deemed by management to be ongoing, major, or central to the provision of health care services are reported as revenues and expenses. Peripheral or incidental transactions are reported as gains and losses.

Donor-restricted funds—Donor-restricted funds are used to differentiate resources, the use of which is restricted by donors or grantors, from resources of general funds on which donors or grantors place no restriction or that arise as a result of the operations of the Hospital for its stated purposes. Restricted gifts and other restricted resources are recorded as additions to the restricted fund.

Resources restricted by donors for plant replacement and expansion are added to the general fund balance to the extent expended within the period.

Resources restricted by donors or grantors for specific operating purposes are reported in other revenue to the extent used within the period.

Net patient services revenues—Net patient services revenues are reported as the estimated net realizable amounts from patients, third-party payers, and others for services rendered, including estimated retroactive adjustments under reimbursement agreements with third-party payers. Retroactive adjustments are accrued on an estimated basis in the period during which the related services are rendered and adjusted in future periods as final settlements are determined.

Charity care—The Hospital provides care to patients who meet certain criteria under its charity care policy without charge or at amounts less than its established rates. Because the Hospital does not pursue collection of amounts determined to qualify as charity care, they are not reported as revenue.

Investments and investment income—Donated investments are reported at fair value at the date of receipt, which is then treated as cost. Investments in commercial paper are stated at cost, adjusted for impairments in value that are deemed to be other than temporary.

Investment income on proceeds of borrowings that are held by a trustee, to the extent not capitalized, is reported as other revenue. Investment income from all other general fund investments is reported as nonoperating gains. Investment income on investments of donor-restricted funds is added to the restricted fund balance.

Estimated malpractice costs—The provision for estimated medical malpractice claims includes estimates of the ultimate costs for both reported claims and claims incurred but not reported.

Costs of borrowing—Deferred financing costs are amortized over the period during which the obligation is outstanding, using the bonds outstanding method. Amortization of deferred financing costs is capitalized during the period of construction of related capital assets.

Patient accounts receivable—Patient accounts receivable arising from revenue for services to patients are reduced by an allowance for uncollectable accounts and contractual allowances based on experience, third-party contractual reimbursement

continues

Exhibit 4–1 continued

arrangements, and any unusual circumstances that may affect the ability of patients to meet their obligations. Accounts deemed uncollectable are charged against this allowance.

Medical supplies—Medical supplies, consisting primarily of medical and surgical inventories, are stated at the lower of cost or market (FIFO [first in, first out]).

Property and equipment—Property and equipment acquisitions are recorded at cost. Property and equipment donated for Hospital operations are recorded as additions to the restricted fund at fair value at the date of receipt and as a transfer to the general fund balance when the assets are placed in service.

Depreciation is provided over the estimated useful life of each class of depreciable asset and is computed on the straight-line method.

Assets whose use is limited—Assets whose use is limited include assets set aside by the board of trustees for malpractice costs and capital improvements over which it retains control and may at its discretion subsequently use for other purposes, assets set aside in accordance with agreements with third-party payers, and assets held by a trustee under an indenture agreement.

Income taxes—The Hospital is a not-for-profit corporation as described in Section 501(c)(3) of the Internal Revenue Code and is exempt from federal income taxes on related income pursuant to Section 501(a) of the Code.

Statement of cash flows—For purposes of the statement of cash flows, the Hospital considers all highly liquid investments (certificates of deposit and repurchase agreements) with maturity dates of three months or less as cash and cash equivalents, except for amounts whose use is limited by board designation, trust agreements, or third-party payers.

Reclassification—Certain amounts on the December 31, 1991 financial statements have been reclassified to conform to the December 31, 1992 financial statement presentation.

Note 2: Net Patient Services Revenues

The Hospital has agreements with third-party payers that provide for payments to the Hospital in amounts different from its established rates. A summary of the payment arrangements with major third-party payers is as follows:

- *Medicare*—Inpatient acute care services rendered to beneficiaries of the Medicare program are paid at prospectively determined rates per discharge. These rates vary according to a patient classification system that is based on clinical, diagnostic, and other factors. Inpatient nonacute services, certain outpatient services, and defined capital costs related to Medicare beneficiaries are paid on the basis of a cost reimbursement methodology. The Hospital is reimbursed for cost-reimbursable items at a tentative rate, with final settlement determined after submission of annual cost reports by the Hospital and audits thereof by the Medicare fiscal intermediary. The Hospital's classification of patients under the Medicare program and the appropriateness of their admission are subject to an independent review by a peer review organization. Gross revenues billed under the Medicare program totaled approximately $16,011,552 and $14,600,080 for 1992 and 1991, respectively. The Hospital's Medicare cost reports have been audited by the Medicare fiscal intermediary through 1989.

Exhibit 4–1 continued

- *Medicaid*—Inpatient acute care services rendered to beneficiaries of the Medicaid program are paid on a prospective payment system similar to that for Medicare. Outpatient services are paid on a percentage of allowed charges based on a ratio of the Hospital's operating expenses to total revenue for outpatient services. Gross revenues billed under the Medicaid program totaled approximately $12,172,410 and $10,097,393 for 1992 and 1991, respectively.

- *Blue Cross*—Inpatient services rendered to Blue Cross subscribers are reimbursed at prospectively determined rates per admission under a preferred hospital agreement. The prospectively determined rates are not subject to retroactive adjustment. Generally, outpatient services are paid on an agreed-on percentage. However, certain other outpatient services are paid on an agreed-on fee schedule.

During 1992, the Hospital revised its estimate of amounts anticipated to be received for Medicare and Medicaid services rendered in 1990 and 1991 by $631,000, resulting in a reduction of 1992 contractual allowances. The Hospital's Medicare cost reports have been audited by the Medicare fiscal intermediary through 1989.

The Hospital has also entered into payment agreements with certain commercial insurance carriers and preferred provider organizations. The basis for payment to the Hospital under these agreements includes prospectively determined rates per discharge, discounts from established charges, and prospectively determined daily rates.

A summary of gross and net patient service revenue follows:

	December 31	
	1992	*1991*
Gross patient services revenue	$48,818,416	$42,524,209
Contractual adjustments and other	(2,723,089)	(3,439,448)
Net patient services revenue	$46,095,327	$39,084,761

Note 3: Charity Care

The Hospital maintains records to identify and monitor the level of charity care it provides. These records include the amount of charges forgone for services and supplies furnished under its charity care policy and the estimated cost of those services and supplies. The following information measures the level of charity care provided:

	December 31	
	1992	*1991*
Charges forgone, based on established rates	$1,097,568	$659,524
Estimated costs and expenses incurred to provide charity care	$1,040,000	$630,000
Equivalent percentage of charity care patients to all patients served	2.20%	1.53%

continues

Exhibit 4-1 continued

Note 4: Patient Accounts Receivable

The Hospital accounts receivable are reported net of the subsequent allowances and contractual adjustments, as follows:

	December 31	
	1992	*1991*
Patient accounts receivable	$9,246,910	$7,511,297
Allowance for bad debt and other	(1,030,837)	(587,944)
Allowance for contractual adjustments	(531,885)	(848,058)
	$7,684,188	$6,075,295

Note 5: Property and Equipment

Property and equipment consist of the following:

	December 31	
	1992	*1991*
Land and land improvements	$ 3,572,503	$ 2,585,534
Buildings and building improvements	14,575,611	11,544,642
Fixed equipment	12,538,364	9,930,282
Major movable and minor equipment	15,871,475	13,974,225
	46,557,953	38,034,683
Less accumulated depreciation	19,762,441	17,283,825
	26,795,512	20,750,858
Construction in progress	3,178,754	3,272,677
	$29,974,266	$24,023,535

Construction in progress commitments: Various construction projects were in progress at December 31, 1992, with an estimated additional cost to complete of $4,800,000.

Note 6: Assets Whose Use Is Limited

Assets whose use is limited that are required for obligations classified as current liabilities are reported in current assets. The composition of assets whose use is limited at December 31, 1992 and 1991 is set forth below. Investments are stated at cost that approximates market.

Exhibit 4–1 continued

	December 31	
	1992	*1991*
By board for malpractice costs		
Cash and short-term investments	$ 233,369	$ 215,585
By board for capital improvements		
Cash and short-term investments	$2,183,639	$ 1,976,543
By agreements with third-party payer for funded depreciation		
Cash and short-term investments	$6,929,210	$11,677,476
U.S. Treasury obligations	332,000	29,295
Interest receivable	162,625	255,397
	$7,423,835	$11,962,168
Under indenture agreement (held by trustee)		
U.S. Treasury obligations	$ 638,966	$ 631,100

The terms of the Series 1990 bonds (Note 7) require that certain funds for bond debt service and acquisition or replacement of Hospital property be established, maintained at certain minimum levels, and funded by the Hospital as follows:

	December 31	
	1992	*1991*
Principal account—Funds must be maintained at levels sufficient to meet principal payments due annually on January 1. The Hospital is required to make quarterly deposits into this account totaling $290,000 for the bond year ending January 1, 1993.	$145,000	$202,500
Interest account—Funds must be maintained at levels sufficient to meet semiannual interest payments totaling $212,787 on January 1, 1993, and $204,087 on July 1, 1993, through quarterly Hospital deposits.	12,803	121,604
Reserve account—Funds at an amount equal to the lesser of the maximum annual debt service or 125% of the average annual debt service must be maintained in the reserve accounts. Deficiencies in other bond fund accounts will be funded from these accounts.	638,966	631,100

continues

Exhibit 4–1 continued

| | December 31 | |
	1992	1991
Series 1985 bond account held by trustee	—	357,096
	796,769	1,312,300
Less assets whose use is limited and that are required for current liabilities	157,803	681,200
	$638,966	$631,100

The bond agreement authorizes the trustees to establish other bond accounts as they may be required. These include an optimal redemption account and a capital replacement fund. No funds were required to be deposited into these accounts as of December 31, 1992 and 1991.

Note 7: Long-Term Debt

Long-term debt consists of the following:

| | December 31 | |
	1992	1991
Series 1990 bonds—California Health Care Facilities Authority revenue bonds, 5.40% to 7.875% due to January 1, 2005	$5,765,000	$6,035,000
Series 1985 bonds—California Health Care Facilities Authority revenue bonds, 5.75% to 8.00%	—	275,200
Miscellaneous notes payable to various individuals, collateralized by real estate	68,913	103,913
	5,833,913	6,414,113
Less current portion	358,913	649,113
	$5,475,000	$5,765,000

The California Health Care Facilities Authority (the Authority) issued special-obligation Series 1990 revenue bonds whose proceeds (totaling $6,310,000) were loaned by the Authority to the Hospital. The Series 1990 bonds are payable solely from payments made by the Hospital.

The Series 1990 bonds include serial bonds maturing from 1993 through 1999 and term bonds maturing in 2005. The bonds bear interest, payable semiannually, at rates from 6% on serial bonds maturing in 1993 to 7.875% on term bonds maturing in 2005. The bonds are collateralized by an interest in the Hospital's gross receivables and

Exhibit 4–1 continued

gross receipts and equipment, and by funds held by the trustee under the bond indenture agreement (Note 6).

The restrictive covenants of the loan and security agreement and the trust indentures require, among other matters, that the Hospital maintain a minimum debt to service coverage ratio.

Principal maturities of long-term debt are as follows:

Year Ending December 31	
1993	$ 358,913
1994	305,000
1995	325,000
1996	345,000
1997	370,000
Thereafter	4,130,000
	$5,833,913

Note 8: Pension Plan

The Hospital has a noncontributory, defined-benefit pension plan covering substantially all employees. The plan calls for benefits to be paid to eligible employees at retirement based primarily on years of service with the Hospital and compensation rates throughout the employment period. Contributions to the plan reflect benefits attributed to employees' services to date, as well as services expected to be earned in the future. Plan assets consist primarily of common and preferred stock, investment-grade corporate bonds, and U.S. Government obligations. Plan information is presented by the projected unit credit method as required by generally accepted accounting principles.

Pension expenses include the following components:

	December 31	
	1992	*1991*
Service costs of the current period	$527,043	$402,970
Interest cost on the projected obligation	523,418	416,168
Actual return on assets held in the plan	(1,103,755)	(835,542)
Net amortization of prior service cost, transition liability, and net gain	572,225	181,560
Pension expense	$518,931	$165,156

continues

Exhibit 4–1 continued

The funded status of the plan and the amounts shown in the general fund balance sheet are as follows:

	December 31	
	1992	1991
Actuarial present value of benefit obligations		
Vested benefits	$5,280,717	$4,471,029
Nonvested benefits	90,934	80,248
Accumulated benefit obligation	5,371,651	4,551,277
Effect of anticipated future compensation levels and other events	1,802,158	1,689,480
Projected benefit obligation	7,173,809	6,240,757
Fair value of assets held in the plan	7,951,109	6,764,658
Plan assets in excess of projected benefit obligation	$ 777,300	$ 523,901

The funded excess consists of the following:

	December 31	
	1992	1991
Unamortized prior service cost	$ (223,514)	$ (251,453)
Net unrecognized loss from past experience different from assumed	226,021	(463,318)
Unamortized liability at transition	1,224,219	1,238,672
Pension liability included in balance sheet	(449,426)	—
	$ 777,300	$ 523,901

Assumptions used in the accounting were as follows:

	December 31	
	1992	1991
Discount rates	8.5%	8.5%
Rates of increase in compensation levels	5.5%	5.5%
Expected long-term rate of return on assets	8.5%	8.5%

Note 9: Self-Insured Plans

Health and dental—The Hospital has a self-insured dental plan covering its employees. An employee self-funded health care plan has been established that is

Exhibit 4–1 continued

administered by direct administrators. Payments are irrevocably deposited into a trust depository account for the benefit of Hospital employees. The trust is tax-exempt under Section 501(c)(9) of the Internal Revenue Code. Payments are charged to employee benefit expense. The Hospital also has stop-loss coverage through an insurance company that provides coverage for employee claims in excess of $25,000. Payments for health and dental insurance coverage totaled $1,213,834 and $1,003,711 in 1992 and 1991, respectively.

Workers' compensation—The Hospital has a self-insured workers' compensation plan for its employees. The Hospital pays its share of actual injury claims, maintenance of reserves, administrative expenses, and reimbursement premiums. Amounts paid by the Hospital for workers' compensation expense were $246,777 and $91,272 in 1992 and 1991, respectively.

Unemployment—The Hospital has a self-insured unemployment plan for its employees. The Hospital pays its share of actual unemployment claims, maintenance of reserves, and administrative expenses. Payments by the Hospital charged to unemployment expense were $46,856 and $5,783 in 1992 and 1991, respectively.

Note 10: Estimated Malpractice Costs

The Hospital is a member of the California Hospital Insurance Fund (the Fund). Members' financial obligations to the Fund are limited to their respective costs for malpractice insurance coverage. The Fund provides claims-based malpractice insurance coverage that covers only asserted malpractice claims. The Hospital recognizes expenses associated with unasserted malpractice claims in the period in which the incidents are expected to have occurred rather than when a claim is asserted. Expenses associated with these incidents are estimated and based on actuarial assumptions of current settlement costs.

Other Assets

Other assets are assets that are neither current nor involve property and equipment. Typically, they are either investments or intangible assets. Omega Hospital has three categories of investments. It has some land that is being held for a future expansion, an investment in a partnership, and cash value of life insurance. Omega also has some deferred financing costs. Deferred financing costs are costs incurred initially by a borrower to issue bonds. Such costs include legal fees, accounting fees, and underwriter's costs. The costs are amortized over the life of the bonds, much like depreciation.

Two major intangible asset items that show up in some health care facility balance sheets are goodwill and organization costs. Goodwill represents the difference between the price paid to acquire another entity and the fair market value of the acquired entity's assets, less any related obligations or liabilities. Goodwill shows up mainly in proprietary facilities, although it is also being increasingly seen in voluntary not-for-profit organizations as they acquire other health care entities. Organization costs are expended for legal and accounting fees and other items incurred at the formation of the entity. The cost of these items is usually amortized over some allowable life.

Current Liabilities

Current liabilities are obligations that are expected to require payment in cash during the coming year or operating cycle, whichever is longer. Like current assets, they are generally expected to be paid in one year's time.

Accounts Payable

Accounts payable may be thought of as the counterpart of accounts receivable. They represent the entity's promise to pay money for goods or services it has received.

Accrued Liabilities

Accrued liabilities are obligations that result from prior operations. They are thus a present right or enforceable demand. The accruing of interest expense with the passage of time, discussed in Chapter 3, is an example. Other examples of accrued expenses are payroll, vacation pay, tax deductions, rent, and insurance. In some cases, especially payroll, accrued liabilities are disaggregated to show material categories. Omega Hospital classifies accrued liabilities into four categories: (1) salaries and wages, (2) employee benefits, (3) interest, and (4) other.

Current Portion of Long-Term Debt

Current portion of long-term debt represents the amount of principal that will be repaid on the indebtedness within the coming year. It does not equal the total amount of the payments that will be made during that year. Total payments include both interest and principal; current portion of long-term debt includes just the principal portion. For example, if at the June 30 fiscal year close, a total of $360,000 ($30,000 per month) will be paid on long-term indebtedness during the coming year and, of this amount, only $120,000 is principal payment, then $120,000 would be shown as a current portion of the long-term debt.

Noncurrent Liabilities

Noncurrent liabilities include obligations that will not require payment in cash for at least one year or more. Omega Hospital shows two types of noncurrent liabilities, estimated malpractice costs and long-term debt.

Estimated Malpractice Costs

Omega Hospital has recorded $988,241 of estimated malpractice costs at the close of 1992. In Exhibit 4–1, Note 10 describes this account and its derivation in more detail. The amount reported for estimated malpractice costs represents the present value of expected or "estimated" claims that the organization will be responsible for paying. In the case of Omega Hospital, there are $988,241 of estimated claims that Omega will be responsible for paying that are not covered by their insurer.

Long-Term Debt

Long-term debt represents the amount of long-term indebtedness that is not due in the next year. Omega Hospital reported $5,475,000 in 1992. When the current portion of long-term debt ($358,913) is added to the long-term portion, the total amount of debt is determined. The note to long-term debt (Note 7, Exhibit 4–1, for Omega Hospital) usually provides additional information on maturities, interest rates, and types of outstanding debt.

Fund Balance

Fund balance, as discussed earlier, represents the difference between assets and the claim to those assets by third parties or liabilities. Increases in this account balance usually arise from one of two sources: (1) contributions or (2) earnings.

In the nonprofit health care industry, there is usually no separation in the fund balance account to recognize these two sources. Thus, there is no indication of how much of Omega Hospital's fund balance of $40,513,054 was earned and how much was contributed. Financial statements prepared for proprietary entities do show this breakdown. Earnings of prior years, reduced by dividend payments to stockholders, are shown in an account labeled *retained earnings*.

In any given year, however, it is possible to determine the sources of change in fund balance by examining the statement of changes in fund balance. Table 4–2 shows that Omega Hospital's increase in its general fund balance resulted totally from the excess of revenues over expenses in both 1991 and 1992.

The value of the fund balance account at any point in time is often confused with the cash position of the entity. However, cash and fund balance will hardly ever be equal. In most situations, the cash balance will be far less than the fund balance. For example, in Table 4–2, Omega Hospital has $40,513,054 in fund balances at December 31, 1992, but only $1,304,403 in cash (Table 4–1) at the same date. Thus, the assumption that the $40,513,054 reported as fund balances can be converted into cash is a false one.

STATEMENT OF REVENUES AND EXPENSES

The statement of revenues and expenses (Table 4–3) has become a financial statement of increasing importance in both the proprietary and nonproprietary sectors. It gives a better picture of operations in a given time period than does a balance sheet. A balance sheet summarizes the wealth position of an entity at a given point in time by delineating its assets, liabilities, and fund balance. An income statement provides information concerning *how* that wealth position was changed through operations.

Table 4–2 Statement of Changes in Fund Balances for Omega Hospital

	General Fund	Restricted Funds	Total
Balances, December 31, 1990	$34,266,944	$391,677	$34,658,621
Additions and deductions			
Excess of revenues over expenses	2,887,135	—	2,887,135
Gifts and grants	—	61,770	61,770
Investment income	—	45,102	45,102
Balances, December 31, 1991	$37,154,079	$498,549	$37,652,628
Additions and deductions			
Excess of revenues over expenses	3,358,975	—	3,358,975
Gifts and grants	—	89,848	89,848
Investment income	—	61,843	61,843
Balances, December 31, 1992	$40,513,054	$650,240	$41,163,294

Table 4-3 Statement of Revenues and Expenses for Omega Hospital: General Fund

	December 31	
	1992	*1991*
Revenue from operations		
Net patient service revenue (Notes 1 and 2*)	$46,095,327	$39,084,761
Other revenue	2,607,489	2,041,106
	$48,702,816	$41,125,867
Operating expenses		
Professional care of patients	24,265,447	20,969,882
Dietary services	1,753,806	1,560,697
General services	6,448,329	4,662,888
Fiscal and administrative services	4,869,205	4,744,064
Employee health and welfare	4,155,523	2,958,193
Medical malpractice costs	716,100	924,183
Depreciation	2,470,733	2,162,895
Interest	430,725	475,666
Provision for bad debts	1,208,468	921,144
	$46,318,336	$39,379,612
Income from operations	$ 2,384,480	$ 1,746,255
Nonoperating gains (losses) (Note 1)		
Interest earnings	975,061	1,136,126
Unrestricted donations	23,332	52,389
Rental income	18,336	22,362
Gain (loss) on disposal of assets	9,561	(35,092)
Foundation expenses	(62,369)	—
Other income (expense)	10,574	(34,905)
	974,495	1,140,880
Excess of revenues over expenses	$ 3,358,975	$ 2,887,135

*Note numbers refer to those in Exhibit 4-1.

An entity's ability to earn an excess of revenue over expenses is an important variable in many external and internal decisions. A series of income statements indicates this ability well. Creditors use income statements to determine the entity's ability to pay future and present debts; management and rate-regulating agencies use them to assess whether current and proposed rate structures are adequate.

The *entity principle* is an important factor in analyzing and interpreting the statement of revenue and expense. Income, the excess of revenue over expenses, comes from a large number of individual operations within a health care entity and is aggregated in the statement of revenues and expenses. For example, reports on minor breakdowns may be required on a departmental basis for some decisions; little can be said about specific rates and their adequacy within a health care facility if department statements of revenues and expenses are not available. Such statements are in fact frequently available and should be used. Here, however, our focus is on the general purpose statement of revenues and expenses, which is an aggregate of individual departments' income.

Revenue

Generally speaking, revenue in a health care facility comes from three sources:

1. patient services revenue
2. other revenue
3. nonoperating gains (losses)

Patient Services Revenue

Patient services revenue represents the amount of revenue that results from the provision of health care services to patients. It is often shown on a net basis in the statement of revenues and expenses with additional detail in the footnotes. Omega Hospital reported net patient services revenue of $46,095,327 in fiscal year 1992. Note 2 in Exhibit 4–1 shows that Omega Hospital really had $48,818,416 in charges or gross patient services revenue. A portion of the revenue was not deemed collectable and was written off. The primary source was derived from contractual adjustments, which represent the difference between what a third-party payer pays and what the actual charges are. For example, a Medicare patient may receive services with charges of $4,000, but Medicare may pay only $3,000 for those services. The $1,000 difference represents the contractual allowance.

Charity care represents services provided for which payment was never expected. Most health care organizations have some stated policy regarding charity care. There is no charge generated for a charity patient because payment is not pursued, but it is sometimes useful to identify the amount of charges or costs incurred to provide charity care. Note 3 in Exhibit 4–1 shows that Omega Hospital provided $1,097,568 in charges to charity patients; that is, 2.2 percent of all patients were charity patients.

It should be emphasized that bad debts are different from charity care. Bad debts are incurred on patients for whom services were provided and payment was expected, but no payment was forthcoming. Bad debts are not reported as a deduction from gross patient services revenue. Instead, bad debts are reported as an expense. As shown in Table 4–3, Omega Hospital had $1,208,468 of bad debt expense in 1992. This value represents the amount of charges to patients who are not expected to pay.

The value that is reported for net patient services revenue is part fact and part estimate. At the close of the fiscal year, someone must estimate what amounts will actually be paid by third-party payers under existing contracts. This is not an easy task in most situations, and there is likely to be some error. This is important to recognize when revenue figures are examined for periods of time shorter than one year (e.g., monthly) and when those statements are not audited by an independent auditor. This does not mean that the data are not valid, only that some caution should be exercised in using them.

Usually it is important to get some information about major third-party payers, such as how they pay and what their relative volume is. Oftentimes the footnotes can be very helpful in this regard. Note 2 in Exhibit 4–1 shows that Omega Hospital billed gross charges of $16,011,552 to Medicare in 1992 and $12,172,410 to Medicaid. Medicare and Medicaid thus account for 57.7 percent of Omega Hospital's total gross patient revenue of $48,818,416. Material in Note 2 also explains how Medicare and Medicaid make payments to the hospital.

Other Revenue

Other revenue is generated from normal day-to-day operations not directly related to patient care. In Table 4–3 Omega Hospital reports $2,607,489 of other revenue for 1992. There is no indication as to the source of this revenue in the financial statements, but the usual sources include revenue from

- educational programs
- research and grants
- rentals of space or equipment
- sales of medical and pharmacy items to nonpatients
- cafeteria sales
- gift shop sales
- parking lot sales
- investment income on borrowed funds held by a trustee
- investment income on malpractice trust funds

It is not entirely clear in all cases whether an item should be categorized as other revenue or as nonoperating gain or loss. The general rule is that items are categorized as nonoperating gains or losses when they are peripheral or incidental to the activities of the health care provider. For example, donations could be classified as a gain to some organizations and as other revenue in other organizations.

Nonoperating Gains (Losses)

Gains and losses result from peripheral or incidental transactions. The exact definitions of *peripheral* and *incidental* are not exactly clear, and the terms could be treated inconsistently. For example, Omega Hospital reports $975,061 of interest earnings in 1992 (Table 4–3). Most likely these earnings resulted from funds restricted by the board for capital improvements and by third-party payers for funded depreciation. Is the investment of funded depreciation or capital replacement reserves incidental to Omega Hospital? Omega Hospital must believe that it is, but another organization with exactly the same situation might choose to categorize it differently.

In general the following items are often categorized as nonoperating gains or losses:

- contributions or donations that are unrestricted
- income from endowments
- income from the investment of unrestricted general funds
- gains or losses on sale of property
- net rentals of facilities not used in the operation of the facility

Operating Expenses

In these days of increasing concern over health care costs, decision makers are paying more attention to health care facilities' operating expenses. Generally speaking, there are two ways that expenses may be categorized: (1) by cost or responsibility center or (2) by object or type of expenditure.

In most general purpose financial statements, costs are reported by cost center or department. Omega Hospital breaks down expenses into four major categories of departments:

1. professional care of patients
2. dietary services
3. general services
4. fiscal and administrative services

Professional services could also be classified as revenue departments. They provide services directly to patients, for which there is a charge. General, fiscal, and administrative services are indirect or support services; they are not direct patient services, but rather support the nursing and other professional service areas.

Omega Hospital also has identified five major types of expenses:

1. employee health and welfare
2. medical malpractice costs
3. provision for bad debts
4. depreciation
5. interest

Employee health and welfare costs represent amounts for employee benefits and tax payments. Among items included here are social security, unemployment tax, workers' compensation, retirement costs, health insurance, and other fringe benefit programs.

Medical malpractice costs represent the amount paid to an insurance company for professional liability coverage during the year, or an actuarial estimate of the amount that will be paid in the future from claims that will have had their basis in the current year. Since many hospitals are partially self-insured and partially commercially insured, the reported malpractice costs may be a mix of both types of coverage.

Bad-debt provisions recognize the amount of gross charges that will not be collected from patients from whom payment was expected. For example, if a patient had commercial insurance coverage that paid 80 percent of her bill of $10,000, the hospital would bill the patient for $2,000. If the patient refused to pay the $2,000 and no payment was expected, the $2,000 charge would be written off as a bad debt.

Depreciation and interest are two special accounts that have great importance in financial analysis and are discussed in Chapter 6.

It should be noted that expense and expenditure (or payment and cash) may not be equivalent in any given period. For example, a health care facility may incur an expenditure of $1,000,000 to buy a piece of equipment but may charge only $200,000 as depreciation expense in a given year. In general, expenditure reflects the payment of cash, while expense recognizes prior expenditure that has produced revenue. Three major categories of expenditures usually are not treated as expenses:

1. retirement or repayment of debt
2. investment in new fixed assets
3. increases in working capital or current assets

One major category of expense—depreciation of fixed assets—does not involve a cash expenditure. In addition, other normal accruals, such as vacation and sick leave benefits, may be recognized as expense but involve no immediate cash outlay.

STATEMENT OF CASH FLOWS

The statement of cash flows is designed to give additional information on the flow of funds within an entity. As we have noted, the concept of expense does not necessarily give decision makers information on funds flow. The statement of cash flows is designed to give information on the flow of funds within an entity and to summarize the sources that make funds available and the uses for those funds during a given period.

Omega Hospital reports its statement of cash flows in Table 4-4. In general there are three activities that generate or use cash flows for an organization: (1) operating activities, (2) investing activities, and (3) financing activities. Omega Hospital derived $4,228,882 of cash flow from operating activities during 1992. It then spent $3,310,764 on investments, primarily property and equipment. It also spent $580,200 for retirement of principal on long-term debt during 1992. The difference is the net increase in cash and cash equivalents during the year, or $337,918. A statement of cash flows can be thought of very simply as a statement that explains the sources for changes in the cash accounts during the year.

It is also useful to review "Reconciliation of excess of revenues over expenses to net cash provided by operating activities and gains and losses" in Table 4-4. This is just an alternative way of looking at the change in cash and cash equivalents that have resulted from operating activities.

The amount of cash flow generated from operating activities can be thought of as the amount of excess of revenues over expenses subject to several adjustments: The first adjustment is for expenses that did not involve an actual outlay of cash. The biggest items here are depreciation and provision for bad debts. Provision for bad debts is added back because the expense did not involve an outlay of cash, merely a write-off of a receivable. For example, Omega Hospital added back $442,893 of its provision for bad debts in 1992 as a noncash charge. This amount is $765,575 less than the amount of bad-debt expense reported in Table 4-3 ($1,208,468). The remaining $765,575 worth of accounts receivables were written off during the year against accounts receivable and no longer remain on the books as a deduction from accounts receivable.

Another major use of cash flow involves working capital items, the difference between current assets and current liabilities. Omega Hospital experienced an increase of $2,051,786 in its patient accounts receivable. This amount exceeds the increase shown in the balance sheet (Table 4–1), but the difference is again attributed to bad-debt expense. In general, the following equation will define the amount of cash flow used to increase

Table 4–4 Statement of Cash Flows for Omega Hospital: General Fund

	December 31	
	1992	1991
Cash flows from operating activities and gains and losses		
Cash received from patients and third-party payers	$42,909,975	$37,689,609
Cash received from other operating revenue	2,607,489	2,041,106
Cash paid to employees and suppliers	(41,831,168)	(35,016,326)
Interest received	859,926	1,136,399
Interest paid	(446,863)	(490,656)
Unrestricted donations and other	129,523	52,839
Net cash provided by operating activities and gains and losses	$ 4,228,882	$ 5,412,971
Cash flows from investing activities		
Purchase of property and equipment	(7,806,660)	(6,599,939)
Proceeds from sale of assets	13,412	—
Cash invested in assets whose use is limited	4,828,984	516,057
Purchase of land held for investment	(189,194)	(136,612)
Capital contribution to investment in partnership	(139,301)	25,309
Increase in cash surrender value of life insurance	(18,005)	(14,177)
Net cash used for investing activities	(3,310,764)	(6,209,362)
Cash flows from financing activities		
Principal payments on long-term debt	(580,200)	(685,767)
Net cash used for financing activities	(580,200)	(685,767)
Net increase (decrease) in cash and cash equivalents	337,918	(1,482,158)
Cash and cash equivalents, beginning of year	966,485	2,448,643
Cash and cash equivalents, end of year	$ 1,304,403	$ 966,485

continues

Table 4–4 continued

	December 31	
	1992	1991
Reconciliation of excess of revenues over expenses to net cash provided by operating activities and gains and losses		
Excess of revenues over expenses	$3,358,975	$2,887,135
Adjustments to reconcile excess of revenue over expenses to net cash provided by operating activities and gains and losses		
Depreciation	2,470,733	2,162,895
Provision for bad debts	442,893	51,506
Provision for malpractice liability	(98,759)	67,000
Gain (loss) on disposal of assets	(9,561)	35,092
Increase (decrease) in cash due to changes in assets and liabilities		
Patient accounts receivable, net	(2,051,786)	(847,313)
Other receivables	(52,811)	273
Third-party payer settlements, net	(367,991)	322,249
Medical supplies	(99,844)	(22,010)
Prepaid expenses	16,164	(54,338)
Interest earned but not received on assets whose use is limited	(16,138)	(14,990)
Accounts payable	(166,550)	603,043
Accrued liabilities	803,557	222,429
Net adjustment	869,907	$2,525,836
Net cash provided by operating activities and gains and losses	$4,228,882	$5,412,971

patient accounts receivable:

[Ending accounts receivable − Beginning accounts receivable + Provision for bad debts reported in reconciliation]

[$7,684,188 − $6,075,295 + $442,893] = $2,051,786

Other working capital items such as a decrease in accounts payable can use cash and reduce cash flow.

STATEMENT OF CHANGES IN FUND BALANCES

The statement of changes in fund balances for both unrestricted and restricted funds merely accounts for the changes in fund balances during the year. Information on flows between restricted and unrestricted funds and flows into the entity that are restricted can be obtained from this statement.

During the last two fiscal years Omega Hospital received no transfers of funds into its general fund. The only source of increase was excess of revenues over expenses. The restricted funds have received some gifts and grants in each year and also some investment income.

SUMMARY

In this chapter we have discussed the contents of four general purpose financial statements:

1. balance sheet
2. statement of revenues and expenses
3. statement of cash flows
4. statement of changes in fund balances

Primary attention was directed at the first two, balance sheet and statement of revenues and expenses, which provide a basis for most financial information.

Our attention in this chapter was directed at understanding the basic information available in these four financial statements. The next two chapters describe how that information can be interpreted and used in actual decision making.

ASSIGNMENTS

1. Determine the amount of net operating income that would result for a hospital whose payer mix and expected volume (100 cases) is as follows:

30 Medicare cases	pay $2,000 per case
30 Blue Cross cases	pay average cost
20 commercial cases	pay 100 percent of charges
10 Medicaid cases	pay average cost
8 self-pay cases	pay 100 percent of charges
2 charity cases	pay nothing

Average cost per case is expected to be $2,200, and the average charge per case is $2,500.

2. How could you determine the amount of debt principal that will be retired during the next year through an examination of the financial statements?

3. What are the titles of the four financial statements that are usually included in an audited financial report?

4. Shady Rest nursing home has just acquired a home health firm for $850,000 in cash. The balance sheet of the home health firm looked as follows just prior to the acquisition:

Current assets	$200,000
Net fixed assets	100,000
Total	$300,000
Current liabilities	$100,000
Shareholder's equity	200,000
Total	$300,000

Assume that the fair market value of the net fixed assets is $300,000. Describe how this acquisition might be reflected on the balance sheet of Shady Rest.

5. Describe several items that are treated as expenses in the income statement but do not require any expenditure of cash in the present period.

6. A major medical supplier has donated $45,000 worth of medical supply items to your firm. These items are then used in the treatment of patients. Explain how this transaction would be recorded in your firm's financial statements.

7. Your local Blue Cross plan reimburses you on the basis of average cost per patient day. An interim rate of $400 per day has been established. Charges to Blue Cross patients have been averaging $465 per day. At the end of the year, an audit was conducted and the actual cost per Blue Cross patient day was found to be $415. During the year, 45,000 Blue Cross patient days were billed and paid for at the interim rate. There are 3,000 Blue Cross patient days that were not billed at the end of the fiscal year. With this information, determine the following amounts:

- gross Blue Cross revenue
- Blue Cross contractual adjustment from revenue
- net Blue Cross revenue
- net receivable due from Blue Cross

8. Your HMO is experiencing a critical shortage of funds. Using the statement of cash flows as a framework for discussion, explain how you might attempt to reduce the need for additional funds.

9. Your hospital has experienced negative levels of net income for the last five years. The total amount of accumulated deficits is $5 million, but you have noticed that your fund balance has increased $2 million during the same period. How might this situation be explained?

10. You have been reading the footnotes to your hospital's financial statements and were surprised to see that the actuarial present value of accumulated pension plan benefits is $4,500,000. A footnote cites a fund of $8,500,000 that has been established to pay these

benefits. However, you can find no mention of either the liability or the fund in the balance sheet. What might explain this situation?

SOLUTIONS AND ANSWERS

1. The calculations to determine the hospital's net operating income would be as follows:

Gross patient revenue	
Medicare (30 × $2,500)	$ 75,000
Blue Cross (30 × $2,500)	75,000
Commercial (20 × $2,500)	50,000
Medicaid (10 × $2,500)	25,000
Self-pay (8 × $2,500)	20,000
Charity (2 × $2,500)	5,000
Total	$250,000
Deductions from gross patient revenue	
Medicare [30 × ($2,500 − $2,000)]	$ 15,000
Blue Cross [30 × ($2,500 − $2,200)]	9,000
Commercial [20 × ($2,500 − $2,500)]	0
Medicaid [10 × ($2,500 − $2,200)]	3,000
Self-pay [8 × ($2,500 − $2,500)]	0
Charity [2 × ($2,500 − 0)]	5,000
Total	$ 32,000
Net patient revenue	$218,000
Total expenses (100 × $2,200)	$220,000
Excess of revenues over expenses	$ (2,000)

2. The value reported for current maturities of long-term debt in the balance sheet should represent the value of debt principal that will be retired during the next fiscal year.

3. The four financial statements are

1. balance sheet
2. statement of revenues and expenses
3. statement of cash flows
4. statement of changes in fund balances

4. First, fair market value of the assets acquired by Shady Rest would be determined. In this example, we will assume that the current asset value would not change but the fixed assets would be restated to $300,000 at fair market value. Shady Rest is thus acquiring total assets worth $500,000 and assuming liabilities of $100,000 for a net book value of $400,000. Since Shady Rest is paying $850,000 for these assets, there would be a goodwill account of $450,000 created for the residual. The following account changes would occur:

- cash—decrease of $850,000
- current assets—increase of $200,000
- net fixed assets—increase of $300,000
- goodwill—increase of $450,000
- current liabilities—increase of $100,000

The goodwill value would be charged to expense in future time periods.

5. Pension expense would not require an actual expenditure of cash at the present time, although a payment may be made to a trustee for investment. Other accruals—such as vacation benefits, sick leave benefits, and FICA (Federal Insurance Contributions Act) accruals—may not require immediate cash expenditures.

6. The fair market value of the items donated would be treated as other operating revenue. In this case, if $45,000 is the fair market value, that amount would be shown as other operating revenue.

7. The following values for the four sources of revenue would result:

Gross revenue (48,000 × $465)	$22,320,000
Contractual adjustment [48,000 × ($465 − $415)]	2,400,000
Net revenue (48,000 × $415)	$19,920,000
Net receivable ((3,000 × $415) + (45,000 × $15))	$ 1,920,000

8. Major categories of fund usage in the statement of changes in financial position are

- repayment of debt
- purchase of fixed assets
- increase in working capital items such as accounts receivable

Conservation of funds could occur in any one of these three areas. For example, the HMO could postpone or delay new fixed-asset acquisitions. It could also try to restructure its debt, especially in situations where a large proportion of the debt is short-term. Finally, it could attempt to reduce the amount of funds necessary for working capital increases. This could be accomplished through a reduction in the HMO's receivable cycle or through an increase in its payable cycle.

9. In this example, the hospital has increased its total equity by $7 million through sources other than income. The most likely sources of these funds are transfers from restricted funds, such as from plant replacement, or from direct equity transfers from related parties, such as a holding company. It is important to note that the funds were not derived from unrestricted contributions. Unrestricted contributions would have been shown as nonoperating revenue and thus included in the computation of excess of revenues over expenses.

10. Pension funds in a defined benefit plan are often held by a trustee and are not shown on the firm's financial statements. This is most likely the situation here. It is important to examine periodically the relationship between the pension fund and the actuarial present value of the pension fund liability. Changes in actuarial assumptions—for example, in mortality, investment yield, or inflation rates—can have a dramatic influence over the size of the liability. The relevant information can be found in the footnotes to the financial statements.

Chapter 5

Accounting for Inflation

To adjust for the effects of changing price levels, the Financial Accounting Standards Board (FASB) has issued a number of pronouncements over the last 30 years. In September 1979, the FASB issued Statement 33, which required large public enterprises to provide supplemental information on the effects of changing price levels in their annual financial reports. This was a major step for the FASB and represented the first time that firms were required to report price level effects in their financial reports.

In 1986, the FASB modified substantially its initial position set forth in Statement 33 with the publication of Statement 89. This pronouncement left intact much of Statement 33, except that it made the reporting voluntary. Business enterprises were encouraged but not required to report supplementary information on the effects of changing prices in the following areas for the most recent five years:

- net sales and operating revenues, using constant purchasing power
- income from continuing operations on a current cost basis
- purchasing power gains or losses from holding monetary items
- increases in specific prices of net plant, property, and equipment net of inflation
- foreign currency translation adjustments on a current cost basis
- net assets (assets less liabilities) on a current cost basis
- income per common share from continuing operations on a current cost basis
- cash dividends per common share
- market price per common share at year end

The rationale for these changes in financial reporting stems from the inaccuracy and inability of present unadjusted historical cost reports to measure financial position accurately in an inflation-riddled economy. Unless inflationary pressures in the economy are removed, it seems logical to assume that alternative financial reporting systems that can account for the effects of changing price levels will be adopted. It also seems logical to expect that the accounting profession will eventually extend alternative reporting requirements to all business organizations. Hospitals and other health care organizations will, in all probability, be included.

At present, the effect of these financial reporting changes has not been clearly demonstrated. Thus, many individuals have formed beliefs and expectations about financial reporting changes that may not be accurate.

The major purpose of this chapter is to discuss and describe the major alternatives for reflecting the effects of inflation in financial statements. Specific methods are described, and the adjustments that need to be made to convert historical cost statements are illustrated. This discussion should provide a basis for understanding and using financial statements that have been adjusted for inflation.

REPORTING ALTERNATIVES

Methods of financial reporting can be categorized along two dimensions: (1) the method of asset valuation and (2) the unit of measurement. Two major methods of asset valuation are (1) acquisition (or historical) cost and (2) current (or replacement) value.

Asset valuation at acquisition cost means that the value of the asset is not changed over time to reflect changing market values. Amortization of the value may take place, but the basis is the acquisition cost. Depreciation is recorded, using the acquisition (historical) cost of the asset. Use of an acquisition cost valuation method postpones the recognition of gains or losses from holding assets until the point of sale or retirement. Current valuation of assets revalues the assets in each reporting period. The assets are stated at their current value rather than their acquisition cost. Likewise, depreciation expense is based on the current value, not the historical cost. Current valuation recognizes gains or losses from holding assets prior to sale or retirement.

There are also two major alternative units of measurement in financial reporting: (1) nominal (unadjusted) dollars and (2) constant dollars measured in units of general purchasing power. Use of a nominal dollar unit of measurement simply means that the attribute being measured is the number of dollars. From an accounting perspective, a dollar of one year is no different from a dollar of another year. No recognition is given to changes in the purchasing power of the dollar, because the attribute is not measured. The major outcome associated with the use of this measurement unit is that gains or losses, regardless of when they are recognized, are not adjusted for changes in purchasing power. For example, if a piece of land that was acquired for $1 million in 1977 were sold for $5 million in 1997, it would have generated a $4 million gain, regardless of changes in the purchasing power of the dollar during the 20-year period.

A constant dollar measuring unit reports the effects of all financial transactions in terms of constant purchasing power. The units that are usually used are the purchasing power of the dollar at the end of the reporting period or the average during the fiscal year. The measurement is made by multiplying the unadjusted, or nominal, dollars by a price index to convert to a measure of constant purchasing power. In periods of inflation, when using a constant dollar measuring unit, gains from holding assets are reduced, while losses are increased. Thus, in the above land sale example, the initial acquisition cost would be restated to 1997 dollars to reduce the gain:

Sale price of land (1997 dollars)	$5,000,000
Less acquisition cost restated (1997 dollars)	2,038,504
Gain on sale	$2,961,496

Constant dollar measurement has a further significant effect on financial reporting: The gains or losses created by holding monetary liabilities or assets during periods of purchasing power changes are recognized in the financial reporting. For example, an entity that owed $25 million during a year when the purchasing power of the dollar decreased by 10 percent would report a $2.5 million (0.10 × $25 million) purchasing power gain. All gains or losses would be recognized, regardless of the valuation basis used.

Monetary assets and liabilities are defined as those items that reflect cash or claims to cash that are fixed in terms of the number of dollars, regardless of changes in prices. Almost all liabilities are monetary items, whereas monetary assets consist primarily of cash, marketable securities, and receivables. Purchasing power gains or losses are recognized on monetary items because there is an assumption that the gains or losses are already realized, since repayments or receipts are fixed.

The interfacing of the valuation basis and the unit of measurement basis produces four alternative financial reporting methods (Table 5–1). Each of the four methods is a possible basis for financial reporting. The unadjusted historical cost (HC) method represents the present method used by accountants; the other three methods are alternatives that would provide

Table 5-1 Alternative Financial Reporting Bases

Unit of Measurement	Asset Valuation Method	
	Acquisition Cost	Current Value
Nominal dollars	Unadjusted historical cost (HC)	Current value (CV)
Constant dollars	Historical cost general price level adjusted (HC-GPL)	Current value general price level adjusted (CV-GPL)
	Constant dollar accounting	Current cost accounting

some degree of inflationary adjustment not present in the HC method. The HC-general price level adjusted (GPL) method is referred to as historical cost/constant dollar accounting, while the current value (CV)-GPL method is referred to as current cost accounting.

Table 5-2 summarizes the effects the four reporting methods would have on three major income statement items: (1) depreciation expense, (2) purchasing power gains or losses, and (3) unrealized gains in replacement values. However, the net effect of the changes in these items on net income for an individual institution cannot be predicted; the composition and age of the assets, as well as the prior patterns of financing, will determine whether the net effect will be positive or negative and to what degree.

USES OF FINANCIAL REPORT INFORMATION

The measurement of financial position is an important function, and its results are useful to a great variety of decision makers, both internal and external to the organization. Changes in financial reporting methods will unquestionably alter the resulting measures of financial position reported in financial statements. These changes are quite likely to produce changes in the decisions that are based on the financial reports (Figure 5-1).

Lenders represent an important category of financial statement users who may change their decisions on the basis of a new financial reporting method. The lender's major concern is the relative financial position of both the individual firm and the industry. A decrease in the relative

Table 5–2 Major Effects of Alternative Reporting Methods on Net Income Measurement

	Impact Variables		
Reporting Methods	*Depreciation Expense*	*Purchasing Power Gains/Losses*	*Unrealized Gains in Replacement Value*
Unadjusted historical cost (HC)	No change	No change/Not recognized	No change/Not recognized
General price level adjusted historical cost (HC-GPL)	Increase/GPL depreciation is recognized	Gain or loss/ Depends on the *net* monetary asset position	No change/Not recognized
Current value (CV)	Increase/Will recognize current replacement cost	No change/Not recognized	Gain/Will recognize increase in replacement cost
General price level adjusted current value (CV-GPL)	Increase/Will recognize current replacement cost	Gain or loss/ Depends on the *net* monetary asset position	Gain/Will recognize increase in replacement cost but will reduce the amount by changes in the GPL

financial position of the industry could seriously affect both the availability and the cost of credit. If, for a variety of reasons, new measurements of financial position make the health care industry appear weaker than other industries, financing terms could change. Particularly for the health care industry, which is increasingly dependent on debt financing, the importance of financial reporting method changes cannot be overstated. Research on the results of changing to an HC-GPL method has shown that the relative financial positions of individual firms and industries are also likely to change.

Changes in financial reporting methods could also have an effect on decisions reached by regulatory and rate-setting organizations. As a result of such changes, comparisons of costs across institutions may be more meaningful than they were before. For example, the capital costs of institutions that operate in relatively new physical plants cannot be compared with the unadjusted historical capital costs of older facilities. Without these adjustments, new facilities may appear to have higher costs and thus be less efficient, whereas in fact the opposite may be true.

The actions of interested community leaders who have access to, and make decisions based on, financial statements might also be affected by

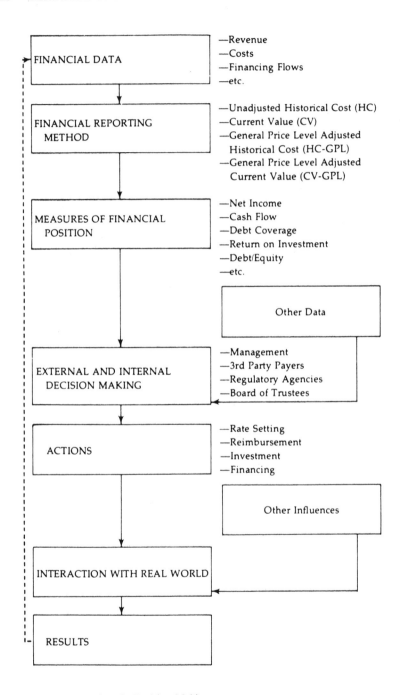

Figure 5–1 Financial Data in Decision Making

reporting method changes. For example, suppose that individual, corporate, and public agency giving is in part affected by reported income. Many in fact regard reported income as a basic index of need, and the relationship between income and giving seems logical. Thus, since each of the alternative financial reporting methods we have discussed will produce a different measure of income, total giving in each case could be affected.

Internal management decisions might also change with a new financial reporting method. Perhaps the most obvious example of such a change would be in rate setting. Organizations that have control over pricing decisions and are not reacting to market-determined prices should set prices at levels at least high enough to recover their costs. The use of a current cost basis of reporting will raise reported cost levels and therefore raise rates.

CASE EXAMPLE: WILLIAMS CONVALESCENT CENTER

In the remainder of this chapter, we show how adjustments are made in the income statement and balance sheet of Williams Convalescent Center, a 120-bed skilled and intermediate care facility, to take into account the effects of inflation. The center's two financial statements are shown in Tables 5–3 and 5–4. You will note that values are reported for each of three reporting methods: (1) HC; (2) HC-GPL, (3) CV-GPL. In this discussion, we do not describe or apply the CV method. This method is not being seriously considered by the accounting profession at this time, and it is not likely to be considered in the future. The CV method suffers from a serious flaw: it does not recognize the effects of changing price levels on equity. In short, the CV method would treat increases in the replacement cost of assets as a gain and not restate them for changes in purchasing power.

Table 5–5 presents a table of values for the consumer price index (CPI). The CPI is the price index that is used by the accounting profession at the present time to adjust financial statements for the effects of inflation.

Price Index Conversion

Both of the two methods (CV-GPL and HC-GPL) we have selected to adjust the financial statements of the Williams Convalescent Center utilize

Table 5-3 Statement of Income for Williams Convalescent Center (000s Omitted)

	HC 19Y4	Constant Dollar (HC-GPL) 19Y4	Current Cost (CV-GPL) 19Y4
Operating revenues	$3,556	$3,625	$3,625
Operating expenses	3,253	3,316	3,316
Depreciation	74	177	185
Interest	102	104	104
Net income	$ 127	$ 28	$ 20
Purchasing power gain from holding net monetary liabilities during the year	—	$ 43	$ 43
Increase in specific prices of property, plant, and equipment during the year	—	—	$ 136
Less effect of increase in general price level	—	—	$ 144
Increase in specific prices over (under) increase in the general price level	—	—	$ (8)
Change in equity due to income transactions	$ 127	$ 71	$ 55

a constant dollar as the unit of measurement. This means that purchasing power, not the dollar, is the unit of measurement. That is, all reported values in the financial statements are expressed in dollars of a specified purchasing power. Usually the purchasing power used is the period end value. In our case example, Williams Convalescent Center uses the purchasing power as of December 31, 19Y4.

Restatement of nominal or unadjusted dollars to constant dollars is a relatively simple process, at least conceptually. All that is required are three pieces of information:

1. the unadjusted value of the account in historical or nominal dollars
2. a price index that reflects the purchasing power in which the unadjusted value is currently expressed
3. a price index that reflects the purchasing power at the date the account is to be restated

For example, Williams Convalescent Center's long-term debt at December 31, 19Y3, is $1,203 (see Table 5-4). To express that amount in constant

Table 5–4 Balance Sheet for Williams Convalescent Center (000s Omitted)

	HC		Constant Dollar (HC-GPL)	Current Cost (CV-GPL)
	19Y3	19Y4	19Y4	19Y4
Current assets				
Cash	$ 98	$ 21	$ 21	$ 21
Accounts receivable	217	249	249	249
Supplies	22	27	27	27
Prepaid expenses	36	36	36	36
Total current assets	$ 373	$ 333	$ 333	$ 333
Property and equipment				
Land	200	200	530	525
Building and equipment	2,102	2,228	5,333	5,570
	2,302	2,428	5,863	6,095
Less accumulated				
depreciation	783	844	2,020	2,186
	1,519	1,584	3,843	3,909
Investments	161	596	596	596
Total assets	$2,053	$2,513	$4,772	$4,838
Current liabilities	412	493	493	493
Long-term debt	1,203	1,478	1,478	1,478
Partners' equity	438	542	2,801	2,867
	$2,053	$2,513	$4,772	$4,838

dollars as of December 31, 19Y4, the following adjustment would be made:

$$\text{Unadjusted amount} \times \frac{\text{Price index converting to}}{\text{Price index converting from}} = \text{Constant dollar value}$$

or

$$\$1,203 \times \frac{315.5}{303.5} = \$1,251$$

The value of the beginning long-term debt for the center would be $1,251, expressed in purchasing power as of December 31, 19Y4. The adjustment method described above is the same for all other accounts. The

Table 5–5 Consumer Price Index, Year-End Values

Year	CPI
19X0	119.1
19X1	123.1
19X2	127.3
19X3	138.5
19X4	155.4
19X5	166.3
19X6	174.3
19X7	186.1
19X8	202.9
19X9	229.9
19Y0	258.4
19Y1	283.4
19Y2	292.4
19Y3	303.5
19Y4	315.5

Source: United States Department of Labor, Bureau of Labor Statistics

price index to which the conversion is made is usually the price index at the ending balance sheet date (December 31, 19Y4, in our example). The price index from which the conversion is made represents the purchasing power in which the account is currently expressed. This value will vary depending on the classification of the account as either monetary or nonmonetary.

Monetary versus Nonmonetary Accounts

When restating financial statements from one based on an HC method to one based on a constant dollar method, it is critical to distinguish between monetary accounts and nonmonetary accounts. Monetary accounts are automatically stated in current dollars and therefore require no price level adjustments. Monetary items, discussed earlier in this chapter, consist of cash or claims to cash or promises to pay cash that are fixed in terms of dollars, regardless of price level changes. Nonmonetary accounts require price level adjustments in order to be stated in current dollars.

Because of the fixed nature of monetary items, holding them during a period of changing price levels creates a gain or loss. This can be seen in the following data from Williams Convalescent Center (000s omitted):

	Unadjusted	Conversion Factor	Constant Dollars
Beginning long-term debt (12/31/Y3)	$1,203	315.5/303.5	$1,251
− Repayment (6/30/Y4)	152	315.5/309.5	155
+ New debt (6/30/Y4)	427	315.5/309.5	435
Ending long-term debt (12/31/Y4)	$1,478		$1,531
− Actual ending long-term debt (12/31/Y4)			$1,478
Purchasing power gain			$ 53

The above data assume that a repayment and new issue occurred at the midpoint of the year, June 30, 19Y4. The price index at that point would have been approximately 309.5. This resulted from taking the average of the beginning and ending values (303.5 + 315.5)/2. In constant dollars, the Williams Center would have reported $1,531 of long-term debt at December 31, 19Y4. However, the actual value of the long-term debt at that date was $1,478. The difference of $53 represents a purchasing power gain to the Center during the year. Because the price level increased during 19Y4, the value of the long-term debt actually owed by the Center declined when measured in constant purchasing power.

Nonmonetary asset accounts must always be restated to purchasing power at the current date. The price index at the time of acquisition represents the price index from which the conversion is made. The price index at the current date represents the index to which the conversion is made. To illustrate the adjustment, assume that the building and equipment account of Williams Convalescent Center has the following age distribution:

Year Acquired	Cost	Conversion Factor	Constant Dollar Cost (12/31/Y4)
19X0	$1,500	315.5/119.1	$3,974
19X8	401	315.5/202.9	624
19Y1	201	315.5/283.4	224
19Y4	126	315.5/315.5	126
	$2,228		$4,948

The above data show that assets with a historical cost of $2,228 represent $4,948 of cost when stated in dollars as of December 31, 19Y4. The latter value is much more meaningful than the former as a measure of actual asset cost in 19Y4. It provides the Center with a measure of cost that is expressed in dollars as of the current date and thus better represents its actual investment. Depreciation expense should also be restated in 19Y4 dollars in order to portray accurately the Center's actual cost of using its building and equipment in the generation of current revenues.

Adjusting the Income Statement

Operating Revenues

If one assumes that revenues are realized equally throughout the year, it simplifies the restatement significantly. If the assumption is valid, and in most cases it is, it means that the revenues can be considered realized at the midpoint of the year, in our case, June 30, 19Y4. As already noted, the price index at June 30, 19Y4, can be assumed to be the average of the beginning and ending price index, or 309.5. The restated operating revenue would be calculated as follows:

$$\$3,556 \times 315.5/309.5 = \$3,625$$

Operating Expenses

Based on the same assumption that we used with operating revenues, the adjustment for operating expenses would be

$$\$3,253 \times 315.5/309.5 = \$3,316$$

Operating expenses do not include depreciation or interest. Separate adjustments for these two items may be required.

Depreciation

The depreciation expense adjustment is different from the earlier adjustments in two ways. First, depreciation expense represents an amortization of assets purchased over a long period of time, usually many years. This means that the midpoint conversion method used for operating revenues and operating expenses is clearly not appropriate. Second, the adjustment methods for the constant dollar and current cost methods diverge. Depreciation expense may vary considerably because the current cost of the assets may differ dramatically from the constant dollar cost. Remember, a price index represents price changes for a large number of goods and services; specific price changes of individual assets may vary significantly from that index.

Constant Dollar Adjustment. Two methods can be used to adjust depreciation expense to a constant dollar amount. The most accurate method is to perform an adjustment for each asset. This can be a time-consuming process, however, and may not be worth the effort. Alternatively, an average acquisition date can be estimated by first determining the average age of the assets, as follows:

$$\text{Average age} = \frac{\text{Accumulated depreciation}}{\text{Depreciation expense}} = \frac{\$844}{\$74} = 11.4 \text{ years}$$

If one uses straight-line depreciation, this way of estimating average age is reasonably reliable. For Williams Convalescent Center, an average of 11.4 years would imply that the assets were purchased sometime in 19X3. Interpolation would yield a price index of 131.8. Depreciation expense in 19Y4, expressed in constant dollars, thus would be:

$$\$74 \times 315.5/131.8 = \$177$$

Current Cost Adjustment. The identification of the current cost of existing physical assets is a subjective and complex process. To many individuals, the current cost method provides little additional value, compared with the constant dollar method. Whether it will be eventually eliminated and replaced by the constant dollar method is not clear at this time.

The first issue to address in the adjustment is the definition of current cost. By and large, current cost can be equated to the replacement cost of the assets. In short, we must determine what the cost of replacing assets in today's dollars would be. This could be estimated through a variety of techniques, using, for example, insurance appraisals or specific price indexes. In the case of Williams Convalescent Center, we will assume a recent insurance appraisal indicated a replacement cost of $5,570 for buildings and equipment. With this estimate, depreciation expense could be adjusted as follows:

$$\frac{\text{Appraisal cost}}{\text{Historical cost}} \times \text{Depreciation expense} = \text{Restated depreciation expense}$$

or

$$\frac{\$5,570}{\$2,228} \times \$74 = \$185$$

Interest Expense

We will again assume that interest expense is paid equally throughout the year. This assumption would produce the following interest expense adjustment:

$$\$102 \times 315.5/309.5 = \$104$$

Purchasing Power Gains or Losses

A purchasing power gain results if one is a net debtor during a period of rising prices, while a purchasing power loss results if one is a net creditor during such a period. In most health care firms, purchasing power gains result because liabilities exceed monetary assets. A firm is thus paying its debts with dollars that are cheaper than the ones it received.

To calculate purchasing power gains or losses, net monetary asset positions must first be calculated. The net monetary position for Williams Convalescent Center is presented below:

	Beginning (12/31/Y3)	Ending (12/31/Y4)
Monetary assets		
Cash	$ 98	$ 21
Accounts receivable	217	249
Prepaid expenses	36	36
Investments	161	596
Total monetary assets	$ 512	$ 902
Monetary liabilities		
Current liabilities	$ 412	$ 493
Long-term debt	1,203	1,478
Total monetary liabilities	$ 1,615	$ 1,971
Net monetary assets	$(1,103)	$(1,069)

The actual calculation of the purchasing power gain for Williams Convalescent Center is as follows:

	Actual Dollars	Conversion Factor	Constant Dollars
Beginning net monetary liabilities	$1,103	315.5/303.5	$1,147
− Decrease	34	315.5/309.5	35
Ending net monetary liabilities	$1,069		$1,112
− Actual			$1,069
Purchasing power gain			$ 43

Because the center was in a net monetary liability position during the year, it experienced a purchasing power gain of $43. This value is not an element of net income; it is rather shown below the net income line in Table 5–3. It thus affects the change in equity.

Increase in Specific Prices Over General Prices

The adjustment to take into account an increase in specific prices over general prices is made only in the current cost method. The constant dollar method does not recognize any increases (or reductions) in prices that are different from the general price level. In short, no gains or losses from holding assets are permitted in the constant dollar method.

The calculations involved in this adjustment can be terribly complex. In our Williams Convalescent Center example, we will make some assumptions to simplify the arithmetic without impairing the reader's conceptual understanding of the adjustment. We will assume the following data:

Insurance appraisal of buildings and equipment, 12/31/Y3	$5,015
Insurance appraisal of buildings and equipment, 12/31/Y4	$5,570
Appraised value of land, 12/31/Y3	$ 500
Appraised value of land, 12/31/Y4	$ 525
New equipment bought on 12/31/Y4	$ 126

The following data show the increase in specific prices over general prices:

	Building and Equipment	Land	Total
Ending appraised value less acquisitions	$5,444	$525	$5,969
– Accumulated depreciation on appraised value	2,186	5—	2,186
Ending net appraised value	$3,258	$525	$3,783
Beginning appraised value	$5,015	$500	$5,515
– Accumulated depreciation on appraised value	1,868	—	1,868
Beginning net appraised value	$3,147	$500	$3,647
Increase in specific prices during the year			$ 136
Effect of increase in general price level	$3,647 × [(315.5/303.5) − 1.0]		$ 144
Increase in specific prices over general price level			$ (8)

These data show that, during 19Y4, the value of physical assets held by Williams Convalescent Center did not increase more than the general price level. This may be a positive sign for the Center if it is not contemplating a sale. The replacement cost for its assets is increasing less than the general price level. Therefore, revenues could increase less than the general price level and replacement could still be ensured.

Adjusting the Balance Sheet

Monetary Items

None of the monetary items—cash, accounts receivable, prepaid expenses, investments, current liabilities, or long-term debt—requires adjustment. The values of these items already reflect current dollars.

Land

In our discussion of the increase in specific prices over the general price level in the Williams Center's income statement, we assumed an appraisal value for land of $525. That value will be used here with the current cost method. With the constant dollar method, we will assume that the land was acquired in 19X0 for $200. To restate that amount to purchasing power as of December 31, 19Y4, the following calculation would be made:

$$\$200 \times 315.5/119.1 = \$530$$

Buildings and Equipment

Values for the Center's buildings and equipment and the related accumulated depreciation have already been cited for the current cost method. We will assume those same values here. This produces a value for buildings and equipment of $5,570 (000s omitted) based on an appraisal. The value for accumulated depreciation was derived as follows:

$$\text{Adjusted accumulated depreciation} =$$

$$\text{Unadjusted accumulated depreciation} \times$$

$$\frac{\text{Appraised value} - \text{Current year acquisitions}}{\text{Historical cost} - \text{Current year acquisitions}}$$

or

$$\$2,186 = \$844 \times \frac{(\$5,570 - \$126)}{(\$2,228 - \$126)}$$

The constant dollar method values can be derived by using the estimated average age of the plant. In earlier discussions relating to depreciation expense, we computed the average age to be 11.4 years and the related price index at acquisition to be 131.8. With this information the following values result:

Buildings and equipment = $2,228 × 315.5/131.8 = $5,333

Accumulated depreciation = $844 × 315.5/131.8 = $2,020

Equity

Equity calculations are not discussed in any detail here. It is enough for our purposes to recognize that equity is a derived figure. Equity must equal total assets less liabilities. In our Williams Center example, this generates values of $2,801 for the constant dollar method and $2,867 for the current cost method.

SUMMARY

Financial reporting suffers from its current reliance on the HC valuation concept. Inflation has made many of the reported values in current financial reports meaningless to decision makers. The example used in this chapter illustrates this point. The total asset investment of Williams Convalescent Center is approximately 100 percent larger when adjusted for inflation under the current cost or constant dollar method. Net income, on the other hand, decreased. The result is a dramatic deterioration in return on investment—the single most important test of business success.

The following table summarizes return on assets and return on equity for Williams Convalescent Center:

	Historical Cost	Constant Dollar	Current Cost
Net income/Total assets	5.1%	0.6%	0.4%
Change in equity due to income transactions/Total assets	5.1	1.5	1.1
Net income/Equity	23.4	1.0	0.7
Change in equity due to income transactions/Equity	23.4	2.5	1.9

These reductions are so drastic that they would prompt an investor seriously to question the continuation of the present investment, let alone replacement. More profitable avenues of investment very likely may be available.

To the extent that our Williams Center example is representative of many health care firms—and it probably is—decisions regarding health care business continuation must be evaluated seriously. It is imperative that health care companies, like all other businesses, adjust their financial reports to reflect inflation. Whether the method used is current cost or constant dollar is not the issue. The important point is that ignoring the effects of inflation is unwise at best.

ASSIGNMENTS

Use the data and information presented in Table 5–6 to answer the following questions:

1. What index was used to restate to constant dollars?

2. What method was used to determine current cost values?

3. Is NME a net debtor or a net creditor?

4. In 1981, NME showed a minus $24 million value for the increase in specific prices over general prices. What does this mean?

5. Why are NME's net operating revenues in 1984 identical for the HC, constant dollar, and current cost methods of reporting?

6. Why is depreciation expense greater in the current cost method than in the constant dollar method?

SOLUTIONS AND ANSWERS

1. NME used the CPI—all urban consumers. This index is required by Financial Accounting Standards Board Statement 33 to restate historical costs to constant dollars.

2. NME used specific price indexes to restate historical costs to current costs. This method contrasts with the use of appraisals discussed in the chapter example.

3. NME is a net debtor. It has experienced a purchasing power gain in each year from 1980 to 1984. Since prices were increasing during that period, NME must have had a net monetary liability position in each year.

4. In 1981, the specific prices of NME's fixed assets must have increased less than the general price level as determined by using the CPI.

5. NME does not restate revenues or expenses to the fiscal year end, May 31. Instead, they restate to the midpoint of the fiscal year, November 30. Since it is usually assumed that revenues are received equally throughout the year, the midpoint (November 30) would represent the index from which the conversion is made. Since NME is converting to the

Table 5–6 Supplementary Financial Information for National Medical Enterprises (NME)

<table>
<tr><td>Effects of
Changing
Prices</td><td colspan="3">The company's financial statements have been prepared in accordance with generally accepted accounting principles and reflect historical cost. The goal of the supplemental information that follows is to reflect the decline in the purchasing power of the dollar resulting from inflation. This information should be viewed only as an indication, however, and not as a specific measure of the inflationary impact.</td></tr>
</table>

Effects of
Changing
Prices

The company's financial statements have been prepared in accordance with generally accepted accounting principles and reflect historical cost. The goal of the supplemental information that follows is to reflect the decline in the purchasing power of the dollar resulting from inflation. This information should be viewed only as an indication, however, and not as a specific measure of the inflationary impact.

The constant dollars were calculated by adjusting historical cost amounts by the CPI—all urban consumers. Current costs, on the other hand, reflect the changes in specific prices of land, buildings, and equipment from the date acquired to the present; they differ from constant dollar amounts to the extent that prices in general have increased more or less rapidly than specific prices. The current cost of buildings and equipment was determined by applying published indices to the historical cost.

Net income has been adjusted only for the change in depreciation expense. Other operating expenses, which are the result of current transactions, are, in effect, recorded in amounts approximating current purchasing power on the primary financial statements. Depreciation expense was determined by applying primary financial statement depreciation rates to restated building and equipment amounts. Since only historical costs are deductible for income tax purposes, the income tax expense in the primary financial statements was not adjusted.

During a period of inflation, the holding of monetary assets (cash, receivables, etc.) results in a purchasing power loss, while owing monetary liabilities (current liabilities, long-term debt, deferred credits, etc.) results in a gain. Net monetary gains or losses are not included in the adjusted net income amounts reported.

Consolidated
Statement of
Income
Adjusted
for Changing
Prices

	For the Year Ended May 31, 1984		
(dollar amounts are expressed in millions)	*As Reported in Primary Statements (Historical Cost)*	*Adjusted for General Inflation (Constant $)*	*Adjusted for Changes in Specific Prices (Current Costs)*
Net operating revenues	$2,065	$2,065	$2,065
Operating and administrative expenses	1,698	1,698	1,698
Depreciation and amortization	84	98	111
Interest	91	91	91
Total costs and expenses	1,873	1,887	1,900
Income from operations	192	178	165
Investment earnings	24	24	24

continues

Table 5–6 continued

(dollar amounts are expressed in millions)	As Reported in Primary Statements (Historical Cost)	Adjusted for General Inflation (Constant $)	Adjusted for Changes in Specific Prices (Current Costs)
		For the Year Ended May 31, 1984	
Income before taxes on income	216	202	189
Taxes on income	95	95	95
Net income	$ 121	$ 107	$ 94
Effective income tax rate	44%	47%	50%
Changing price gains not included in adjusted income: Increase in specific prices (current cost) of property, plant, and equipment held during the year*			$ 139
Less effect of increase in general price level			68
Excess of increase in specific prices over increase in the general price level			$ 71

*At May 31, 1984, current cost of property, plant, and equipment, net of accumulated depreciation, was $1,915 (historical cost $1,349). "Property, plant, and equipment" in the data above and below includes land held for expansion.

Selected Supplementary Financial Data Adjusted for Effects of Changing Prices	(dollar amounts, except pre-share amounts, are expressed in millions)				
	For the years ended May 31	1984	1983	1982	1981	1980
	Net operating revenues Adjusted for general inflation	$2,065	$1,852	$1,271	$1,070	$832
	Net Income Adjusted for general inflation	107	85	73	54	36
	Adjusted for changes in specific prices	94	73	64	46	27
	Earnings per share Adjusted for general inflation	1.54	1.29	1.18	.95	.82
	Adjusted for changes in specific prices	1.35	1.12	1.04	.82	.61
	Purchasing power gain from holding net monetary liabilities during the year	28	15	16	22	32

Table 5–6 continued

(dollar amounts, except pre-share amounts, are expressed in millions)

For the years ended May 31	1984	1983	1982	1981	1980
Increase in specific prices of property, plant, and equipment over (under) increases in the general price level	68	85	16	(24)	77
Net assets at year end (total assets less total liabilities)					
Adjusted for general inflation	1,095	972	756	657	413
Adjusted for changes in specific prices	1,332	1,162	894	809	470
Cash dividends declared per common share					
Adjusted for general inflation	$ 0.43	$ 0.39	$ 0.34	$ 0.28	$ 0.21
Market price per common share at year end:					
adjusted for general inflation	$20.24	$29.41	$12.39	$24.30	$11.66
Average CPI—all urban consumers	303.9	293.4	280.3	257.5	230.0

Source: National Medical Enterprises (NME) annual report 1984.

midpoint index, the adjustment is 1.0. This can be seen in the following equation:

$$\text{Historical revenues} \times \frac{\text{CPI at } 11/30/83}{\text{CPI at } 11/30/83} = \text{Historical revenues}$$

6. Depreciation expense under the current cost method exceeds depreciation expense under the constant dollar method because the current cost value of depreciable assets exceeds the constant dollar value of depreciable assets.

Chapter 6

Analyzing Financial Statements

The major purpose of this chapter is to introduce some analytical tools for evaluating the financial condition of health care entities. Think for a moment how confusing and difficult it would be, without a key, to reach any conclusions about financial position from any of the financial statements presented in Chapter 4. Unless your training is in business or finance, the statements may look like a mass of endless numbers with little meaning. In short, there may be too much information in most financial statements to be digested easily by a general purpose user.

An exhaustive list of people who might use general purpose financial information would be difficult to prepare. Some of the potential users and their reasons for measuring financial condition are

- boards of trustees, to evaluate the solvency of their facilities and establish a framework for various decisions, such as those relating to investment, financing, and pricing
- creditors, to determine the amounts and terms of credit to be granted health care facilities and to evaluate the security of presently outstanding credit obligations
- employee unions, to evaluate the financial condition of a health care facility and its ability to meet increasing demands for higher wages; also to assess the capability of the facility to meet existing contractual relationships for deferred compensation programs, such as pension plans
- departmental managers, to understand better how operations and activities under their direct control contribute to the entity's overall financial position

- rate-regulating agencies, to assess the adequacy of existing and proposed rates of a health care facility that is subject to rate review
- grant-giving agencies (public and private), to determine a grantee's ability to continue to provide services supported by a grant and to assess the need for additional funding
- public, to determine a community health care facility's financial condition and assess its need to rate increases and its use of prior funds to enhance and improve the delivery of health care services; as a basis for assessing the need for money in a fund drive.

RATIO ANALYSIS

The technique used to assess financial condition is financial ratio analysis, the examination of the relation of two pieces of financial information to obtain additional information. In this process, the new information is both easier to understand and usually more relevant than the unrelated, free-standing information found in general purpose financial statements. For example, the values of fund balance and total assets may have little meaning when stated independently in a balance sheet. When the ratio of the two is taken, however, it is possible to indicate the proportion of assets that have been financed with sources other than debt.

Financial ratios are not another attempt by financial specialists to confuse and confound decision makers. Financial ratios have been empirically tested to determine their value in predicting business failure. The results to date have been quite impressive: financial ratios can, in fact, discern potential problems in financial condition even five years in advance of their emergence.

A sad fact is that much financial information is never really subjected to financial ratio analysis; the mass of figures just seems too voluminous ever to be synthesized. Decision makers tend to assume that, if the entity is breathing at the end of the year and is capable of publishing a financial statement, all must be well. If something goes wrong later, the accountant is blamed for not warning the decision makers. Sometimes the accountant *is* at fault. However, it is often the decision makers' fault for not analyzing and interpreting the financial information given to them in published financial statements.

The accounting profession was bombarded with criticism after the Penn Central collapse in 1970. To many it seemed that reporting standards must be too loose if the imminent financial collapse of a $7 billion business could not be determined from its financial statements. However, Paul Dasher, in the March–April 1972 issue of the *Financial Analyst's Journal*, showed that anyone who could apply normal financial ratios to published financial statements could have detected the impending failure. At the conclusion of this chapter, the reader should be able to examine selectively a few specific financial ratios to better assess the financial condition of a health care entity.

Meaningful ratio analysis relies heavily on the existence of relevant, comparable data. Absolute values of ratios are usually more valuable than the underlying financial information, but they are even more valuable when they can be compared with existing standards. For example, the statement that a hospital earned 3 percent on its revenues in the previous year is useful, but a statement of the relationship of this 3 percent to some standard would be far more valuable.

Usually the analysis of financial ratios involves two types of comparisons. Temporal comparison of ratios, the comparison of year-end ratios to prior-year values, gives the analyst some idea of both trend and desirability. A projected financial ratio similarly may be compared with prior actual values to test the validity of the projection and the desirability of the proposed plan of operation.

A second method of comparison uses industry averages as the relevant standards for comparison. The Financial Analysis Service (FAS), a comparative ratio service of the Healthcare Financial Management Association (HFMA), provides an excellent set of financial ratio averages for both hospitals and nursing homes.

For some time, the lack of uniformity in financial reporting has inhibited meaningful financial analysis in the health care industry. Specifically, the use of fund accounting has made it difficult to separate the financial effects of operations from the financial effects of other activities of the organization, such as those supported by endowment or grant monies. To some extent, this problem was solved with the publication of the American Institute of Certified Public Accountants' *Audits of Providers of Health Care Services* in 1989. This publication is applicable to hospital financial statements and those of other health care entities. One major feature is the requirement that funds be separated into general and donor-restricted categories, as discussed in Chapter 4. In most situations, focusing the financial analysis on the general fund categories provides a better basis for evaluating actual health care operations.

Financial ratios can be classified into five major categories for the purposes of this chapter:

1. liquidity ratios
2. capital structure ratios
3. activity ratios
4. profitability ratios
5. other ratios

In the following discussion, individual ratios within each of these categories are defined with respect to their assessment of financial condition. The specific indicators described are a subset of the 30 ratios used in the FAS. Additional information about FAS can be obtained by contacting the Healthcare Financial Management Association in Westchester, Illinois. The financial statement of Omega Hospital, shown in Tables 4–1 and 4–3, illustrate the discussion.

It may seem to some that undue emphasis is being placed on financial reporting and financial analysis in the hospital sector. In terms of coverage in this chapter, this is true. However, ratios are general in nature and are just as relevant in other health care settings. For example, use of a current ratio that measures an entity's liquidity is valid and helpful not only for hospitals but also for nursing homes, HMOs, outpatient clinics, and surgicenters. Furthermore, understanding the application of financial ratios in the relatively more complex hospital environment makes their application in other settings easier.

Liquidity Ratios

Liquidity is a term frequently used by business and financial people. It refers to the ability of a firm to meet its short-term maturing obligations. The more liquid a firm, the better it is able to meet its short-term obligations or current liabilities. Liquidity is an important dimension in the assessment of financial condition. Most firms that experience financial problems do so because of a liquidity crisis; they are unable to pay current obligations as they become due. Measuring an entity's liquidity position is central to determining its financial condition. Other long-term factors, such as a poor accounts receivable collection policy, may explain a poor liquidity position, but the worsening of a liquidity position is usually the first clue that something more basic is wrong.

Current Ratio

One of the most widely used measures of liquidity is the current ratio:

$$\frac{\text{Current assets}}{\text{Current liabilities}}$$

For Omega Hospital, the current ratio values for 1992 and 1991 are as follows:

1992	*1991*
$\frac{10,587,463}{5,045,039} = 2.10$	$\frac{9,027,558}{5,082,361} = 1.78$

The higher the ratio value, the better the firm's ability to meet its current liabilities. A value commonly used in industry as a standard is 2.00; this means that two dollars of current assets (assets expected to be realized in cash during the year) are available for each one dollar of current liabilities (obligations expected to require cash within the year). The 1990 FAS national median was 2.00. On both a trend basis and a standard comparison basis, Omega Hospital is in a favorable position (Table 6–1).

The current ratio is a basic measure that is widely used. However, if used alone, it does not tell the whole story. Some types of assets—cash and marketable securities, for example—are more liquid than accounts receivable or inventory. The current ratio does not account for these differences.

Days in Patient Accounts Receivable Ratio

The current ratio is a useful measure of a firm's liquidity, but it does not differentiate between categories of current assets. For example, cash is much more liquid than inventory or accounts receivable. In many situations, high current ratios result from excessive investment in accounts receivable. Days in patient accounts receivable is a liquidity ratio that further refines liquidity measurements and may pinpoint an area for correction. It is defined as all net patient accounts receivable divided by average daily net patient revenue:

$$\frac{\text{New patient accounts receivable}}{\text{Net patient revenue}/365}$$

Table 6-1 Financial Ratio Analysis of Omega Hospital

Ratio	1992	1991	1990 HFMA National Median	Evaluation Trend	Evaluation Standard
Liquidity					
Current	2.10	1.78	2.00	Favorable	Favorable
Days in patient accounts receivable	60.8	56.7	74.4	Unfavorable	Favorable
Average payment period	42.0	49.8	58.3	Favorable	Favorable
Days' cash on hand	12.2	19.9	19.6	Unfavorable	Unfavorable
Capital structure					
Equity financing	.78	.76	.52	Favorable	Favorable
Long-term debt to equity	.14	.16	.54	Favorable	Favorable
Times interest earned	8.79	7.07	2.85	Favorable	Favorable
Debt service coverage	6.19	4.76	3.06	Favorable	Favorable
Cash flow to debt	.55	.47	.20	Favorable	Favorable
Activity					
Total asset turnover	.95	.86	.94	Favorable	Unfavorable
Fixed-asset turnover	1.66	1.76	1.99	Unfavorable	Unfavorable
Current asset turnover	4.69	4.68	3.45	Favorable	Favorable
Other asset turnover	4.34	2.64	4.74	Favorable	Unfavorable
Average age of plant	8.00	7.99	7.62	Unfavorable	Unfavorable
Profitability					
Total margin	.068	.068	.042	Stable	Favorable
Operating margin	.048	.041	.023	Favorable	Favorable
Operating margin, price-level-adjusted	.030	.027	.002	Favorable	Favorable
Nonoperating gain	.020	.027	.018	Unfavorable	Favorable
Return on equity	.083	.078	.082	Favorable	Favorable
Reported income index	1.00	1.00	.996	Stable	Unfavorable
Other					
Restricted equity	.016	.013	.004	Favorable	Favorable
Replacement viability	.72	1.20	.35	Unfavorable	Favorable

For Omega Hospital, days in accounts receivable for 1992 and 1991 are

$$\underset{1992}{\frac{7,684,188}{(46,095,327/365)} = 60.8} \qquad \underset{1991}{\frac{6,075,295}{(39,084,761/365)} = 56.7}$$

Values for this ratio indicate the number of days in the average collection period. For example, Omega Hospital in 1992 had 60.8 days outstanding in accounts receivable at year end. This implies that it took the hospital 60.8 days on average to turn its accounts receivable into cash. High values for this ratio could indicate problems in collection time that may be due to faulty collection policies and billing systems of the entity. However, a high value might also indicate that the underlying quality of the accounts receivable is poor; that is, their collectability may be in doubt. This might imply that the write-off policy of the entity should be re-examined.

A good way to evaluate the collectability of accounts receivable is to perform an aging of accounts receivable by payer. For example, let us assume that an aging of Omega Hospital's accounts receivable as of December 31, 1992, was performed (Table 6–2). The aging of accounts receivable as shown in Table 6–2 casts doubt on the collectability of much of the $700,000 in self-pay accounts receivable that is over one year past due. It might also raise a question of why $600,000 of third-party payer receivables over one year old are still outstanding. The answer could be a poor collection policy for payment by such third parties as Medicaid, or it may be due to an unresolved dispute between the provider and the payer over the amount actually due.

Omega Hospital's 1992 days in patient accounts receivable compares favorably with the 1990 FAS median of 74.4 days, but in 1992 value is up 4.1 days from the 1991 value. This increase absorbed a significant portion of Omega's short-term cash. If Omega had been able to maintain its 1991 days in patient accounts receivable value, it would have been able to realize an additional $517,783 in cash:

$$\frac{\text{1992 Revenue}}{365} \times \text{Change in days in patient accounts} = \frac{46,095,327}{365} \times 4.1$$

Care must be exercised in using any of the liquidity ratios if seasonality is a factor. For example, if the dates for financial statement presentation

---

Table 6–2 Aging of Accounts Receivable for Omega Hospital as of December 31, 1992 (000s Omitted)

	Gross	Self-Pay	Third-Party
Less than 30 days	$3,000	$ 800	$2,200
31–90 days	4,400	700	3,700
91–365 days	500	300	200
Over 365 days	1,300	700	600
Total	$9,200	$2,500	$6,700

occur during a slack period of the year, certain values of current assets may be understated and others overstated. In particular, the values of accounts receivable and inventory might be at their lowest point of the year, and the corresponding values of cash and marketable securities at their highest, or vice versa, giving a biased view of the liquidity position of the firm. In addition, standards may vary by type of health care facility and region of the country. Clinics and HMOs can be expected to have significantly fewer days in accounts receivable than most hospitals. The collection period also depends heavily on the composition of payers and their payment practices. Medicaid may pay on a prompt and timely basis in one state and yet be delinquent in another. The same holds true for Blue Cross and other major third-party payers.

Average Payment Period Ratio

Another index that provides information about causes of a worsening liquidity position is the average payment period ratio:

$$\frac{\text{Current liabilities}}{(\text{Total operating expenses} - \text{Depreciation})/365}$$

For Omega Hospital, the values of this ratio for 1992 and 1991 are

1992	*1991*
$\dfrac{5,045,039}{(46,318,336 - 2,470,733)/365} = 42.0$	$\dfrac{5,082,361}{(39,379,612 - 2,162,895)/365} = 49.8$

For a financial condition standpoint, low values of this ratio are better than higher values. Creditors often use a slight adaptation of this ratio:

$$\frac{\text{Accounts payable}}{\text{Purchases}/365}$$

If the data are available, both of the above ratios should be calculated. However, in the Omega Hospital example, a separate listing of purchases for the year is not available.

The average payment period ratio indicates the length of time an entity takes to pay its obligations. The denominator, which is total expenses less depreciation divided by 365, provides an index of average daily cash expenses. (Remember, depreciation is a noncash expense.) The numerator (current liabilities) represents obligations for expenditures during the coming year. Most normal supply items are expensed within the year in which they are purchased. The same is true of payroll expenses, which usually constitute the largest single element of accrued liabilities and expenses. A standard value for this ratio derived from FAS is 58.3. On this basis, Omega Hospital has a favorable trend and a favorable standard comparison.

Days' Cash on Hand Ratio

A final measure of liquidity is days' cash on hand:

$$\frac{\text{Cash} + \text{marketable securities}}{(\text{Total operating expenses} - \text{Depreciation})/365}$$

For Omega Hospital, the values of this ratio for 1992 and 1991 are

1992	1991

$$\frac{1,304,403 + 157,803}{(46,318,336 - 2,470,733)/365} = 12.2 \qquad \frac{966,485 + 681,200}{(39,379,612 - 2,162,895)/365} = 19.9$$

Higher values of this ratio imply a more liquid position, other factors remaining constant. The ratio measures the number of days an entity could meet its average daily expenditures (as measured by the denominator) with existing liquid assets, namely cash and marketable securities. It attempts to define a maximum period of safety, assuming the worst of all conditions—for example, no conversion of accounts receivable into cash.

Omega Hospital's current days' cash on hand ratio is well below the 1990 FAS national median of 19.6. The hospital also experienced a significant decline in 1992 to 12.2 days from 19.9 days. Much of this decline can most likely be attributed to the increase in days in patient accounts receivable.

A key concern for Omega might be the adequacy of its present short-term cash position. It is usually helpful to relate days' cash on hand ratio values to replacement viability ratio values (see "Other Ratios" later in this chapter). Sizable values for replacement viability indicate that long-term investment funds could be used to supplement short-term cash reserves in a liquidity crisis. Omega has an above-average replacement viability ratio that lessens the impact of the short-term cash deficiency.

Capital Structure Ratios

Capital structure ratios are useful in assessing the long-term solvency or liquidity of a firm. Although the liquidity ratios just discussed are useful in detection of immediate solvency problems, the capital structure ratios are especially useful in longer term assessment of financial condition. They are also valuable in detecting some short-term problems. Capital structure ratios are carefully evaluated by long-term creditors and bond-rating agencies to determine an entity's ability to increase its amounts of debt financing. In the last 20 years, the hospital and health care industries have increased their percentages of debt financing. This trend makes capital structure ratios vitally important to many individuals. Evaluation of these ratios may well determine the amount of credit available to the industry and thus directly affect its rate of growth.

Equity Financing Ratio

A basic capital structure ratio is the equity financing ratio:

$$\frac{\text{Fund balance}}{\text{Total assets}}$$

For Omega Hospital the values for this ratio in 1992 and 1991 are

1992	*1991*
$\dfrac{40,513,054}{52,021,334} = .78$	$\dfrac{37,154,079}{49,088,440} = .76$

Higher values for this ratio are regarded as positive indicators of a sound financial condition, all other things being equal. After all, if an entity had zero debt or a fund balance to total assets ratio of 1.0, there would not be any possible claimants on the entity's assets and thus no fear of bankruptcy or insolvency. The ratio indicates the percentage of total assets that have been financed with sources other than debt. In segments of the health care industry in which there is a greater stability in earnings, lower equity financing ratios may be permitted.

Omega Hospital's values are very high and increasing, which is favorable. Approximately 78 percent of all assets are financed with equity. The primary cause for this low level of debt is a conservative board policy that keeps debt at relatively low levels. Omega is paying off its existing long-term debt and not borrowing any more on a long-term basis. Omega may have to use more debt in the near future because of its high average age of plant (see Table 6–1).

Long-Term Debt to Equity Ratio

Another capital structure ratio used by many analysts is the long-term debt to equity ratio:

$$\frac{\text{Long-term debt}}{\text{Fund balance}}$$

For Omega Hospital, the values for this ratio in 1992 and 1991 are

1992	1991
$\frac{5,475,000}{40,513,054} = .14$	$\frac{5,765,000}{37,154,079} = .16$

One deficiency of the equity financing ratio is that it includes short-term sources of debt financing, such as current liabilities. When assessing solvency and the ability to increase long-term financing, it is sometimes desirable to focus on "permanent capital." Permanent capital consists of sources of financing that are not temporary, including long-term debt and fund balance. Low values for the long-term debt to equity ratio may indicate to creditors an entity's ability to carry additional long-term debt.

The average value for this ratio in the Standard & Poor's 400 Industrials was 42 percent; that is, for every one dollar of long-term debt, two dollars came from equity. In the health care industry this value may be higher, especially for hospitals. A value used by some investment bankers is 2.0. In other words, they are willing to allow two dollars of long-term debt for every one dollar of equity for some hospitals. In part, this reflects the stability of the industry. It also reflects the relative difficulty in acquiring equity capital in a largely nonprofit industry.

Omega Hospital has very low long-term debt to equity ratios when compared with the 1990 FAS national median of .54. Assuming that Omega could demonstrate satisfactory debt service coverage, the hospital should have significant additional debt capacity available to it. For example, if Omega could reach a long-term debt to equity ratio of 2.0, Omega could have approximately $81 million in long-term debt, or $75.5 million more than its existing value of $5.475 million.

Times Interest Earned Ratio

A traditional capital structure ratio that attempts to measure the ability of an entity to meet its interest payment is the times interest earned ratio:

$$\frac{\text{Excess of revenues over expenses + Interest expense}}{\text{Interest expense}}$$

For Omega Hospital, the values for this ratio in 1992 and 1991 are

1992	*1991*
$\dfrac{3,358,975 + 430,725}{430,725} = 8.79$	$\dfrac{2,887,135 + 475,666}{475,666} = 7.07$

Even though a firm has a very low percentage of debt financing, it may not be able to carry additional debt because its profitability cannot meet the increased interest payment. Repayment of interest expense is a very important consideration in long-term financing. Failure to meet interest payment requirements on a timely basis could result in the entire principal value of the loan's becoming due. Meeting the fixed annual interest expense obligations is thus highly critical to solvency. The times interest earned ratio measures the extent to which earning could slip and still not impair the entity's ability to repay its interest obligations. High values for this ratio are obviously preferable. An absolute minimum standard in general industry is 1.5. The 1990 FAS national median for the times interest earned ratio was 2.85.

Omega Hospital had both a favorable trend and a favorable comparison with the national norm. Omega's 1992 times interest earned increased significantly in 1992 because of two factors: (1) decline in interest expense and (2) increase in excess of revenues over expenses. Omega appears to have both low debt and good coverage of existing debt. This confirms an earlier observation regarding the additional debt capacity of Omega.

Debt Service Coverage Ratio

A commonly used capital structure ratio that measures the ability to pay both components of long-term indebtedness—interest and principal—is the debt service coverage ratio:

$$\frac{\text{Excess of revenues over expenses} + \text{Depreciation} + \text{Interest}}{\text{Principal payment} + \text{Interest expense}}$$

Values for Omega's debt principal repayments in 1992 and 1991 can be identified in Table 4–4 (statement of cash flows). By using these values, debt service coverage ratios for Omega Hospital in 1992 and 1991 are

1992	*1991*
$\dfrac{3,358,975 + 2,470,733 + 430,725}{580,200 + 430,725} = 6.19$	$\dfrac{2,887,135 + 2,162,895 + 475,666}{685,767 + 475,666} = 4.76$

The debt service coverage ratio is a broader measure of debt repayment ability than the times interest earned ratio because it includes the second component of a debt obligation—the repayment of debt principal. The numerator of the debt service coverage ratio defines the funds available to meet debt service requirements of principal and interest. The ratio indicates the number of times that the debt service requirements can be met from existing funds. Higher ratios indicate that an entity is better able to meet its financing commitments.

A standard minimum debt service coverage ratio value used by investment bankers in the hospital industry is 1.5. The 1990 FAS national median for the debt service coverage ratio was 3.06. With this value as a standard, Omega Hospital has both a favorable trend and a favorable standard comparison evaluation.

Values for Omega Hospital's debt service coverage ratio corroborate our earlier findings for the times interest earned ratio. The hospital is in a good position to assume additional long-term debt. Ultimately, further improvement in these ratios may be linked directly to improvements in profitability.

Cash Flow to Debt Ratio

One of the best predictors of financial failure is the cash flow to debt ratio:

$$\frac{\text{Excess of revenues over expenses} + \text{Depreciation}}{\text{Current liabilities} + \text{Long-term debt}}$$

For Omega Hospital, the values of the cash flow to debt ratio in 1992 and 1991 are

1992	*1991*
$\frac{3{,}358{,}975 + 2{,}470{,}733}{5{,}045{,}039 + 5{,}475{,}000} = .55$	$\frac{2{,}887{,}135 + 2{,}162{,}895}{5{,}082{,}361 + 5{,}765{,}000} = .47$

The cash flow to debt ratio has been found to be an excellent predictor of financial failure, even as much as five years in advance of such failure. The numerator (cash flow) can be thought of as the firm's source of total funds, excluding financing. The denominator (total debt) provides a measure of a major need for future funds, namely, debt retirement. A low value for this ratio often indicates a potential problem in meeting future debt payment requirements.

Omega Hospital's values for cash flow to total debt are increasing and are significantly above the 1990 FAS national median of .20. Omega again is seen to have very good coverage and should not experience any difficulty in servicing its existing debt.

Activity Ratios

Activity, or turnover, ratios measure the relationship between revenue and assets. The numerator is always revenue; it may be thought of as a surrogate measure of output. The denominator is investment in some category of assets; it may be thought of as a measure of input. These ratios are also referred to as efficiency ratios, since efficiency ratios measure output to input. As noted in a later context, activity ratios also have a very important relationship to measures of profitability.

Total Asset Turnover Ratio

The most widely used activity ratio is the total asset turnover ratio:

$$\frac{\text{Total revenue}}{\text{Total assets}}$$

where total revenue = net patient revenue + other revenue + net nonoperating gains.

For Omega Hospital, the values of the total asset turnover ratio in 1992 and 1991 are

$$
\begin{array}{cc}
\textit{1992} & \textit{1991} \\[4pt]
\dfrac{48,702,816 + 974,495}{52,021,334} = .95 & \dfrac{41,125,867 + 1,140,880}{49,088,440} = .86
\end{array}
$$

A high value for this ratio implies that the entity's total investment is being used efficiently; that is, a large number of services is being provided to the community from a limited resource base. However, the ratio can be deceptive. For example, a facility that is relatively old, with most of its plant assets fully depreciated, is quite likely to show a high total asset turnover ratio; yet it may not be nearly as efficient as a newer facility that has plant and equipment assets that are largely undepreciated.

A measure that may be used to evaluate partially the existence of this problem by detecting the age of a given physical plant is

$$\frac{\text{Allowance for depreciation}}{\text{Depreciation expense}} = \text{Average age of plant}$$

By using this measure for Omega Hospital, the values for 1992 and 1991 are

1992	*1991*

$$\frac{19,762,441}{2,470,733} = 8.0 \qquad \frac{17,283,825}{2,162,895} = 7.99$$

The 1990 FAS national median for the average age of plant ratio was 7.6 Omega is therefore slightly older than the U.S. norm. All other factors being equal, this should suggest that the total asset turnover and fixed-asset turnover ratios should be higher. Omega's total asset turnover ratio is slightly higher than the national median of .94, but its fixed asset turnover ratio is lower. This finding is surprising and suggests that it is not Omega's efficiency with respect to fixed-asset investment that has created its overall favorable asset efficiency. As Table 6–1 shows, current asset efficiency, especially receivables, has helped Omega achieve a superior total asset turnover.

Fixed-Asset Turnover Ratio

Another common turnover ratio is the fixed-asset turnover ratio:

$$\frac{\text{Total revenue}}{\text{Net fixed assets}}$$

For Omega Hospital, the values of the fixed-asset turnover ratio in 1992 and 1991 are

1992	*1991*

$$\frac{48,702,816 + 974,495}{29,974,266} = 1.66 \qquad \frac{41,125,867 + 1,140,880}{24,023,535} = 1.76$$

The fixed-asset turnover ratio is identical to the total asset turnover ratio, except that fixed assets, a specific subset of total assets, is substituted in the denominator. This substitution is an attempt to assess the relative efficiency of an individual category of assets. In fact, all the turnover ratios discussed subsequently are further segregations of various categories of assets.

Fixed assets represent the number one investment in most health care entities. The fixed-asset turnover ratio can thus be of major importance in assessing the relative efficiency of plant investments. The 1990 FAS national median for the fixed-asset turnover ratio was 1.99. Because

Omega's average age of plant is older than the U.S. norm, Omega has a problem with respect to fixed-asset investment, as evidenced by a low fixed-asset turnover ratio. This problem may be attributed to one of three areas:

1. excessive investment in fixed assets
2. inadequate volume for existing capacity
3. low prices for services

Omega's low fixed-asset turnover is primarily a result of low prices, as is shown later.

Current Asset Turnover Ratio

The complement of the fixed-asset turnover ratio is the current asset turnover ratio:

$$\frac{\text{Total revenue}}{\text{Current assets}}$$

For Omega Hospital, the values of this ratio in 1992 and 1991 are

1992	1991
$\frac{48,702,816 + 974,495}{10,587,463} = 4.69$	$\frac{41,125,867 + 1,140,880}{9,027,558} = 4.68$

The current asset turnover ratio focuses on the relative efficiency of the investment in current assets with respect to the generation of revenue. The valuation of current assets is not subject to the same difficulties encountered in the measurement of fixed assets. The ratio is thus more comparable across facilities. Omega Hospital has a very favorable comparison with the 1990 FAS national median of 3.45. The primary reason for this favorable comparison is the relatively smaller investment in patient accounts receivable and cash. Omega had 60.8 days in patient accounts receivable in 1992 and 12.2 days' cash on hand. Both values are well below the national median.

Other Asset Turnover Ratio

The last activity ratio to be discussed is the other asset turnover ratio:

$$\frac{\text{Total revenue}}{\text{Other assets}}$$

Other assets are defined as

Total assets − Current assets − Fixed assets

For Omega Hospital, the values of this ratio in 1992 and 1991 are

1992   *1991*

$$\frac{48,702,816 + 974,495}{11,459,605} = 4.34 \qquad \frac{41,125,867 + 1,140,880}{16,037,347} = 2.64$$

In most situations, a high other asset turnover ratio is desirable because it signals an ability to provide services with minimal investment. If the cause of a high other asset turnover ratio is the lack or absence of replacement funds, the high other asset turnover ratio may not be desirable. Omega Hospital increased significantly its other asset turnover ratio in 1992. Unfortunately, the primary cause for the increase was the removal of $4,538,333 ($11,962,168 − $7,423,835) of funded depreciation. Omega is still below the 1990 FAS national median of 4.74 in 1992. This does not appear to be a problem, however, because Omega still has far larger replacement reserves set aside, as evidenced by a higher replacement viability ratio (see "Other Ratios").

Profitability Ratios

To talk of profit in a largely nonprofit industry appears to many to be a contradiction in terms. Yet few, if any, health care facilities could remain liquid and solvent if profits were held to zero. In such a situation, cash flow would not be sufficient to meet normal nonexpense cash flow requirements, such as repayment of debt principal and investment in additional fixed and current assets.

However, recognizing the basic need for profit is not the same thing as determining how much is needed. It is not healthy either for the public or for the health care entity if the entity's profitability is either too great or too small. Discussion of the need for profitability thus centers on a definition of financial requirements. Here we are concerned only with the interpretation of several commonly used financial ratios of profitability.

Total Margin Ratio

A common profitability ratio is the total margin ratio:

$$\frac{\text{Excess of revenues over expenses}}{\text{Total revenue}}$$

For Omega Hospital, total margin ratios in 1992 and 1991 are

1992	*1991*
$\dfrac{3,358,975}{48,702,816 + 974,495} = .068$	$\dfrac{2,887,135}{41,125,867 + 1,140,880} = .068$

The total margin ratio defines the percentage of total revenue plus net nonoperating gains that has been realized in the form of net income, or revenues and gains in excess of expenses and losses. It is used by many analysts as a primary measure of total profitability. Although this measure is extremely useful, we believe that income should be related to some measure of investment to be meaningful. An alternative measure of profitability, discussed later, that does provide a measure of investment in the denominator is the return on equity ratio.

It is possible to improve the total margin ratio by either improving operating margin performance or increasing nonoperating gains. For most hospitals, short-term improvements will result primarily from increases in operating margins. The total margin ratio will, in most situations, be equal to

Operating margin ratio + Nonoperating gain ratio

There may be some limited circumstances in which an item affects excess of revenues over expenses but does not appear in either net nonoperating gains or income from operations.

Omega Hospital's total margin exhibited a stable and very favorable comparison with the 1990 FAS national median of .042. Although the total margin is constant, it is useful to notice the two components, operating margin and nonoperating gain. A large gain in the operating margin ratio was offset by a large decline in the nonoperating gain ratio.

Operating Margin Ratio

The most commonly cited measure of profitability is the operating margin ratio:

$$\frac{\text{Net operating income}}{\text{Total revenue}}$$

For Omega Hospital, the values of this ratio in 1992 and 1991 are

1992	*1991*
$\dfrac{2,384,480}{48,702,816 + 974,495} = .048$	$\dfrac{1,746,255}{41,125,867 + 1,140,880} = .041$

To realize an increase in operating margins, one of two options exists: (1) raise net prices or (2) reduce cost per unit. An increase in volume is sometimes cited as a third option, but an increase in volume has the effect of reducing cost per unit when fixed costs exist. For many health care firms the primary way to enhance profitability is through cost reduction, because prices may be fixed by external payers such as Medicare.

Omega Hospital has exhibited a favorable trend in its operating margin. Its 1992 value of .048 is well above the national FAS median of .023. Omega's high operating margin is almost totally attributed to low costs, as is discussed shortly.

Operating Margin, Price-Level-Adjusted Ratio

It is often useful to adjust the operating margin ratio to reflect replacement cost depreciation. The operating margin, price-level-adjusted ratio does this:

$$\frac{\text{Operating income} + \text{Depreciation} - \text{Price level depreciation}}{\text{Total revenue}}$$

For Omega Hospital, the values for this ratio in 1992 and 1991 are

1992

$$\frac{2,384,480 + 2,470,733 - 3,364,894}{48,702,816 + 974,495} = .030$$

1991

$$\frac{1,746,255 + 2,162,895 - 2,767,948}{41,125,867 + 1,140,880} = .027$$

The operating margin, price-level-adjusted ratio is identical to the operating margin ratio except that it substitutes price level depreciation for depreciation expense reported on an unadjusted historical cost basis. The ratio defines the proportion of operating revenue net of deductions that is retained as income after deducting price-level-adjusted depreciation. Although not totally accurate, this measure of operating profitability attempts to reflect the replacement costs of operating fixed assets in the calculation of the operating margin.

Values of this ratio that are below zero imply that the organization is not currently earning enough operating income to provide funds for the eventual replacement of its fixed assets. Future replacement needs may have to be met from an increased reliance debt (if available) or from other equity sources, such as grants and contributions (if available). Values for this ratio that exceed zero are not to be interpreted as a guarantee of future fund availability for replacement. To the extent that increased working capital needs are financed with equity, an erosion of the replacement potential of the hospital will occur. Also, it should be remembered that the index used for price level restatement is the consumer price index for urban wage earners, which may understate the real replacement cost of the hospital.

Omega Hospital has both a favorable trend and a favorable comparison with the 1990 FAS national median. This further reinforces the earlier conclusions reached regarding unadjusted operating margins. Omega is generating a reasonable level of profit to replace its existing fixed assets.

Nonoperating Gain Ratio

A profitability ratio that provides a means of analyzing the source of profit is the nonoperating gain ratio:

$$\frac{\text{Net nonoperating gains}}{\text{Total revenue}}$$

For Omega Hospital, the values for this ratio in 1992 and 1991 are

1992	*1991*
$\dfrac{974,495}{48,702,816 + 974,495} = .020$	$\dfrac{1,140,880}{41,125,867 + 1,140,880} = 0.27$

The nonoperating gain ratio defines the proportion of total revenue plus net nonoperating gains that was derived from net nonoperating gains. The major sources of nonoperating gains will most likely be donations, income on nonborrowed funds, and other gains and losses. Some firms may report negative values for this ratio if they experience large losses in a given year.

To some extent, nonoperating gains can be used to subsidize poor operating margins, if net nonoperating gains are consistently sizable. For many health care firms, development activity has become increasingly important as a source of income to supplant eroding operating profits. Improvements in the nonoperating gain ratio will have a positive impact on most profitability ratios.

Omega Hospital experienced a large drop in its nonoperating gain ratio in 1992. Much of this decline was caused by a $161,065 decline in interest earnings. Most likely this decline resulted from a reduction in funded depreciation. Although Omega is slightly above the 1990 FAS national median of .018, the decline is cause for some concern.

Return on Equity Ratio

One of the primary tests of profitability for both voluntary and investor-owned health care firms is the return on equity ratio:

$$\frac{\text{Excess of revenues over expenses}}{\text{Fund balance}}$$

For Omega Hospital, the values for this ratio in 1992 and 1991 are

1992	*1991*
$\dfrac{3,358,975}{40,513,054} = .083$	$\dfrac{2,887,135}{37,154,079} = .078$

The return on equity ratio defines the amount of net income or excess of revenues over expenses earned per dollar of equity investment. This ratio has been discussed by decision makers in some hospitals, especially investor-owned hospitals, as an alternative way to establish rates. Many financial analysts consider the return on equity ratio the primary test of profitability. Failure to maintain a satisfactory value for this ratio may prevent the hospital from obtaining equity capital in the future.

The return on equity ratio can be expressed as a product of four ratios:

$$(\text{Operating margin ratio} + \text{Nonoperating gain ratio}) \times \frac{\text{Total asset turnover ratio}}{\text{Equity financing ratio}}$$

For health care firms without access to donor-restricted funds, government tax support, or other sources of new equity, asset growth will be limited to return on equity. This principle is referred to as "sustainable growth." The principle simply says that a firm cannot generate a growth rate in assets greater than its growth rate in equity for a prolonged period of time. If a firm can generate a return on equity of only 5 percent per year, its new growth in asset investment will be limited to 5 percent per year.

Omega Hospital has both a favorable trend and a favorable comparison against the 1990 FAS national median of .082. Initially, one might have thought the comparisons with the FAS median would have been better, but Omega has a very high equity financing ratio. In Omega's case, a little more financial leverage might help Omega achieve higher returns on equity values and, as a result, greater growth in assets.

Reported Income Index Ratio

Given the peculiar nature of fund accounting in the hospital and health care industry, another valuable profitability ratio is the reported income index ratio:

$$\frac{\text{Excess of revenue over expenses}}{\text{Change in fund balance}}$$

For Omega Hospital, the values for this ratio in 1992 and 1991 are

1992	*1991*
$\dfrac{3,358,975}{3,358,975} = 1.00$	$\dfrac{2,887,135}{2,887,135} = 1.00$

As noted in Chapter 4, there are situations in which funds may be transferred to the general fund from a restricted fund and not be shown as income to the general fund. An important example of this is the purchase of fixed assets with dollars from a restricted plant replacement fund. The fixed assets purchased would be transferred to the general fund and shown as general plant property and equipment; a corresponding direct charge or increase in fund balance of the general fund would also occur. This increase in fund balance is necessary if the basic accounting equation is to be kept in balance; assets must equal liabilities plus fund balance. If this situation occurs frequently, the financial condition of the entity is far more favorable than its profitability ratios would indicate. The ratio of excess of revenue over expenses to changes in fund balance is designed to determine to what extent such transactions are occurring. Values consistently, and significantly, less than 1.0 indicate that a very important unreported source of income is being used by the entity.

Omega Hospital has not shown any transfer of funds during the last two years. It is possible in some cases to have a transfer out of equity. Investor-owned organizations that pay dividends will transfer out equity and have reported income index ratios greater than 1.

Other Ratios

Two ratios do not fit neatly into the four categories discussed above. These ratios are nevertheless useful in providing additional information about the overall assessment of financial position.

Restricted Equity Ratio

To assess the availability of capital from third-party donor-restricted funds, the restricted equity ratio is often used:

$$\frac{\text{Total donor-restricted fund balances}}{\text{General fund balance}}$$

For Omega Hospital, the values for this ratio in 1992 and 1991 are

1992	1992

$$\frac{650,240}{40,513,054} = .016 \qquad \frac{498,549}{37,154,079} = .013$$

High values for restricted equity ratios are usually desirable. An underlying assumption about the desirability of high restricted equity ratios is that the entity must already have adequate levels of unrestricted equity. This can be evaluated by analyzing the equity financing ratio. Restricted equity will usually improve hospital profitability in one of two ways: First, if the restricted equity is an endowment, it may provide a very stable flow of investment income that will be reported as nonoperating revenue. Second, if the restricted equity is for plant purposes, there will be future credits to the general fund balance and will show up as reported income index ratios, being less than 1.

Replacement Viability Ratio

To assess the feasibility of future plant replacement, the replacement viability ratio is frequently used:

$$\frac{\text{Restricted plant fund balance + Unrestricted investments}}{\text{Price-level-adjusted accumulated depreciation} \times 0.50}$$

For Omega Hospital, the values for replacement viability in 1992 and 1991 are

1992	1991

$$\frac{0 + (2,183,639 + 7,423,835)}{26,687,428 \times .50} = .72 \qquad \frac{0 + (1,976,543 + 11,962,168)}{23,231,185 \times .50} = 1.20$$

The replacement viability ratio is used to measure the adequacy of current investments to meet replacement needs. The numerator (restricted plant fund balance plus unrestricted investments) is a measure of current funds available to meet potential replacement needs. The denominator is a measure of the present need. Price-level-adjusted accumulated depreciation is a measure of the current cost of fixed assets that has been written off as depreciation. It is not a perfect measure of a hospital's replacement need, but it gives a far better estimate than that produced by simply using unadjusted historical cost accumulated depreciation. Its value is multiplied by 0.50 to recognize that debt financing may be used, the assumption being that 50 percent of replacement needs will be financed with debt.

A standard value for the replacement viability ratio is 1.0. This implies a situation in which exactly enough funds are available for replacement needs. Values greater than 1.0 may indicate more than adequate levels of investment, whereas values less than 1.0 indicate deficiencies. Hospitals may adjust this ratio to reflect their own desired future financing patterns. This is done by multiplying the calculated replacement viability ratio as follows:

$$\text{Replacement viability ratio} \times \frac{0.50}{\text{Expected proportion of equity financing}}$$

Omega Hospital's replacement viability ratio compares favorably with the 1990 FAS national median of .35, but it does have an unfavorable trend, as discussed earlier. Omega liquidated $4,538,333 in funded depreciation during 1992, which caused the decline. Although Omega has more replacement reserves than the average U.S. hospital, its 1992 value of .72 implies that only 36 percent (.72/2) of its present replacement cost need is funded. Additional funding should be made, especially if the hospital's board wishes to keep debt financing lower than 50 percent.

SOME CAVEATS

In this chapter, we have demonstrated, through an examination of 22 separate financial ratios, the use of financial ratio analysis in the assessment of the financial condition of health care facilities. At this point, it is appropriate to add some general limitations that should be recognized when evaluating financial condition through financial ratio analysis.

Validity of Standards

The standards used in this chapter should be helpful in many health care settings. They are, however, of special importance in the hospital industry, since that is where they were derived. These ratios will vary by region of the country and time period. This implies that standards should be updated frequently. It also implies the importance of using adequate trend data.

Financial ratios should be calculated over a minimum of five years if meaningful trends are to be discovered. The two-year comparisons developed in this chapter were used only to discuss basic methodology and are clearly inadequate. In this connection, participation in a financial service, such as the HFMA's FAS, is strongly encouraged.

Cost Valuation

The values reported in a balance sheet are usually stated in unadjusted historical cost. Although this valuation does have some advantages in terms of objectivity of reporting, it limits the utility of comparisons across facilities when inflation is a predominant factor. The need for adjustment of ratios that use balance sheet values, especially fixed-asset values, cannot be overstated.

Projections

Financial ratio analysis uses historical data. It provides a picture of where the entity has been; it does not necessarily tell where it is going. Budgetary data are required for this purpose. The value of financial ratio analysis as a predictor rests on the assumption that past behavior validly indicates future behavior.

Accounting Alternatives

It should be recognized that there are available a number of acceptable accounting alternatives for measuring the financial effects of various transactions. The use of different accounting methods can create significantly different values for financial ratios, even when the underlying financial events are identical. There may even be situations in which differences in accounting methods impair the comparability of financial ratios across health care facilities or over time. Consistent use of a given set of accounting methods can help a health care facility avoid such comparability problems and should be encouraged.

OPERATING INDICATORS

Before this discussion of measuring financial position is concluded, attention should be focused on cost control. In most health care firms, the most likely cause of either good or bad financial performance is traceable to operating income. As results from operations improve, so does overall financial performance. Operating income can be defined very simply as

$$Revenue - Costs$$

where

$$Revenue = Output \times Price\ per\ unit\ of\ output$$

$$Cost = Prices\ paid\ for\ inputs \times Number\ of\ inputs\ required\ per\ unit\ of\ service$$
$$\times Services\ provided\ per\ unit\ of\ output \times Output$$

The above equations suggest five categories of factors that may influence operating profit:

1. Prices of inputs
2. Efficiency
3. Volume
4. Intensity of service
5. Prices of outputs

Ideally, management will monitor actual performance in all of these areas through a comparison of actual indicator values to budgeted values. When significant deviations occur, some management action should be taken to correct the situation. In our discussion, 12 macroindicators are defined and suggested for monitoring. These values should be compared with those of the budget on a fairly frequent basis, at least quarterly and ideally monthly.

It is also useful to compare these indicators with industry averages when they are available. We will again use comparative national medians for the 12 indicators, which were taken from the HFMA's strategic operating indicator data set. Data used to define the indicator values for Omega Hospital are presented in Table 6–3. Data from Omega for only one year are used in this analysis. The indicators, their definitions, Omega-calculated values for 1992, and the 1990 HFMA Far West regional medians for hospital bed sizes between 200 and 299 are presented in Table 6–4.

Table 6-3 1992 Operating Indicator Data for Omega Hospital

Indicator	Inpatient	Outpatient	Total
Gross patient revenue	$36,719,000	$13,197,000	$49,916,000
Bad debt and charity	2,010,438	722,561	2,733,000
Contract allowance	1,688,973	607,026	2,296,000
Total deductions	3,699,412	1,329,587	5,029,000
Net patient revenue	33,019,587	11,867,412	44,887,000
Other revenue			3,581,000
Total revenue			$48,468,000
Operating expenses			
Salary and wages	$15,737,029	$ 5,655,970	$21,393,000
Fringe benefits	3,057,219	1,098,780	4,156,000
Interest	317,050	113,949	431,000
Depreciation	1,817,706	653,293	2,471,000
Professional liability insurance	526,700	189,299	716,000
Other operating expenses	11,727,923	4,215,076	15,943,000
Total operating expenses	$33,183,630	$11,926,369	$45,110,000
Medicare discharges			2,697
Total discharges			12,395
Outpatient visits			93,450
Licensed beds			224
Staffed beds			224
Patient days			51,917
Case mix index			0.8147
Full-time equity	580.4	208.5	789.0

1. *Occupancy*—Occupancy can be either a measure of volume or a measure of productivity, depending on one's view. If actual occupancy levels are below budgeted levels, an adverse impact on average costs may result. This occurs because a significant percentage of total cost is usually fixed in the short run: costs will not decline proportionally with a change in volume. Usually significant and permanent declines in occupancy signal a need for management to alter the cost structure of the hospital. In addition, some adjustment in the rate structure may be necessary to maintain desired levels of profitability.

Table 6–4 1992 Cost Control Indicators for Omega Hospital

Indicator	Definition	1990 HFMA Far West 200 to 299-Bed Median	1992 Omega Value
1. Occupancy %	$\dfrac{\text{Patient days}}{365 \times \text{Licensed beds}} \times 100$	63.3	63.5
2. Length of stay, case-mix-adjusted	$\dfrac{\text{Patient days}}{\text{Case mix index} \times \text{Discharges}}$	4.7	5.1
3. Net price per discharge, case-mix-adjusted	$\dfrac{\text{Net inpatient revenue}}{\text{Total discharges} \times \text{Case mix index}}$	$ 4,130	$ 2,664
4. Cost per discharge, case-mix-adjusted	$\dfrac{\text{Inpatient operating expenses}}{\text{Total discharges} \times \text{Case mix index}}$	$ 4,131	$ 3,286
5. Inpatient man-hours per discharge, case-mix-adjusted	$\dfrac{\text{Inpatient FTEs} \times 2{,}080}{\text{Total discharges} \times \text{Case mix index}}$	130.2	119.6
6. FTE's* per occupied bed	$\dfrac{\text{Inpatient FTEs}}{\text{Average daily census}}$	5.14	4.08
7. Salary per FTE	$\dfrac{\text{Salaries}}{\text{FTEs}}$	$26,271	$27,114
8. Capital costs per discharge	$\dfrac{\text{Inpatient capital costs}}{\text{Total discharges}}$	$ 386	$ 172
9. Net price per visit	$\dfrac{\text{Net outpatient revenue}}{\text{Total visits}}$	$ 198	$ 127
10. Cost per visit	$\dfrac{\text{Total outpatient costs}}{\text{Total visits}}$	$ 197	$ 128
11. Outpatient man-hours per visit	$\dfrac{\text{Outpatient FTEs} \times 2{,}080}{\text{Total visits}}$	5.82	4.64
12. Outpatient revenue %	$\dfrac{\text{Net outpatient revenue} \times 100}{\text{Total revenue}}$	19.5	24.4

*FTEs = full-time equivalents.

Omega Hospital has a 1992 occupancy percentage of 63.5. This value is almost identical to the HFMA median for the region. Although Omega clearly has some additional capacity to service more inpatients, its values do not suggest a major problem with utilization.

2. *Length of stay, case-mix-adjusted*—This measure is identical to the traditional length-of-stay measure, except that it is adjusted for case-mix differences. This enhances the comparability across hospitals with different case mixes.

Increasing values for length of stay, case-mix-adjusted data will almost always have a negative impact on profitability because most hospitals receive a fixed fee per case. Medical staff involvement in evaluating length of stay and treatment protocols is no longer only desirable; it is an absolute necessity.

Omega Hospital has a 1992 length of stay, case-mix-adjusted value of 5.1, which is above the regional median of 4.7. Although this value is not significantly above the regional median, it does suggest a closer examination of individual case types. A reduction in this value could lower Omega's costs.

3. *Net price per discharge, case-mix-adjusted*—This indicator provides management and the board with a measure of the average amount of revenue realized per discharge. This measure is case-mix-adjusted, so that differences due to kinds of cases seen should be eliminated. Values that differ from norms may reflect areas with higher costs of living or a different payer mix. Hospitals with heavy Medicare and Medicaid patient loads may find it harder to generate more revenue per case because Medicare and Medicaid pay a fixed price per diagnosis-related group that is not negotiable.

Omega Hospital has an extremely low net price per discharge, case-mix-adjusted, in 1992. The value is well below the regional median of $4,130. Further information reveals that Omega has a relatively small percentage of Medicare and Medicaid patients. Omega could and probably should raise its rates to increase its operating profitability. Although its operating margins are already higher than the U.S. median, it should be remembered that this hospital wishes to finance the majority of its future capital expenditures with equity. Its replacement viability position indicates a deficiency in this area, so future profits could be used to build replacement funds.

4. *Cost per discharge, case-mix-adjusted*—Hospitals that fail to control their costs are often more likely to fail. With increasing percentages of hospital revenue coming from payers who pay fixed prices, it is

very important to monitor and compare costs. Hospitals with high costs per discharge must realize higher prices per discharge. If price competition exists in the market area, or if the vast majority of patients pay fixed non-negotiable prices, higher costs will certainly lead to much lower profit per discharge. The case-mix adjustment will remove much of the interhospital variation that stems from case-mix differences; however, severity may still be a problem.

Omega Hospital's cost per discharge, case-mix-adjusted ratio is very low relative to the regional median. The basis for this conclusion is related to low capital costs and low staffing, or, stated alternatively, excellent productivity. Please note that the total costs reported in Table 6–3 do not match those reported in Omega Hospital's income statement in Table 4–3. The difference is bad debts. Bad debts in Table 6–3 are treated as a deduction from revenue and not an expense. This lowers costs and lowers revenues. Also note from Table 6–3 that Omega actually lost money from patient operations in 1992. Net revenues from patients were $44,887,000, compared with costs from patient operating expenses of $45,110,000. Were it not for other revenues, Omega would have lost money in 1992.

5. *Inpatient man-hours per discharge, case-mix-adjusted*—The inpatient man-hours per discharge, case-mix-adjusted indicator, provides an overall measure of inpatient labor productivity. Because of the labor intensity of hospital services, control over labor costs and staffing is critical to efficient and financially viable operations.

This measure assumes that the measure of activity or volume is a case-mix-adjusted discharge. This adjustment should make comparisons across hospitals reasonably valid. Hospitals with high values for inpatient man-hours per discharge adjusted for case mix may want to examine several areas. First, is the hospital using more staffing but lower cost staffing? For example, a hospital that employs more lower cost employees, such as aides, might have more hours worked per adjusted discharge but still have lower costs. This situation could be examined through a review of the salary per FTE indicator. Second, high staffing could result from excessive length of stay. In this regard, length of stay adjusted for case mix should be reviewed. Third, staffing may vary depending on the extent of contract services. Hospitals with low staffing ratios may have larger amounts of contract labor. This should be reflected in higher values for other costs per discharge adjusted for case mix.

Omega Hospital used 10.6 fewer man-hours per case-mix-adjusted discharge in 1992 than the regional median (130.2 − 119.6).

Omega might improve this value further if its length of stay could be reduced as discussed earlier.

6. *Full-time employees per occupied bed*—The number of full-time equivalents (FTEs) per occupied bed is a traditional measure of inpatient labor productivity. Labor productivity in the hospital industry is extremely important because hospital operations are very labor intensive. Control over staffing is thus a very critical element of management control.

   The FTE per occupied bed measure implicitly assumes that the major factor creating staffing need is the number of patients in the hospital. Clearly this argument is not totally valid. Case-mix intensity and patient illness severity can and do have a profound impact on staffing.

   A hospital with a high value for FTEs per occupied bed may not necessarily have a staffing problem. It is possible to employ more lower-paid personnel in the overall labor mix and still have lower costs. It is also possible to have a high number of FTEs per occupied bed but not be overstaffed when case-mix intensity is considered. In this light, it is very useful to evaluate jointly FTEs per occupied bed and inpatient man-hours per discharge adjusted for case mix. If the two measures provide different signals, the inpatient man-hours per discharge case-mix-adjusted measure may be the more relevant. This is especially true when one considers that revenues are more likely to be related to discharges adjusted for case mix than to patient days.

   Omega hospital demonstrates strong productivity when the FTEs per occupied bed indicator is examined. This variation is even larger on a relative basis than the earlier man-hours per discharge indicator. The reason is related to length of stay. Omega is achieving excellent productivity with respect to the level of patient care provided, but if length of stay could be reduced, additional gains would be realized.

7. *Salary per FTE*—The salary per FTE indicator provides a basic measure for the per-unit cost of the largest resource item used in producing hospital services. Control over wage rates is an important element in overall cost control.

   It is important to recognize that many factors may influence salary per FTE. First, wage rates may vary significantly by geographical region. Hospitals in New York City will clearly have higher salaries than hospitals in less expensive cost of living areas. It is therefore critical to ensure that a relevant peer group is matched with your hospital for comparison purposes. Second, labor mix may also impact the values for salary per FTE. Hospitals that employ all-RN staffs may have higher salary per FTE values but should experience lower staffing as measured by inpatient man-hours per discharge adjusted for case mix. Finally, the extent of contract labor services may also affect reported values of salaries per FTE. Hospitals that contract out relatively low-paid areas, such as housekeeping, may experience higher salary per FTE values.

Hospitals with high salary per FTE values should consider all of the comparability factors cited above, but they should also evaluate their present wage and salary structure. In today's competitive environment it is difficult to survive paying employees $15.00 per hour when your competitors are paying an average wage rate of $13.50 per hour if there are no differences in productivity.

Omega Hospital has a slightly higher salary per FTE than the regional median. This may reflect higher wages in the community or a higher skilled labor force. If the cause is attributed to labor force skill this may explain Omega's better productivity.

8. *Capital costs per discharge*—The capital costs per discharge indicator measures the total amount of interest and depreciation expense per discharge. This measure is not adjusted for case-mix differences and may be higher in hospitals with higher case-mix indices. High values for capital costs per discharge may be the result of several factors. First, as already mentioned, case-mix intensity may be a cause. Hospitals with higher case-mix severity often have a larger investment in fixed assets on a per-discharge basis. Second, low volume may also be a causal factor in high capital costs per discharge. Since capital costs are largely fixed costs, low volume would mean that the fixed capital costs of interest and depreciation would be spread over fewer units. Third, age of the plant may also be an issue. Hospitals with relatively new plants often will have both higher depreciation and interest costs. Fourth, the percentage of debt financing and the relative cost of that debt often will affect measures of capital costs per discharge. Hospitals with heavy percentages of debt financing and/or expensive costs of debt frequently will have higher capital costs per discharge. Finally, the use of operating leases also will have an impact. If the hospital leases assets on an operating basis, its depreciation and interest may be lower, resulting in lower capital costs per discharge.

Omega has very low capital costs per discharge because it has very little debt and an older plant. It is therefore not surprising to see values in this range for Omega. Future reliance on debt would increase these values significantly.

9. *Net price per visit*—Net price per visit defines the amount of revenue collected per outpatient visit. A key to the comparability of this indicator across hospitals is a uniform definition of an outpatient visit. The definition used by HFMA is related to an "encounter" concept and is defined as follows: "Each outpatient visit to each clinic or service is counted as one. For example, a patient who visits the emergency room, cardiology clinic and ophthalmology clinic on the same or subsequent day(s) would be counted as three visits."

It is usually very important to monitor prices in the outpatient area. Quite often there is a greater price sensitivity in outpatient services compared with inpatient services because patients frequently pay all or a greater portion of the bill directly because of lower insurance coverage.

Omega Hospital has low net prices per outpatient visit. If comparison of specific procedures corroborates this conclusion, Omega should explore raising prices in the outpatient area, too.

10. *Cost per visit*—The cost per visit measure is an analogue to the cost per discharge measure. It provides an overall measure of the cost of production in the outpatient area. The basic unit of production in the outpatient area is the visit. Unfortunately, a visit is not always identified in the same manner across hospitals. Care must be exercised in making comparisons with group medians. It is possible that the definitions of an outpatient visit are not uniform within the group. Over time we expect there to be increasing standardization in the definition of an outpatient visit.

There is also no adjustment for case mix in the outpatient area. A hospital seeing a high percentage of emergency patients may have a much higher cost per visit. Hospitals with extensive nonemergency patients may have significantly lower costs per visit.

Omega has a 1992 cost per visit of $128, compared with the regional median of $197. Although there may be some output comparison problems here, it does seem likely that Omega is more efficient in supplying outpatient services, also. It appears to be a very productive and well-managed firm.

11. *Outpatient man-hours per visit*—The outpatient man-hours per visit measure provides an overall measure of labor productivity for outpatient services. A high value would tend to imply excessive staffing and should be investigated. There are, however, several possible causes for high values that may not be related to poor labor productivity. First, it is possible that a visit in one hospital may not be comparable to a visit in other hospitals. This problem has already been discussed for other indicators measured on a per-visit basis.

Great care should be exercised to ensure that visits are at least defined consistently over time and, ideally, consistently across hospitals.

Second, the complexity of a visit may vary. There is no case-mix adjustment for an outpatient visit as there is for inpatient discharges. Third, if outpatient expenses, including labor costs, are allocated according to outpatient revenue percentages, there may be some bias.

Omega Hospital has achieved superior productivity, as seen in the outpatient man-hours per visit. In 1992 Omega used only 4.64 hours per visit, compared with the regional norm of 5.82.

12. *Outpatient revenue percentage*—The outpatient revenue percentage provides a measure of the hospital's reliance on outpatient revenue. A high value is not necessarily good or bad. The indicator merely provides a measure of the hospital's current reliance on outpatient revenue.

In general, the hospital industry has been increasing its overall reliance on outpatient revenue sources in the past. Many of the new growth areas are concentrated in the outpatient areas as the location of many health care services shifts from inpatient to outpatient settings.

A hospital experiencing an increase in outpatient revenue percentages needs to determine the cause. An increase that results totally from a decline in inpatient business is of course not a favorable indication. An increase resulting from substantial relative growth in outpatient care may be highly favorable if the inpatient care side of the equation is stable to increasing. The key to assessment is profitability. Expansion in any business line, inpatient or outpatient, is beneficial if reasonable returns are being generated.

Omega Hospital derived 24.4 percent of its total revenue from outpatient areas in 1992. There were 93,450 outpatient visits in 1992, compared with 75,669 in 1991. Omega has seen dramatic growth in the outpatient area and is wisely trying to capitalize on the expected growth.

SUMMARY

Assessing the financial condition of a firm is a joint management and board responsibility. It is essential that periodic evaluations be performed to enable better long-term strategic decisions and midcourse corrections to avert financial problems. Many of the indicators described in this chapter should be helpful in the measurement of financial position. Comparative data, such as those provided by HFMA, should also be sought to provide some relevant bench marks for assessing performance.

<hr>

ASSIGNMENTS

1. Operating margins in your hospital have been consistently below national norms for the past three years. Discuss the factors that might have created this situation and the ways in which you might determine specific causes.

2. Table 6–5 contains financial statements and some key financial ratios for Multiplan, an HMO corporation. Analyze the data and describe areas of strength and weakness.

3. An income index ratio of 1.5 is reported by a health care entity. What could account for this value?

4. How could a firm have a negative times interest earned ratio and a positive debt service coverage ratio?

5. Your firm's current liquidity ratio is 1.2. Is your liquidity position poor? What other factors would you check?

6. Your total asset turnover ratio has been declining over the past few years. How might you determine the cause for this decline?

7. Your firm has a replacement viability ratio of .20. If you were to replace your fixed assets today, what percentage of debt financing would you use?

8. Howard Ruhl has just been selected as the new chief executive officer (CEO) of Suburban Hospital, a well-known, 600-bed teaching hospital located in the suburb of a stable Western city of approximately 1.5 million population. Howard is concerned about the future of the hospital. He fears that, over the years, it has relied too much on its good location and excellent medical staff. Although all the operating indicators point to a good future—for example, outpatient and inpatient volumes are up—Howard is specifically concerned about the financial welfare of the hospital.

   The man whom Howard is replacing is well respected and was unquestionably a good manager. He personally brought the hospital through a significant growth period and is probably the major cause of its current success. He was, however, not well versed in finance and did not recruit competent fiscal help. The present chief fiscal officer is an old friend of the outgoing CEO and has no financial background; he received an MHA more than 20 years ago from the same school as the outgoing CEO.

   Suburban Hospital has borrowed very little in the past. Most of its present plant was financed with county general-obligation bonds. That financing vehicle is no longer available.

   At the present time, Suburban has a fairly active outpatient clinic operation. It does not have an attached medical office building. Howard believes that major growth in a number of areas is essential if Suburban is to remain strong. However, he is not certain which areas of growth to suggest to his fiscally conservative board, or how to suggest them. As a first step, Howard has asked for and received the two most recent financial statements. His present fiscal officer has calculated some key financial ratios for him to consider in his review. These statements and ratios are shown in Table 6–6.

Table 6–5 Financial Statements and Ratios for Multiplan, Inc.

(Dollar amounts in thousands except per-share data)

	Years ended December 31	
	1992	1991
Consolidated statements of income		
Revenue		
Premiums	$188,018	$113,482
Hospital services	4,786	3,936
Pharmacy sales	1,022	1,014
Other income	2,898	3,118
Total revenue	196,724	121,550
Costs and expenses		
Medical services	74,838	45,963
Hospital services	72,378	42,905
Outpatient services	11,761	8,159
Other health care expense	7,386	6,161
Salary expense	9,174	5,766
Marketing, general, and administrative	7,981	5,281
Depreciation and amortization	1,689	1,237
Interest	1,597	1,519
Total costs and expenses	186,804	116,991
	9,920	4,559
Minority interests	523	588
Income before income taxes	10,443	5,147
Provision for income taxes	(5,057)	(2,640)
Net income	$ 5,386	$ 2,507
Net income per common share	$ .35	$ .17
Consolidated balance sheets		
Assets		
Current assets		
Cash and cash equivalents	$ 34,264	$ 15,996
Accounts receivable (net of allowance for doubtful accounts 1992, $1,367 and 1991, $173)	14,069	9,664
Inventory	715	529
Prepaid expenses	2,435	814
Total current assets	51,483	27,003

Table 6–5 continued

(Dollar amounts in thousands except per-share data)

	Years ended December 31	
	1992	1991
Property and equipment		
Land	1,725	1,682
Building and leasehold improvements	7,350	4,847
Furniture and equipment	6,822	5,044
	15,897	11,573
Less accumulated depreciation and amortization	(2,947)	(1,718)
Total property and equipment	12,950	9,855
Other assets		
Intangible assets	12,183	12,985
Long-term receivables	1,494	1,747
Other assets	508	570
Total other assets	14,185	15,302
Total assets	$ 78,618	$ 52,160
Liabilities and shareholder's equity		
Current liabilities		
Estimated claims payable	$ 16,977	$ 12,275
Accounts payable	1,306	2,068
Accrued income taxes	2,740	2,470
Current portion of long-term debt	940	961
Accrued hospital incentive	2,370	511
Accrued salary expense	1,627	1,293
Other current liabilities	1,969	1,640
Total current liabilities	27,929	21,218
Long-term debt	11,475	12,567
Deferred income taxes	352	293
Other long-term liabilities	807	1,292
Total liabilities	40,563	35,370

continues

Table 6–5 continued

(Dollar amounts in thousands except per-share data)

	Years ended December 31	
	1992	*1991*
Shareholders' equity		
Preferred stock; 6,000,000 shares authorized, none issued		
Common stock, no stated value; authorized 60,000,000 shares; 1992, 16,186,000 shares, and 1991, 15,000,000 shares, and outstanding	18,581	2,702
Additional paid-in capital	11,581	11,581
Retained earnings	7,893	2,507
Total shareholders' equity	38,055	16,790
Total liabilities and shareholders' equity	$ 78,618	$ 52,160
Financial ratios		
Liquidity		
Current	1.843	1.273
Quick	1.818	1.248
Acid test	1.227	.754
Days in patient accounts receivable	26.494	29.784
Average payment period	53.752	65.740
Days' cash on hand	65.945	49.561
Capital structure		
Equity financing	.484	.322
Cash flow to debt	.176	.107
Long-term debt to equity	.323	.825
Fixed-asset financing	.948	1.406
Times interest earned	4.373	2.650
Debt service coverage	3.390	2.140
Activity		
Total asset turnover	2.502	2.330
Fixed-asset turnover	15.191	12.334
Current asset turnover	3.821	4.501
Inventory	275.138	229.773
Profitability		
Operating margin	.027	.021
Reported income index	.253	.165
Return on total assets	.069	.048
Return on equity	.142	.149
Other		
Average age of plant	1.745	1.389

Table 6-6 Financial Statements and Ratios for Suburban Hospital

(Dollar amounts in thousands)	1992	1991
Income statement		
Operating revenues		
Routine services	$28,453	$22,914
Ancillary services	33,376	27,133
Total patient revenues	$61,829	$50,047
Deductions from revenue		
Charity and bad debts	$ 2,160	$ 1,549
Contractual adjustments	3,263	2,388
Other	229	63
Total deduction from revenue	(5,652)	(4,000)
Net patient revenue	56,177	46,047
Other operating revenues	2,547	48
Total operating revenues	$58,724	$46,095
Operating expenses		
Salaries	$30,620	$24,670
Supplies and other	27,026	20,723
Total operating expenses	57,646	45,393
Net operating gain	1,078	702
Nonoperating revenues—net excess	1,363	497
of revenues over expenses before	2,441	1,199
changes in method of accounting	671	—
Excess of revenues over expenses	$ 3,112	$ 1,199
Balance sheet		
Unrestricted funds		
Assets		
Current assets		
Cash and cash equivalents	$ 974	$ 2,606
Accounts receivable	8,734	6,398
Other current assets	988	1,829
Current assets	10,696	10,833

continues

Table 6–6 continued

(Dollar amounts in thousands)		
	1992	1991
Other assets		
Replacement funds	4,668	7,215
Other funds	2,256	1,182
Other assets	6,924	8,397
Property, plant, and equipment	36,579	31,508
Total assets	54,199	50,738
Liabilities and current liabilities		
Accounts payable	1,948	2,644
Accrued expenses	3,005	2,174
Current maturities of long-term debt	1,031	837
Other	85	792
Current liabilities	6,069	6,447
Long-term debt	13,658	13,213
State equity	1,408	1,372
Fund balance	33,064	29,706
Total liabilities and fund balance	54,199	50,738
Restricted funds		
Total restricted funds	773	665
Fund balance	$ 773	$ 665
Financial ratios		
Liquidity		
Current	1.760	1.680
Quick	1.600	1.400
Acid test	.160	.400
Days in patient accounts receivable	56.700	50.700
Average payment period	40.100	54.200
Days' cash on hand	6.400	21.900
Capital structure		
Equity financing	.610	.590
Long-term debt to equity	.420	.450
Fixed-asset financing	.370	.420
Times interest earned	4.430	4.350
Debt service coverage	3.660	2.880
Cash flow to total debt	.260	.150

continues

Table 6-6 continued

(Dollar amounts in thousands)	1992	1991
Activity		
Total asset turnover	1.080	.910
Fixed-asset turnover	1.610	1.460
Current asset turnover	5.490	4.260
Inventory turnover	76.900	85.000
Profitability		
Deductible	.091	.080
Markup	1.117	1.104
Operating margin	.018	.015
Nonoperating revenue	.440	.410
Reported income index	.970	.270
Return on total assets	.057	.024
Return on equity	.094	.040
Other		
Average age of plant	8.500	9.090
Operating margin, price-level-adjusted	− .029	− .029
Restricted equity	.023	.022
Replacement viability	.212	.394

(a) Define key areas of concern for Suburban Hospital and state the rationales for your concern.

(b) Propose a set of possible actions that may correct the problems in these key areas.

SOLUTIONS AND ANSWERS

1. Operating margins are related to the values of markup and deductible ratios. A low operating margin ratio could result from a low markup ratio, a high deductible ratio, or some combination of the two. Low markup ratios in turn result from low prices or high expenses. A high deductible ratio results from large write-offs of revenue to third-party payers for contractual allowances or from large bad debt and charity care write-offs. Ideally, operating margins should be broken down by major product lines, such as pediatrics, obstetrics, ambulatory surgery, and so on.

2. An examination of Multiplan's financial data yields the following conclusions:

   • Multiplan has experienced a sizable growth in equity during the last two years, as evidenced by the reported income index. The funds involved resulted from the issuance of stock.

   • Multiplan has a low days in accounts receivable ratio, but this is based on a comparison with hospital norms. HMOs usually have a low days in accounts receivable ratio because of the prepayment nature of their business. However, the trend is still favorable.

- Multiplan has a relatively good total asset turnover compared with hospital norms. Again, HMOs usually have far less investment in fixed assets than do hospitals. This can be seen from an analysis of the fixed-asset turnover ratio.

- Multiplan has shown significant improvement in its operating margin. The 1992 value of 2.7 percent is comparable with that of hospitals, but it probably should be higher to finance future growth needs. No deductible or markup ratios are calculated because Multiplan does not have significant contractual allowances and provides only net revenue measures.

- Multiplan appears to have significant additional debt capacity available, as can be seen from an examination of its capital structure ratios. This additional debt capacity is, however, contingent on the maintenance and improvement of existing operating margins.

3. A transfer of funds out of the entity may have taken place. This is often the case in investor-owned companies, due to the payment of dividends. It may also occur in a voluntary entity because of a corporate restructuring. A positive reported income index can result if there is a positive transfer of funds into the firm when a loss occurs. For example, a firm may have a loss of $15 million and transfer of $5 million into the firm. The resulting reported income index would be 1.5 ($-15.0 / -10.0$).

4. The firm may have an extensive amount of depreciation and very low debt principal payments. This is often the case in the early years immediately after a major construction program.

5. A low current ratio is not always an indication of a poor liquidity position. If significant cash reserves are available, as measured by a high acid test ratio or a high replacement viability ratio, a liquidity problem may not exist. Alternatively, a high current ratio that results from a high days in patient accounts receivable position may not indicate good liquidity.

6. A declining total asset turnover can usually be traced to a declining fixed-asset turnover ratio or a declining current asset turnover ratio. A declining fixed-asset turnover ratio often results from declining utilization or from new plant investment, which should be associated with a declining average age of plant ratio. A declining current asset turnover ratio can be traced to an increasing days in patient accounts receivable, an increasing days' cash on hand, or a declining inventory turnover ratio.

7. The required percentage of debt financing for the firm would be 90 percent, or, alternatively, 10 percent equity financing. The following formulas can be used:

$$\text{Required debt financing \%} = [1.0 - .5 \times \text{Replacement viability ratio}] \times 100.0\%$$

$$= [1.0 - .5 \times .20] \times 100.0\%$$

$$= 90.0\%$$

8. (a) The major areas of concern for Suburban Hospital are
   - relatively low operating profitability
   - relatively old physical plant
   - dramatic decline in liquid assets, as evidenced by days' cash on hand

(b) Possible courses of action to be considered are

- Improve markup position through an increase in rates or curtailment of operating expenses. Suburban's markups have been historically low.

- Investigate the reasons for the buildup of accounts receivable. The increase appears to have required Suburban to expend more of its cash reserves to meet operating expenses.

- Consider additional debt financing to meet physical asset replacement and expansion needs. Suburban appears to have additional debt capacity at the present time. However, a successful financing package is highly contingent on an improvement in operating profitability.

Chapter 7

Strategic Financial Planning

Is there a need to define corporate financial policy in a health care firm? If so, who should be responsible—the board of trustees, the chief executive officer, the chief financial officer, or some combination of these? How should the definition of financial policy be accomplished? What are the steps required?

These kinds of questions are only now beginning to surface in the health care industry. Finance and financial management have long been areas of concern, but their orientation has recently shifted. Reimbursement and payment system management has given way to financial planning. Survival tomorrow is no longer a guaranteed option. Health care firms must establish realistic and achievable financial plans that are consistent with their strategic plans. The primary purpose of this chapter is to help provide a basis for the very crucial task of financial policy formation in health care firms.

THE STRATEGIC PLANNING PROCESS

Most observers would probably agree that financial policy and financial planning should be closely integrated within the strategic planning process. Understanding the strategic planning process is thus a first step in defining and developing financial policy and financial planning. It would be ideal if there was agreement among leading experts regarding the definition of strategic planning, but such is not the case. The literature on strategic planning is fairly recent; most of it has appeared since 1965. And the application of strategic planning principles to the health care industry is even more recent; the bulk of the literature on such applications has been published since 1980.

One trend in health care strategic planning does appear clear, however: there is a definite movement away from "facilities planning" to a more market-oriented approach. Health care firms can no longer decide which services they want to deliver without assessing need or market. This requirement appears consistent with the concept of strategic planning as it is used in general industry. Indeed, as the business environments of the health care industry and general industry become more alike, strategic planning in the two areas should become increasingly similar.

Much of the literature that deals with the strategic planning process in business organizations appears to be concerned with two basic decision outcomes: first, a statement of mission and/or goals is required to provide guidance to the organization. Second, a set of programs or activities to which the organization will commit resources during the planning period is defined.

Figure 7–1 shows the integration of the financial planning process with the strategic planning process. Financial planning is fashioned by the definition of programs and services and then assesses the financial feasibility of those programs and services. In many cases, a desired set of programs and services may not be financially feasible. This may cause a redefinition of the organization's mission and its desired programs and services. For example, a hospital may decide to change from a full-scale hospital to a specialty hospital, or it may decide to drop specific clinical programs, such as pediatrics or obstetrics.

Three points concerning the integration of strategic and financial planning should be emphasized. First, both strategic planning and financial planning are the primary responsibility of the board of trustees. This does not exclude top management from the process, since they should be active and participative members of the board. Second, strategic planning should precede financial planning. In some situations, the board may make strategic decisions based on the availability of funding. Although this may be fiscally conservative, it can often inhibit creative thinking. Third, the board should play an active, not a passive, role in the financial planning process. The board should not await word concerning the financial feasibility of its desired programs and services; it should actively provide guidelines for management and/or its consultants to use in developing the financial plan. Specifically, the board should establish key financial policy targets in three major areas:

1. growth rate
2. debt capacity
3. profitability objective (return on equity)

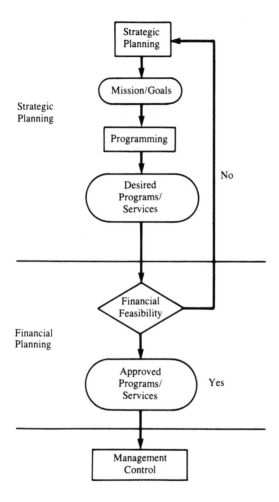

Figure 7-1 Integration of Strategic and Financial Planning

Financial Policy Targets

The term *financial feasibility* is often associated with an expensive study performed by a consulting firm in conjunction with the issue of debt. In such cases, the financial projections are so incredibly complex that few people profess to understand them, and even fewer actually do. In many people's minds, financial planning consists of a large number of mathematical relationships that can simulate future financial results, given certain key inputs. The validity of the projections is dependent on the reliability of the mathematical relationships, or model, and on the accuracy of the assumptions. Most financial feasibility studies developed in this way are never reviewed and never updated.

But conditions are changing and changing very rapidly. A large number of health care firms are now beginning to develop formal strategic plans. They are beginning to redefine, or at least reconsider, their basic mission and to identify future market areas. It is increasingly clear that their financial plans and financial strategies must be integral parts of their overall strategic plan. With the elimination of cost reimbursement and increased competition among health care providers, board members are beginning to insist on a greater role in financial policy making. Future financial viability is no longer a virtual certainty; some analysts predict that as many as one out of four existing hospitals will not survive.

Granted that health care board members and health care executives have an urgent need to understand financial policy and financial planning, can the requisite body of knowledge be conveyed in a manner that is capable of being understood? Must board members and executives remain passive observers in financial planning, or can they be given the means to establish key policy directives?

The simplest way to categorize and describe key financial relationships in a financial plan is through a balance sheet presentation. A financial plan can be thought of as a bridge between a current balance sheet and a balance sheet at some future date (see Figure 7-2). The bridge consists of three spans: first, the plan must specify what the *growth rate* and level of investment in assets should be at future dates. This span is directly linked to the strategic planning outcome that defines desired programs. Second, the plan must specify debt targets for the organization. Quite often the debt targets are split into two categories, current debt and long-term debt. The third and final span defines the amount of equity or fund balance required and the feasibility of generating the required equity. Having defined total assets in step 1 and debt levels in step 2, the amount of required equity or fund balance is predetermined. However, the plan must determine whether that level of new equity can be generated. For example, the organization described in Figure 7-2 must generate $25 million of new equity during the five-year plan. The key question to answer is whether there is a reasonable plan of operations that can earn that much new equity. In many cases the initial answer is no, and management and the board must rethink their investment levels in new assets or change their debt policy.

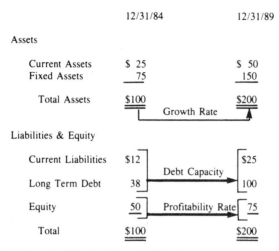

Figure 7–2 Bridge Spans in Effective Financial Planning

Requirements for Effective Policy Making

The preceding discussion of the elements of financial planning and the three major target areas of financial policy suggests certain requirements for effective financial planning and policy making. The following ten requirements are of special importance.

1. The Accounting System Should Be Capable of Providing Data on Cost, Revenue, and Investment along Program Lines

Programs, or "strategic business units," are the basic building blocks of any strategic plan. The financial plan must be developed on a basis consistent with the strategic plan. Unfortunately, present accounting systems are geared to provide data along responsibility center or departmental lines. For example, psychiatry may represent a program in the strategic plan, but the financial data on costs, investments, and revenues for the program may be intertwined with those of many departments, such as dietary, housekeeping, occupational therapy, and pharmacy. Still, this problem is not unique to the hospital and health care industry. Many organizations have programs that cut across departmental lines. In such cases, the financial data can be accumulated along programmatic lines, but some adjustments in cost and revenue assignments are necessary.

With the advent of the diagnosis-related group (DRG) payment system, the hospital industry has been making major advancements in the accumulation of financial data in terms of DRG categories. It is now possible to define major programs or product lines in a hospital as consisting of a specific set of DRGs. For example, if obstetrics were a program, it might be defined as DRG #370 (cesarian section with CC) to DRG #391 (normal newborns).

The important point to note here is that, although problems exist in obtaining financial data along program lines, they are not insurmountable. The health care industry is, of course, different from the automotive industry, but the differences do not necessarily imply greater difficulties.

2. No Growth Does Not Imply a Zero Growth Rate in Assets

The fact that no growth does not necessarily imply zero growth in assets is so obvious that it is often overlooked by many planning committees. Inflation will create investment needs that exceed present levels, even though the organization's strategic plan may call for program stabilization or an actual retrenchment. An annual rate of inflation equal to 7 percent means a doubling of investment values every ten years. For example, a nursing home with assets of $25 million today should plan on being a $50-million-asset firm ten years from now. Just because the investment involved may not represent a real increase in value does not negate the need for a plan of finance that will generate $25 million in new equity and debt financing over the next ten years.

Over time, of course, expectations about future rates of inflation may change. The financial plan should reflect the best current thinking in this area. This may necessitate periodic changes in the financial plan (requirement 9). It is also important to recognize that there may be differences in investment inflation rates across programs. In some programs, such as oncology, in which dramatic technological changes are likely to occur, a greater relative inflation rate may have to be assigned.

3. Working Capital Is a Major Element in Computing Total Future Asset Needs

In computing future investment needs, it is not uncommon to omit the working capital category. Most investment in any strategic plan is usually in bricks, mortar, and equipment. However, working capital can still be a rather sizable component, accounting for 20 to 30 percent of total investment in many health care firms.

The term *net working capital* is often used to describe the amount of permanent financing required to finance working capital or current assets. Net working capital is defined as current assets less current liabilities. It is important to remember this, since some current liability financing is automatic or un-negotiated. Just as inflation increases the dollar value of outstanding accounts receivable, it also increases wages or salaries payable and accounts payable. It is the net amount that must be financed. In the example depicted in Figure 7–2, the increase in net working capital was $12 ($25 − $13).

Working capital requirements vary by program. New programs usually have significant working capital requirements, whereas existing programs may experience only modest increases resulting from inflation. One of the primary causes for failure in new business ventures is often an inadequate amount of available working capital. New programs also may have significantly different working capital requirements. For example, a home health program may require little fixed investment in plant and equipment, but significant amounts of working capital may be required to finance a long collection cycle and initial development costs. Many firms that rushed into the development of home health agency programs have become acutely aware of this problem.

If inadequate amounts of working capital are included in the financial plan, the entire plan may be jeopardized. For example, an unanticipated $2 million increase in receivables requires an immediate source of finance, such as the liquidation of investments. If those investments are essential to provide needed equity in a larger financing program, certain key investments may be delayed or canceled in the future. A number of firms have had to reduce the scope of their strategic plans because of unanticipated demands for working capital.

4. Some Accumulation of Funds for Future Investment Is Critical to Long-Term Solvency

Saving for a rainy day has not been a policy practiced by many health care firms to any significant degree. As of 1990 the average hospital had approximately 35 percent of its replacement needs available in investments assuming 50 percent debt financing. This implies that the average hospital would need to borrow 82.5 percent of its replacement needs. This level of debt financing may no longer be feasible in the hospital industry as lenders reassess the relative degree of risk involved.

It is critical that health care boards and management establish formal policies for retention of funds for future investment. Health care firms can no longer expect to finance all of their investment needs with debt. They must set aside funds for investment to meet future needs in the same manner that pension plans are funded. An actuarially determined pension funding requirement is analogous to a board policy of replacement reserve funding. Yet very few hospitals have seriously undertaken to set aside funds for future investment needs, which partially explains the dramatic growth in debt in the hospital industry.

5. A Formally Defined Debt Capacity Ceiling Should Be Established

Few health care firms have formally defined their debt capacity or debt policy. This is in sharp contrast to most other industries. Without such a formally established debt policy, one of two unfavorable outcomes may result. First, debt may be viewed as the balancing variable in the financial plan. If a firm expects a $25 million increase in its investment and a $5 million increase in equity, $20 million of debt is required to make the strategic plan financially feasible. The firm will then try to arrange for $20 million of new debt financing. This is the situation in which many hospitals have found themselves. In such cases, additional debt could usually be obtained and adequate debt service could be demonstrated to lenders. Cost reimbursement had its advantages in that it could be used to provide payment for debt service costs. The strategic plan could remain un-changed, but a potential problem was that the debt to equity ratio might increase significantly.

Second, the balancing variable in the financial plan may shift to the investment side, but on an ex post facto basis. An approved financial plan may be unrealistic because the level of indebtedness required to finance the strategic plan exposes the hospital to excessive risks. Management may not realize this until the actual financing is needed. At that point, a scaling down of the programs specified in the strategic plan may be required. If a realistic debt capacity ceiling had been established earlier, existing funded programs might have been canceled or cut back to make funds available for more desirable programs.

Debt capacity can be defined in a number of ways. It can be expressed as a ratio, such as a long-term debt to equity ratio, or it can be defined in terms of demonstrated debt service coverage. Whatever the method used, some limit on debt financing should be established. That limit should represent a balance between the organization's desire to avoid financial risk exposure and the investment needs of its strategic plan. Debt policy should be clearly and concisely established before the fact; it should not be an ad hoc result.

6. Return on Investment by Program Area Should Be an Important Criterion in Program Selection

The principle that return on investment by program area should govern program selection is related to the need for accounting data along product lines, as discussed above. In order to calculate return on investment along program lines, financial data on revenues, expenses, and investment must be available along program lines. Return on investment should be used as part of an overall system of program evaluation and selection.

Portfolio analysis is a buzzword that has been used lately to categorize programs in terms of market share and growth rate. Health care writers have applied the concept to the literature on health care planning and marketing. However, one difficulty with the application of portfolio analysis in the health care industry is in the selection of the dimensions for developing the portfolio matrix. In most portfolio matrices, the dimensions used are market share and growth. Market share and growth are assumed to have an explicit relationship to cash flow. High market share is associated with high profitability and thus with good cash flow. High market growth is assumed to require cash flow for investment. For example, a program with a high market share and low growth is regarded as a "cash cow." It produces high cash flow but requires little cash flow for reinvestment because of its low growth needs.

Here we will employ a slight modification of the portfolio analysis paradigm, incorporating the dimension of profitability. Figure 7–3 illustrates the revised portfolio analysis matrix. Its two dimensions are (1) return on investment and (2) community need. Return on investment is used as the measure of profitability because it has the most direct tie to strategic and financial planning. Profit is merely new equity that can be used to finance new investment. Absolute levels of profit or cash flow mean little unless they are related to the underlying investment. For example, if program A has a profit of $100,000 and an investment of $2,000,000 while program B has a profit of $50,000 and an investment of $100,000, which program is a better cash cow if both programs have low community need?

In our revised portfolio analysis matrix, community need replaces the traditional marketing dimensions of growth and market share. Community need may be difficult to measure quantitatively, but the concept appears closely aligned to the missions of most voluntary health care firms—firms that were usually formed to provide health care services to some reasonably well-defined market.

Figure 7–3 categorizes programs as "dogs," "cash cows," "stars," and "Samaritans." With the exception of *Samaritan*, these terms are identical to those used in the existing literature. An example of a Samaritan program is one with a small or negative return on investment but a high community need. Thus, a hospital may provide a drug abuse program that loses money but meets a community need not met by any other health care provider. The program can continue if—and only if—the hospital has some stars or cash cows to subsidize the program's poor profitability. Dogs, that is, programs with low community need and low profit, should be considered in light of the resources they draw from potential Samaritans. The new payment environment makes this kind of analysis mandatory.

7. Nonoperating Sources of Equity Should Be Included in the Financial Plan

In the preceding discussion of return on investment, we were concerned primarily with operating profitability. However, in most voluntary health care firms, nonoperating income can also be extremely important. In fact, in 1990 nonoperating revenue accounted for 43 percent of total reported net income in the hospital industry. If nonoperating income can be improved, a significant new source of funding will be available to help finance the strategic plan. This could mean either that a greater percentage of desired programs can be undertaken or that reduced levels of indebtedness are possible.

The investment portfolio of many health care firms is quite large. Funds are available for retirement plans, professional liability self-insurance plans, funded depreciation, bond funds, endowments, and other purposes. Thus, small increases in investment yields can create sizable increases in income. For example, a 1 percent improvement in the yield on invested pension funds may reduce annual pension expense by as much as 10 percent. Clearly, hospital management should formally establish and incorporate target investment yields in its financial plans.

New equity can come from sources other than operating and nonoperating income. Corporate restructuring arrangements can create proprietary subsidiaries that can issue stock. Joint venture relationships with medical staff and others can be used to finance plant assets. It is important that both board members and executives have a clear understanding of the possible alternatives available for raising new equity to finance the strategic plan. Raising new equity through stock or partnerships is no longer the exclusive domain of proprietary entities.

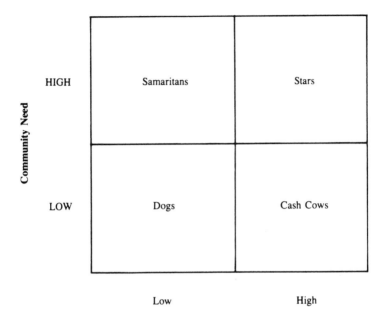

Figure 7–3 Revised Portfolio Analysis Matrix

---

8. The Financial Plan Must Be Integrated with the Management Control System

The integration of the financial plan with the management control system is an obvious requirement, but it is often overlooked. Frequently, a large fee is paid to a consultant, or enormous amounts of internal staff time are used to develop a financial plan that is never used.

Ideally, the financial plan is the basis for the annual budget. The key link between the budget and the financial plan should be the return on investment (ROI) targets specified in the financial plan. These ROI targets are critical to the long-run fulfillment of the strategic plan. Failure to achieve the targeted levels of profit will require revisions in the strategic plan.

Health care boards would not have to be involved in pricing debates if approved financial plans were available. In such situations, the profitability targets by program already would have been approved in the plans. The primary issues in the budgeting process should be the translation of profit targets by program lines to departmental lines via pricing allocations and the assessment of departmental operating efficiencies. Long, involved discussions about whether budgeted profit is too much or not enough should not be necessary.

9. The Financial Plan Should Be Updated at Least Annually

Management should have the most recent financial road map available at all times. Few people would plan a drive to San Francisco from Boston with a five-year-old road map, yet many organizations operate either with no long-range financial plan or with an outdated one. This can be especially dangerous for health care firms at the present time, as the business environment continues to change rapidly. Today, financial plans based on yesterday's financial environment may be useless, or even misleading. In all financial plans, a careful reassessment of relative program profitability is periodically required, possibly prompting major revisions of the strategic plan. Knowing both where you are going and how you expect to get there is critical to survival in a competitive environment.

10. The Financial Plan Is a Board Document and Should Be Formally Approved by the Board

In many firms the financial plan, if it exists, is regarded as a management document. The board may be only mildly interested in reviewing it and not interested at all in relating it to a strategic plan. This is rather strange behavior. Most boards would never dream of letting management operate without a board-approved annual budget for fear of failing to fulfill their board responsibilities. Yet planning for periods of time greater than one year is not regarded as important.

A recent hospital board meeting that followed a two-day strategic planning retreat illustrates this traditional perspective. During the retreat, strategic discussions about the future were held. The board and management agreed on a plan for the future that called for significant expansion into new market areas, such as long-term care. At the subsequent board meeting the chief executive officer and the chief finance officer presented the strategic plan and the related financial plan. The board members regarded approval of the financial plan as a waste of time. They did approve it, but in body only, not in spirit. Their rationale for apathy was clear. They could not foresee any problem with the financing. Most of them had been board members for a long time. Whenever money was needed in the past they raised rates or borrowed, and they could not see any reason to change this policy in the future. It is hoped that behavior today would be different.

Fortunately, this kind of reaction is becoming less common. Board members today are beginning to realize that the financial plan and the strategic plan are integrally related. It is impossible to develop one without the other, and both are ultimately the responsibility of the board.

DEVELOPING THE FINANCIAL PLAN

In this section we describe in some detail the steps involved in preparing a financial plan, using an actual case example. For our purposes, a financial plan may be defined as the bridge between two balance sheets. Here we limit our attention to the financial plan as a projection of the balance sheet; discussion of methods used to project other financial statements, such as those involving income or cash flow, is beyond the scope of this chapter.

The Developmental Process

Four steps are involved in the development of a financial plan:

1. Assess financial position and prior growth patterns.
2. Define growth needs in total assets for the planning period.
3. Define acceptable level of debt, for both current and long-term categories.
4. Assess reasonableness of required growth rate in equity.

Assessment of Present Financial Position

The first step in the development of a financial plan is the assessment of present financial position. It is extremely important to determine the present financial health and position of the firm. Without such information, projections about future growth can be dangerous at best. In most situations, past performance is usually a good basis for projecting future performance. For example, a financial plan may call for a future growth rate in equity of 15 percent per year. If, however, the prior five-year period showed an average annual growth rate in equity of only 5 percent, there may be some doubt about the validity of the 15 percent assumption and thus about the reasonableness of the financial plan.

Three categories of financial information need to be assembled to assess present financial position:

1. financial statements for the past three to five years
2. compounded growth rates in individual balance sheet accounts
3. financial evaluation of the firm, using ratio analysis

To illustrate the application of this information in financial planning, the balance sheets presented in Table 7–1 are used. These balance sheets provide information for Omega Hospital for the years 1988 through 1992. The column at the far right identifies the average four-year compounded growth rate. This average rate of growth can be determined by using financial mathematics tables (see Chapter 12), by using a calculator with financial functions, or by solving the following equation:

$$(1 + i)^4 = \frac{1992 \text{ Value}}{1988 \text{ Value}}$$

where i equals the average annual compounded rate of growth.

Tables 7–1, 7–2, and 7–3 present some useful historical data that will be helpful in assessing the present financial position and projecting asset growth rates. After a review of the three tables, the following summary may help to organize our thinking about Omega Hospital's 1992 financial position:

- Omega's short-term cash position has fallen dramatically over the last five years. Table 7–1 indicates that cash and short-term investments dropped an average of 4.0 percent per year during the last four years. Present days' cash on hand is a modest 12.2 (Table 7–3), but significant long-term liquidity exists to ensure that a short-term cash payment problem will not happen. Omega has a replacement viability ratio of .717 in 1992, which guarantees funding for any short-term cash crisis.

- Accounts receivable have been increasing at rates in excess of revenue growth, but present days in accounts receivable are very low (60.8 days). Management's ability to keep accounts receivable days below national norms will play a major role in any financial plan.

Table 7-1 Historical Balance Sheets for Omega Hospital (000s Omitted)

	1988	1989	1990	1991	1992	Annual Compound Growth Rate (%)
Assets						
Cash and short-term investments	$ 1,724	$ 3,640	$ 2,449	$ 1,648	$ 1,462	−4.0
Net patient accounts receivable	4,719	4,923	5,204	6,075	7,684	13.0
Supplies	608	663	659	681	780	8.9
Other current assets	299	538	570	624	661	21.9
Total current assets	$ 7,350	$ 9,764	$ 8,882	$ 9,028	$10,587	9.6
Gross property and equipment	30,052	31,494	36,659	41,307	49,737	13.4
Accumulated depreciation	12,901	14,744	16,302	17,284	19,762	11.3
Net property and equipment	17,151	16,750	20,357	24,023	29,975	15.0
Replacement reserves	11,203	13,381	14,007	13,939	9,607	−3.8
Other assets	4,122	4,242	4,210	2,099	1,852	−18.1
Total assets	$39,826	$44,137	$47,456	$49,089	$52,021	6.9
Liabilities and fund balance						
Current liabilities	$ 3,366	$ 5,040	$ 5,467	$ 5,082	$ 5,045	10.7
Long-term debt	7,572	6,910	6,310	5,765	5,475	−7.8
Estimated malpractice costs	0	0	1,020	1,087	988	Infinite
Fund balance	28,888	32,187	34,659	37,155	40,513	8.8
Total liabilities and fund balance	$39,826	$44,137	$47,456	$49,089	$52,021	6.9

- It would seem likely that Omega will face major capital expenditures for new plant, property, and equipment in the future. Their average age of plant is 8.0 years, which is well above comparative values for other hospitals. Although significant capital expenditure growth was made during the last four years (net property and equipment increased at an annual rate of 15.0 percent), more remains to be done if Omega is to remain competitive in its present market.
- Omega has excellent capital structure ratios, which would indicate its ability to finance new capital growth with debt should its board so

Table 7-2 Historical Income Statement for Omega Hospital (000s Omitted)

	1988	1989	1990	1991	1992
Revenues					
Gross patient revenue	$33,992	$36,671	$38,245	$42,524	$48,818
Contractual adjustments	4,231	3,718	4,179	3,439	2,723
Net patient revenue	29,761	32,953	34,066	39,085	46,095
Other revenue	1,823	1,874	1,983	2,041	2,607
Total operating revenue	$31,584	$34,827	$36,049	$41,126	$48,702
Expenses					
Interest expense	842	788	590	476	431
Bad-debt expense	0	0	0	1,208	921
Depreciation	1,993	1,911	1,785	2,163	2,471
Other operating expense	27,399	30,096	32,258	35,533	42,495
Total operating expense	$30,234	$32,795	$34,633	$39,380	$46,318
Income from operations	1,350	2,032	1,416	1,746	2,384
Nonoperating income	1,177	1,266	1,055	1,141	974
Excess of revenues over expenses	$2,527	$3,298	$2,471	$2,887	$3,358

choose. Coverage ratios are extremely high because Omega has very little debt and has experienced excellent levels of operating profitability.

- Omega has recorded good operating margins during the last five years. The degree of operating profitability is oftentimes the most critical assumption in any financial plan. Organizations that project higher operating margins than they realize will experience major financial shock. While it may be dangerous to overestimate operating margins, there is also a problem with underestimating margins. Underestimations can produce capital plans that miss the mark in terms of meeting the organization's goals or that rely too much on debt financing.

- Omega has set aside significant levels of funds to meet future replacement needs. Over the last four years it has financed all its capital expenditures from either current cash flow or replacement reserves. Although the present replacement reserve of $9.6 million is down sharply from 1991's year-end value of $13.9 million, it is still a sizable pool of funds that enhances the long-term liquidity position of Omega Hospital greatly. Investment income from this pool of funds is also the major source of Omega's nonoperating income.

Table 7-3 Historical Financial Ratios for Omega Hospital

Ratio	1988	1989	1990	1991	1992	1990 HFMA* National Median
Profitability						
Total margin	.077	.091	.067	.068	.068	.042
Operating margin	.041	.056	.038	.041	.048	.014
Operating margin, price-level-adjusted	.018	.031	.009	.027	.030	.003
Nonoperating gain	.036	.035	.028	.027	.020	.018
Reported income index	.620	1.000	1.000	1.157	1.000	.994
Return on equity	.087	.102	.071	.078	.083	.082
Liquidity						
Current	2.184	1.937	1.625	1.776	2.099	1.91
Days in accounts receivable	57.878	54.529	55.757	56.732	60.845	73.7
Average payment period	43.504	59.565	60.726	49.841	41.997	60.5
Days' cash on hand	22.282	43.019	27.213	16.163	12.170	18.8
Capital structure						
Equity financing	.725	.729	.730	.757	.779	.48
Long-term debt to equity	.262	.215	.182	.155	.135	.72
Cash flow to debt	.413	.436	.362	.466	.554	.170
Times interest earned	4.000	5.185	5.190	7.065	8.791	2.48
Activity						
Total asset turnover	.823	.818	.782	.861	.955	.910
Fixed-asset turnover	1.910	2.155	1.823	1.759	1.657	1.94
Other asset turnover	2.138	2.048	2.037	2.635	4.335	4.18
Current asset turnover	4.457	3.697	4.178	4.682	4.692	3.45
Other ratios						
Average age of plant	6.473	7.715	9.133	7.991	7.998	7.23
Replacement viability	1.262	1.234	1.063	1.199	.717	.35

*HFMA = Healthcare Financial Management Association.

Definition of Growth Rate of Assets

The preceding summary of Omega's present financial position gives us a good basis for projecting growth rates for individual asset categories. These growth rates should be related to Omega's financial plan. Ideally, we should know what new programs and services will be introduced in the coming planning period, usually five years. These broad policy projections must be translated into specific financial requirements.

Many hospitals and other health care firms have developed five-year capital budgets. These budgets may represent a useful starting point for the development of the financial plan; however, they should be regarded as a starting point only. Most long-term capital budgets are wish lists of what would be nice to have and are not usually realistic in terms of what the organization can afford to purchase. Before incorporating capital budgets into the long-term financial plan, the budgets must be fine-tuned and—most important—related to the organization's strategic plan. The strategic plan should define spending priorities that will maximize attainment of organizational goals and objectives.

We now define the assumptions used to forecast individual asset categories for Omega during the next five years. Remember that the investment requirements should be identified first, before any consideration is given to the financing of those investments. In short, ask yourself what is required first to accomplish the set of goals and objectives defined for the organization. After that list is developed, you may discuss the financing of those needs.

- *Cash and investments.* Omega's management believes that it can operate safely with 10.0 days' cash on hand. Although this value is below its present level of 12.2 and well below the national hospital median of 18.8, Omega believes that with its cushion of long-term replacement reserves, it will not jeopardize its ability to meet short-term maturing obligations.
- *Net patient accounts receivable.* Omega believes that it can maintain days in accounts receivable values that are very close to their present position of 60.8 days. Therefore, Omega has forecast future patient accounts receivable at 62.0 days for all five forecast years.
- *Supplies.* Omega has historically maintained approximately 1.56 percent of its total operating revenue in supplies. This relationship between revenue and supplies is believed to be fairly stable and is used to predict supplies in the forecast period.
- *Other current assets.* Omega has forecast its other current assets to be 1.36 percent of total operating revenue. This is based on a historical pattern that is believed to be stable.
- *Gross property and equipment.* These values were taken directly from Omega's five-year capital expenditure plan, after that plan was revised to reflect reasonableness. Omega would like to fund all projects included in the plan. The schedule below summarizes the five-year forecast (000s omitted):

	1993	*1994*	*1995*	*1996*	*1997*
Beginning gross property, plant and equipment	$49,737	$67,018	$78,809	$85,696	$93,541
+ Capital Expenditures	18,081	11,791	8,887	7,845	3,500
− Disposals	800	0	2,000	0	0
Ending gross property, plant, and equipment	$67,018	$78,809	$85,696	$93,541	$97,041

• *Accumulated depreciation.* These values were taken directly from Omega's five-year capital expenditure plan. The values reflect the amount of annual depreciation to be taken on Omega's depreciable assets netted from any accumulated depreciation on assets sold or disposed of during the year (000s omitted).

	1993	1994	1995	1996	1997
Beginning accumulated depreciation	$19,762	$21,948	$26,350	$29,445	$34,829
+ Depreciation	2,986	4,402	5,095	5,384	5,431
− Disposals	800	0	2,000	0	0
Ending accumulated depreciation	$21,948	$26,350	$29,445	$34,829	$40,260

• *Replacement reserves.* Omega currently has a replacement viability ratio of .717. Omega ideally would like to attain a replacement viability ratio of 1.0. This means that in 1992, Omega should have had $13.4 million in replacement funds ($9,607,000/.717). Omega has set an initial target of achieving the following balances for replacement funds (000s omitted):

	1993	1994	1995	1996	1997
Replacement reserves	$11,000	$12,000	$13,000	$14,000	$15,000

• *Other assets.* Omega has projected its other assets to increase in the following pattern (000s omitted):

	1993	1994	1995	1996	1997
Other assets	$2,000	$2,200	$2,400	$2,700	$3,000

Definition of Debt Policy

Having defined the desired levels of investment for Omega Hospital, the next step to be undertaken is the definition of debt policy during the five-year forecast period. Debt should not be viewed as the balancing variable in the financial plan. That is, the financial plan should not project assets and equity and then balance the equation with debt. Sound financial policy requires that the board and management define in advance what their position is regarding the assumption of debt. Presented below is Omega's management and board policy on debt for the next five years.

• *Current liabilities*: Omega's management people believe that an average payment period ratio of 50.0 would be a reasonable target for their current liabilities. They presently have an average payment period ratio of 42 and believe that this could be increased without jeopardizing the firm or exposing it to unnecessary risk. Current liabilities will therefore be defined as

$$\frac{\text{Total operating expenses} - \text{Depreciation}}{365} \times 50$$

Omega's board members have recently accepted the idea of a major capital financing program. They have stated that they will not create long-term debt in an amount that is greater than their fund balance at that point in time. This is stated formally in a long-term debt to equity ratio target of less than 1.0. Management has requested that an initial offering of $32.075 million be placed in 1993. A part of the proposed financing will be used to retire the present long-term bonds of $5,475,000. Interest and principal payments for the next five years are presented below (000s omitted):

	1993	1994	1995	1996	1997
Beginning long-term debt	$5,045	$32,075	$31,475	$30,775	$29,975
Debt principal payments	5,045	600	700	800	900
New long-term debt	32,075	0	0	0	0
Ending long-term debt	$32,075	$31,475	$30,775	$29,775	$29,075
Interest payments	1,200	2,309	2,266	2,216	2,158

- *Estimated malpractice costs.* Although they are not usually thought of as a formal liability, estimated malpractice costs do represent a form of financing. Omega has recognized malpractice expenses at levels beyond its payments. This deferral represents a timing difference, but it can have significant cash flow implications. Omega believes that estimated malpractice costs will increase at 8 percent per year over the next five years.

Assessment of the Reasonableness of Required Equity Growth

Determining whether the equity growth rate is reasonable is without question the most crucial step in the financial planning process. Defining the amount of required equity capital is actually quite simple. Once the level of total assets has been projected and the organization's debt policy has been defined, the required amount of equity is a residual figure. Assets must equal liabilities plus equity, which we identified as the basic accounting equation in Chapter 2.

The best way to identify the amount of equity that will be available at the end of each year is to think of the individual components in the following equation:

Beginning fund balance	$100
+ Excess of revenues over expenses	10
+ / − Transfers of equity	2
Ending fund balance	$112

The initial starting point is the projection of excess of revenues over expenses (net income) during each of the forecast years. Some of the items that determine net income have an important effect on the asset growth projections. In fact, several asset categories are dependent on either a revenue or an expense projection. For example, accounts receivable cannot be forecast until projected revenues are forecast, because accounts receivable forecasts result from multiplying forecasted daily revenue by the expected days in accounts receivable.

- *Gross patient revenue.* Gross patient revenue was forecast to grow at 9.5 percent per year. Of this 9.5 percent, 7.0 percent reflected a true price increase and 2.5 percent was a volume increase for new services.
- *Contractual adjustments.* Contractual adjustments are forecast to be a percentage of gross patient revenue. The percentages used for each year will be increasing to reflect the historical trend and also to recognize a growing reluctance of third-party payers to increase their payments at rates matching cost increases. The percentages used are 6.0, 6.4, 6.8, 7.2, and 7.6 for each of the five years commencing in 1993.
- *Other revenue.* Other revenue is forecast to grow at 8.0 percent per year.
- *Interest expense.* Interest expense has already been defined in the section on long-term debt. These numbers should be exact, given the proposed debt service schedule.
- *Bad-debt expense.* Bad-debt expense was not shown as an operating expense until 1991. Prior to that year, bad-debt expense was shown as a deduction from gross patient revenue. Bad-debt expense was forecast at 2.8 percent of gross patient revenue. This value was based on the 1991 relationship and is more conservative than the 1992 percentage of 1.89.

- *Depreciation.* Depreciation was given in a schedule presented in the section identifying projected values for accumulated depreciation.
- *Other operating expense.* Other operating expense was projected to grow at 8.0 percent per year. This rate reflects a 6.5 percent growth in prices and wages and a 1.5 percent for volume. The 6.5 percent is believed to be appropriate because Omega currently has a wage and salary structure that is ahead of most nearby competitors, and it believes that wage and salary increase can be held at 6.0 percent or lower. Projecting a 1.5 percent increase in cost due to volume effects may also appear too low in light of the expected 2.5 percent volume increase. However, not all costs will go up proportionately with an increase in volume. Some costs are fixed and will not change. In this case, Omega has assumed that 60 percent (1.5/2.5) of its costs are variable and 40 percent are fixed.
- *Nonoperating income.* Nonoperating income is primarily derived from replacement reserves. Interest rates on those investments have been unusually high in the past, and management believes that 8.0 percent will be a reasonably safe yield for board-designated investments in the future. In addition to the investment income, management also believes that $50,000 of contributions will be forthcoming on an annual basis over the forecast period. Interest income will be forecast by using the following relationship:

$$\frac{\text{Beginning investment balance} + \text{Ending investment balance}}{2} \times .08$$

Tables 7–4 and 7–5 present the balance sheet and income statement for the initial projection. The income statement of Table 7–5 shows that the present financial plan is not feasible with its current set of assumptions. In two years, 1995 and 1996, transfers of outside equity would be required in the amounts of $944,000 and $2,632,000, respectively.

Management now has several options that it could consider.

- Leave the plan as is and seek equity transfers in the required amounts. This will probably not be realistic, given prior levels of giving.
- Reduce the amount of required investment to match the availability of funds. Most likely this would mean reducing the amount of board-designated funds to accommodate the reduction. This reduction would not be very serious because the balance sheet of Table 7–4 indicates

Table 7-4 Forecasted Balance Sheet for Omega Hospital (000s Omitted)

	1993	1994	1995	1996	1997
Assets					
Cash and short-term investments	$ 1,331	$ 1,466	$ 1,578	$ 1,698	$ 1,829
Net patient accounts receivable	8,535	9,306	10,147	11,063	12,062
Supplies	829	904	985	1,073	1,169
Other current assets	722	786	857	934	1,018
Total current assets	$11,417	$12,463	$13,567	$14,768	$16,078
Gross property and equipment	67,018	78,809	85,696	93,541	97,041
Accumulated depreciation	21,948	26,350	29,445	34,829	40,260
Net property and equipment	45,070	52,459	56,251	58,712	56,781
Trustee-held funds	2,800	2,800	2,800	2,800	2,800
Board-designated replacement reserves	22,651	15,671	13,000	14,000	18,179
Other assets	1,200	1,400	1,600	1,900	2,200
Total other assets	26,651	19,871	17,400	18,700	23,179
Total assets	$83,138	$84,793	$87,218	$92,180	$96,038
Liabilities and fund balance					
Current liabilities	$ 6,656	$ 7,331	$ 7,889	$ 8,492	$ 9,144
Long-term debt	32,075	31,475	30,775	29,975	29,075
Estimated malpractice costs	1,067	1,152	1,245	1,344	1,452
Fund balance	43,340	44,835	47,309	52,369	56,367
Total liabilities and fund balance	$83,138	$84,793	$87,218	$92,180	$96,038

that in 1997 there is $18,179,000 of board-designated funds. This balance reflects the approximately $4.0 million of equity transfers in 1995 and 1996, but the present value is above the target of $15.0 million by about $3.0 million. This implies that if the equity transfers were not forthcoming, Omega would only be about $1.0 million short of its replacement reserve target in 1997.

• Increase operating income to generate the required additional equity. Most likely this would have to come from either a price increase or an

Table 7-5 Forecasted Income Statement for Omega Hospital (000s Omitted)

	1993	1994	1995	1996	1997
Revenues					
Gross patient revenue	$53,456	$58,534	$64,095	$70,184	$76,851
Contractual adjustments	3,207	3,746	4,358	5,053	5,841
Net patient revenue	50,249	54,788	59,737	65,131	71,010
Other revenue	2,816	3,041	3,284	3,547	3,831
Total operating revenue	$53,065	$57,829	$63,021	$68,678	$74,841
Expenses					
Interest expense	1,200	2,309	2,266	2,216	2,158
Bad-debt expense	1,497	1,639	1,795	1,965	2,152
Operating expense	45,895	49,566	53,531	57,814	62,439
Depreciation	2,986	4,402	5,095	5,384	5,431
Total operating expense	$51,578	$57,916	$62,687	$67,379	$72,180
Income from operations	1,487	-87	334	1,299	2,661
Investment income	1,290	1,533	1,147	1,080	1,287
Contributions	50	50	50	50	50
Nonoperating income	1,340	1,583	1,197	1,130	1,337
Excess of revenues					
over expenses	$ 2,827	$ 1,496	$ 1,531	$ 2,429	$ 3,998
+Beginning fund balance	40,513	43,340	44,835	47,309	52,369
+Transfers required	0	0	944	2,632	0
Ending fund balance	$43,340	$44,836	$47,310	$52,370	$56,367

expense reduction. Since Omega is already a low-cost provider, the expense cutting may not be reasonable.

Assuming that Omega decides to reduce its required investment in board-designated funds to match current projected funding, the final income statement and balance sheet are presented in Tables 7-6 and 7-7. A forecasted set of financial ratios is presented in Table 7-8.

Omega Hospital is about $1.0 million short of its targeted $15.0 million in board-designated funds in 1997. This is the only target originally set by management and the board that was not met in the first draft of the financial plan. It is very unusual to have an initial plan be so close to the one finally adopted. Usually, major changes in spending and income assumptions are required before a reasonable plan results.

Table 7-6 Adjusted Forecasted Balance Sheet for Omega Hospital (000s Omitted)

	1993	1994	1995	1996	1997
Assets					
Cash short-term investments	$ 1,331	$ 1,466	$ 1,578	$ 1,698	$ 1,829
Net patient accounts receivable	8,535	9,306	10,147	11,063	12,062
Supplies	829	904	985	1,073	1,169
Other current assets	722	786	857	934	1,018
Total current assets	$11,417	$12,463	$13,567	$14,768	$16,078
Gross property and equipment	67,018	78,809	85,696	93,541	97,041
Accumulated depreciation	21,948	26,350	29,445	34,829	40,260
Total accumulated depreciation	21,948	26,350	29,445	34,829	40,260
Net property and equipment	45,070	52,459	56,251	58,712	56,781
Trustee-held funds	2,800	2,800	2,800	2,800	2,800
Board-designated					
replacement reserves	22,651	15,671	12,017	10,194	14,056
Other assets	1,200	1,400	1,600	1,900	2,200
Total other assets	26,651	19,872	16,417	14,894	19,056
Total assets	$83,138	$84,793	$86,235	$88,374	$91,915
Liabilities and fund balance					
Current liabilities	$ 6,656	$ 7,331	$ 7,889	$ 8,492	$ 9,144
Long-term debt	32,075	31,475	30,775	29,975	29,075
Estimated malpractice costs	1,067	1,152	1,245	1,344	1,452
Fund balance	43,340	44,835	46,326	48,563	52,244
Total liabilities and					
fund balance	$83,138	$84,793	$86,235	$88,374	$91,915

INTEGRATION OF THE FINANCIAL PLAN WITH MANAGEMENT CONTROL

The development of a financial plan is a useless exercise unless that plan is integrated into the management control process. Management needs to know whether the plan is being realized and, if it is not, what corrective action can be taken. In some cases, there is little that management can do. For example, assume that the entity has experienced an unusually large reduction in its operating margins as a result of increased competition. In this case, perhaps the only course of action open to management is to revise its plan to reflect more accurately the current situation. Indeed, it is important for management to assess the accuracy of

Table 7-7 Adjusted Forecasted Income Statement for Omega Hospital (000s Omitted)

	1993	1994	1995	1996	1997
Revenues					
Gross patient revenue	$53,456	$58,534	$64,095	$70,184	$76,851
Contractual adjustments	3,207	3,746	4,358	5,053	5,841
Net patient revenue	50,249	54,788	59,737	65,131	71,010
Other revenue	2,816	3,041	3,284	3,547	3,831
Total operating revenue	$53,065	$57,829	$63,021	$68,678	$74,841
Expenses					
Interest expense	1,200	2,309	2,266	2,216	2,158
Bad-debt expense	1,497	1,639	1,795	1,965	2,152
Operating expense	45,895	49,566	53,531	57,814	62,439
Depreciation	2,986	4,402	5,095	5,384	5,431
Total operating expense	$51,578	$57,916	$62,687	$67,379	$72,180
Income from operations	1,487	−87	334	1,299	2,661
Investment income	1,290	1,533	1,108	888	970
Contributions	50	50	50	50	50
Nonoperating income	1,340	1,583	1,158	938	1,020
Excess of revenues					
over expenses	$ 2,827	$ 1,496	$ 1,492	$ 2,237	$ 3,681
+Beginning fund balance	40,513	43,340	44,835	46,326	48,563
+Transfers required	0	0	0	0	0
Ending fund balance	$43,340	$44,836	$46,327	$48,563	$52,244

its financial plan annually and to make appropriate changes in it as needed.

To integrate the financial plan with the management control process, some structure is needed. Financial ratios provide that structure. The chart in Figure 7-4 depicts detailed targets for Omega Hospital, reflecting its financial plan. In the chart, specific ratio values are delineated. The primary targets involve the five major ratios that together determine the hospital's equity growth rate. The secondary targets are concerned with additional data that can be used to monitor actual performance and detect possible problems.

To see how the chart in Figure 7-4 might be used in management control, let us assume that 1993 has just ended and the financial data essential to the calculation of the ratios are now available. Omega's actual growth rate in equity for 1993 is assumed to be 5.9 percent, which represents an unfavorable variance from the required value of 6.5 percent.

Table 7-8 Forecasted Financial Ratios for Omega Hospital

Ratio	1993	1994	1995	1996	1997
Profitability					
Total margin	.052	.025	.023	.032	.049
Operating margin	.027	−.001	.005	.019	.035
Operating margin, price-level-adjusted	−.010	−.024	−.011	−.001	.013
Nonoperating gain	.025	.027	.018	.013	.013
Reported income index	1.000	1.000	1.000	1.000	1.000
Return on equity	.065	.033	.032	.046	.070
Liquidity					
Current	1.715	1.700	1.720	1.739	1.758
Days in accounts receivable	62.000	62.000	62.000	62.000	62.000
Average payment period	50.000	50.000	50.000	50.000	50.000
Days' cash on hand	10.000	10.000	10.000	10.000	10.000
Capital structure					
Equity financing	.521	.529	.537	.550	.568
Long-term debt to equity	.740	.702	.664	.617	.557
Cash flow to debt	.150	.152	.170	.198	.238
Times interest earned	3.356	1.648	1.658	2.009	2.706
Activity					
Total asset turnover	.654	.701	.744	.788	.825
Fixed-asset turnover	1.207	1.133	1.141	1.186	1.336
Other asset turnover	2.041	2.990	3.909	4.674	3.981
Current asset turnover	4.765	4.767	4.731	4.714	4.718
Other ratios					
Average age of plant	7.350	5.986	5.779	6.469	7.413
Replacement viability	1.229	.914	.675	.468	.533

Actual values for the primary indicators are

	1993 Values
Operating margin ratio	.023
Total asset turnover ratio	.654
Equity financing ratio	.521
Nonoperating gain	.024
Reported income index ratio	1.00

The major cause of the unfavorable variance in the equity growth rate is a deviation from the expected operating margin of .004, from .027 to .023. In addition, the nonoperating gain ratio was also below expectations, actual value of 2.4 percent compared with an expected value of 2.5 percent. All other ratio targets that determine equity growth were met. This would narrow any corrective actions to the two areas of operating margins and nonoperating gains.

It is extremely important to remember the concept of "sustainable growth" introduced in Chapter 6: Sustainable growth simply means that no

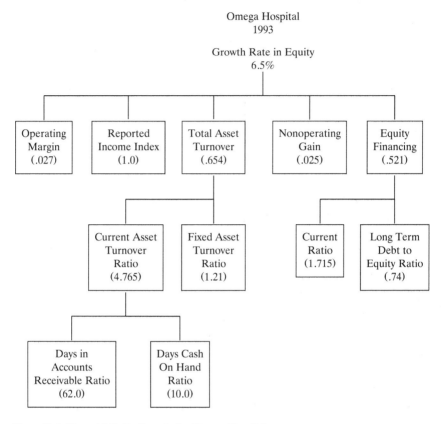

Figure 7–4 Financial Ratio Targets for Omega Hospital

organization can generate a growth rate in assets that exceeds its growth rate in equity for a prolonged period of time. Ultimately, an organization is limited by the rate at which it can generate new equity.

Equity growth can be defined as follows:

$$\text{Equity growth rate} = \frac{[\text{OM} + \text{NOR}] \times \text{TAT}}{\text{RII} \times \text{EF}}$$

where OM = operating margin ratio, NOR = nonoperating gain ratio, TAT = total asset turnover ratio, RII = reported income index ratio, and EF = equity financing ratio.

Top management and board concentration on this simple formula and the key relationships represented by it will dramatically improve financial focus and direction.

SUMMARY

In the process of identifying the requirements for effective financial policy formulation in health care firms, it is especially important to relate the strategic plan to the financial plan. The financial plan should not be developed in isolation from strategic planning, nor should the strategic plan be developed in isolation from the financial plan. Both plans need to be developed together, reflecting in that context their individual requirements and assumptions. A strategic plan is not valid if it is not financially feasible, and a financial plan is of little value if it does not reflect the strategic decisions reached by management and the board.

A financial plan should be updated at least annually, projecting a forecast period of three to five years. Financial plans that are not updated stand a good chance of becoming invalid. The environment of health care delivery is changing, and a health care entity's financial plan must reflect the changes. In fact, a failure to update its financial plan can have disastrous consequences for an entity, leading perhaps to market share retrenchment or even financial failure.

Finally, financial plans should be integrated into the management control process. Financial ratios can be very useful in this regard. In particular, specific ratios can be usefully related to the key financial planning target of growth rate in equity.

ASSIGNMENTS

1. A financial plan may be thought of as a bridge between two balance sheets. What are the major categories of assumptions that must be specified to project a future balance sheet, given a current balance sheet?

2. What problems result from the present responsibility center orientation of most accounting systems in providing data for financial planning?

3. Your director of marketing is urging you to develop a new drug abuse program. She has argued that there is no capital investment involved in the development of the new service. Do you believe this is an accurate statement?

4. Your hospital has a current replacement viability ratio of .20. What are the implications of this indicator for your hospital's financial planning?

5. Your controller has just provided you with ROI figures for your firm's major product lines. You have noticed that obstetrics has a very low ROI. What factors should be considered before you drop this service?

6. You are in the process of developing your firm's financial plan for the next five years. As an initial step, you are analyzing financial ratios for the last five years. You notice that, over the five-year period, the average age of plant ratio has increased from 8.5 years to 12.2 years. What are the implications of this for your financial plan?

7. If current assets are expected to increase by $4 million over the next five years and you wish to increase your current ratio from 1.5 to 2.0, what additional amount of new equity must be generated to finance the increase in the current ratio on the incremental $4.0?

8. Beginning equity is $50 million and equity in five years is projected to be $100 million. What is the annual rate of growth implied by these values?

9. You are assessing the financial plan developed for you by a prestigious "Big 6" accounting firm. You are especially interested in the attainability of the projected growth rate in equity. You know that, if that growth rate is not realistic, the financial plan is not valid and you may have to scale back your projected increase in assets. The following schedule summarizes your findings:

	Historical Average	Five-Year Projections
Reported income index ratio	1.000	.900
Operating margin ratio	.025	.027
Total asset turnover ratio	1.100	1.200
Nonoperating gain ratio	.011	.011
Equity financing ratio	.500	.500
Equity growth rate	7.86%	10.29%

Does the accounting firm's plan appear to be reasonable?

10. During the next five years, Meredith Hospital must spend $2 million to renovate its plant. Data for the most recent two years are presented in the hospital's financial statements in Tables 7-9 through 7-12. Based on these data, develop a projected balance sheet for 1997. Assume that Meredith Hospital will be experiencing a general inflationary rate of 8 percent over the next five years. Does it appear that the hospital can realistically finance its asset needs?

11. Using the Omega Hospital example of this chapter, project the income statement and balance sheet for the years 1993 to 1997. Assume that all final assumptions reflected in Tables 7-6 and 7-7 stay the same, except that gross patient revenue now increases at 8.5 percent instead of 9.5 percent per year. All funding deficiencies will be met through reductions in board-designated replacement funds.

SOLUTIONS AND ANSWERS

1. Projection of a future balance sheet requires assumptions in three categories:

   (a) rates of growth for individual asset accounts
   (b) debt financing policy for both current and long-term debt
   (c) realizable rate of growth in equity that is factored into five ratio areas: (1) operating margins, (2) nonoperating revenue, (3) equity financing, (4) total asset turnover, and (5) reported income index.

2. Strategic financial planning is usually done along program or product lines, not responsibility centers. This requires the financial planner to transfer revenue, cost, and invest-

Table 7-9 Balance Sheet for Meredith Hospital, December 31, 1992 and 1991

Assets	1992	1991
Unrestricted funds		
Current assets		
Cash		
Demand deposits	$ 4,855	$ 49,953
Savings	22,948	79,849
Certificates of deposit	9,187	103,362
Accounts receivable		
Patient accounts	910,596	634,867
Less allowance for uncollectable accounts and		
contractual allowance	52,000	75,000
	858,596	559,867
Other	83,845	40,445
	942,441	600,312
Inventory	115,356	101,542
Prepaid expenses	24,128	42,369
Total current assets	1,118,915	977,387
Other assets		
Other	69,085	71,501
Property, plant, and equipment less accumulated		
depreciation of $1,474,395 in 1992 and		
$1,473,063 in 1991	2,008,589	1,850,819
	$3,196,589	$2,899,707
Restricted funds		
Special purpose funds		
Investments	$ 169	$ 169
Endowment funds		
Cash and investments	$ 155,302	$ 155,302

ment assignments from responsibility centers to product lines. This can be a very difficult and inexact process.

3. Although there may be a little new investment in fixed assets required to start a drug abuse program, the investment in working capital may be sizable. Some projection of the investment should be made to assess the potential return on investment that is likely to result.

4. A replacement viability ratio of .20 implies that your hospital will need to borrow 90 percent of its replacement needs in the future. The percentage of debt financing is derived by the following formula:

$$\text{Debt financing} = 100\% - .5 \times \text{replacement viability ratio}$$

This directly affects the debt policy assumptions that will be used in the financial plan. It will also have an impact on the firm's operating margins because of the potentially large increase in debt and the resulting increase in interest expense.

Table 7–10 Statement of Liabilities and Fund Balances for Meredith Hospital, Years Ended December 31, 1992 and 1991

	1992	1991
Unrestricted funds		
Current liabilities		
Current maturities of long-term debt	$ 20,282	$ 0
Trade accounts payable	299,607	138,655
Accrued expenses		
Salaries and wages	61,618	119,709
Other	270,327	175,769
Amounts due Blue Cross, Blue Shield, Medicare, and Medicaid from adjustments of interim payments	144,402	77,851
Total current liabilities	796,236	511,984
Long-term debt, less current maturities	121,415	0
Fund balance	2,278,938	2,387,723
	$3,196,589	2,899,707
Restricted funds		
Special purpose funds		
Fund balance	$,196,169	$,196,169
Endowment funds		
Fund balance	$ 155,302	$ 155,302

5. Eliminating a product line solely on the basis of an inadequate return on investment may not be consistent with the firm's goals and objectives. Specifically, obstetrics may meet a community need and may be essential to the firm's mission; it may in fact be classified as a Samaritan (see Figure 7–3). Alternatively, a low return on investment can sometimes be deceiving. The product line may have important externalities. For example, obstetrics may lose money, but gynecology may be very profitable. Removing obstetrics may mean that the firm's gynecology line, and its profits, would be reduced.

6. The current average age of plant ratio implies that the firm has a very old plant relative to industry norms. This will almost certainly mean that significant new investment will be required in the planning period.

7. Use of a current ratio of 2.0 implies that the incremental investment of $4.00 million in current assets would be financed with $2.00 million of current liabilities. Use of a current ratio of 1.5 would imply current liability financing of $2.67 million. Therefore, the change in the current ratio implies that an additional equity requirement of $670,000 would be required.

8. The implied annual rate of growth is 14.86 percent.

9. The accounting firm's plan specifies a 30 percent increase in the annual growth rate in equity, compared with the historical five-year average (7.86 percent versus 10.29 percent). The major changes are in the reported income index and total asset turnover ratios. In the past five years, the firm has had no unreported income, since the value for the reported income index is 1.0. It is very important to find out what the source of the new equity is expected to be. The increase in total asset turnover, although not large, does

Table 7–11 Statement of Revenue and Expense and Changes in Unrestricted Fund Balances for Meredith Hospital, Years Ended December 31, 1992 and 1991

	1992	1991
Operating revenue		
Patient revenue	$6,116,268	$4,476,208
Revenue deductions	785,465	430,380
Net patient revenue	5,330,803	4,045,828
Other operating revenue	138,179	103,259
Total operating revenue	5,468,982	4,149,087
Operating expenses		
Nursing service	1,572,884	1,106,979
Emergency service	354,441	268,728
Ancillary service	1,100,823	793,752
Medical administration	129,259	114,344
General service	799,767	674,755
Administrative and fiscal services	811,718	620,180
Interest	3,151	0
Depreciation	190,583	165,896
Other operating expense	497,920	453,847
Total operating expense	5,460,546	4,198,481
Income (loss) from operations	8,436	(49,394)
Net nonoperating income (expense)	(133,913)	124,385
Excess of revenues over expenses (expenses over revenues)	(125,477)	74,991
Fund balance		
Beginning	2,387,723	2,298,255
Transfer from restricted fund	16,692	14,477
Ending	$2,278,938	$2,387,723

Table 7–12 Statement of Changes in Fund Balances, Restricted Funds, for Meredith Hospital, Years Ended December 31, 1992 and 1991

	Special Purpose Funds		Endowment Funds	
	1992	1991	1992	1991
Balance, beginning	$169	$169	$155,302	$155,302
Additions (deductions)				
Interest income	20	20	16,019	13,940
Contributions	653	517	0	0
Transfer to unrestricted funds	(673)	(537)	(16,019)	(13,940)
Balance, ending	$169	$169	$155,302	$155,302

play an important role in the higher projected growth rate in equity. Reasons for this increase should be verified.

10. The data in Table 7–13 are the results of a financial ratio analysis conducted for Meredith Hospital. The ratios indicate that the hospital's cash position is presently very weak. A significant buildup in cash may be required to meet liquidity concerns. There is very little long-term debt, but profitability is very weak, which means that debt service coverage is marginal. Virtually no replacement funds are present to finance future asset growth. Table 7–14 shows data for the projected balance sheet for Meredith Hospital with supporting assumptions. From these data, the projected growth rate in equity is fairly modest, 2.32 percent per annum. This rate appears feasible, provided the hospital can increase its operating margin and not lose money from nonoperating sources. A key concern is the ability of the hospital to borrow long-term debt. Its present levels of income may not justify additional long-term debt in the amount required in the plan.

11. Tables 7–15 and 7–16 reflect the reduction of gross patient revenue growth to 8.5 percent per year.

Table 7–13 Financial Ratios for Meredith Hospital

Ratio	1991	1992
Liquidity		
Current	1.909	1.405
Days in patient accounts receivable	50.509	58.788
Average payment period	46.341	55.148
Days' cash on hand	21.104	2.562
Capital structure		
Equity financing	.823	.713
Cash flow to debt	.470	.071
Long-term debt to equity	.000	.053
Fixed-asset financing	.000	.060
Times interest earned	NA	− 38.821
Debt service coverage	NA	20.662
Activity		
Total asset turnover	1.474	1.669
Fixed-asset turnover	2.308	2.656
Current asset turnover	4.372	4.768
Inventory	42.085	46.241
Profitability		
Operating margin	− .012	.002
Nonoperating revenue	.029	− .025
Reported income index	.838	1.153
Return on total assets	.026	− .039
Return on equity	.031	− .055
Other		
Average age of plant	8.879	7.736
Operating margin, price-level-adjusted	− .056	− .033
Restricted equity	.065	.068
Replacement viability	.046	.047

Table 7–14 Projected Balance Sheet for Meredith Hospital (000s Omitted)

	1992	1997
Current assets		
Cash and certificates of deposit	$ 37	$ 217[a]
Accounts receivable	942	1,384[b]
Inventory	115	169[c]
Prepaid expenses	24	35[d]
Total current assets	$1,118	$1,805
Other	69	852[e]
Property, plant, and equipment	2,009	2,456[f]
Total assets	$3,196	$5,113
Current liabilities	$ 796	$1,002[g]
Long-term debt	121	1,555[h]
Fund balance	2,279	2,556[i]
Total liabilities and fund balance	$3,196	$5,113

Assumptions

[a]Present cash should be around $148 to yield a 10.5 days' cash on hand position. Inflating that value forward at 8 percent yields $217.

[b]Present days in accounts receivable is acceptable. Present receivables are inflated at 8 percent.

[c]Present inventory may be excessive, but this is not significant. Current value is inflated at 8 percent.

[d]Prepaid expenses are inflated at 8 percent.

[e]Other assets represent replacement funds. Their present position is inadequate, given their low replacement viability ratio. To be near normal, the present level of investments should be near $580. Inflating $580 at 8 percent yields the 1997 projected value.

[f]The hospital expects to add $2,000,000 in new investment over the five-year period. This would yield $4,009,000 in 1997 before subtracting depreciation. Present depreciation expense is $190,583. The assumption that the new assets will be put in operation in year 3 and have an average ten-year life means $200,000 of additional depreciation expense in years 3, 4, and 5. Total depreciation expense would be $1,552,915 [(5 × $190,583) = (3 × $200,000)]. This means the net plant would be $2,456,085 in 1997.

[g]The current ratio will be 1.8 in 1997.

[h]It is assumed that the hospital desires an equity financing ratio of .5. Therefore, current liabilities plus long-term debt cannot exceed $2,557 (50 percent of $5,113). Long-term debt is therefore $1,555.

[i]Equity is a residue figure (5113-1002-1555).

Table 7–15 Forecasted Balance Sheet for Omega Hospital

	1993	1994	1995	1996	1997
Assets					
Cash and short-term investments	1,331	1,465	1,577	1,697	1,826
Net patient accounts receivable	8,457	9,137	9,872	10,665	11,521
Supplies	822	888	959	1,036	1,120
Other current assets	715	773	835	902	975
Total current assets	11,326	12,263	13,242	14,300	15,442
Gross property and equipment	67,018	78,809	85,696	93,541	97,041
Accumulated depreciation	21,948	26,350	29,445	34,829	40,260
Net property and equipment	45,070	52,459	56,251	58,712	56,781
Trustee-held funds	2,800	2,800	2,800	2,800	2,800
Replacement reserves	22,281	14,374	9,100	4,809	5,177
Other assets	1,200	1,400	1,600	1,900	2,200
Total other assets	26,281	18,574	13,500	9,509	10,177
Total assets	82,676	83,296	82,994	82,522	82,400
Liabilities and fund balance					
Current liabilities	6,654	7,327	7,883	8,483	9,130
Long-term debt	32,075	31,475	30,775	29,975	29,075
Estimated malpractice costs	1,067	1,152	1,245	1,344	1,452
Fund balance	42,880	43,342	43,091	42,720	42,743
Total liabilities and fund balance	82,676	83,296	82,994	82,522	82,400

Table 7–16 Forecasted Income Statement for Omega Hospital

	1993	1994	1995	1996	1997
Gross patient revenue	52,968	57,470	62,355	67,655	73,406
Contractual adjustments	3,178	3,678	4,240	4,871	5,579
Net patient revenue	49,789	53,792	58,115	62,784	67,827
Other revenue	2,816	3,041	3,284	3,547	3,831
Total operating revenue	52,605	56,833	61,399	66,331	71,657
Interest expense	1,200	2,309	2,266	2,216	2,158
Bad-debt expense	1,483	1,609	1,746	1,894	2,055
Operating expense	45,895	49,566	53,531	57,814	62,439
Depreciation expense-other asset	2,986	4,402	5,095	5,384	5,431
Total operating expense	51,564	57,886	62,638	67,308	72,083

Table 7–16 continued

	1993	1994	1995	1996	1997
Income from operations	1,041	−1,054	−1,240	−978	−426
Investment income	1,276	1,466	939	556	399
Contributions	50	50	50	50	50
Nonoperating income	1,326	1,516	989	606	449
Excess of revenues over expenses	2,367	462	−251	−371	23
+Beginning fund balance	40,513	42,880	43,342	43,091	42,720
+Transfers required	0	0	0	0	0
Ending fund balance	42,880	43,342	43,091	42,720	42,743

Chapter 8

Cost Concepts and Decision Making

In the last five chapters, we have focused on understanding and interpreting the financial information prepared by the financial accounting system and presented in general purpose financial statements. This chapter is directed more narrowly at the utilization of cost information in decision making. Cost information is produced by the cost accounting system of an entity. In most situations, it is shaped by the financial accounting system and the generally accepted principles of financial accounting. However, it is flexible, since it usually provides information for identifiable and specific decision-making groups, such as budgetary cost variance reports to department managers, cost reports to third-party payers, and forecasted project cost reports to planning agencies.

Cost is a noun that never really stands alone. In most situations, two additional pieces of information are added that enhance the meaning and relevance of the cost statistic. First, the object being costed is defined. For example, we might say that the cost of routine nursing care in Willkram Hospital is $200. Objects of costing are usually of two types: (1) products (outputs or services) and (2) responsibility centers (departments or larger units). Quite often, we oversimplify this classification system and refer to cost information about products as planning information and cost information about responsibility centers as control information.

Second, usually an adjective is added to modify cost. For example, we might say that the direct cost of routine nursing care in Willkram Hospital is $100. A number of major categories of adjective modifiers refine the concept of cost; they are all used to improve the decision-making process by precisely defining cost to make it more relevant to decisions.

This chapter discusses some of the basic concepts of cost used in cost analysis. It is important to explain this jargon if decision makers are to use cost information correctly. Different concepts of cost are required for different decision purposes. In most situations, these concepts require specific, unique methodologies of cost measurement.

CONCEPTS OF COST

Cost may be categorized in a variety of ways to meet decision makers' specific needs. However, in most situations, the total value of cost is the same. Using one cost concept in place of another simply slices the total cost pie differently. For example, in Table 8–1, the total cost of a laboratory for June 1992 was $21,360. Of that amount, $20,000 could be classified as direct cost and $1,360 as indirect cost. However, classifying

Table 8–1 Cost Report, Laboratory, June 1992

	Amount
Direct costs	
Salaries	$10,000
Supplies	5,000
Other	5,000
Total	$20,000
Depreciation	
Building and Fixed Equipment	100
Major Movable Equipment	60
Total	160
Allocated costs	
Employee Benefits	150
Administration	500
Maintenance	250
Housekeeping	200
Laundry	100
Total	1,200
Total costs	$21,360
Relative value units (RVU) produced	10,000
Average cost per RVU	$ 2,136

costs by controllability might determine that $15,000 of the laboratory cost was controllable and $6,360 was not controllable. The total cost, however, is the same in both cases.

This brings us to another important point. Since, in most cases, different concepts of cost simply slice total cost in different ways, there may be underlying relationships between the various concepts of costs. For example, direct costs and controllable costs may be related. In many situations, there are standard rules of thumb that may be used to relate cost measures.

The difference between cost and expense is another crucial definitional point. Accountants have traditionally defined cost in a way that leads one to think of cost as an expenditure. However, in most reported cost statistics, the definition is usually one of expense, not necessarily expenditure. For example, in Table 8–1, depreciation is listed as a cost. However, depreciation is not an actual expenditure of cash but an amortization of prior cost. In the present context, unless otherwise indicated, when we are discussing cost statistics the terms *costs* and *expenses* may be used interchangeably.

For purposes of discussion, we examine below the four major categories within which costs can be classified:

1. traceability to the object being costed
2. behavior of cost to output or activity
3. management responsibility for control
4. future costs versus historical costs

Traceability

Of all cost classifications, traceability is the most basic. Two major categories of costs classified by traceability are (1) direct costs and (2) indirect costs. A direct cost is specifically traceable to a given cost objective. For example, the salaries, supplies, and other costs in Table 8–1 are classified as direct costs of the laboratory. Indirect costs cannot be traced to a given cost objective without resorting to some arbitrary method of assignment. In Table 8–1, depreciation, employee benefits, and costs of other departments would be classified as indirect costs.

Not all costs classified as indirect may actually be indirect, however. In some situations, they could be redefined as direct costs. For example, it might be possible to calculate employee benefits for specific employees; these costs could then be charged to the departments in which the employees work and thus become direct costs. However, the actual costs of performing these calculations might be prohibitive.

The classification of a cost as either direct or indirect depends on the given cost objective. This is a simple observation, but one that is forgotten by many users of cost information. For example, the $20,000 of direct cost identified in Table 8–1 is a direct cost only with respect to the laboratory department. If another cost objective is specified, the cost may no longer be direct. For example, dividing the $20,000 of direct costs by the number of relative value units (RVUs) yields a direct cost per RVU of $2.00, but this is not really a true figure. The direct cost of any given RVU may be higher or lower than the $2.00 calculated, which is the average value for all RVUs and not necessarily the cost for any specific unit.

Incorrect classification is a common problem in cost accounting. Costs are accumulated on a department or responsibility center basis and may be direct or indirect with respect to that department. However, it can be misleading to say that the same set of direct costs is also direct with respect to the outputs of that department.

The major direct cost categories of most departments would include the following:

- salaries
- supplies
- other (usually fees and purchased services such as utilities, dues, travel, and rents)

Indirect cost categories usually include

- depreciation
- employee benefits
- allocated costs of other departments

The concept of direct versus indirect cost may not appear to have much specific relevance to decision makers. To some extent this is true; however, the concept of direct versus indirect costs is pervasive. It influences both the definition and measurement of other alternative cost concepts that do have specific relevance.

Cost Behavior

Cost is also classified by the degree of variability in relation to output. The actual measurement of cost behavior is influenced by a department's classification of cost, which provides the basis for categorizing costs as direct or indirect.

For our purposes, we can identify four major categories of costs that are classified according to their relationship to output:

1. variable
2. fixed
3. semifixed
4. semivariable

Variable costs change as output or volume changes in a constant, proportional manner. That is, if output increases by 10 percent, costs should also increase by 10 percent; that is, there is some constant cost increment per unit of output. Figure 8-1 illustrates, graphically and mathematically, the concept of variable cost for the laboratory example of Table 8-1. It is assumed that all supply costs in this case are variable. For each unit increase in RVUs, supply costs will increase by $.50.

Fixed costs do not change in response to changes in volume. They are a function of the passage of time, not output. Figure 8-2 illustrates fixed cost behavior patterns for the depreciation costs of the laboratory example. Each month, irrespective of output levels, depreciation cost will be $160.

Semifixed (step) costs do change with respect to changes in output, but they are not proportional. A semifixed cost might be considered variable or fixed—depending on the size of the steps relative to the range of volume under consideration. For example, in Figure 8-3, it is assumed that the salaries cost of the laboratory is semifixed. If the volume of output under consideration for a specific decision were between 6,000 and 8,000 RVUs, salary costs could be considered fixed at $9,000. Some semifixed costs may be considered variable for cost analysis purposes. For example, if smaller units of people could be employed instead of full-time equivalents (FTEs), such as on the basis of hours generated by an available part-time pool, the size of the steps might be significantly smaller than 2,000 RVUs in our laboratory example. At present, it is assumed that one additional FTE must be employed for every increment of 2,000 RVUs. Treating salary costs as variable in this situation might not be a bad procedure (see Figure 8-3).

Semivariable costs include elements of both fixed and variable costs. Utility costs are good examples. There may be some basic, fixed requirement per unit of time, (month, year) regardless of volume—such as normal heating and lighting requirements. But there is also likely to be a direct, proportional relationship between volume and the amount of the utility

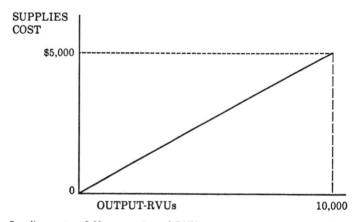

Note: Supplies cost = $.50 × number of RVUs.

Figure 8–1 Cost Behavior of Supplies Cost, Variable

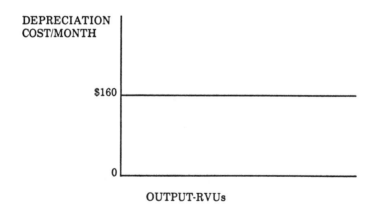

Note: Depreciation cost = $160 per month.

Figure 8–2 Cost Behavior of Depreciation, Fixed

cost. As volume increases, costs go up. Figure 8–4 illustrates semivariable costs in our laboratory example.

In many situations, we do not focus on specific cost elements but aggregate several cost categories of interest. It is interesting to see what type of cost behavior pattern emerges when we do this. Figure 8–5 aggregates the four cost categories discussed earlier: variable, fixed, semi-fixed, and semivariable. A semivariable cost behavior pattern closely approximates the actual aggregated cost behavior pattern; this is true for

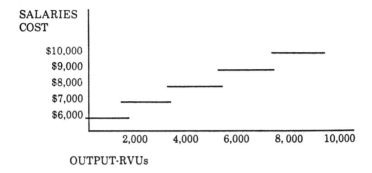

Note: Salary costs = $6,000 if RVUs are less than 2,000, $7,000 if RVUs are between 2,001 and 4,000, $8,000 if RVUs are between 4,001 and 6,000, $9,000 if RVUs are between 6,001 and 8,000, and $10,000 if RVUs are between 8,001 and 10,000.

Figure 8–3 Cost Behavior of Salary Costs, Semifixed

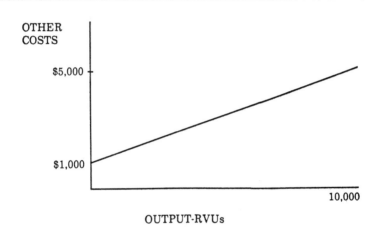

Note: Other costs = $1,000 per month + $.40 × RVUs.

Figure 8–4 Cost Behavior of Other Costs, Semivariable

many types of operations. In the next section, we discuss some very simple but useful methods for approximating this cost function.

Controllability

One of the primary purposes of gathering cost information is to aid the management control process. To facilitate evaluation of the management

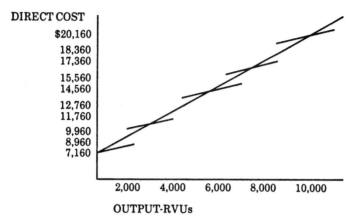

Note: Direct cost and depreciation = $7,160 per month + $1.30 × RVUs (approximation).

Figure 8–5 Cost Behavior of Aggregated Costs, Direct Cost, and Depreciation

control process, costs must be assigned to individual responsibility centers, usually departments, where a designated manager is responsible for cost control. A natural question that arises is, for what proportion of the total costs charged to a department is the manager responsible? The answer to this question requires that costs be separated into two categories: controllable costs and noncontrollable costs.

Controllable costs can be influenced by a designated responsibility center or departmental manager within a defined control period. It is said that all costs are controllable by someone at some time. For example, the chief executive officer of a health care facility, through the authority granted by the governing board, is ultimately responsible for all costs.

The matrix of costs shown in Figure 8–6 categorizes the laboratory cost report data of Table 8–1. All costs must fall into one of the six cells; however, it may be possible to categorize an aggregated cost category into more than one cell. In the laboratory example, other cost was viewed as semivariable, implying that part of the cost would be described as a direct variable cost ($4,000) and part as a direct fixed cost ($1,000).

There is a tendency in developing management control programs, especially in the health care industry, to use one of three approaches in designating controllable costs. First, controllable costs may be defined as the total costs charged to the department; the department manager would view all costs in the above six categories as controllable. In our example, all $21,360 of cost would be viewed as controllable by the laboratory manager. In most normal situations, however, this grossly overstates the

Traceability	Variable		Fixed		Semifixed		Total
Direct	Other Supplies	$4,000 5,000 $9,000	Other	$1,000 $1,000	Other	$10,000 $10,000	$20,000
Indirect	Employee Benefits Housekeeping	$150 $100 $250	Depreciation Administration Housekeeping	$160 $500 $100 $760	Maintenance Laundry	$250 $100 $350	$1,360
Totals		$9,250		$1760		$10,350	$21,360

Figure 8–6 Laboratory Cost Behavior Categorization

amount of cost actually controllable by a given department manager. The result of this overstatement has been negative in many situations. Department managers have rightfully viewed this basis of control as highly inequitable.

Second, controllable costs may be limited to those costs classified as direct. This system is also not without fault: specifically, there may be fixed costs attributed directly to the department that should not be considered controllable. Rents on pieces of equipment, for example, may not be under the department manager's control. There may also be indirect costs, especially costs that are variable, that the department manager can control. For example, employee benefits may legitimately be the department manager's responsibility.

Third, in some situations, controllable costs may be defined as only those costs that are direct/variable. This limits costs that are controllable by the department manager to their lowest level. However, it excludes what could be a relatively large amount of cost influenced by the department manager. Failure to include the latter cost in the manager's control sphere may weaken management control.

Future Costs

Decision making involves selection among alternatives; it is a forward-looking process. Actual historical cost may be useful as a basis for projecting future costs, but it should not be used without adjustment unless it can be assumed that future conditions will be identical to past conditions.

A variety of concepts and definitions have been used in current discussion of costs for decision-making purposes. The following four types of costs appear to be basic to the process of selecting among alternative decisions.

1. avoidable costs
2. sunk costs
3. incremental costs
4. opportunity costs

Avoidable Costs

Avoidable costs will be affected by the decision under consideration. Specifically, they are costs that can be eliminated or saved if an activity is discontinued; they will continue only if the activity is left unchanged. For example, if a hospital were considering curtailing its volume by 50 percent in response to cost containment pressures, what would it save? The answer is those costs that are avoidable. In most situations, multiplication of current and average cost per unit of output (patient days or admissions) by the projected change in output would overstate avoidable costs; a considerable proportion of the cost may be classified as sunk. Variable costs are almost always a subset of avoidable costs, but avoidable costs might include some fixed costs. For example, administrative staffing might be drastically reduced in a nursing home if 50 percent of the beds were taken out of service. Most likely administrative staffing costs would have been classified as fixed, given earlier expectations regarding volume.

Sunk Costs

Sunk costs are unaffected by the decision under consideration. In the example above, large portions of cost—depreciation, administrative salaries, insurance and others—are sunk or not avoidable in the proposed 50 percent reduction in volume.

The distinction between fixed and variable costs, on the one hand, and sunk and avoidable costs, on the other, is not perfect. Many costs classified as fixed may also be thought of as sunk, but some are not. For example, malpractice insurance premiums generally may be considered fixed cost, given an expected normal level of activity. However, if the institution is considering a drastic reduction in volume, malpractice premiums may not be entirely fixed. In summary, sunk costs are almost a subset of fixed costs, but not all fixed costs need be sunk. In the evaluation of a decision to close a hospital, most of the hospital's costs (both fixed and variable) probably would be eliminated and therefore would be categorized as avoidable and not sunk with respect to the closure decision.

Incremental Costs

Incremental costs represent the change in cost that results from a specific management action. For example, someone might want to know the incremental cost of signing a managed-care contract that would generate 200 new admissions a year. There is a strong relationship between incremental and avoidable costs. They can be thought of as different sides of the same coin. We use the term *incremental costs* to reference the change in costs that results from a management action that *increases* volume. The term *avoidable costs* defines the change in cost that results from a management action that *reduces* volume. For decisions involving only modest changes in output, incremental costs and variable costs may be used interchangeably. In most situations, however, incremental costs are more comprehensive. A decision to construct a surgi-center adjacent to a hospital would involve fixed and variable costs. Depreciation of the facility would be a fixed cost but it would be incremental to the decision to construct the surgi-center.

Opportunity Costs

Opportunity costs are values foregone by using a resource in a particular way instead of in its next best alternative way. Assume that a nursing home is considering expanding its facility and would use land acquired 20 years ago. If the land had a historical cost of $1 million but a present market value of $10 million, what is the opportunity cost of the land? Practically everyone would agree that if sale of the land constituted the next best alternative, the opportunity cost would be $10 million, not $1 million. Alternatively, a hospital might consider converting part of its acute care facility into a skilled nursing facility because of a reduction in demand or obsolescence in the facility. The question arises, what is the value, or what would be the cost of the facility, to the skilled nursing facility operation? If there is no way that the facility can be renovated or if the facility is not needed for the provision of acute care, its opportunity cost may be zero. This could contrast sharply to the recorded historical cost of the facility.

COST MEASUREMENT

In this section, we examine the methods of cost measurement for two cost categories: (1) direct and indirect full cost and (2) variable and fixed cost. Both of these cost categories are useful in financial decisions, but the cost accounting system does not directly provide estimates for them.

Direct and Indirect Full Cost

In most cost accounting systems, costs are classified by department or responsibility center or by the object of expenditure. When costs are classified primarily along departmental lines, individual cost items are charged to the departments to which they are traceable. When costs are classified by object of expenditure, they may be identified as relating to supplies, salaries, rent, insurance, or some other category.

Departments in a health care facility can be classified generally as direct or indirect departments, depending on whether or not they provide services directly to the patient. Sometimes the terms *revenue* and *nonrevenue* are substituted for direct and indirect. In the hospital industry, the following breakdown is used in general purpose financial statements.

Operating Expense Area	Type of Department
Nursing services area	Direct/revenue
Other professional services	Direct/revenue
General services	Indirect/nonrevenue
Fiscal services	Indirect/nonrevenue
Administrative services	Indirect/nonrevenue

Whatever the nomenclature used to describe the classification of departments, cost allocation is a fundamental need. The costs of the indirect, nonrevenue departments need to be allocated to the direct revenue departments for many decision-making purposes. For example, some payers reimburse on the basis of the full costs of direct departments and are interested in the costs of indirect departments only insofar as they affect the calculation of the direct departments' full costs. Pricing decisions need to be based on full costs, not just direct costs, if the costs of the indirect departments are to be covered equitably. It is also critical to include indirect costs when evaluating the financial return of specific programs or product lines. For example, some indirect costs would need to be assigned to an ambulatory surgery program to evaluate properly whether the program was financially viable.

Equity is a key concept in allocating indirect department costs to direct departments. Ideally, the allocation should reflect as nearly as possible the actual cost incurred by the indirect department to provide services for a direct department. Department managers who receive cost reports showing indirect allocations are vitally interested in this equity principle, and for good reason. Even if indirect costs are not regarded as controllable by the department manager, the allocation of costs to a given direct department can have an important effect on a variety of management decisions. Pricing, expansion or contraction of a department, the purchase of new equipment, and the salaries of department managers are all affected by the allocation of indirect costs.

Costs of indirect departments are in most cases not traceable to direct departments. If they were, they could be reassigned. In such cases, they must be allocated to the direct departments in some systematic and rational manner. In general, two allocation decisions must be made: (1) selection of the allocation basis and (2) selection of the method of cost apportionment.

Table 8-2 provides sample data for a cost allocation. In this example, there are four departments: two are indirect (laundry/linen and housekeeping) and two are direct (radiology and nursing). Pounds of laundry is the only allocation basis under consideration for the laundry and linen department. The housekeeping department can use one of two allocation bases, either square feet of area served or hours of service actually worked.

In general, there are only three acceptable methods of cost allocation:

1. step-down method
2. double-distribution method
3. simultaneous-equations method

Most health care facilities still use the step-down method of cost allocation. In this method, the indirect department that receives the least amount of service from other indirect departments and provides the most service to other departments allocates its cost first. A similar analysis follows to determine the order of cost allocation for each of the remaining indirect departments. This determination can be subjective to allow some flexibility, as we shall see shortly.

In the step-down allocation process illustrated below, laundry/linen allocates its cost first. Then, housekeeping allocates its direct cost, plus the allocated cost of laundry and linen, to the direct departments of radiology and nursing, based on the ratio of services provided to those departments.

Table 8–2 Cost Allocation Example

Department	Direct Costs	Pounds of Laundry Used	Square Feet	Hours of Housekeeping Used
Laundry/linen	$ 15,000	$ —	$ 50,000	$ 150
Housekeeping	30,000	5,000	—	—
Radiology	135,000	5,000	10,000	900
Nursing	270,000	90,000	140,000	1,950
Total	$450,000	$100,000	$200,000	$3,000

The allocation proportions are given in parentheses.

	Direct Costs	Laundry/Linen	Housekeeping	Total
Laundry/Linen	$ 15,000	$15,000		
Housekeeping	30,000	750 (.05)	$30,750	
Radiology	135,000	750 (.05)	9,711 (.3158)	$145,461
Nursing	270,000	13,500 (.90)	21,039 (.6842)	304,539
Total	$450,000	$15,000	$30,750	$450,000

The order of departmental allocation can be an important variable in a step-down method of cost allocation. Shown below is an alternative step-down cost allocation in which housekeeping allocates its cost first, preceding laundry/linen.

	Direct Costs	Housekeeping	Laundry/Linen	Total
Housekeeping	$ 30,000	$30,000		
Laundry/Linen	15,000	1,500 (.05)	$16,500	
Radiology	135,000	9,000 (.30)	868 (.053)	$144,868
Nursing	270,000	19,500 (.65)	15,632 (.947)	305,132
Total	$450,000	$30,000	$16,500	$450,000

The double-distribution method of cost allocation is just a refinement of the step-down method. Instead of closing the individual department after allocating its costs, it is kept open and receives the costs of other indirect departments. After one complete allocation sequence, the former departments are then closed, using the normal step-down method. The simultaneous-equations method of cost allocation is used in an attempt to be exact about the cost allocation amounts. A system of equations is established, and mathematically correct allocations are computed. In the above example, if simultaneous equations had been used, the cost of radiology would be $145,075 and the cost of nursing would be $304,925.

Finally, it should be noted that using a different allocation base can create differences in cost allocation. For example, the use of square footage for housekeeping, instead of hours served, produces the following pattern of cost allocation when housekeeping allocates its cost first, using the step-down method:

	Direct Cost	*Housekeeping*	*Laundry/Linen*	*Total*
Housekeeping	$ 30,000	$30,000		
Laundry/Linen	15,000	7,500 (.25)	$22,500	
Radiology	135,000	1,500 (.05)	1,125 (.05)	$137,625
Nursing	270,000	21,000 (.70)	21,375 (.95)	312,375
Total	$450,000	$30,000	$22,500	$450,000

The important point in this discussion is that full cost is not as objective and exact a figure as one might normally think. Indirect costs can be allocated in a variety of ways that can create significant differences in full costs for given departments. This flexibility should be remembered when examining and interpreting full-cost data.

Variable and Fixed Cost

A very important and widely used cost concept is variability with respect to output. It is involved in determining for decision-making purposes such costs as avoidable, sunk, incremental, and controllable. However, accounting records do not directly yield this type of cost information. Instead, the costs are classified by department and by object of expenditure. Thus, in order to develop estimates of variable and fixed costs, the relevant data must be analyzed in some way.

Our discussion of cost concepts classified by variability with respect to output indicated that a semivariable cost pattern may be a good representation of many types of costs. A semivariable cost function is one that has both a fixed and variable element in it. A semivariable cost function often results when various types of costs are aggregated together.

Estimating Methods

Estimation of a semivariable cost function requires separation of the cost into variable and fixed components. A variety of methods, varying in complexity and accuracy, may be used. Three of the simplest methods are (1) visual-fit, (2) high-low, and (3) semiaverages.

To illustrate each of these methods, assume that we are trying to determine the labor cost function for the radiology department and we have the following six biweekly payroll data points:

Pay Period	No. of Films	Hours Worked
1	300	180 (low)
2	240	140 (low)
3	400	230 (high)
4	340	190 (high)
5	180	110 (lowest)
6	600	320 (highest)

In the visual-fit method of cost estimation, the above individual data points are plotted on graph paper. A straight line is then drawn through the points to provide the best fit. Visual fitting of data is a good first step in any method of cost estimation. Figure 8–7 shows a visual fitting of the above radiology data.

The high-low method is a simple technique that can be used to estimate the variable and fixed-cost coefficients of a semivariable cost function. The variable cost parameter is solved first. It equals the change in cost from the highest to the lowest data point, divided by the change in output. In the above radiology example, the variable hours worked would be calculated as follows:

$$\frac{\text{Variable labor hours}}{\text{Film}} = \frac{320 - 110}{600 - 180} = \frac{210}{420} = .50$$

The fixed-cost parameter may then be solved by subtracting the estimated variable cost (determined by multiplying the variable cost parameter estimate by output at the high level) from total cost. In our radiology example, fixed cost would equal

$$\text{Fixed labor hours} / \text{Biweekly pay period} = 320 - (.50 \times 600) = 320 - 300 = 20$$

Alternatively, it is possible to plot the high and low points and then draw a straight line through them.

The semiaverages method is very similar to the high-low method in terms of its mathematical solution. To derive the estimate of variable cost, the difference between the mean of the high-cost points and the mean of the low-cost points is divided by the change in output from the mean of the high-cost points to the mean of the low-cost points. In the radiology

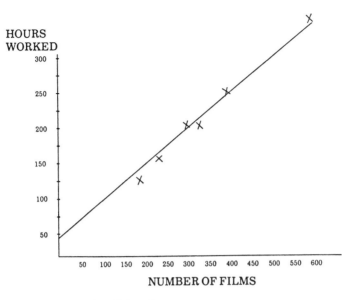

Figure 8–7 Visual Fitting of Radiology Data

example, variable cost would be calculated as follows:

$$\text{Variable labor hours/film} = \frac{\dfrac{320 + 230 + 190}{3} - \dfrac{180 + 140 + 110}{3}}{\dfrac{600 + 400 + 340}{3} - \dfrac{300 + 240 + 180}{3}}$$

$$= \frac{246.67 - 143.33}{446.67 - 240.00} = .50$$

Fixed cost is solved in a manner identical to that used in the high-low method. In the radiology example, fixed cost would equal

$$\text{Fixed labor hours/}$$
$$\text{Bi-weekly pay period} = 246.67 - (.50 \times 446.67) = 23.34$$

These three methods of estimating variable and fixed cost are highly simplistic. They are useful in only limited ways to provide a basis for further discussion and analysis of what the true cost behavioral pattern might be. However, in most situations a limited attempt, based on simplistic methods, to discover the underlying fixed/variable cost patterns is better than no attempt.

Data Checks

When any of the above methods are used, several data checks should be performed. First, the cost data being used to estimate the cost behavior pattern should be stated in a common dollar. If the wages paid for employees have changed dramatically from one year to the next, the use of unadjusted wage and salary data from the two years can create measurement problems. In our radiology example, we used a physical quantity measure of cost, namely, hours worked. A physical measure of cost should be used whenever possible.

Second, cost and output data should be matched; the figures for reported cost should relate to the activity of the period. In most situations, accounting records provide this type of relationship, based on the accrual principle of accounting. However, in some situations this may not happen; supply costs may be charged to a department when the items are purchased, not when they are used.

Third, the period of time during which a cost function is being estimated should be one of a stable technology and case mix. If the technology under consideration has changed dramatically during that period, there will be measurement problems.

BREAK-EVEN ANALYSIS

Certain techniques can be applied in analyzing the relationships among cost, volume, and profit. These techniques rely on categorizing costs as fixed and variable. They can serve as powerful management decision aids and may be valuable in a wide range of decisions. An understanding of these techniques is crucial for decision makers whose choices affect the financial results of health care facilities.

Profit in a health care facility is influenced by various factors, including

- rates
- volume
- variable cost
- fixed cost
- payer mix
- bad debts

The primary value of break-even analysis, or, as it is sometimes called, cost-volume-profit analysis, is its ability to quantify the relationships among the above factors and profit.

Traditional Applications

Break-even analysis has been used in industry for decades with a high degree of satisfaction. Its name comes from the solution to an equation that sets profit equal to zero and revenue equal to costs. To illustrate, assume that a hospital has the following financial information:

Variable cost per case	$1,000.00
Fixed cost per period	$100,000.00
Rate per case	$2,400.00

The break-even volume can be solved by dividing fixed costs by the contribution margin, which is the difference between rate and variable cost:

$$\text{Break-even volume in units} = \frac{\text{Fixed cost}}{\text{Rate} - \text{Variable cost}}$$

Thus, in our hospital example, break-even volume would be

$$\text{Break-even volume in units} = \frac{\$100,000}{\$2,400 - \$1,000} = 71.4 \text{ Cases}$$

If volume exceeds 72 cases, the hospital will make a profit; but if volume goes below 71 cases it will incur a loss. Sometimes, a revenue-and-cost relationship is put into graphic form to illustrate profit at various levels. Such a presentation is referred to as a break-even chart. For our hospital example, a break-even chart is shown in Figure 8–8.

In many cases, some targeted level of net income or profit is desired. The break-even model is easily adapted to this purpose; the new break-even point would become

$$\text{Break-even volume in units} = \frac{\text{Fixed cost} + \text{Targeted net income}}{\text{Rate} - \text{Variable cost}}$$

In our example, assuming that a profit of $6,000 were required, the new break-even point would be

$$\text{Break-even volume in units} = \frac{\$100,000 + \$6,000}{\$1,400} = 75.7 \text{ Cases}$$

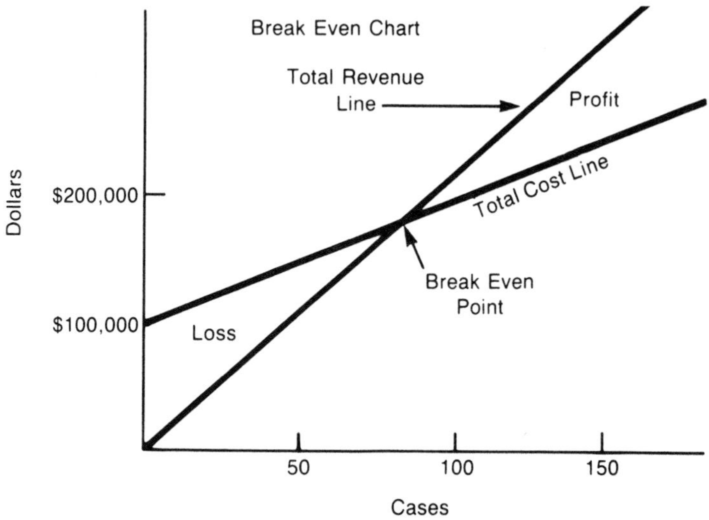

Figure 8–8 Break-Even Chart

Multiple-Payer Model

Although break-even analysis is a powerful management tool, it cannot be employed in the health care industry without adaptation. The major revision required relates to the revenue function. The preceding discussion of break-even analysis assumed that there was only one payer or purchaser of services. That payer was assumed to pay a fixed price per unit of product. However, this situation does not exist in the health care industry, where there may be three or more major categories of payers. For our purposes, we will assume that there are three categories of payers:

1. cost payers (paying average cost of services provided)
2. fixed-price payers (paying an established fee per unit of service, for example, a fixed price per diagnosis-related group (DRG))
3. charge payers (paying on the basis of internally set prices)

The break-even formula in these three payer situations can be generalized as follows:

$$\text{Break-even volume in units} = \frac{(1 - CO)F + NI}{CH \times P_I + FP \times P_E - (1 - CO)V}$$

This formula may look complex at first glance, but it is really very similar to the previous one-payer break-even formula. In fact, the above equation can be used in the one-payer situation and provides an identical result. To aid in our understanding of the formula, we should first define the individual variables:

V = Variable cost per unit of output
F = Fixed cost per period
NI = Targeted net income
P_I = Internally set price that is paid by charge payers
P_E = Externally set price paid by fixed-price payers
CO = Proportion of cost payers
CH = Proportion of charge payers
FP = Proportion of fixed-price payers

Let us now examine each term in the equation:

- $(1 - CO)F$—This term represents the proportion of fixed costs (F) that is not paid by cost payers (CO). Cost payers are assumed to pay their proportionate share of fixed costs. This leaves the residual portion $(1 - CO)$ unpaid; it is included in the numerator as a financial requirement that must be covered before break even takes place. If there were no cost payers, $(1 - CO)$ would be 1, and all of the fixed costs would be included. This is the case in traditional break-even analysis.
- NI—This term, targeted net income, is included as a financial requirement as in the traditional break-even formula. NI is not reduced by the cost payer portion because it is assumed that cost payers are not contributing toward meeting the net income requirement. Cost payers pay cost, nothing less and nothing more.
- $CHxP_I$—This term represents the weighted price paid by charge payers. When added to the next term ($FPxP_E$), we have a measure of the price paid by the two price-paying categories of customers—charge payers and fixed-price payers. It should be emphasized that P_I represents the price received, not the charge made. For example, if 10 percent of the patients paid established charges of \$2,400 per case and 20 percent paid 90 percent of established charges of \$2,400 per case, the following values would result:

$$CH = .10 + .20 = .30$$

$$P_I = (1.0 \times \$2{,}400) \times 1/3 + (.90 \times \$2{,}400) \times 2/3 = \$2{,}240$$

- $FPxP_E$—This term represents the weighted price paid by fixed-price payers. The addition of this term to $CHxP_I$ yields a measure of the price received for price-paying patients. The summation of the two terms can be compared with the rate term used in the traditional break-even formula. Again, there may be circumstances in which a subweighting may be necessary. For example, assume that Medicare pays $2,000 per case and that 40 percent of the cases are Medicare. Also assume that 10 percent of the cases are from an HMO that pays $2,200 per case. The following values would result:

$$FP = .40 + .10 = .50$$

$$P_E = .8 \times \$2,000 + .2 \times \$2,200 = \$2,040$$

- $(1 - CO)V$—This term represents the net variable cost that remains after reflecting the proportion paid by cost payers. Cost payers pay their share of both fixed and variable cost. If there were no cost payers, the entire value of the variable cost per unit would be subtracted to yield the contribution margin per unit.

To see that the traditional break-even formula is actually derived from our more general three-payer model, let us compute the break-even point using the data from the case example developed in our discussion of traditional break-even analysis:

$$\text{Break-even volume in units} = \frac{(1 - 0) \times \$100,000 + \$6,000}{1.0 \times \$2,400 + 0 \times \$0 - (1 - 0) \times \$1,000}$$

$$= 75.7 \text{ cases}$$

Now, having tested the accuracy of the three-payer break-even formula in a one-payer situation, let us expand our initial case example to a more realistic multiple-payer situation. The following data are assumed:

Payer Proportion	Payment Method
.20	Pay average cost
.40	Pay $2,000 per case (fixed-price payer)
.10	Pay $2,200 per case (fixed-price payer)
.10	Pay 100% of charges, $2,400 per case
.20	Pay 90% of charges, $2,160 per case

Also assume that the variable cost is $1,000 per case and fixed costs are $100,000 per period. In addition, the firm needs a profit of $6,000 to meet other financial requirements. The use of these data in our break-even model would produce the following result:

$$\text{Break-even volume in cases} = \frac{(.8 \times \$100,000) + \$6,000}{(.3 \times \$2,240) + (.5 \times \$2,040) - (.8 \times \$1,000)}$$

$$= \frac{\$86,000}{\$892} = 96.413$$

To demonstrate the accuracy of the break-even formula, we can derive the following income statement for our case example, assuming 96.4 cases as the break-even volume:

Patient revenue	
.20 × 96.4 × $2,037.34*	$39,279.92
.40 × 96.4 × $2,000.00	77,120.00
.10 × 96.4 × $2,200.00	21,208.00
.10 × 96.4 × $2,400.00	23,136.00
.20 × 96.4 × $2,160.00	41,644.80
Net patient revenue	$202,388.72
Fixed cost	100,000.00
Variable cost (96.4 × $1,000)	96,400.00
Net income	$ 5,988.72

*Average cost × ($100,000 + $96,400)/96.4 × $2,037.34

This income statement demonstrates that, at a volume of 96.4 patients, the firm's net income would be $5,988.72. This value does not exactly match the targeted net income level of $6,000.00 because of a small rounding error; the actual break-even volume was 96.413, not 96.4.

Before concluding this discussion of break-even analysis, some mention of output determination would be useful. For the break-even model to be applicable, there must be one measure of output. It makes no difference whether the measure of activity is macro, such as a case or patient days, or whether the measure of activity is micro, such as a treatment or laboratory test. Two conditions, however, must hold:

1. It must be possible to define an average price paid for that unit for both fixed-price payers and charge payers. For example, both Medicare and Medicaid may pay a fixed rate per case, but all charge payers may pay some percentage of the billed charges. This would require someone to aggregate average charge-payer amounts to an expected price per case. It might also require an assignment of a per-case amount paid by Medicare to an estimated amount per, for

example, physical therapy treatment if the focus of analysis was at the treatment level.

2. A variable cost per unit of the defined output measure can be established. This may mean aggregating across departments to create a variable cost value for an aggregated output measure such as a case or a patient day. Disaggregation is not nearly as great a problem in variable cost measurement because costing systems usually provide reasonably good detail at the departmental level.

Special Applications

The break-even formula has many applications other than that of computing break-even points. Two specific applications are in (1) the computation of marginal profit of volume changes and (2) rate-setting analysis.

Computation of Marginal Profit of Volume Changes

In most business situations, executives are very concerned about the impact of volume changes on operating profitability. At the beginning of a budget period, management may not be sure what its actual volumes will be, but it still needs to know how sensitive profit will be to possible swings in volume. If the payer mix is expected to remain constant, the following simple formula can be used to calculate the marginal changes in profit associated with volume swings:

Change in profit = Change in units $\times$ Profitability index
where:
Profitability index = $CH(P_I - V) + FP(P_E - V)$

The profitability index remains constant and is simply multiplied by pro-jected volume change to determine the profit change. Using our earlier case example, the profitability index would be

Profitability index = $.3(\$2,240 - \$1,000) + .5(\$2,040 - \$1,000) = \$892$

The value for the profitability index is really the weighted contribution margin per unit of output. This fact is easily seen by comparing the value calculated above with that from our three-payer break-even example. The values are the same, \$892 in each case. This means that for every one unit change in output the profit increases by \$892. An increase of one unit will raise profit by \$892, and a decrease of one unit will lower profit by \$892. A useful question to raise at this point is, how large a reduction in volume can the firm experience before its profit falls to $2,000? Using the preceding formula, the answer would be:

Change in profit   = Volume change × Profitability index
($6,000 − $2,000) = Volume change × $892
Volume change   = 4.48 cases

If volume falls by 4.48 cases, the firm's profit will fall to $2,000. Further analysis could be used to portray other scenarios or to answer other what-if type questions. In each case, the resulting data could be displayed in a table or graph.

Rate-Setting Analysis

Rate setting is an extremely important activity for most health care organizations. Usually the objective is not profit maximization but rather fulfillment of financial requirements. In general, pricing services can be stated in the following conceptual terms:

Price = Average cost + Profit requirement + Loss on fixed-price patients

If Q represents total budgeted volume in units, we can use our earlier break-even model to develop the following pricing formula:

$$P_I = AC + \frac{NI}{CHxQ} + \frac{(AC - P_E) \times FP \times Q}{CHxQ}$$

where:

$$AC = \text{Average cost per unit} = \frac{F}{Q} + V$$

Again, it is useful to examine the individual terms in order to understand their conceptual relationship:

- *AC*—This term represents the average cost per unit. Average cost is the basis on which the firm marks up to establish a price that can meet its financial requirements.
- $NI/(CHxQ)$—This term divides the target net income (NI) by the number of charge-paying units (CHxQ). This payment source generates the firm's profit. Internally set prices will not affect the amount of payment received from cost payers or fixed-price payers.
- $(AC - P_E) \times (FPxQ)/(CHxQ)$—This term is complex but has a simple interpretation. The difference between average cost (AC) and the fixed price (P_E) represents an additional requirement that must be

covered by the firm's charge-paying units. This difference per unit is then multiplied by total fixed-price payer units (FPxQ) to generate the total loss resulting from selling services to fixed-price payers. Dividing by the number of charge payers (CHxQ) translates this loss into an additional pricing increment that must be recovered from the charge payers. It is important to note that, if the fixed price paid by fixed-price payers exceeds average cost, this term will be negative. Prices to the charge payers could then be reduced because the fixed-price payers would be making a positive contribution to the firm's profit requirement.

To test the validity of the pricing formula, let us apply it to the data in our earlier three-payer break-even example. Assume that the volume is 96.4 cases:

$$P_1 = \$2,037.34 + \frac{\$6,000}{.3 \times 96.4} + \frac{(\$2,037.34 - 2,040) \times .5 \times 96.4}{.3 \times 96.4}$$

$$= \$2,037.34 + \$207.47 - 4.43 = \$2,240.38$$

The required price as determined above, $2,240.38, is approximately equal to the price established for charge payers, $2,240. Again, a small discrepancy exists because of rounding errors.

It should be noted that $2,240 is not the actual charge or price set per case. The actual posted charge is $2,400. P_1 represents the net amount actually received. Because the firm had one category of payers who paid 90 percent of charges, the effective price realized was only $2,240. When using this pricing formula to define hospital charges, the defined price must be increased to reflect write-offs due to discounts, bad debts, or charity care. The following general formula represents the markup requirement:

$$Price = P_1/(1 - \text{write-off proportion})$$

The write-off proportion is not based on total revenue; it is based only on the revenue from charge payers. For example, in our case example, the charge payers represented 30 percent of total cases. Of that 30 percent, 10 percent paid 100 percent of charges and 20 percent paid 90 percent of charges. The write-off percentage is thus:

$$(1/3) \times (1.0 - 1.0) + (2/3) \times (1.0 - .9) = .0667$$

Using this value to mark up the required net price of $2,240 would yield $2,400 ($2,240/[1 - .0667] = $2,400), which is the firm's established charge.

An important issue for many health care organizations concerns the maximization of profit per dollar of rate increase. In a number of states and regions, rate regulations impose restraints on a firm's ability to raise its rates. In addition, boards may wish to minimize rate increases in any given budgetary cycle.

The percentage of any price increase that will be realized as profit can be expressed as follows:

$$\% \text{ Price increase realized as profit} = (\% \text{ Charge payers})$$
$$\times (1 - \text{Write-off proportion})$$
$$- \text{Physician fee } \%$$

Let us assume that a nursing home is interested in learning what effect a $5 increase in its per diem would have on its profitability. Its present payer mix and write-off proportions are

Payer Percentage	Payer Mode	Write-off Proportion
10%	Medicare—pays cost	.00
50%	Private payer—pays charges	.10
40%	Medicaid—pays fixed charge per diem	.00

Thus, a $5.00 per diem increase would generate a 45 percent increase in profit, or $2.25 per day:

$$50\% \times (1 - .10) = 45\%$$

Evaluating Incremental Profit of New Business

One of the most common examples of the use of marginal analysis methods is evaluating the profitability of new business. Many health care providers are being approached on an almost daily basis with a proposal for a new block of patients. For example, a preferred provider organization (PPO) may approach a hospital with an opportunity for it to be in the PPO's network if the hospital is willing to accept a discount from its present price structure. It is very easy to define a conceptual model to organize the financial evaluation of this proposal or a similar one:

$$\text{Change in profit} = \text{Change in volume [Price per unit} - \text{Incremental cost per unit]}$$
$$- \text{Change in existing price} \times \text{Volume affected}$$

The terms are defined as follows:

- *Change in volume*—In many cases there will be a reasonably good measure of what the new volume will be. For example, the PPO may be able to deliver 20 new cases per year. It is important to structure a contract that has a volume trigger related to the range of discounts. If high volumes are realized, then the full discount will be granted. However, if volumes are significantly lower than expected, the discount will get smaller. This provides an incentive for the contractor to send as much volume as possible to the hospital.
- *Price per unit*—This variable is almost always known with some degree of precision. In many instances, it may actually be a given figure. Prices for services are established in the contract itself.
- *Incremental cost per unit*—This variable is often hard to calculate, but not impossible. If the expected change in volume is relatively small, variable cost per unit would be a good approximation.
- *Change in existing price*—Once a contract is signed and new business is serviced, there may be a negative effect on existing prices. If the organization has granted a discount to attract the client, it may find itself facing similar demands for discounts from all of its existing clients. In many areas of the country, Blue Cross has a most-favored-nation clause that guarantees it the lowest price charged by a hospital. Any hospital that lowers prices to another payer below the Blue Cross payment rate may find itself facing an immediate reduction in price to Blue Cross and a possible lawsuit. Utilization by cost payers will also create an automatic reduction in price. As more volume is delivered, the cost per unit will fall as fixed costs are spread over more units. This means that cost payers will automatically benefit from increases in volume. Many hospitals have some sizable blocks of cost payers. For example, there is still a substantial block of Medicare outpatient business that is cost reimbursed.

SUMMARY

Cost accounting systems can be designed to provide different measures of cost for different decision-making purposes. This is a desirable characteristic, not an exercise in numbers playing. To understand what measure of cost is needed for a specific purpose, the decision maker must have some knowledge of the variety of alternative concepts of cost. The terms covered in this chapter should be useful in helping decision makers define their needs more precisely.

Break-even analysis presents management with a set of simple analytical tools to provide information about the effects of costs, volume, and prices on profitability. In this chapter, we examined the application of several break-even models for health care providers with three categories of payers. Use of these models should help analysts understand the conceptual framework for improving profitability in their health care organization.

ASSIGNMENTS

1. What are the two major categories of decisions that utilize cost information?

2. What does it mean to say that a cost is direct?

3. Define the terms *variable costs* and *fixed costs*. Give some examples of each.

4. Is it true that indirect costs should never be included in the determination of controllable costs?

5. A hospital is considering using a vacant wing to set up a skilled nursing facility. What is the cost of the space?

6. A free-standing ambulatory care center averages $60 in charges per patient. Variable costs are approximately $10 per patient, and fixed costs are about $1.2 million per year. Using these data, how many patients must be seen each day, assuming a 365-day operation, to reach the break-even point?

7. Howard Hamilton, administrator of Harding Hospital, is assessing the adequacy of the hospital's rate structure for fiscal year 1993. Harding has three primary clinical service lines with abbreviated budgeted volumes, as indicated in Table 8–3.

   The hospital's projected gross revenue, using last year's prices and this year's projected volume, is depicted in Table 8–4.

   Harding's budgeted costs by department are shown in Table 8–5.

Table 8–3 Budgeted Clinical Service Volumes for Harding Hospital

Service	Medicare	Medicaid	Charge	Total
Cardiology				
DRG #127—Heart failure	20	5	15	40
DRG #140—Angina	15	2	3	20
Pulmonary				
DRG #88—Chronic obstruction	20	2	8	30
Surgery				
DRG #115—Pacemaker implant	15	3	12	30
DRG #209—Major joint	20	3	17	40

Table 8–4 Projected Gross Revenue for Harding Hospital

	Nursing ($300 / Day)	Surgery ($1,000 / Hr.)	Ancillary ($20 / Unit)	Total
DRG #127				
Medicare	$ 48,000	$ 0	$ 6,000	$ 54,000
Medicaid	10,500	0	1,500	12,000
Other	31,500	0	4,500	36,000
DRG #140				
Medicare	27,000	0	3,000	30,000
Medicaid	3,000	0	400	3,400
Other	4,500	0	600	5,100
DRG #88				
Medicare	42,000	0	8,000	50,000
Medicaid	4,200	0	800	5,000
Other	16,800	0	3,200	20,000
DRG #115				
Medicare	67,500	67,500	6,000	141,000
Medicaid	10,800	13,500	1,200	25,500
Other	43,200	54,000	4,800	102,000
DRG #209				
Medicare	108,000	10,000	2,000	120,000
Medicaid	11,700	1,500	300	13,500
Other	66,300	8,500	1,700	76,500
	$495,000	$155,000	$44,000	$694,000

Harding Hospital's Medicaid patients are reimbursed on a ratio of a charges-to-charges formula, applied departmentally. Assume that indirect costs are allocated proportionately to nursing, surgery, and ancillary. Medicare patients use the following rates for payment:

DRG #	Price
127	$2,520
140	1,800
88	2,500
115	9,360
209	5,520

Charge payers have an average 10 percent write-off.

Given the above background and data:

a. Project Harding Hospital's operating income at last year's prices.
b. Develop a rate increase proposal that will generate $50,000 of income. Prices must

Table 8-5 Budgeted Costs for Harding Hospital, by Department

	Activity Unit	Projected Volume	Projected Cost	Variable Cost/Unit	Fixed Cost
Nursing	Patient day	1,650	$325,000	$100	$160,000
Surgery	Hours	155	100,000	300	53,500
Ancillary	Unit	2,200	30,000	6	16,800
Dietary and housekeeping	Patient day	1,650	150,000	50	67,500
Business office	Cases	160	20,000	60	10,400
Overhead	None	—	80,000	0	80,000
			$705,000		$388,200

exceed cost in each area. Minimize the total value of the revenue increase above the present $694,000.

8. Your hospital's board of trustees has just determined that the maximum revenue increase it will permit next year is 5 percent. It has also specified maximum and minimum rate increases by department. Data for the hospital's five departments are:

	Current Charges	Budgeted Cost	Cost	Fixed Price	Charge	Bad Debt	Physician Fee	Min.	Max.
Nursing	$2,00	$2,200	30	30%	40%	10%	0%	5	20%
Emergency room	200	190	70	10	20	10	0	0	10
Operating room	300	330	35	40	25	20	0	10	25
Laboratory	1,000	750	50	30	20	15	10	−10	20
Anesthesiology	360	300	40	30	30	10	30	0	10
	$3,860	$3,770							

Payer Composition % columns: Cost, Fixed Price, Charge, Bad Debt, Physician Fee. *Rate Change %* columns: Min., Max.

Given the above information, develop a rate change plan that will maximize the hospital's net income yet still adhere to the board's guidelines.

9. Develop an estimate of fixed and variable costs for labor expenses, based on the following data. Develop your estimates by using the high-low and the semiaverages methods:

Period	Output in Units	Hours Worked
1	16,156	3,525
2	19,160	4,151
3	17,846	3,829
4	20,238	4,454
5	21,198	4,657
6	14,640	3,406

10. An interdepartmental service structure and its direct costs are as follows:

Department	Direct Costs	% of Service Consumed by S_1	S_2	S_3	R_1	R_2	R_3
Service center 1	$10,000	—	10	10	40	20	20
Service center 2	12,000	10	—	10	20	40	20
Service center 3	10,000	10	10	—	20	20	40
Revenue center 1	30,000						
Revenue center 2	25,000						
Revenue center 3	50,000						

Compute the total costs, direct and allocated, for each of the three revenue centers, using the direct and step-down methods of cost apportionment.

11. Your hospital was denied a contract with an HMO last year. Legal counsel believes that there was a breach of contract and wishes to bring suit against the HMO for damages. The chief executive officer has asked you to work with the controller to develop a defensible measure of the damages experienced during the last year. Explain how you would go about organizing your work to estimate the amount of damages.

SOLUTIONS AND ANSWERS

1. The two major categories of decisions that use cost data are planning and control. Planning decisions usually require costs that are accumulated by program or product line, whereas control decisions usually require costs that are accumulated by responsibility centers or departments.

2. A direct cost is one that can be traced or associated with a specific cost objective, usually related to a department or responsibility center.

3. A variable cost is one that changes proportionately with volume. Common examples are materials and supplies. A fixed cost does not change with volume but remains constant. Common examples are rent, depreciation, and interest. Fixed costs are usually constant only for some "relevant range" of volume. For example, depreciation will probably increase if a facility experiences volume increases that exceed existing capacity.

4. It is not invariably true that indirect costs should never be included in the determination of controllable costs. There are some costs that may be classified as indirect but could be controlled by a manager. For example, housekeeping costs may be classified as an indirect cost to the physical therapy department. However, the actual amount of housekeeping services required by the physical therapy department may be affected by the actions of the physical therapy department manager.

5. The opportunity cost of the space—that is, its value in the next best alternative use—should be measured. Possible alternative uses might be use as physician offices or as sleeping accommodations for patient families.

6. The number of patients that must be seen is 65.75 patients per day, based on the following calculation:

$$\text{Annual break-even volume} = \frac{1,200,000}{\$50} = 24,000 \text{ patients per year}$$

$$\text{Daily break-even volume} = \frac{24,000}{365} = 65.75 \text{ patients per day}$$

7. a. The projection of Harding Hospital's operating income at last year's prices is developed in the following financial statements:

- Cost allocation

	Initial	Overhead	Business Office	Dietary and Housekeeping	Total
Overhead	$ 80,000	—	—	—	—
Business office	20,000	—	—	—	—
Dietary and housekeeping	150,000	—	—	—	—
Ancillary	30,000	5,275	1,319	9,893	46,487
Surgery	100,000	17,582	4,396	32,970	154,948
Nursing	325,000	57,143	14,285	107,137	503,565
	$705,000	$80,000	$20,000	$150,000	$705,000

- Medicaid net patient revenue

	Medicaid Revenue	Medicaid Proportion (Medicaid Revenue/ Total Revenue)	Medicaid Cost Share (Medicaid Proportion × Total Cost)
Nursing	$40,200	.08121	$40,896
Surgery	15,000	.09677	14,995
Ancillary	4,200	.09545	4,437
	$59,400		$60,328

- Charge payer net patient revenue

	Collected Revenue Charge Revenue	.9 × Charge Revenue
Nursing	$162,300	$146,070
Surgery	62,500	56,250
Ancillary	14,800	13,320
		$215,640

- Medicare net patient revenue

DRG #	Price	Volume	Revenue
124	$2,520	20	$50,400
140	1,800	15	27,000
88	2,500	20	50,000
115	9,360	15	140,400
209	5,520	20	110,400
			$378,200

- Projected income

Gross patient revenue	$694,000
Less deductions	39,832
Net patient revenue	654,168
Less cost	705,000
Loss	($50,832)

b. The rate increase proposal could be developed as shown in the following calculations:

- Percentage of price realized as profit

$$\text{Nursing} = (162,300/495,000) \times (1 - .10) = .29509 = 29.509\%$$
$$\text{Surgery} = (62,500/155,000) \times (1 - .10) = .362903 = 36.2903\%$$
$$\text{Ancillary} = (14,800/44,000) \times (1 - .10) = .30273 = 30.273\%$$

- Initial rate increases/set rate equal costs

	Cost	Present Revenue	Increase	New Rate/Unit
Nursing	$503,565	$495,000	$ 8,565	$ 305.19
Surgery	154,948	155,000	00	$1000.00
Ancillary	46,487	44,000	2,487	21.13
	$705,000	$694,000	$11,052	

- Required profit increment

$$\text{Increase} = 50,832 + 50,000 = \$100,832$$

- Profit generated from initial rate increase

Nursing	$8,565 × .29509 = $2,527
Ancillary	2,487 × .30273 = 753
	$3,280

- Remaining profit required

$100,832
− 3,280
$ 97,552

- Price strategy
  Load into surgery because surgery has the highest profit potential:

$$.362903 \times \text{Price increase} = \$97,552$$
Price increase = $268,809 or $1,734 per hour
New surgery price = $2,734 per hour

- Charge revenue

$$\text{Nursing } \$305.19 \times \frac{162{,}300}{300} \times .9 = \$148{,}597$$

$$\text{Surgery } \$2{,}734 \times \frac{62{,}500}{1{,}000} \times .9 \quad = \$153{,}788$$

$$\text{Ancillary } \$21.13 \times \frac{14{,}800}{20} \times .9 \quad = \quad \underline{14{,}073}$$

$$\underline{\$316{,}458}$$

- Projected income with new price structure

Net Medicaid revenue	$ 60,328
Net Medicare revenue	378,200
Net charge revenue	316,458
Net patient revenue	754,986
Less cost	705,000
Net operating income	$ 49,986

8. The rate change plan could be developed in the following manner:

- Percentage of price realized as profit

Department	% Price Realized As Profit
Nursing	40.0% × .9 = 36.0%
Emergency room	20.0% × .9 = 18.0%
Operating room	25.0% × .8 = 20.0%
Laboratory	(20.0% × .85) − 10.0% = 7.0%
Anesthesiology	(30.0% × .9) − 30.0% = −3.0%

- Results of loading as much of the rate increase as possible into nursing

Department	Current Charges	Required Minimum	Additional Charges	Final Charges
Nursing	$2,000	100	163	$2,263
Emergency room	200	0	0	200
Operating room	300	30	0	330
Laboratory	1,000	− 100	0	900
Anesthesiology	360	0	0	360
	$3,860	$ 30	$163	$4,053

9. The following estimates of fixed and variable costs for labor expenses could be developed:

	Variable Hours/Unit	Fixed Hours
High-low method	.1908	613
Semiaverages method	.2093	193

10. The total costs for the three revenue centers would be as follows:

	Cost Apportionment Method	
	Direct	Step-Down
Revenue center 1	$ 40,500	$ 40,000
Revenue center 2	36,000	35,889
Revenue center 3	60,500	61,111
	$137,000	$137,000

11. A reasonable framework for the estimation of damages would be the equation introduced earlier in this chapter:

$$\text{Change in profit} = \text{Change in volume [Price per unit} - \text{Incremental cost per unit]} - \text{Change in existing price} \times \text{Volume affected}$$

Chapter 9

Product Costing

Since the implementation of the prospective payment system, there has been a rapidly growing interest in cost accounting. The increased interest in developing sophisticated cost accounting systems is not limited to the hospital industry; it has infected all health care industry sectors. Most, if not all, of this interest is due to the establishment of fixed prices for services and to the increasing economic competition among health care providers.

A variety of terms have been used to describe the new methodology in cost accounting. Some refer to it as costing by diagnosis-related groups (DRGs), others call it standard costing, and still others refer to it as costing by product line or as product costing. For the purposes of this chapter, we shall use the term *product costing*. A product or product line is more generic, compared with the terms used in the other definitions. Also, the concept of product costing can be related to costing in other industries; most of the principles of product costing have been examined and debated for many years in the manufacturing sector. Thus, we do not have to reinvent the wheel in order to develop costing principles for the health care industry.

RELATIONSHIP TO PLANNING, BUDGETING, AND CONTROL

Cost information is of value only as it aids in the management decision-making process. Figure 9-1 presents a schematic that summarizes the planning-budgeting-control process in a business. Of special interest is the decision output of the planning process. The planning process should

Figure 9–1 The Planning-Budgeting-Control Process

detail the products or product lines that the business will produce during the planning horizon.

Products and Product Lines

The terms *product* and *product line* seem fairly simple and easy to understand in most businesses. For example, a finished car is the product of the automobile company; individual types of cars may then be grouped to form product lines, such as the Chevrolet product line of General Motors.

Can this definition of a product be transposed to the health care sector? Many individuals feel very strongly that products cannot be defined so easily in health care firms. The major dilemma seems to arise in the area of patients versus products. In short, is the product the patient, or is it the individual services provided, such as laboratory tests, nursing care, and meals? In most situations, we believe that the patient is the basic product of a health care firm. This means that the wide range of services provided to patients—such as nursing, prescriptions, and tests—are to be viewed as intermediate products, not final products. There is in fact little difference between this interpretation and that applied in most manufacturing settings. For example, automobile fenders are, on one hand, a final product; on the other, they are only an intermediate product in preparation of the final product, the completed automobile. Ultimately, it is the automobile that is sold to the public, not the fenders. In the same vein, it is the treated patient who generates revenue, not the individual service provided in isolation. Indeed, a hospital that provided only laboratory tests would not be a hospital but rather a laboratory. In short, it takes patients to be a health care provider.

Product lines represent an amalgamation of patients in a way that makes business sense. Sometimes people use the term *strategic business units* to refer to areas of activity that may stand alone. For our purpose, a product line is a unit of business activity that requires a go or no-go decision. For example, eliminating one DRG is probably not possible, because that DRG may be linked to other DRGs within a clinical specialty area; it may be impossible to stop producing DRG #36 (Retinal Procedures) without also eliminating other DRGs, such as DRG #39 (Lens Procedure). Thus, in many cases, it is the clinical specialty, for example, ophthalmology, that defines the product line.

Budgeting and Resource Expectations

The budgeting phase of operations involves a translation of the product-line decisions reached earlier into a set of resource expectations. The primary purpose of this is twofold. First, management must assure itself that there will be a sufficient funds flow to maintain financial solvency. Just as you and I must live within our financial means, so must any health care business entity. Second, the resulting budget serves as a basis for management control. If budget expectations are not realized, management must discover why not and take corrective actions. A budget or set of resource expectations can be thought of as a standard costing system. The budget represents management's expectations of how costs should behave, given a certain set of volume assumptions.

The key aspect of budgeting is the translation of product-line decisions into precise and specific sets of resource expectations. This involves five basic steps:

1. Define the volumes of patients by case type to be treated in the budget period.
2. Define the standard treatment protocol by case type.
3. Define the required departmental volumes.
4. Define the standard cost profiles for departmental outputs.
5. Define the prices to be paid for resources.

The primary output of the budgeting process is a series of departmental budgets that spell out what costs should be during the coming budget period. Three separate sets of standards are involved in the development of these budgets (the three sets of standards are described later in the chapter).

We will now use a simple hypothetical nursing home example to illustrate how these five steps would be integrated into the budgeting process. We will assume that our nursing home is a 100-bed facility with a very simple organizational structure. It only has three departments: a dietary department, a nursing department, and an administration department.

Define Volumes of Patients (Step 1)

The first step in any budgetary process is the estimation of critical volume statistics. These statistics, when defined, will enable managers to determine levels of activity in each of the departments. In our nursing home example, we will assume that the facility will average 95 percent occupancy, or 34,675 patients during the next year. For most nursing homes, patient days would be the critical measure of patient volume. In a hospital it might be discharges, patient days, and outpatient visits. Ideally, these macro measures would then be broken down further into more specific case types. For example, in a nursing home we might categorize patients by their acuity, whereas a hospital might use DRG categories.

Define Standard Treatment Protocol (Step 2)

The second step in the budgetary process is the definition of the relationship between patient volumes and departmental volumes. If 34,675 patients are seen in our nursing home next year, what does that mean in terms of individual departmental activity for dietary, nursing, and administration?

The major connection here is the determination of "standard treatment protocol." What departmental service is required to provide a patient day of care? In our nursing home example, we will assume that there are only two real products required to treat a nursing home patient: (1) three patient meals per patient day and (2) two hours of nursing.

Define Required Departmental Volumes (Step 3)

Given the standard treatment protocol defined in step 2 above, it is relatively easy to determine departmental volumes. In order to treat 34,675 patients our nursing home will need to provide the following service:

$$3 \text{ Meals} \times 34{,}675 = 104{,}025 \text{ Meals in dietary}$$

$$2 \text{ Nursing hours} \times 34{,}675 = 69{,}350 \text{ Nursing hours}$$

Define Standard Cost Profiles (Step 4)

Given the level of activity required in the departments, it is now time to define the "standard cost profiles." This set of standards simply relates departmental volume to expected resource levels. In short, what resources are required to provide a patient day of care? We will assume that the departmental managers have developed the following standard cost profiles. Dietary will be purchasing individual food packages from an outside vendor for every meal.

Dietary
   1 Purchased food package
   30 Minutes of dietary labor
Nursing
   1 Hour of RN labor
   1 Hour of aide labor
Administration
   5 Full-time equivalents (FTEs) to provide 34,675 patient days of care

You will notice that administration has a requirement for resources, but it did not specify any service required in step 2, standard treatment protocol specification. There will be a number of areas, such as administration, in which there is no really clear connection between service and patient volume. It is possible only on a macro basis to determine staffing or resource profiles for a specified range of activity, e.g., 34,675 patient days.

Define Resource Prices (Step 5)

The last step in completing the budget is to determine the expected resource prices to be in effect during the budget period. Those prices are determined below:

Purchased food package	$2.00/meal
Dietary labor	$6.00/hour
RN labor	$15.00/hour
Aide labor	$8.00/hour
Administrative labor	$28,000/FTE

Presented below is a summary of the completed budget for the nursing home example, assuming that 34,675 patient days of care are provided next year:

Dietary		
Purchased food packages	$ 208,050	
Dietary labor	104,025	
Total dietary	$ 312,075	
Nursing		
RN labor	$ 520,125	
Aide labor	277,400	
	$ 797,525	
Administration		
Salaries	$ 140,000	
Total cost	$1,249,600	

Control and Corrective Action

The control phase of business operations monitors actual cost experience and compares it with budgetary expectations. If there are deviations from expectations, management analyzes the causes of the deviation. If the deviation is favorable, management may seek to make whatever created the variance a permanent part of operations. If the variance is unfavorable, action will be taken in an attempt to prevent a recurrence. Much of the control phase centers around the topic of variance analysis, which is explored in depth in Chapter 11.

THE COSTING PROCESS

Most firms, whether they are hospitals, nursing homes, or steel manufacturers, have fairly similar costing systems. In fact, in most cases, the similarities outweigh the differences. Figure 9-2 presents a schematic of the cost measurement process that exists in most businesses.

Valuation

Valuation has always been a thorny issue for accountants, one that has not been satisfactorily resolved even today. We need only to look at the current controversy over replacement costs versus historical costs to see

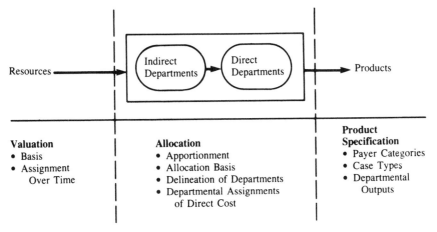

Valuation
- Basis
- Assignment
  Over Time

Allocation
- Apportionment
- Allocation Basis
- Delineation of Departments
- Departmental Assignments
  of Direct Cost

Product
Specification
- Payer Categories
- Case Types
- Departmental
  Outputs

Figure 9–2 The Cost Measurement Process

the problem in full bloom. Here, for discussion purposes, we have chosen to split the valuation process into two areas: (1) basis and (2) assignment over time. These two areas are not mutually exclusive; to some degree they overlap. However, both areas determine the total value of a resource that is used to cost a final product.

The valuation basis is the process by which a value is assigned to each and every resource transaction occurring between the entity being accounted for and another entity. In most situations this value is historical cost.

Having established a basis value for the resource transaction, there are two major types of situations in which that value will have to be assigned over time: First, the value may be expended prior to the actual reporting of expense; the best example of this is depreciation. Second, the expense may be recognized prior to an actual expenditure. Normal accruals such as wages and salaries are examples of this situation.

Allocation

The end result of the cost allocation process is to assign to direct departments all costs or values determined in the valuation phase of costing. Two phases of activity are involved in this assignment: First, all resource values to be recorded as expense in a given period are assigned or allocated to the direct and indirect departments as direct expenses. Second, once the initial cost assignment to individual departments has been made, a further allocation is required. In this phase the expenses of the indirect departments are assigned to the direct departments.

By using this framework for analysis, costing issues may be subcategorized. In the initial cost assignment phase, there appear to be two major action categories involved in the costing process: (1) assigning the cost to departments and (2) defining the indirect and direct departments.

In the first category, a situation may arise in which the departmental structure currently specified is not questioned, but some of the initial value assignments are. For example, premiums paid for malpractice insurance might be charged to the administration and general department, or they may be charged directly to the nursing and professional departments that are involved. In the second category, a situation may arise in which the existing departmental structure has to be revised. For example, the administration and general department may be split into several new departments, such as nonpatient telephone, data processing, purchasing, admitting, business office, and other.

In the second phase of cost allocation, the reassignment from indirect departments to direct departments, there are also two primary categories of action involved: (1) selection of the cost apportionment method and (2) selection of the appropriate allocation basis. With respect to the first category, cost apportionment methods—such as step-down, double-distribution, and simultaneous-equations—are simply mathematical algorithms that redistribute cost from existing indirect departments to direct departments, given defined allocation bases. An example of the second action category is the selection of square feet or hours worked for housekeeping as an appropriate allocation basis for an indirect department.

Product Specification

In most health care firms, there are two phases in the production (or treatment) process. The schematic in Figure 9–3 illustrates this process and also introduces a few new terms.

In stage 1 of the production process, resources are acquired and consumed within departments to produce a product, defined as a service unit. Here, two points need to be emphasized. First, all departments have service units, but not all departments have the same number of service units. For example, nursing may provide four levels of care: acuity levels 1, 2, 3, and 4. Laboratory, in contrast, may have a hundred or more separate service units that relate to the provision of specific tests. Second, not all service units can be directly associated with the delivery of patient care;

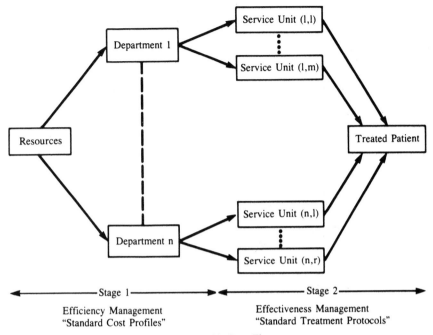

Figure 9–3 The Production Process for Health Care Firms

some of the service units may be only indirectly associated with patient treatment. For example, housekeeping cleans laboratory areas, but there is no direct association between this function and patient treatment. However, the cleaning of a patient's room could be regarded as a service that is directly associated with a patient.

Stage 2 of the production process relates to the actual consumption of specific service units in the treatment of a patient. Much of the production process is managed by the physician. This is true regardless of the setting (hospital, nursing home, home health care firm, or clinic). The physician prescribes the specific service units that will be required to treat a given patient effectively.

The lack of management authority in this area complicates management's efforts to budget and control its costs. This is not meant to be a negative criticism of current health care delivery systems; all of us would prefer to have a qualified physician rather than a lay health care executive direct our care. Yet this is perhaps the area of greatest difference between health care firms and other business entities. Management at General Motors can decide which automobiles will have factory-installed air conditioning and tinted glass and which will not. In contrast, a hospital manager will have great difficulty in attempting to direct a physician to either prescribe or not prescribe a given procedure in the treatment of a patient.

Health care products to be costed may vary depending on the specific decision under consideration. At one level, management may be interested in the cost of a specific service unit or departmental output. Prices for some service units (for example, for x-ray procedures) may have to be established, and to do that management must know their costs. In other situations, the cost for one treated patient or a grouping of treated patients may be desired. For example, management may wish to bid on a contract to provide home health services to an HMO. In this case, it is important for management to understand what the costs of treating HMO patients are likely to be. If the contract is signed, management then needs to determine the actual costs of treating the patients from the HMO in order to measure the overall profitability from that segment of the business. Alternatively, a grouping of patients by specialty may be necessary. A hospital may wish to know whether it is losing money from treating a particular DRG entity or some grouping of DRGs, such as obstetrics. This kind of cost information is especially critical to management decision making involving the expansion or contraction of specific clinical service areas and the recruitment of new medical staff.

STANDARD DEVELOPMENT

The key to successful product costing is management's ability to develop and maintain two systems: (1) a system of standard cost profiles and (2) a system of standard treatment protocols. The relationship between these two systems is shown in Figure 9–3. The linchpin between them is the service unit (SU) concept. Specifically, management must know what it costs to produce an SU, and it must know what particular SUs are needed to treat a given patient.

Standard Cost Profiles

The standard cost profile (SCP) is not a new concept; it has been used in manufacturing cost accounting systems for many years. For our purposes, there are two key elements in an SCP: (1) the definition of the SU being costed and (2) the profile of resources required to produce the SU.

As noted earlier, the number of SUs in a given department may vary; some departments may have one, while others may have a hundred or more. If the number of SUs is very large, however, there may be an unacceptable level of costing detail involved to make the system feasible. In these situations, it may be useful to aggregate some of the SUs. For example, the laboratory may perform a thousand or more tests. In this situation, it may make sense to develop cost profiles for only the most commonly performed tests and to employ some arbitrary assignment method for the remaining noncommon tests.

The SU does not have to be a product or service that is directly performed for a patient. Many indirect departments do not provide services or products to the patient; instead, their products or services are consumed by other departments, both direct and indirect. However, many indirect departments have SUs that are provided directly to the patient. For example, dietary, often regarded as an indirect department, may not have revenue billed for its product to the patient. However, a meal furnished by it to a patient is an SU that is just as direct as a laboratory test or a chest x-ray. In a similar vein, housekeeping may provide cleaning for a patient's room that is, in effect, a direct service consumed by the patient.

Thus, SUs may be categorized as either direct or indirect. A direct SU is one that is associated with a given patient. An indirect SU is one provided to another department of the hospital, as opposed to a patient. The differentiation between direct and indirect SUs is important, not only in the development of standard cost profiles but also in the development of standard treatment protocols. Direct SUs must be identified when standard treatment protocols are defined, whereas indirect SUs need not be specifically identified, although some estimate of allocated cost is often required.

In the development of an SCP for a given SU, the following resource expense categories are listed: (1) direct expenses (labor, materials, and departmental overhead) and (2) allocated overhead. Ideally, the expense should also be categorized as variable or fixed. This distinction is particularly important in certain areas of management decision making, as pointed out in Chapter 8. Specifically, the differentiation between variable and fixed cost is critical to many incremental pricing and volume decisions. It is also important in flexible budgeting systems and management control. These topics are explored in greater depth in Chapters 10 and 11.

Table 9–1 presents an SCP for a regular patient meal in a dietary department. The total cost of providing one regular patient meal, or SU #181, is $2.50. The variable cost per meal is $1.30, and the average fixed cost per meal is $1.20.

In most situations, direct labor is the largest single expense category. In our dietary meal example, this is not true because the direct material cost, mostly raw food, is larger. It is possible, and in many cases desirable, to

Table 9–1 Standard Cost Profile for a Dietary/Regular Patient Meal SU #181

Cost Category	Quantity Required		Unit Cost	Variable Cost	Average Fixed Cost	Average Total Cost
	Variable	Fixed				
Direct labor	.05	.05	$6.00	$ .30	$ .30	$ .60
Direct materials	1.00	.00	1.00	1.00	.00	1.00
Department overhead	.00	1.00	.50	.00	.50	.50
Allocated costs						
Housekeeping	.00	.10	1.00	.00	.10	.10
Plant operation	.00	1.00	.10	.00	.10	.10
Administration	.00	.02	10.00	.00	.20	.20
Total				$1.30	$1.20	$2.50

define direct labor costs by labor category. Thus, in our dietary meal example, we might provide separate listings for cooks, dietary aides, and dishwashers.

An important point here is the division of cost into fixed and variable quantities. Table 9–1 indicates that .05 unit of variable labor time is required per meal, and .05 unit of fixed labor is required per meal. (In Chapter 8 we discussed several methods for splitting costs into fixed and variable elements.) The fixed-cost assignment is an average based on some expected level of volume. This is an important point to remember when developing SCPs; a decline in volume below expected levels will raise the average cost of production.

The third column of Table 9–1 presents unit cost. This represents management's best guess as to the cost or price of the resources to be used in the production process. Our dietary meal SCP indicates a price of $6 per unit of direct labor. This value reflects the expected wage per hour to be paid for direct labor in the dietary department. Again, it might be possible and desirable to break out direct labor further into specific job classifications. This usually permits better costing, but it also requires more effort.

Any fringe benefit cost associated with labor should be included in the unit cost. For example, the average direct hourly wage in our dietary meal example might be $5 per hour, but fringe benefits may average 20 percent. In this case, the effective wage would be $6 per hour.

Departmental overhead consists of expenses that are charged directly to a department and do not represent either labor or materials. Common examples are equipment costs, travel allowances, expenses for outside purchased services, and cost of publications. Usually these items do not vary with level of activity or volume but remain fixed for the budgetary period. If this is the case, assignment to an SCP can be based on a simple average. For example, assume that our dietary department expects to provide 200,000 regular patient meals next year. Assume further that the department has been authorized to spend $100,000 in discretionary areas that constitute departmental overhead. The average cost per meal for these discretionary costs would be $.50 and would be fixed.

Allocated costs are probably the most difficult to assign in most situations. In our dietary example, we include only three allocated cost areas. This is probably a low figure; a number of other departments would most likely provide service to dietary and should properly be included in the SCP.

There are two major alternatives to the use of estimates of allocated costs in an SCP. First, individual costing studies could be performed, and services from one department to another could be recorded. This process may be expensive, however, and not worth the effort. For example, if separate meters were installed, utility costs could be associated with each user department. However, the installation of such meters is probably not an effective expenditure of funds; costing accuracy would not be improved enough to justify the extra expenditure.

The second alternative would be a simple averaging method. All overhead costs might be aggregated and apportioned to other departments on the basis of direct expenses, FTEs, or some other criterion. This method is relatively simple, but its accuracy would be suspect if significant variation in departmental utilization exists.

We believe that the best approach to costing is to identify all possible direct SUs. These SUs, which can be directly associated with a patient, are far more numerous than one would suspect. For example, a meal provided to a patient is a direct SU but is currently treated as an indirect product in most costing systems. Laundry and linen have certain SUs that are directly associated with a patient, such as clean sheets and gowns. Housekeeping provides direct services to patients when its personnel clean rooms. Administration and medical records also provide specific direct services to patients in the form of processed paper work and insurance forms. If such costs, currently regarded as indirect, were reclassified as direct, there would be a substantially lower level of indirect costs that would require allocation. This would improve the costing of patients—the health care product—and make the allocation of indirect costs less critical. Currently, indirect costs in many health care settings are in excess of 50 percent of total cost. With better identification of services or SUs, we believe that level could be reduced to 25 percent or lower.

Standard Treatment Protocols

There is an analogy between a standard treatment protocol (STP) and a job order cost sheet used in industrial cost accounting. In a job order cost system, a separate cost sheet is completed for each specific job. This is necessary because each job is different from jobs performed in the past and jobs to be performed in the future. Automobile repairs are an excellent example of a job order cost system. A separate cost sheet is prepared for each job. That cost sheet then serves as the bill or invoice to the customer.

Health care firms also operate in a job cost setting. Patient treatment may vary significantly across patients. The patient's bill may be thought of as a job order cost sheet in that it reflects the actual services provided during the course of the patient's treatment. Of course, not all of the services provided are shown in the patient's bill. For example, meals provided are rarely charged for as a separate item.

In a typical job order cost setting, standards may not always be applied. When you drop your car off for servicing, the dealer does not prepare a standard job order cost sheet. Dealers have no incentive to do this because they expect that customers will pay the actual costs of the service when they drop by to pick up their cars. If they do not, the dealer may take possession of the car as collateral.

In the past, a similar situation existed among health care firms; the client or patient would pay for the actual cost of services provided. Today this is no longer true for the majority of health care products. Today, most health care firms are paid a fixed fee or price regardless of the range of services provided. Medicare's DRG payment system is an example of this type of payment philosophy.

Because the majority of health care revenue is derived from fixed-price payers, we need to define specific STPs wherever possible. Table 9–2 shows a hypothetical STP for DRG #208 (Disorder of Biliary Tract). (This STP is for illustrative purposes only; it should not be regarded as a realistic STP for DRG #208.)

In the Table 9–2 STP, costs are split into fixed and variable components. Thus, the STP requires 25 patient meals at a variable cost of $1.30 per meal and a fixed cost of $1.20 per meal. The basis for these data is the SCP (see Table 9–1). As noted earlier, this breakout into fixed and variable costs is extremely valuable for management in making its planning and control decisions. For example, if Medicare paid the hospital $1,400 for every DRG #208 treated, we would conclude that, at least in the short run, the hospital would be financially better off if it continued to treat

Table 9–2 Standard Treatment Protocol for DRG #208 / Disorder of Biliary Tract

Service Unit No.	Service Unit Name	Quantity	Variable Cost / Unit	Fixed Cost / Unit	Total Cost / Unit	Total Variable Cost	Total Fixed Cost	Total Cost
1	Admission process	1	$48.00	$52.00	$100.00	$ 48.00	$ 52.00	$,100.00
7	Nursing care level 1	1	80.00	40.00	120.00	80.00	40.00	120.00
8	Nursing care level 2	7	85.00	45.00	130.00	595.00	315.00	910.00
9	Nursing care level 3	1	110.00	45.00	155.00	110.00	45.00	155.00
29	Pharmacy prescriptions	1	38.00	19.00	57.00	38.00	19.00	57.00
38	Chest x-ray	1	12.00	8.00	20.00	12.00	8.00	20.00
46	Laboratory complete blood count	1	4.00	3.50	7.50	4.00	3.50	7.50
49	Other laboratory tests	1	85.00	55.00	140.00	85.00	55.00	140.00
57	Patient meals	25	1.30	1.20	2.50	32.50	30.00	62.50
65	Clean linen changes	5	.60	.50	1.10	3.00	2.50	5.50
93	Room preparation	1	7.00	3.00	10.00	7.00	3.00	10.00
	Totals					$1,014.50	$573.00	$1,587.50

DRG #208 cases, since the payment of $1,400 exceeds the variable cost of $1,014.50 and is therefore making a contribution to fixed costs.

Table 9–2 depicts two areas in which no actual quantity is specified: pharmacy prescriptions and other laboratory tests. In these instances, the total cost of the services is instead divided between fixed and variable costs. Because of the large number of products provided in each of these two areas, it would be impossible to develop an SCP for each product item. However, some of the heavier volume laboratory tests or pharmacy prescriptions may be separately identified and costed; for example, laboratory complete blood count is listed as a separate SU.

Some of the items shown in Table 9–2 may not be reflected in a patient's bill. For example, patient meals, clean linen changes, room preparation, and admission processing would not usually be listed in the bill. Also, separation of nursing care by acuity level may not be identified in the bill; many hospitals do not distinguish between levels of nursing care in their pricing structures.

A final point to emphasize is that not all SUs will show up in an STP. Only those SUs that are classified as direct are listed. A direct SU is one that can be directly traced or associated with patient care. The costs associated with the provision of indirect SUs are allocated to the direct SUs. At the same time, the objective should be to create as many direct SUs as possible.

VARIANCE ANALYSIS

In general, given the systems of standards discussed above, four types of variances may be identified in the variance analysis phase of control:

1. Price (rate)
2. Efficiency
3. Volume
4. Intensity

The first three types of variances are a direct result of the development of the SCPs; they are the product of departmental activity. A rate or price variance is the difference between the price actually paid and the standard price multiplied by the actual quantity used:

$$\text{Price variance} = (\text{Actual price} - \text{Standard price}) \times \text{Actual quantity}$$

For example, assume that our dietary department of Table 9–1 produced 1,500 patient meals for the period in question. To produce these meals, it used 180 hours of labor and paid $6.25 per hour. In this case, the price or rate variance would be

$$(\$6.25 - \$6.00) \times 180 \text{ hours} = \$45.00$$

This variance would be unfavorable because the department paid $6.25 per hour when the expected rate was $6.00.

An efficiency variance reflects productivity in the production process. It is derived by multiplying the difference between actual quantity used and standard quantity by the standard price:

$$\text{Efficiency variance} = (\text{Actual quantity} - \text{Standard quantity}) \times \text{Standard price}$$

In our dietary example, the efficiency variance would be

$$(180 \text{ hours} - 155 \text{ hours}) \times \$6 = \$150$$

Standard labor is derived by multiplying the variable labor requirement of .05 times the number of meals produced, or 1,500. To this sum is added the budgeted fixed-labor requirement of 80 hours (.05 × 1,600 meals). In our example, the department used 25 more hours of labor than had been expected. As a result, it incurred an unfavorable efficiency variance of $150.

The volume variance reflects differences between expected output and actual output. It is a factor to be considered in situations with fixed costs. If no fixed costs existed, the resources required per unit would be constant. This would mean that the cost per unit of production should be constant. For most situations, this is not a reasonable expectation; normally fixed costs are present.

The volume variance is derived by multiplying the expected average fixed cost per unit times the difference between budgeted volume and actual volume:

$$\text{Volume variance} = (\text{Budgeted volume} - \text{Actual volume}) \times \text{Average fixed cost per unit}$$

In the case of direct labor in our dietary example, the volume variance would be an unfavorable $30 ([1,600 Meals − 1,500 Meals] × $.30).

Notice that in our example, the total of these variances equals the difference between actual costs incurred for direct labor and the standard cost of direct labor assigned to the SU, a patient meal:

Actual direct labor ($6.25 × 180 hours)	$1,125
Standard cost ($.60 × 1,500 meals)	900
Total variance	$ 225
Price variance	$ 45.00
Efficiency variance	150.00
Volume variance	30.00
Total variance	$225.00

The intensity variance is the difference between the quantity of SUs actually required in treating a patient and the quantity called for in the STP. For example, if 20 meals were provided to a patient categorized in DRG #208, there would be a favorable variance of five meals, given the STP data of Table 9–2.

Intensity variances are generically defined as follows:

Intensity variance = (Actual SUs − Standard SUs) × Standard cost per SU

Thus, in our example, the intensity variance for a patient with respect to meals would be a favorable $12.50 ([20 meals − 25 meals] × $2.50).

It may be useful to split intensity variances into fixed and variable elements. In our example, it is probably not fair to say that $12.50 was realized in savings because five fewer meals were delivered. Five times $1.30, the variable cost, may be a better reflection of short-term realized savings.

One final word on variance analysis: It is important to specify the party responsible for variances. This is, after all, part of the rationale for standard costing—to be able to take corrective action through individuals to correct unfavorable variances. In our example, three variances—price, efficiency, and volume—are distinguished in the departmental accounts. However, the department manager may not be responsible for all of this variation, especially in the volume area. Usually, department managers have little control over volume; they merely react to the volume of services requested from their departments.

The intensity variance can be largely associated with a given physician. Most of the SUs are of a medical nature, resulting from physician decisions regarding testing or length of stay. It may be very helpful, therefore, to accumulate intensity variances by physicians. Periodic discussions regarding these variations can be most useful to both the health care executive and the physician. Ideally, physicians should participate actively in the development of STPs.

SUMMARY

Product costing has become much more critical to health care executives today than it was prior to 1983. The emphasis on prospective prices and competitive discounting creates a real need to define costs. For health care purposes, the product is a treated patient. Various aggregations of patients may also be useful. For example, we may want to develop cost data by DRG, by clinical specialty, or by payer category.

To develop a standard cost system in a health care firm, two sets of standards must be defined. First, a series of SCPs must be developed for all SUs (intermediate departmental products) produced by the firm. This part of standard costing is analogous to that of most manufacturing systems. Second, a set of STPs must be defined for major patient treatment categories. These STPs must identify all the service units to be provided in the patient treatment. Physician involvement is critical in this area.

The purpose of standard costing is to make planning decisions, such as those involved in pricing and product mix, more precise and meaningful. Standard costing is also useful in making control decisions. Variance analysis is based on the existence of standard cost and the periodic accumulation of actual cost data. Timely analysis of variances can help management achieve desired results.

ASSIGNMENTS

1. An HMO has asked your hospital to provide all of its obstetrical services. It has offered to pay your hospital $2,000 for a normal vaginal delivery without complications (DRG #373). You have looked at the STP for this DRG and discovered that your hospital's cost is $2,400. What should you do?

2. Dr. Jones is scheduled to meet with you this afternoon. He has been an active admitter, but you would like to see his practice increase. After reviewing Dr. Jones's financial report, shown in Table 9–3, what recommendations would you make?

3. Using the data presented in Table 9–4, explain why some DRGs have negative values for deductions.

4. In Table 9–4, DRG #14 has the largest revenue of all the case types listed, yet it lost money, Why?

5. The data in Table 9–5 represent a cost accountant's effort to define the variable cost for DRG #104 (Cardiac Valve Procedures with Cardiac Cath). Evaluate this method.

SOLUTIONS AND ANSWERS

1. Hopefully, the STP for DRG #373 separates the costs into variable and fixed elements. If the variable cost is below $2,000, some marginal profit may be earned by your hospital on the additional business. However, a close examination of the STP should be made by the

Table 9–3 Dr. Jones's Financial Report

Case No.	Type Description	No. of Discharges	ALOS*	Comp LOS	LOS Var	Total Charges	Deductions	Net Revenue	Variable Cost	Gross Margin	Fixed Cost	Net Income
0316	Renal Failure w/	7	11.7	6.7	5.0	$ 19,371	$ 4,484	$ 14,887	$ 7,372	$ 7,515	$ 6,926	$ 589
0315	Other Kidney Uri	5	42.4	12.7	29.7	28,945	6,270	22,675	12,375	10,300	8,866	1,434
0468	Unrelated OR Pro	5	32.2	11.3	20.9	87,309	12,739	71,570	33,421	38,149	30,955	7,194
0130	Periph Vascular	3	6.0	8.8	-2.8	8,166	1,834	6,332	3,055	3,277	3,297	-20
0138	Cardiac Arrhythm	3	4.3	7.4	-3.1	3,524	1,027	2,497	1,351	1,146	985	161
0182	Esophagitis GI + D	3	7.3	6.7	.6	14,171	3,427	10,744	5,308	5,436	5,503	-67
0331	Other Kid + Urina	3	8.7	7.6	1.1	10,983	2,539	8,444	3,900	4,544	4,390	154
0024	Seizure + Headache	2	16.0	6.8	9.2	4,625	1,156	3,469	1,651	1,818	1,459	359
0127	Heart Failure +	2	4.0	10.4	-6.4	1,827	592	1,235	606	629	348	281
0140	Angina Pectoris	2	7.0	6.6	.4	5,290	1,179	4,111	2,079	2,032	1,765	267
0188	Other Digest/sys	2	9.5	6.5	3.0	4,733	1,148	3,585	1,551	2,034	1,926	108
0296	Nutri + Misc Met	2	8.0	8.9	-.9	2,840	625	2,215	1,103	1,112	995	117
0321	Kid + Urinary Tra	2	23.0	4.6	18.4	12,377	248	12,129	4,103	8,026	4,505	3,521
0442	Other OR Proc In	2	6.5	11.6	-5.1	11,415	2,629	8,786	4,533	4,253	4,082	171
0443	Other OR Proc In	2	8.5	5.6	2.9	8,974	2,227	6,747	3,392	3,355	3,225	130
0452	Complications Tr	2	44.5	6.0	38.5	1,827	482	1,345	562	783	693	90
0467	Other Factors In	2	1.5	3.1	-1.6	1,461	396	1,065	452	613	518	95
0010	Nervous Syst Neo	1	35.0	13.5	21.5	267	99	168	62	106	35	71
0016	Nonspec Cerebrov	1	8.0	11.0	-3.0	4,984	1,093	3,891	2,064	1,827	2,034	-207
0066	Epistaxis	1	7.0	4.6	2.4	302	112	190	86	104	68	36
0085	Pleural Effusion	1	19.0	12.1	6.9	675	251	424	393	31	220	-189
0088	Chronic Obstruct	1	3.0	9.1	-6.1	2,634	694	1,940	1,087	853	946	-93
0112	Vasc Proc No Maj	1	9.0	26.2	-17.2	6,357	1,380	4,977	2,445	2,532	2,482	50
0120	Other OR Procedu	1	71.0	16.4	54.6	10,448	3,461	6,987	2,862	4,125	2,178	1,947
0143	Chest Pain	1	6.0	4.2	1.8	5,659	1,179	4,480	2,333	2,147	2,070	77
0144	Other Circ Diagn	1	2.0	9.3	-7.3	2,085	439	1,646	858	788	713	75
0152	Minor Small + Lar	1	93.0	13.7	79.3	1,084	403	681	241	440	149	291
0171	Other Digest/sys	1	35.0	6.9	28.1	2,136	793	1,343	555	788	358	430
0175	G.I. Hemmorhage A	1	6.0	5.8	.2	3,734	883	2,851	1,676	1,175	1,027	148
0224	Up Extr Proc No	1	23.0	4.3	18.7	10,977	5,544	5,433	3,672	1,761	4,165	-2,404
	OP 30 Case types	62	17.9	8.6	9.3	$276,180	$59,333	$216,847	$105,148	$111,699	$96,883	$14,816

*ALOS = average length of stay.

Table 9–4 Financial Statement by DRG Category

Number	Description	Total Charges	Total Deductions	Net Revenue	Variable Cost	Gross Margin	Total Margin (%)	Fixed Cost	Net Income	Income %
0001	Craniotomy Age 17 No Trau	$ 14,115	$ 3,317	$10,798	$ 4,709	$ 6,089	43.1	$ 4,192	$1,897	13.4
0002	Craniotomy Age 17 W/Trau	1,170	435	735	302	433	37.0	220	213	18.2
0004	Spinal Procedures	5,553	–251	5,804	2,278	3,526	63.4	1,596	1,930	34.7
0005	Extracranial Vasc Procedu	14,814	2,310	12,504	5,641	6,863	46.3	4,898	1,965	13.2
0006	Carpal Tunnel Release	12,488	1,991	10,497	4,441	6,056	48.4	4,649	1,407	11.2
0007	Periph + Cranial Nerv/Syst	2,586	–1,900	4,486	586	3,900	150.8	424	3,476	134.4
0008	Periph + Cranial Nerv/Syst	6,742	605	6,137	2,577	3,560	52.8	2,806	754	11.1
0010	Nervous Syst Neoplasms Ag	36,194	5,602	30,592	13,594	16,998	46.9	13,625	3,373	9.3
0011	Nervous Syst Neoplasms Ag	9,075	2,869	6,206	3,058	3,148	34.6	2,885	263	2.8
0012	Degenerative Nerv/Syst Di	49,084	11,628	37,456	18,392	19,064	38.8	18,500	564	1.1
0013	Multiple Sclerosis & Cere	4,249	532	3,717	1,448	2,269	53.4	1,417	852	20.0
0014	Spec Cerebrovascular Dis	129,884	37,434	92,450	48,146	44,304	34.1	45,014	–710	–.5
0015	Transient Ischemic Attack	39,989	10,813	29,176	13,768	15,408	38.5	14,098	1,310	3.2
0016	Nonspec Cerebrovascular D	7,272	1,713	5,559	2,855	2,704	37.1	2,496	208	2.8
0017	Nonspec Cerebrovascular D	544	11	533	147	386	70.9	223	163	29.9
0018	Cranial + Periph Nerve Diso	12,807	895	11,912	4,305	7,607	59.3	4,680	2,927	22.8
0019	Cranial + Periph Nerve Diso	4,083	–160	4,243	1,311	2,932	71.8	1,535	1,397	34.2
0020	Nerv/Syst Infect No Viral	8,246	619	7,627	2,405	5,222	63.3	2,519	2,703	32.7
0021	Viral Meningitis	3,443	1,334	2,109	1,180	929	26.9	971	–42	–1.2
0022	Hyperten Encephalopathi	589	147	442	194	248	42.1	135	113	19.1

continues

Table 9-4 continued

Number	Description	Total Charges	Total Deductions	Net Revenue	Variable Cost	Gross Margin	Total Margin (%)	Fixed Cost	Net Income	Income %
0024	Seizure + Headache Age > 69	19,427	2,201	17,226	6,071	11,155	57.4	5,299	5,856	30.1
0025	Seizure + Headache Age = 18–69	24,151	2,948	21,203	7,728	13,475	55.7	9,092	4,383	18.1
0026	Seizure + Headache Age = 0–17	5,511	424	5,087	2,310	2,777	50.3	2,139	638	11.5
0027	Traumatic Stupor + Coma >	2,572	318	2,254	1,051	1,203	46.7	798	405	15.7
0028	Traumatic Stupor + Coma <	7,220	1,760	5,460	2,227	3,233	44.7	3,357	–124	–1.7
0029	Traumatic Stupor + < 1H	438	9	429	168	261	59.5	70	191	43.6
0032	Concussion Age = 18–69	6,826	277	6,549	2,345	4,204	61.5	2,279	1,925	28.2
0033	Concussion Age = 0–17	1,513	269	1,244	615	629	41.5	613	16	1.0
0034	Other Disorders Nerv/Sys	34,702	9,918	24,784	15,312	9,472	27.2	10,380	–908	–2.6
0035	Other Disorders Nerv/Sys	18,634	764	17,870	8,342	9,528	51.1	7,935	1,593	8.5
0036	Retinal Procedures	13,240	1,999	11,241	4,428	6,813	51.4	5,463	1,350	10.1
0037	Orbital Procedures	3,284	684	2,600	1,437	1,163	35.4	1,089	74	2.2
0038	Primary Iris Procedures	1,092	226	866	574	292	26.7	466	–174	–15.9
0039	Lens Procedures	118,725	27,289	91,436	43,601	47,835	40.2	48,010	–175	–.1
0040	Extraocular Proc No Orbit	4,455	547	3,908	1,819	2,089	46.8	2,131	–42	–.9
0041	Extraocular Proc No Orbit	4,798	228	4,570	1,683	2,887	60.1	1,574	1,313	27.3
0044	Acute Major Eye Infection	6,953	1,841	5,112	2,178	2,934	42.1	2,900	34	.4
0045	Neurological Eye Disorder	8,995	1,432	7,563	3,153	4,410	49.0	3,425	985	10.9

Table 9-5 Format for Defining Variable Cost for DRG #104
(Cardiac Valve Procedures with Cardiac Cath)

Department	Average Charges	Ratio of Direct Costs to Charges*	Estimated Costs	Estimated Variable Costs (As % of Total Estimated Costs)[†]	Estimated Variable Costs
General nursing	$1,240	.71	$ 880	70	$ 616
Special care unit	1,810	.68	1,231	70	862
Central supply	180	.28	50	75	38
Laboratory	270	.47	127	10	13
EKG	50	.37	19	20	4
EEG	60	.38	23	20	5
Nuclear medicine	190	.37	70	30	21
Diagnostic radiology	95	.38	36	25	9
Operating room	650	.47	306	65	199
Emergency department	105	.49	51	40	21
Transfusion	405	.63	255	70	179
Pharmacy	320	.28	90	75	67
Anesthesiology	180	.44	79	30	24
Respiratory therapy	295	.35	103	25	26
Physical therapy	85	.61	52	25	13
Clinic	110	.53	58	30	17
Totals	$6,045		$3,430		$2,114

Variable cost of other departments (e.g., dietary, housekeeping, admitting, billing, medical records), estimated at $50 per admission plus $30 per day × 9 days.[‡]
   Total estimated variable cost 320 / $2,434

*Ratio of direct costs (not fully allocated costs) to charges, per the general ledger.
[†] Source: estimates prepared by department managers.
[‡] Source: estimates prepared by department managers.

HMO physicians. There may be some patient-management differences, especially with regard to length of stay, that could result in more or less cost. An agreement on the STP with the HMO physicians should be negotiated.

2. Most of the income generated by Dr. Jones is in areas where the LOS is significantly above the normal level. For example, DRG Nos. 468, 321, and 120 accounted for 85 percent of the total income that he generated for the hospital. In each of these three DRG categories his LOS was well above normal. Since these cases were profitable, they must not have been billed to Medicare. If there is a likelihood that some of your major payers may shift to a prospective case payment basis, you may not want to encourage Dr. Jones to increase his practice. The data in his financial report indicate a relatively high LOS in almost all areas.

3. DRG #7 has a minus $1,900 deduction. This means that payment received for treating this DRG category exceeded charges by $1,900. This probably reflects payment by Medicare in excess of charges. This situation may change if other hospitals have a similar experience. At the present time, however, DRG #7 is a very profitable product for the hospital (134.4 percent).

4. One reason DRG #14 lost money can be found in the deductible provision. Approximately 29 percent of the DRG charges were written off. You may want to pay special attention to the firm's STP for this case type. Perhaps the firm's LOS or ancillary services are excessive.

5. The first potential weakness in the cost accountant's method is the use of a cost-to-charge ratio. There is no guarantee that charges for departmental services will always be related to costs. The method also may miss a large block of indirect departmental costs that may be variable. Finally, the method simply does not relate well to the two-stage definition of standard costs involving SCPs and STPs, as discussed in this chapter. In fairness, it must be noted that the cost accountant's method would cost significantly less than other methods. And it is not clear whether the improved accuracy that might result from some other, more sophisticated, system would be worth the extra cost.

Chapter 10

The Management
Control Process

Twenty years ago, the word *budgeting* could not have been found in the vocabularies of many hospital managers and other health care facility administrators. Today, this is no longer true. Most hospitals and other health care facilities now develop and use budgets as an integral part of their overall management control process.

To a large extent, the attention being paid to budgeting by health care providers is attributable to changes in the environment. The recent adoption of prospective payment and the increasing price competition among health care providers have forced many health care firms to monitor and control costs with increasing care. Budgeting is of course a logical way for any business organization to control its costs. Indeed, other parties external to health care providers now require health care firms to prepare and submit budgets and other financial forecasts. For example, rate-setting agencies frequently require hospitals and other health care facilities to submit fairly detailed institutional budgets. The certificate of need also requires a projection of financial information for projects under review.

External forces thus have certainly stimulated the development of budgets in the health care industry, but most likely such budgets would have been developed in any case. Hospitals and health care facilities have grown larger and more complex, in both organization and finances. And budgeting is imperative in organizations in which management authority is delegated to many individuals.

ESSENTIAL ELEMENTS

For our purposes, a budget is defined as a quantitative expression of a plan of action. It is an integral part of the overall management control process of an organization.

275

Anthony and Herzlinger (*Management Control in Nonprofit Organizations* [Homewood, Ill.: Richard D. Irwin, 1976], 16–33) discuss management control in great detail. They define it as "a process by which managers assure that resources are obtained and used effectively and efficiently in the accomplishment of an organization's objectives" (p. 16).

Efficiency and Effectiveness

In the above definition, special emphasis is placed on attaining efficiency and effectiveness. In short, they determine the success or failure of management control.

These two terms have very precise meanings. Often individuals talk about the relative efficiency and effectiveness of their operations as if efficiency and effectiveness were identical, or at least highly correlated. They are not identical, nor are they necessarily correlated. An operation may be effective without being efficient, and vice versa. A well-managed operation should ideally be both effective and efficient. Efficiency is easier to measure and its meaning is fairly well understood; efficiency is simply a relationship between outputs and inputs. For example, a cost per patient day of $110 is a measure of efficiency; it tells how many resources, or inputs, were used to provide one day of care, the measure of output.

Managers and other persons wishing to assess management in the health care industry are increasing their use of efficiency measures. In most situations, efficiency is measured by comparison with some standard. Several basic considerations should be understood if efficiency measures are to be used intelligently. First, output measures may not always be comparable. For example, comparing the costs per patient day of care in a 50-bed rural hospital with those in a 1,000-bed teaching hospital is not likely to be meaningful. A day of care in a teaching hospital typically entails more service. Second, cost measures may not be comparable or useful for the specific decision under consideration. For example, two operations may be identical, but one may be in a newer facility and thus would have a higher depreciation charge, or the two operations may account for costs differently. One hospital may use an accelerated depreciation method, such as the sum of the year's digits, while the other may use straight-line depreciation. Third, the cost concepts used may not be relevant to the decision under consideration. For example, a certificate of need review to decide which of two hospitals should be permitted to build a 50-bed expansion will obviously consider cost. However, comparing the full costs of a day of care in each institution and selecting the lower one could produce bad results: for this specific decision, the full cost concept is wrong. Incremental or variable cost is the relevant cost concept in this case. The focus of interest is on what the future additional cost would be, not what the historical average cost was.

Effectiveness is concerned with the relationship between an organization's outputs and its objectives or goals. A health care facility's typical goals might include solvency, high quality of care, low cost of patient care, institutional harmony, and growth. Measuring effectiveness is more difficult than measuring efficiency for at least two reasons. First, defining the relationship between outputs and some goals may be difficult because many facilities' goals or objectives are not likely to be quantified. For example, exactly how does an alcoholism program contribute to quality of care? Still, objectives and goals can usually be stated more precisely in quantitative terms. In fact, they should be quantified to the greatest extent possible. In the alcoholism program example, quality scales, such as frequency of repeat visits or new patients treated, might be developed. Second, the output must usually be related to more than one organization goal or objective. For example, both solvency and reasonable cost are legitimate objectives for a hospital. Yet continuing an emergency room operation might affect solvency negatively and at the same time positively affect patient treatment costs. How should decision makers weight these two criteria to determine an overall measure of effectiveness?

Control Unit

Most health care facilities have various responsibility centers over which management control is exercised. These centers are generally referred to as departments. Figure 10–1 presents an organizational chart of a hospital and its departments.

Usually the departments perform special functions that contribute to overall organization goals, directly or indirectly. They receive resources or inputs and produce services or outputs:

Responsibility centers are the focus of management control efforts. Emphasis is placed on the effectiveness of their operations. Measurement problems occur when the responsibility structure is not identical to the program structure. Decision makers are frequently interested in a program's total cost. Yet in the case of a burn care program, for example, it is unlikely that all the resources used in the program will be assigned to it directly; the costs of medical support services (such as physical therapy, laboratory, and radiology, as well as other general and administrative

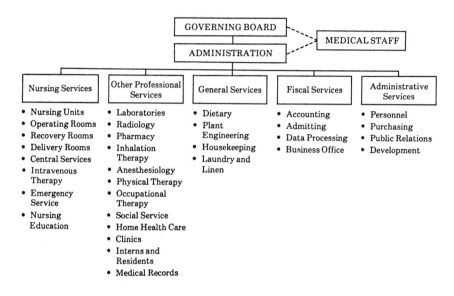

Figure 10–1 Hospital Organization Chart

services) will not likely be contained in the burn care unit. Program lines typically run across responsibility center or departmental lines. This necessitates cost allocations for decisions that require program cost information. It should be remembered that where cost allocations are involved, the accuracy of the information as well as its comparability may be suspect. For example, one may be interested in the specific costs of a burn care program, but then find that those costs must be allocated from various departments or responsibility centers, such as laboratory, radiology, and housekeeping.

Responsibility centers vary greatly, depending on the controlling organization. For a regulatory agency, the responsibility center might be an entire health care facility; for a health care facility manager, it may be an individual department; for a department manager, it may be a unit within the department. The only requirement is that a designated person be in charge of the identified responsibility center.

Phases of Management Control

Figure 10–2 illustrates the relationship of various phases of the management control process to each other and to the planning process. Management control relies on the existence of goals and objectives;

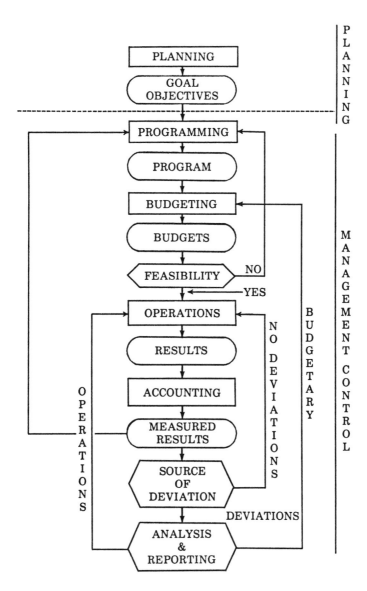

Figure 10–2 The Management Control Process

without them, the structure and evaluation of the management control process is incomplete. Poor or no planning usually limits the value of management control. Effectiveness becomes impossible to assess without stated goals and objectives; in such cases, one can focus only on measuring and attaining efficiency. The organization can assess only whether it has produced outputs efficiently; it cannot evaluate the desirability of those outputs.

For the purposes of this discussion, we shall be concerned with the four phases of management control that Anthony and Herzlinger have identified in their work on management control (see previous citation):

1. programming
2. budgeting
3. accounting
4. analysis and reporting

Programming

Programming is the phase of management control that determines the nature and size of programs an organization will use to accomplish its stated goals and objectives. It is the first phase of the management control process and interrelates with planning. In some cases, the line dividing the two activities may in fact be hard to draw. Programming is usually of intermediate length, three to five years. It lasts longer than budgeting, but is shorter than planning.

Programming decisions deal with new and existing programs. The methodology for programming is different in these two areas. Programming decisions for new programs involve capital investment or capital budget decision making (this process is examined more extensively in Chapter 13). The method for making programming decisions for existing programs is often referred to as zero-base review, or zero-base budgeting (this method is discussed later in this chapter).

To illustrate the programming process, assume that a stated objective of a hospital organization is to develop and implement a program of ambulatory care in the community. The decision makers in the programming phase of management control would take this stated objective and evaluate alternative programs to accomplish it, such as a surgicenter, an outpatient clinic, or a mobile health screening unit. After this analysis, a decision might be made to construct a ten-room surgicenter on a lot adjacent to the hospital. This would be a program decision.

Budgeting

Budgeting is the management control phase of primary interest. It was defined earlier as a quantitative expression of a plan of action. Budgets are usually stated in monetary terms and cover a period of one year.

The budgetary phase of management control follows the determination of programs in the programming phase. In many cases, no real review of existing programs is undertaken; the budgeting phase then may be based on a prior year's budget or on the actual results of existing programs. Proponents of zero-base budgeting have identified this practice as a major shortcoming.

The budgeting phase primarily translates program decisions into terms that are meaningful for responsibility centers. The decision to construct a ten-room surgicenter will affect the revenues and costs of other responsibility centers, such as laboratory, radiology, anesthesiology, and business office. The effects of program decisions thus must be carefully and accurately reflected in the budgets of each of the relevant responsibility centers.

Budgeting may also change programs. A more careful and accurate estimation of revenues and costs may prompt one to re-evaluate prior programming decisions as financially unfeasible. For example, the proposed ten-room surgicenter may be shown, through budget analysis, to produce a significant operating loss. If the hospital cannot or will not subsidize this loss from other sources, the programming must be changed. The size of the surgicenter may be reduced from ten rooms to five to make the operation break even.

Accounting

Accounting is the third phase of the management control process. Once programs have been decided on and budgets developed for them along responsibility center lines, the operations begin. The accounting department accumulates and records information on both outputs and inputs during the operating phase.

It is important to note that cost information is provided along both program and responsibility center lines. Responsibility center cost information is used in the reporting and analysis phase to determine the degree of compliance with budget projections. Programmatic cost information is used to assess the desirability of continuing a given program at its present size and scope in the programming phase of management control.

Analysis and Reporting

The last phase of management control is analysis and reporting. In this phase, differences between actual costs and budgeted costs are analyzed to determine the probable cause of the deviations and are then reported to the individuals who can take corrective action. The method used in this phase is often referred to as variance analysis, which is discussed in greater detail in Chapter 11. Those doing the analysis and reporting rely heavily on the information provided from the accounting phase to break down the reported deviations into categories that suggest causes.

In general, there are three primary causes for differences between budgeted and actual costs:

1. Prices paid for inputs were different from budgeted prices.
2. Output level was higher or lower than budgeted.
3. Actual quantities of inputs used were different from budgeted levels.

Within each of these causal areas, the problem may arise from either budgeting or operations. A budgetary problem is usually not controllable; no operating action can be taken to correct the situation. For example, the surgicenter may have budgeted for ten RNs at $2,100 each per month. However, if there were no way to employ ten RNs at an average wage less than $2,200 per month, the budget would have to be adjusted to reflect the change in expectations. Alternatively, the problem may arise from operations and be controllable. Perhaps the nurses of the surgicenter are more experienced and better trained than expected. If this is true, and the mix of RNs originally budgeted is still regarded as appropriate, some action should be taken to change the actual mix over time.

THE BUDGETING PROCESS

Elements and Participants

Budgeting is regarded by many as the primary tool that health care facility managers can use to control costs in their organizations. The objectives of budgetary programs, as defined by the American Hospital Association, are fourfold:

1. to provide a written expression, in quantitative terms, of the policies and plans of the hospital
2. to provide a basis for the evaluation of financial performance in accordance with the plans
3. to provide a useful tool for the control of costs
4. to create cost awareness throughout the organization

The budgetary process encompasses a number of inter-related but separate budgets. Figure 10–3 provides a schematic representation of the budgetary process and the relationships between specific types of budgets.

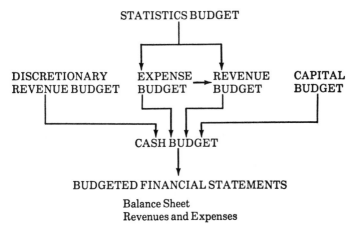

STATISTICS BUDGET

DISCRETIONARY   EXPENSE __ REVENUE   CAPITAL
REVENUE BUDGET   BUDGET   BUDGET   BUDGET

CASH BUDGET

BUDGETED FINANCIAL STATEMENTS
Balance Sheet
Revenues and Expenses

Figure 10–3 Integration of the Budgetary Process

The individuals and roles involved in the budgetary process may vary. In general, the following individuals or parties may be involved:

- governing board
- chief executive officer (CEO)
- controller
- responsibility center managers
- budgetary committee

The governing board's involvement in the budgetary process is usually indirect. The board provides the goals, objectives, and approved programs that are used as the basis for budgetary development. In many cases, it formally approves the finalized budget, especially the cash budget and budgeted financial statements; these are critical in assessing financial condition, which is a primary responsibility of the board.

The CEO or administrator of the health care facility has overall responsibility for budgetary development. The budget is the administrator's tool in the overall program of management by exception, which enables the CEO to focus only on those areas where problems exist.

Controllers often serve as budget directors. Their primary function is facilitation: they are responsible for providing relevant data on costs and outputs and for providing budgetary forms that may be used in budget development. They are not responsible for either making or enforcing the budget.

Responsibility centers are the focal points of control. Managers of departments should be actively involved in developing budgets for their assigned areas of responsibility and are responsible for meeting the budgets developed for their areas.

Many large health care facilities use a special budgetary committee to aid in budget development and approval. Typically, this committee is composed of several department managers, headed by the controller or administrator. A committee structure such as this can help legitimize budgetary decisions that might appear arbitrary and capricious if made unilaterally by management.

Statistics Budget

Development of the statistics budget is the first step in budgeting. It provides the basis for subsequent development of the revenue and expense budgets. Together, these three budgets are sometimes referred to as the operating budget.

The objective of the statistics budget is to provide measures of workload or activity in each department or responsibility center for the coming budget period. There are three parts to this task:

1. controllable nature of output
2. responsibility for estimation
3. problems in estimation methodology

Controllable Nature of Output

Sales forecasts in many businesses reflect management's output expectations—how much of the business's product can be sold, given certain promotional efforts. There is some question about the extent to which health care facilities can determine their volume of service, at least within the usual budgetary period. Although, in the long run, through the development or discontinuation of certain programs, volume may be changed, most health care facilities implicitly assume in the development of their statistics budget that they cannot affect their overall volume during the coming budgetary period. Instead they assume that they will provide services to meet their actual demand. This leads to a reliance on past-period service levels to forecast demand. Assuming that demand patterns in the budget period will be similar to prior periods can, however, be a costly mistake. First, foreseeable but uncontrollable forces may dramatically alter service patterns. For example, retirement of key medical staff with no replacement could drastically reduce admissions. Second, the health care facility may in fact control service levels in the short run and do so in a way that reduces costs. For example, a hospital may decide to use a preadmission testing program that reduces average length of stay in the hospital, thus reducing total volume and total cost.

Responsibility for Estimation

The second issue in the statistics budget is the assignment of responsibility for developing projected output or workload indicators. Should department managers provide this information themselves, or should top management provide it to them? In some situations, department managers may tend to overstate demand. Overstatement of demand implies a greater need for resources within their own area and creates potential budgetary slack if anticipated volumes are not realized. The result of the information coming from top management may be the converse: understatement of demand may result in a lower total cost budget and eventually lower total actual costs. Negotiation thus often becomes necessary in determining demand for budgetary purposes.

Problems in Estimation Methodology

The last area of statistics budget development concerns problems of estimation. In most health care facilities, activity in departments depends on a limited number of key indicators, such as patient days and outpatient visits.

Prior values for these indicators can be related to departmental volume through statistical analysis. The major problem becomes one of accurately forecasting values for the indicators.

The use of seasonal, weekly, and daily variations in volume poses an important estimation problem. Too often, yearly volume is assumed to be divided equally between the monthly periods throughout the year, even when that is clearly not the case. Recognition of seasonal, weekly, and daily patterns of variation in volume can in fact create significant opportunities for cost reduction, especially in labor staffing.

Finally, output at the departmental level is often multiple in nature. In fact, a department normally produces more than one type of output; for example, a laboratory may provide literally thousands of different tests. In such situations, a weighted unit of service is needed, such as the relative value units (RVUs) used in areas such as laboratory and radiology. The need to use weighted unit measures in the statistics budget is especially important when the mix of services is expected to change. Assume that a hospital is rapidly increasing its volume in outpatient clinics. This expansion in volume will increase activity in many other departments, including pharmacy. If, in such a situation, the filling of an outpatient prescription requires significantly less effort than the filling of an inpatient prescription, the use of an unweighted activity measure for prescriptions could provide misleading information for budgetary control purposes. Far more labor than is actually needed might be budgeted.

Expense Budget

With estimates of activity for individual departments developed in the statistics budget, department managers can proceed to develop expense budgets for their areas of responsibility. Expense budgeting is the area of budgeting "where the rubber meets the road." Management cost control efforts are finally reflected in hard numbers that the departments must live with, in most cases for the budget period. Major categories of expense budgets at the departmental level include payroll, supplies, and other. In some situations, a budget for allocated costs from indirect departments may also be included, although this is usually not done by department managers.

In our discussion of expense budgeting, we shall focus on the following four issues of budgeting that are of general interest:

1. length of the budget period
2. flexible or forecast budgets
3. standards for price and quantity
4. allocation of indirect costs

Length of the Budget Period

Generally speaking, there are two alternative budget periods that may be used—*fixed* and *rolling*. Of the two, a fixed budget period is far more frequently used in the health care industry. A fixed budget covers some defined time from a given budget date, usually one year. This contrasts with a rolling budget, in which the budget is periodically extended on a frequent basis, usually a month or a quarter. For example, in a rolling budget period with a monthly update, the entity would always have a budget of at least 11 months in front of it. The same is not true in a fixed budget, in which, at fiscal year end, there may be only one week or one month left.

A rolling budget has a number of advantages, but it requires more time and effort and therefore more cost. Among its major advantages are

- more realistic forecasts, which should improve management planning and control
- equalization of the workload of budget development over the entire year
- improved familiarity and understanding of budgets by department managers

Flexible or Forecast Budgets

The use of a flexible budget versus a forecast budget has received much discussion among health care financial people. At the present time, very few hospitals and other health care facilities use a formal system of flexible budgeting. However, flexible budgeting is a more sophisticated method of budgeting than typical forecast budgeting and is being adopted by more and more health care facilities as they become experienced in the budgetary process.

A flexible budget is a budget that adjusts targeted levels of costs for changes in volume. For example, the budget for a nursing unit operating at 95 percent occupancy would be different from the budget for that same unit operating at an 80 percent occupancy. A forecast budget, in contrast, would make no formal differentiation in the allowed budget between these two levels.

The difference between a forecast and a flexible budget is illustrated by the historical data and projected use levels for the laboratory presented in Table 10-1. The forecast levels of volume in RVUs for 1994 are identical to the actual volumes of 1993, except that a 10 percent growth factor is assumed. The department manager using this statistics budget must develop a budget for hours worked in 1994. A common approach to this task is to assume that past work experience indicates future requirements. In this case, the average value for hours of work required per RVU in 1993 was .5061. A common method for developing a forecast budget is to multiply this value of .5061 by the estimated total workload for the budget period, which is expected to be 72,160, and spread the total product equally over each of the 12 months. This is the forecast budget depicted in Table 10-2.

A major difference between a flexible budget and a forecast budget is that a flexible budget must recognize and incorporate underlying cost behavioral patterns. In this laboratory example, hours worked might be

Table 10-1 Laboratory Productivity Data

| | 1993 Actual | | 1994 |
	Hours Worked	RVUs	Expected RVUs
January	2,825	5,700	6,270
February	2,700	5,200	5,720
March	2,900	6,000	6,600
April	2,875	5,900	6,490
May	2,825	5,700	6,270
June	2,700	5,200	5,720
July	2,750	5,400	5,940
August	2,625	4,900	5,390
September	2,725	5,300	5,830
October	2,750	5,400	5,940
November	2,750	5,400	5,940
December	2,775	5,500	6,050
Total	33,200	65,600	72,160

Note: 1993 average hours/RVU = $\dfrac{33{,}200}{65{,}600}$ = .5061.

written as a function of RVUs:

$$\text{Hours worked} = (1{,}400 \text{ hours per month}) + (.25 \times \text{RVUs})$$

Application of this formula to the budgeted RVUs expected in 1994 yields the flexible budget presented in Table 10-2.

Two points should be made before concluding our discussion of flexible budgeting versus forecast budgeting. First, a flexible budget may be represented as a forecast budget for planning purposes. For example, in the laboratory problem of Table 10-2, the flexible budget would provide an estimated hours-worked requirement of 34,837 hours for 1994. However, in an actual control period evaluation, the flexible budget formula would be used. To illustrate, assume that the actual RVUs provided in January 1994 were 6,500 instead of the forecasted 6,270. Budgeted hours in the flexible budget would then not be 2,967, but 3,025:

$$1{,}400 + (.25 \times 6{,}500) = 3{,}025$$

This value would be compared with the actual hours worked, not the initially forecasted 2,967.

Second, dramatic differences in approved costs can result from the two methods. Recognizing the underlying cost behavioral patterns can change

Table 10–2 Alternative Hours-Worked Budget for Laboratory

	Forecast Budget*	Flexible Budget†
January	3,043	2,967
February	3,043	2,830
March	3,043	3,050
April	3,043	3,022
May	3,043	2,967
June	3,043	2,830
July	3,043	2,885
August	3,043	2,747
September	3,043	2,857
October	3,043	2,885
November	3,043	2,885
December	3,043	2,912
Total	36,516	34,837

*$(.5061 \times 72,160)/12 = 3,043.35$.
†January value = $(1,400) + (.25 \times 6,270)$.

the estimated resource requirements approved in the budgetary process. In our laboratory example in Table 10–2, the forecast budget calls for 36,516 hours versus the flexible budget hours requirement of 34,837. The difference results from the method used to estimate hours worked. In a forecast budget method, the prior average hours per RVU relationship is used. In most situations, average hours or average cost should be greater than variable hours or variable cost. In departments with expanding volume, the estimated requirements for resources could be overstated. The converse may be true in departments with declining volume. In many cases, use of forecast budgeting methods is based on the incorporation of prior average cost relationships. Flexible budgeting methods do not make this error, since their use depends on explicit incorporation of cost behavioral patterns that distinctly recognize variable and fixed costs.

Standards for Price and Quantity

Earlier, three factors were identified that can create differences between budgeted and actual costs: volume, prices, and usage or efficiency. The use of flexible budgeting is an attempt to improve the recognition of deviations caused by changes in volume. The use of standards for prices and wage rates, coupled with standards for physical quantities of usage, is an attempt to improve the recognition of deviations from budget that result from prices and usage.

For example, assume that the flexible budget-hours requirement for the laboratory example is still hours worked = 1,400 + (.25 × RVUs). Assume further that the budget wage rate is $9 per hour and the actual RVUs for January 1994 were 6,500. Total payroll cost for hours worked (excluding vacations and sick pay) are assumed to be $31,000. If the actual hours worked were 3,100, the variance analysis report presented in Table 10-3 would be applicable to the laboratory department.

The total unfavorable variance of $3,775 results from a $3,100 unfavorable price variance and a $675 unfavorable efficiency variance. Splitting the variance in this manner helps management quickly identify possible causes. For example, the $3,100 price variance may be due to a negotiated wage increase of $1 per hour. If this is the case, the department manager is clearly not responsible for the variance. If, however, the difference is due to an excessive use of overtime personnel or a more costly mix of labor, then the manager may be held responsible for the difference and should attempt to prevent the problem from occurring again. The unfavorable efficiency variance of $675 reflects excessive use of the labor input during the month in the amount of 75 hours. An explanation for this difference should be sought and steps taken to prevent its recurrence.

Standard costing techniques have been used in industry for many years as an integral part of management control. Although it is true that input and output relationships may not be as objective in the health care industry as they are in general industry, this does not imply that standard costing cannot be used. In fact, there are many areas of activity within a health care facility that have fairly precise input-output relation-

---

Table 10-3 Standard Cost Variance Analysis for Labor Costs, Laboratory, January 1994

1. Price variance = (Actual hours worked) × (Actual wage rate)
   − (Actual hours worked) × (Budgeted wage rate)
   = (3,100 × $10.00) − (3,100 × $9.00)
   = $3,100 [Unfavorable]

2. Efficiency variance = (Actual hours worked) × (Budgeted wage rate)
   − (Budgeted hours worked) × (Budgeted wage rate)
   = (3,100 × $9.00) − (3,025 × $9.00)
   = $675 [Unfavorable]

3. Total variance = $3,100 + $675 = $3,775 [Unfavorable]

   Note: Actual wage rate = $31,000/3,100 = $10.00
   Budgeted wage rate = $9.00
   Actual hours worked = 3,100
   Budgeted hours worked = (1,400) + (.25 × 6,500) = 3,025

ships—housekeeping, laundry and linen, laboratory, radiology, and many others. Standard costing can prove to be a very valuable tool for cost control in the health care industry, if properly applied (this topic is explored in greater detail in Chapter 11).

Allocation of Indirect Costs

There has probably been more internal strife in organizations over the allocation of indirect costs than over any other single budgetary issue. A comment often heard is, "Why was I charged $3,000 for housekeeping services last month when my department didn't use anywhere near that level of service?"

A strong case can in fact be made for not allocating indirect costs in budget variance reports. In most normal situations, the receiving department has little or no control over the costs of the servicing department. Allocation may thus raise questions that should not be raised. While it is true that indirect costs need to be allocated for some decision-making purposes, such as pricing, they are generally not needed for evaluating individual responsibility center management.

However, an equally strong argument can be made for including indirect costs in the budgets of benefiting departments. They are legitimate costs of the total operation, and department managers should be aware of them. If department managers can influence costs in indirect areas by their decisions, they should be held accountable for them. For example, maintenance, housekeeping, and other indirect costs can be influenced by the decisions of benefiting departments. Ideally, a charge for these indirect services should be established and levied against the using departments, based on their use. Labeling the cost of indirect areas as totally uncontrollable can stimulate excessive and unnecessary use of indirect services and thus have a negative impact on the total cost control program in an organization.

Revenue Budget

The revenue budget can be set effectively only after the expense budget and the statistics budget have been developed. The not-for-profit nature of the health care industry demands that revenue be related to budgeted expenses. Moreover, some of the total revenue actually realized by a health care facility is directly determined by expenses because of the presence of cost reimbursement formulas.

Rate Setting

In this discussion of the revenue budget, we shall focus on only one aspect of revenue budget development—pricing or rate setting. Specifically, we shall illustrate through an additional example the rate-setting model discussed in Chapter 8.

Figure 10–4 illustrates the rate-setting model. Sources of information to define the variables of the model are identified. However, three parameters have no identified source:

1. desired profit
2. proportion of charge-paying patients
3. proportion of charge-paying patient revenue not collected

In many situations, departmental indicators for these three values are not available. Instead, institutionwide values or averages are substituted. In many cases, this may not be a bad approximation, but some serious inequities can result in departments in which the relative proportions of inpatient and outpatient use differ greatly. Typically, departments with high outpatient use experience higher levels of charge reimbursement and higher levels of write-offs on that charge reimbursement, due to the reduced presence of insurance coverage for outpatient types of services. Furthermore, the charge-paying patient reimbursement in inpatient areas may be through commercial insurance, subject to smaller write-offs. The following data illustrate this:

	Department 1	Department 2	Total
Desired profit	$ 500	$ 500	$ 1,000
Budgeted expense	$10,000	$10,000	$20,000
Estimated volume	100	100	—
Percentage bad debt	4%	20%	12%
Percentage charge-paying patients	20%	60%	40%
Percentage bad debt on charge-paying patients	20%	33%	30%

In most situations, separate figures for the percentage of write-offs on charge-paying patients and the percentage of charge-paying patients are not available on a departmental basis. Sometimes the best information available may be the percentage of bad-debt write-offs on total revenue for the institution as a whole. In the above example, a 4 percent write-off on 20 percent of the patients who paid charges in department 1 implies that 20 percent of the charge-paying patient revenue in that department is

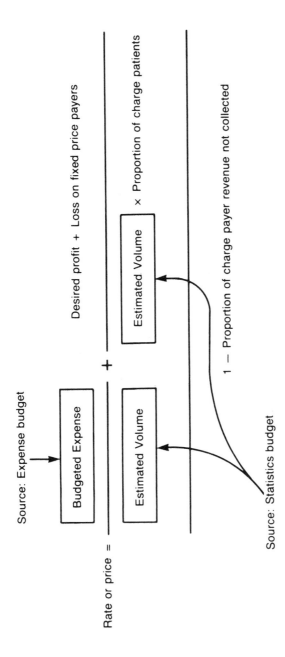

Note: The two source items indicate where values for budgeted expense and estimated volume may be found.

Figure 10–4 Rate Setting in the Revenue Budget

written off. The corresponding figure for department 2 is 33 percent. Using these data, and substituting the total or aggregate values for the percentage write-offs on charge-paying patients and the percentage of charge-paying patients, the following rates would be established:

$$\text{Department 1 price} = \frac{\dfrac{\$10,000}{100} + \dfrac{\$500}{100 \times .4}}{1 - .30} = \$160.71$$

$$\text{Department 2 price} = \frac{\dfrac{\$10,000}{100} + \dfrac{\$500}{100 \times .4}}{1 - .30} = \$160.71$$

However, proper reflection of the departmental values would show the following rates:

$$\text{Department 1 price} = \frac{\dfrac{\$10,000}{100} + \dfrac{\$500}{100 \times .2}}{1 - .2} = \$156.25$$

$$\text{Department 2 price} = \frac{\dfrac{\$10,000}{100} + \dfrac{\$500}{100 \times .6}}{1 - .33} = \$161.69$$

In the former case, the use of aggregate or average values produces an inequitable pricing structure. The price for department 1 was initially overstated, while the price for department 2 was initially understated. If equity in rate setting is an objective, reliance on average values can prevent the development of an equitable rate structure along departmental lines. In many cases, the errors may be significant.

Desired Profit Levels

Determining a desired level of profit is not easy. In many cases, it is a subjective process, made to appear objective through the application of a quantitative profit requirement. For example, desired profit may be arbitrarily set at some percentage of budgeted expenses, such as 2 percent above expenses, or as a certain percentage of total investment. However, desired levels of profit can, in general, be stated as the difference between financial requirements and expenses:

Desired profit = Budgeted financial requirements − Budgeted expenses

Budgeted financial requirements are cash requirements that an entity must meet during the budget period. Four elements usually constitute total budgeted financial requirements:

1. budgeted expenses, excluding depreciation
2. requirements for debt principal payment
3. requirements for increases in working capital
4. requirements for capital expenditures

Budgeted expenses at the departmental level should include both direct and indirect (or allocated) expenses. Depreciation charges are excluded because depreciation is a noncash requirement expense.

Debt principal payments include only the principal portion of debt service due. In some cases, additional reserve requirements may be established, which may require additional funding. Interest expense is already included in budgeted expenses and should not be included in debt principal payments.

Working capital requirements were discussed earlier. The maintenance of necessary levels of inventory, accounts receivable, and precautionary cash balances requires an investment. Changes in the total level of this investment must be funded from cash, additional indebtedness, or a combination of the two. Planned financing of increases in working capital is a legitimate financial requirement.

Capital expenditure requirements may be of two types. First, actual capital expenditures may be made for approved projects. Those projects not financed with indebtedness require a cash investment. Second, prudent fiscal management requires that funds be set aside and invested to meet reasonable requirements for future capital expenditures. This amount should be related to the replacement cost depreciation of existing fixed assets.

Any loss incurred on fixed-price payers, such as Medicare, must be added to the desired profit target. The amount of the loss would represent the projected difference between allocated costs or expenses and net revenue received from fixed-price payers. If revenues exceed costs, the difference would be subtracted from the profit target. For example, if a firm received $5,000,000 in revenue from Medicare and incurred $4,800,000 in costs to provide care to Medicare patients, the difference of $200,000 would be subtracted from the desired profit target. The result would obviously be lower required rates or prices. (Chapter 8 provides more detail on price setting.)

A logical question is, how is the desired profit requirement allocated to individual departments? Usually it is just assigned on the basis of some percentage of budgeted expenses. If a hospital budgets $5 million in expenses and determines that $500,000 profit is required, each department might set its rates to recover 10 percent above its expenses. However, the importance of cost reimbursement and bad debts at the departmental level should also be considered.

Discretionary Revenue Budget and Capital Budget

Discretionary revenue may be important, especially for institutions with large endowments. A good management control system will have a budget for expected return on endowments. Variations from the expected level would then be investigated. In some cases, changes in investment management may be necessary.

Capital budgeting can give many health care managers a major control tool. It can significantly affect the level of cost. This is especially true when not only the initial capital costs associated with given capital expenditures but also the associated operating costs for salaries and supplies are considered. (The capital budgeting process is examined in detail in Chapter 11.)

The Cash Budget and Budgeted Financial Statements

The cash budget is management's best indicator of the organization's expected short-run solvency. It translates all of the above budgets into a statement of cash inflows and outflows. The cash budget is usually broken down by periods, such as months or quarters, within the total budget period. An example of a cash budget is shown in Table 10–4.

Departmental expense budgets, departmental revenue budgets, a discretionary revenue budget, and a capital budget that do not provide a sufficient cash flow can necessitate major revisions. If the organization cannot or will not finance the deficits, changes must be made in the budgets to maintain the solvency of the organization. A poor cash budget could cause an increase in rates, a reduction in expenses, a reduction in capital expenditures, or many other changes. These changes and revisions must be made until the cash budget reflects a position of short-run solvency.

The two major financial statements that are developed on a budgetary basis are the balance sheet and the statement of revenue and expense. These two statements are indicators of both short- and long-run solvency; however, they are more important in assessing long-run solvency. Unfavorable projections in either statement might cause changes in any of the other budgets.

Table 10–4 Cash Budget, Budget Year 1994

| | 1st Quarter | | | | | |
	January	February	March	2nd Quarter	3rd Quarter	4th Quarter
Receipts from operations	$300,000	$310,000	$320,000	$1,000,000	$1,100,000	$1,100,000
Disbursements from operations	280,000	280,000	300,000	940,000	1,000,000	1,000,000
Cash available from operations	$ 20,000	$ 30,000	$ 20,000	$ 60,000	$ 100,000	$ 100,000
Other receipts						
Increase in mortgage payable				500,000		
Sale of fixed assets		20,000				
Unrestricted income—endowment			40,000	40,000	40,000	40,000
Total other receipts	0	$ 20,000	$ 40,000	$1,540,000	$1,140,000	$1,140,000
Other disbursements						
Mortgage payments			150,000	480,000	150,000	
Fixed-asset purchase				130,000	30,000	30,000
Funded depreciation			30,000			
Total other disbursements	0	0	180,000	610,000	180,000	30,000
Net cash gain (loss)	$ 20,000	$ 50,000	$(120,000)	$ (10,000)	$ (40,000)	110,000
Beginning cash balance	100,000	120,000	170,000	50,000	40,000	0
Cumulative cash	$120,000	$170,000	$ 50,000	$ 40,000	$ 0	$ 110,000
Desired level of cash	100,000	100,000	100,000	100,000	100,000	100,000
Cash above minimum needs (financing needs)	$ 20,000	$ 70,000	$ (50,000)	$ (60,000)	$(100,000)	$ 10,000

In short, the budgeted financial statements and the cash budget test the adequacy of the entire budgetary process. Budgets that result in an unfavorable financial position, as reflected by the budgeted financial statements and the cash budget, must be adjusted. Solvency is a goal that most organizations cannot sacrifice. Cash budgeting is explored in greater detail in Chapter 16.

ZERO-BASE BUDGETING

Zero-base budgeting is a term that has gained much publicity. It has been touted as management's most effective cost containment tool. It has also been described as the biggest hoax of the century. The truth lies somewhere in the middle.

Zero-base budgeting or zero-base review, as some like to call it, is a way of looking at existing programs. It is part of programming, but it focuses on existing programs instead of new programs. Zero-base budgeting assumes that no existing program is entitled to automatic approval. Many individuals have identified automatic approval with existing budgetary systems that are based on prior-year expenditure levels.

Zero-base budgeting looks at the entire budget and determines the efficacy of the entire expenditure. It thus requires a tremendous effort and investment of time. It cannot be done well on an annual basis. This is why many refer to it as zero-base review instead of zero-base budgeting. Some individuals have suggested that a zero-base review of a given activity would be appropriate every five years.

Zero-base budgeting is a process of periodically re-evaluating all programs and their associated levels of expenditures. Management decides the frequency of this re-evaluation and may vary it from every year to every five years.

Although most decision makers agree with the concept of zero-base budgeting, in practice it poses two significant questions:

1. What arithmetic should be used in zero-base budgeting?
2. Who should be involved in the actual decision-making process?

In each case, the answers are important to the success or failure of the zero-base budget program. Yet there is still not complete agreement among experts regarding the answers.

In this section, we present what we believe to be the basis of the zero-base budgeting concept in terms of the above two questions. We shall illustrate our discussion with a case example of an actual application of the concept in the data-processing department of a hospital. In this example, significant savings were realized through the application of zero-base budgeting.

Arithmetic of the Zero-Base Budgeting Process

Nearly everyone would agree that cost benefit analysis should be the arithmetic of zero-base budgeting. There are two important issues involved in the application of cost benefit analysis to zero-base budgeting programs: (1) Are the services that are presently provided being delivered in an efficient manner? (2) Are these services being delivered in an effective manner in terms of the organization's goals and objectives? A procedure for quantitatively answering these two questions involves seven sequential steps:

1. Define the outputs or services provided by the program/departmental area.
2. Determine the costs of these services or outputs.
3. Identify options for reducing the cost through changes in outputs or services.
4. Identify options for producing the services and outputs more efficiently.
5. Determine the cost savings associated with options identified in steps 3 and 4.
6. Assess the risks, both qualitative and quantitative, associated with the identified options of steps 3 and 4.
7. Select and implement those options with an acceptable cost/risk relationship.

Definition of Outputs

Table 10–5 lists outputs provided by the data processing department in our case example. Six basic functions or service areas are identified:

1. outpatient systems
2. inpatient systems
3. step-down
4. month-end
5. accounts payable
6. payroll

Table 10–5 Data Processing Outputs and Costs

	Pages	Runs Per Year	Copies	Total Pages	Weighted Pages	$.0113/pg. Direct Supply Cost	$.2894/wtd. pg. cost Labor & Mach.	Total Cost	Cost Reductions
I. Outpatient system									
A. Outpatient maintenance report	2	365	4	2,920	1,460	$ 33.00	$ 422.49	$ 455.49	($8.25)
B. Outpatient error listing for admissions	2	365	4	2,920	1,460	33.00	422.49	455.49	(8.25)
C. Outpatient initial edit summary	1	365	4	1,460	730	16.50	211.24	227.74	(4.13)
1. Admissions summary total	1	365	4	1,460	730	16.50	211.24	227.74	(4.13)
2. Initial cash edit	1								
3. Additional patients added to outpatient history		365	4	1,460	730	16.50	211.24	227.74	(4.13)
D. Daily transaction audit report (AR)—charges	11	365	4	16,060	8,030	181.48	2,323.69	2,505.17	(45.37)
E. Outpatient posting control	40	365	4	58,400	29,200	659.92	8,449.78	9,189.70	(164.95)
F. Daily revenue report	42	365	4	61,320	30,660	692.92	8,872.27	9,565.19	(9,565.19)
G. Outpatient billing balance	4	365	4	5,840	2,920	65.99	844.98	910.27	(16.50)

H.	Patients transferred to AR/history file	5	365	4	7,300	3,650	82.49	1,056.22	1,138.71	(20.62)
I.	Cash receipts and adjustments report	3	365	4	4,380	2,190	49.49	633.73	683.22	(12.37)
J.	AR transaction audit	5	365	4	7,300	3,650	82.49	1,056.22	1,138.71	(20.62)
K.	AR error listing	4	365	4	1,460	730	16.50	211.24	227.74	(4.13)
L.	Self-pay patient statement*	100	365	1	36,500	36,500	3,650.00	10,562.22	14,212.22	
M.	Revenue and usage statistics	42	365	2	30,660	30,660	346.46	8,872.27	9,218.73	
N.	General journal	3	12	2	72	72	81	20.84	21.65	
O.	Outpatient edit report	5	12	2	120	120	1.36	34.73	36.09	
P.	Outpatient activity trial balance	2,500	12	2	60,000	60,000	678.00	17,362.56	18,040.56	
Q.	Outpatient alpha listing (telephone)	800	52	4	166,400	83,200	1,880.32	24,076.08	25,906.00	(25,956.40)
R.	Outpatient alpha listing (balance)	800	52	4	166,400	83,200	1,880.32	24,076.08	25,956.40	(25,956.40)
II.	Inpatient system									
A.	Final census report	27	365	4	39,420	19,710	$ 445.45	$ 5,703.60	$ 6,149.05	($222.75)
B.	Volunteer alpha listing	6	365	3	6,570	4,380	74.24	1,267.47	1,341.71	
C.	Alphabetic census	6	365	6	13,140	4,380	148.48	1,267.47	1,415.95	
D.	Financial class census report	10	365	2	7,300	7,300	82.49	2,112.44	2,194.93	(2,194.93)
E.	Utilization census	6	365	4	8,760	4,380	98.99	1,267.47	1,366.46	(50.00)
F.	Social services census	10	365	1	3,650	7,300	41.25	2,112.44	2,153.69	

continues

Table 10–5 continued

		Runs Per Year	Copies	Total Pages	Weighted Pages	$.0113/pg. Direct Supply Cost	$.2894/wtd. pg. cost Labor & Mach.	Total Cost	Cost Reductions
		Pages							
G.	Statistical census reports	2	365	3	2,190	1,460	24.75	422.49	447.24	(447.24)
H.	Clergy listing	15	365	1	5,475	10,950	61.87	3,168.69	3,230.54	
I.	Admission, discharge, and transfer report	4	365	8	11,680	2,920	131.98	844.98	976.96	
J.	Pap smear admissions control report	1	365	2	730	730	8.25	211.24	219.49	
K.	Census by HICDA code	7	365	2	5,110	5,110	57.74	1,478.71	1,536.45	
L.	Daily charge transaction error listing	5	365	1	1,825	3,650	20.62	1,056.22	1,076.84	
M.	Daily transaction	44	365	1	16,060	32,120	181.48	9,294.76	9,476.24	
N.	Daily dialysis report	1	365	2	730	730	8.25	211.24	219.49	
O.	Inpatient billing balance	8	365	2	5,840	5,840	65.99	1,689.96	1,755.95	
P.	Outpatient billing balance—dialysis	2	365	2	1,460	1,460	16.50	422.49	438.99	
Q.	Summary patient statement*	50	365	2	36,500	36,500	1,825.00	10,562.22	12,387.22	
R.	Detail patient statement*	50	365	2	36,500	36,500	1,825.00	10,562.22	12,387.22	
S.	Noncovered charges	10	365	1	3,650	7,300	41.25	2,112.44	2,153.69	
T.	New accounts receivable report	3	365	2	2,190	2,190	24.75	633.73	658.48	

U.	Cash receipts and adjustments	10	365	3	10,950	7,300	123.74	2,112.44	2,236.18
V.	AR transaction audit	10	365	2	7,300	7,300	82.49	2,112.44	2,194.93
W.	Daily error listing	3	365	2	2,190	2,190	24.75	633.73	658.48
X.	Schedule of preadmission	3	365	2	2,190	2,190	24.75	633.73	658.48
Y.	Medicaid review census	2	365	2	1,460	1,460	16.50	422.49	438.99
III.	Step-down								
A.	Step-down cost center description table	2	12	2	48	48			
B.	Step-down allocations master file	2	12	2	48	48	$ .54	$ 13.89	$ 14.93
C.	Step-down direct expense edit	2	12	2	48	48	.54	13.89	14.43
D.	Step-down cost allocation statistics file	2	12	2	48	48	.54	13.89	14.93
E.	Step-down cost allocation—periodic	2	12	2	48	48	.54	13.89	14.93
IV.	Month-end								
A.	Cumulative monthly statistical census	1	12	2	24	24	.27	6.95	7.22
B.	Monthly statistical census by day	1	12	2	24	24	.27	6.95	7.22

continues

Table 10–5 continued

	Pages	Runs Per Year	Copies	Total Pages	Weighted Pages	$.0113/pg. Direct Supply Cost	$.2894/wtd. pg. cost Labor & Mach.	Total Cost	Cost Reductions
C. Infection control report	1	12	2	24	24	.27	6.95	7.22	
D. Reimbursement summary	1	12	2	24	24	.27	6.95	7.22	
E. Revenue and usage statistics	65	12	2	1,560	1,560	17.63	451.43	469.06	
F. Aged accounts receivable summary	1	12	2	24	24	.27	6.95	7.22	
G. Detail trial balance	105	12	2	2,520	2,520	28.48	729.22	757.70	
H. In-house 21 days billing	25	12	2	600	600	6.78	173.63	180.41	
I. Dialysis billing	89	12	2	2,136	2,136	24.14	618.11	642.25	
J. Zero-balance roster	742	12	4	35,616	17,808	402.46	5,153.21	5,555.67	($5,555.67)
K. Bad-debt report	35	12	2	840	840	9.49	243.08	252.57	
L. General journal	5	12	2	120	120	1.36	34.73	36.09	
V. Accounts payable (AP) system									
A. Vendor master maintenance report	2	156	2	624	624	7.05	180.57	187.62	
B. AP initial edit listing	1	156	2	312	312	3.53	90.29	93.82	
C. AP batch proof	1	156	2	312	312	3.53	90.29	93.82	
D. Cash requirements report	50	12	2	1,200	1,200	13.56	347.25	360.81	

E.	AP monthly reconciliation	30	12	2	720	720	8.14	208.35	216.49	
F.	AP distribution	23	12	2	552	552	6.24	159.74	165.98	
G.	AP trial balance	50	12	2	1,200	1,200	13.56	347.25	360.81	
H.	Vendor master listing	2	12	2	48	48	.54	13.89	14.43	
VI.	Payroll									
A.	Payroll edit summary									
	1. Payroll update controls	1	104	2	208	208	$ 2.35	$ 60.19	$ 62.54	
	2. Payroll master file maintenance	10	104	2	2,080	2,080	23.50	601.90	625.40	
B.	Time card edit report	60	52	4	12,480	6,240	141.02	1,805.71	1,946.73	
C.	Check register	58	52	2	6,032	6,032	68.16	1,745.52	1,813.68	
D.	Department benefits statement	60	52	4	12,480	6,240	141.02	1,805.71	1,946.73	
E.	Labor analysis report	42	52	2	4,368	4,368	49.36	1,263.99	1,313.35	
F.	Payroll journal report	10	12	1	120	240	1.36	69.45	70.81	
G.	Quarterly 941 report	27	4	2	216	216	2.44	62.51	64.95	
H.	W-2 forms	1,091	1	1	1,091	2,182	12.33	631.42	643.75	
I.	Time cards*	1,091	52	1	56,732	56,732	4,252.50	16,416.88	20,669.38	($10,334.69)
J.	Standard payroll checks*	1,091	52	1	56,732	56,732	3,373.65	16,416.88	19,710.53	(9,855.26)

continues

Table 10–5 continued

	Pages	Runs Per Year	Copies	Total Pages	Weighted Pages	$.0113/pg. Direct Supply Cost	$.2894/wtd. pg. cost Labor & Mach.	Total Cost	Cost Reductions
K. Miscellaneous reports									
1. Employee longevity report	10	12	2	240	240	2.70	69.45	72.15	
2. YTD earnings report	1,091	4	2	8,728	8,728	98.68	2,525.67	2,524.29	
3. Union dues paid	8	12	2	192	192	2.17	55.56	57.73	
4. Estimated yearly budget report by status and by grade	60	1	1	60	120	68	34.73	35.41	
5. Sick hour control report (not done)									
6. Prepaid checks	20	104	1	2,080	2,080	138.76	601.90	740.66	
7. LPN listing	2	2	2	8	8	.09	2.31	2.40	
8. Employee address labels (30/pg)	30	2	1	60	60	.68	17.17	17.85	
9. Century club membership labels* (not done)									
				1,077,855	788,900	$24,702.00	$225,367.00	$250,069.00	($90,138.00)

*Items for which supplies were directly costed.
Total pages for these items were 225,044, and the total direct supply cost was $15,065.

Determining the specific outputs of each of these areas, as shown in Table 10−5, is, in general, a useful procedure. And determining the basic factors involved in the establishment and maintenance of each department and program is a good first step in defining specific outputs.

Determination of Costs

The concept of cost that is most relevant in zero-base budgeting is avoidable cost. An attempt is made to discover what the costs of a department's services are now and what cost would be incurred if those services were discontinued. In this context, the direct cost of the department is most useful. Indirect cost in most situations should be ignored because it is unavoidable. In our data processing case example, the three direct cost components are supply cost, labor and machine cost, and other. Of these three, only labor cost, and machine and supply cost can be avoided, given a reduction in services.

The average supply cost per page was derived by dividing total supply cost, less supply cost that could be traced to a specific report, by the total number of pages, less pages associated with reports for which supply cost could be directly traced:

$$\text{Supply cost/Page} = \frac{\$24,702 - \$15,065}{1,077,885 - 225,044} = \$.0113$$

The six reports for which supply cost was directly traceable are

		System
1.	self-pay patient statement	I-L
2.	summary patient statement	II-Q
3.	detail patient statement	II-R
4.	time cards	VI-I
5.	standard payroll checks	VI-J
6.	prepaid checks	VI-K(1)

Labor and machine cost is divided by weighted pages to determine cost per weighted page. Weighted pages is an index that reflects the fact that little or no additional labor and machine cost is incurred for multiple copies of reports. The index uses a base report of two copies to provide the conversion. Thus, a four-copy report consisting of three pages would require twelve total pages, but it would be stated as a six-page report when expressed in weighted pages. In certain situations, the index is modified to reflect a more realistic assessment of cost variation. In our data processing department, the labor and machine cost per weighted page was

$$\text{Labor and machine cost/Weighted page} = \frac{\$225,367}{778,900} = \$.2894$$

Options for Modifying Output

Table 10–6 identifies 11 options for modifying the output of the data processing department. Typical output changes could occur through elimination of the service, reduction in the frequency of the service, reduction in the quality of service, or reduction in the amount of service. All of these types of changes, except reduction in quality, occurred in the data processing case example.

Options for Producing Services More Efficiently

Only after some determination of the need for services is made can efficiency be seriously examined. In our case example, there are no efficiency options identified. Yet the identification of improved ways to

Table 10–6 Options for Reducing Output in a Data Processing Department

Option	Risk	Savings
1. Reduce outpatient report copies I-A–K from four copies to three copies per day.	Small	$ 314.48
2. Change usage demand on outpatient report I-F from daily to monthly.	Small	9,251.02
3. Eliminate two copies of inpatient report II-A—final census.	Small	222.75
4. Discontinue inpatient report II-D— financial class census.	Small	2,194.93
5. Eliminate two copies of inpatient report I-E—utilization census.	Small	50.00
6. Eliminate outpatient report I-Q—alpha listing with telephone number.	Small	25,956.40
7. Eliminate outpatient report I-R—alpha listing with balance.	Small	25,956.40
8. Eliminate inpatient report II-G— statistical census.	Small	447.24
9. Eliminate zero-balance roster report— month-end, Report IV-J.	Small	5,555.67
10. Pay biweekly rather than weekly; cut preparation and usage of time cards by 50%.	Medium	10,334.69
11. Pay biweekly rather than weekly; reduce paycheck preparation and usage by 50%.	Medium	9,855.26
Total estimated savings		$90,138.84

provide services is an important activity in efforts to minimize costs. In a complete zero-base review, efficiency should be considered.

Determination of Cost Savings

Table 10–6 also identifies the cost savings associated with the options for modifying the output of the data processing department. Avoidable cost is the cost concept that is used. The savings are limited to just supply costs when a report is not discontinued but only the number of copies is changed. When a report is discontinued or its frequency is reduced, then labor and machine costs are also reflected in the savings to be realized. Some may question whether significant labor and machine savings could be realized in changes this small. Since many costs of this type are step or semifixed, the actual incremental cost associated with a very slight reduction in volume may indeed be negligible. Still, in reviews of this type, where significant changes in work effort are envisioned, the average cost estimate may be a reasonable expectation of savings. In this example, total cost savings from the identified 11 options is projected to be approximately $90,000.

Risk Assessment

Risk is a function of two factors: the probability of an adverse consequence and the potential severity of that consequence. In most situations, both these factors are highly subjective. Nevertheless, some idea of risk, even subjectively determined, is necessary in the overall assessment of the option's desirability.

Management Decision Making

After concluding the above analysis, someone needs to make decisions concerning the specific options to be selected. This responsibility falls to those in the management structure who are involved in the zero-base review.

In general, with regard to management's participation in the decision-making process of a zero-base budgeting program, three major aspects must be considered:

1. In the case of general service or indirect departments, panels of managers from the using departments should be involved in identifying options for changes in outputs. These individuals have an obvious interest in and a need to know the changes that are likely to be made. In addition, their assessment of risk is important.
2. Individuals from the specific program area under evaluation should also be involved in the zero-base review. Their involvement is essential for two reasons: (1) In many cases, the best ideas for changes in

output or methods of production will come from those who are intimately involved in the delivery of the product. (2) Participation of these individuals in the review process will help ensure cooperation in any decisions that are made.

3. Final decisions on options should be made by top management because it has a total perspective of the organization. Placing responsibility in lower level management may create problems of suboptimization.

SUMMARY

This chapter has focused specifically on budgeting and management control as practiced at the institutional or organizational level. The basic unit in management control is usually a department. However, the application of the principles of management control can be much broader. The control unit may be an entire hospital or region, and the controller may be a health system agency or a rate-setting organization. Even on this broad scale, the general principles of management control and budgeting discussed in this chapter are applicable.

ASSIGNMENTS

1. Under what conditions is a flexible budget likely to be more effective than a forecast budget?

2. Can an organization be efficient but not effective? Discuss the circumstances in which this could be true.

3. The first step in the budgeting process is to develop the statistics budget. Why is this true?

4. Ann Walker, CPA, is the controller for your hospital. For a long time, Ms. Walker has been concerned about management control in the hospital, and she has finally developed a new departmental labor control system. It is based on the following data for the obstetrics nursing unit:

Period	Patient Days	Hours Worked	Rate	Total Cost
1	350	1,550	$13.50	$20,925
2	400	1,700	13.80	23,460
3	300	1,400	13.20	18,480
4	375	1,625	13.80	22,425
5	450	1,850	13.80	25,530
Total	1,875	8,125		$110,820

Average rate = $13.64 = $110,820/8,125
Average hours/Patient day = 4.33 = 8,125/1,875

Using these data, Ms. Walker developed a two-factor variance model for labor costs in the obstetrics department. In period 1, the variances in this model would be as follows:

Labor rate variance = ($13.50 − $13.64) × 1,550 = $217.00 (Favorable)

Labor usage variance = (1,550 − 1,515.5) × $13.64 = $470.58 (Unfavorable)

A similar model for labor control has been adopted in all other departments. As the chief executive officer of the hospital, are you satisfied with this labor control system? What suggestions for revisions would you make?

5. Floyd Farley is the maintenance department head. His department is participating in a wage incentive program in which he and his staff receive 20 percent of the department's income as supplemental income. Net income is defined as $12 times maintenance man-hours charged, less direct departmental expense. Do you see any problems with this system? If so, how might they be solved?

6. You have been asked to prepare a flexible budget for a 40-bed nursing unit. A schedule of staffing requirements by occupancy is presented below:

	Below 60% Occupancy	60–80% Occupancy	80–100% Occupancy
First shift			
Head nurse	1	1	1
Registered nurse	1	1	2
Licensed practical nurse	1	1	1
Aides	1	2	2
Second shift			
Registered nurse	2	2	2
Licensed practical nurse	1	1	1
Aides	2	3	3
Third shift			
Registered nurse	1	1	1
Licensed practical nurse	1	1	1
Aides	0	1	2

Daily personnel costs by job title and shift

Head nurse	$70
Registered nurse—first shift	54
Second and third shifts	62
Licensed practical nurse—first shift	34
Second and third shifts	40
Aides—first shift	28
Second and third shifts	30

Prepare a budget for management that shows expected personnel costs for this nursing unit by occupancy level.

7. You must establish a pricing schedule for laboratory procedures. From a total hospital perspective, management has decided that the hospital must earn 5 percent above costs. The hospital has established that it loses 10 percent on each fixed-price payer (Medicare or Medicaid). That is, for every $100 of cost incurred to treat a fixed-price payer, the hospital receives only $90 in payment. You must build both the required profit and the expected loss on fixed-price payers into your rate structure. Payer mix for the laboratory is expected to be as follows:

| | Budgeted RVUs | | |
	Inpatient	Outpatient	Total
Medicare	200,000	50,000	250,000
Medicaid	40,000	10,000	50,000
Blue Cross	80,000	20,000	100,000
Commercial insurance and HMOs	60,000	10,000	70,000
Bad debt and charity	15,000	15,000	30,000
Total RVUs	395,000	105,000	500,000

Medicare pays on a fixed price per DRG for all inpatients. There is thus no separate payment for laboratory tests. Medicaid pays average costs for both inpatient and outpatient tests. Medicare also pays average costs for outpatient tests. Blue Cross pays 95 percent of charges for both inpatient and outpatient procedures. All other commercial insurance and HMO patients pay 100 percent of charges. If budgeted expenses are $1,000,000 ($2.00 per RVU), what price must be set to meet management's profit expectations?

8. How would you calculate the amount of revenue to be realized as cash from patient sources in a fiscal period?

9. What is the major conceptual difference between zero-base budgeting and conventional budgeting?

10. In a hospital operation, what key variables are important in projecting volume at departmental levels?

SOLUTIONS AND ANSWERS

1. Two conditions are necessary for a flexible budget to be more useful than a forecast budget: First, there must be some indication that costs are variable, at least in part. Second, there must be some variability in activity levels, that is, volume is not expected to be constant in each period.

2. Efficiency relates to the costs per unit of output produced. Effectiveness relates to the attainment of organizational objectives given its outputs. It is quite possible for a firm to be efficient but not effective. For example, a hospital might provide inpatient care at an extremely low cost. However, this might not be effective if the provision of the inpatient care is accomplished at rates that threaten the hospital's goal of financial solvency.

3. Figure 10-3 indicates that the statistics budget provides input for the development of the expense budget and the revenue budget. Projection of both expenses and revenues is a function of expected volume and variability of volume over the budget period. In cases where volume is expected to vary significantly, management may try to make more of their costs variable to maximize their ability to control costs, given volume changes. For

example, more variable staffing may be used through the use of part-time employees, nursing pools, or overtime.

4. The primary weakness of Ms. Walker's model is its failure to incorporate fixed labor requirements. A flexible budgeting system should be put into effect instead. Using a high-low method, the following budget parameters for hours required can be estimated:

$$\text{Variable hours} = \frac{1,850 - 1,400}{450 - 300} = 3.0 \text{ hours per patient day}$$

Fixed hours per period $= 1,850 - 3.0 \times 450 = 500$ hours per period

The deviation in hours worked per period is removed when the fixed labor requirement is recognized:

Period	Actual Hours	Budgeted Hours (500 + 3.0 × PD)	Difference
1	1,550	1,550	0
2	1,700	1,700	0
3	1,400	1,400	0
4	1,625	1,625	0
5	1,850	1,850	0

5. Mr. Farley has an incentive to engage his staff in what might be needless maintenance. This could be controlled by setting limits on the absolute level of incentive payment that could be earned, for example, by basing the incentive payments on the difference between actual and budgeted costs or by establishing control systems for authorizing maintenance work.

6. The following budget could be developed to show daily standard personnel costs by occupancy level for the nursing unit:

	Occupancy		
	Below 60%	*60–80%*	*80–100%*
First shift			
Head nurse	$ 70	$ 70	$ 70
Registered nurse	54	54	108
Licensed practical nurse	34	34	34
Aides	28	56	56
Second shift			
Registered nurse	124	124	124
Licensed practical nurse	40	40	40
Aides	60	90	90
Third shift			
Registered nurse	62	62	62
Licensed practical nurse	40	40	40
Aides	0	30	60
Total Standard Personnel Costs	$512	$600	$684

7. Using the formula in Figure 10–4, the following rate structure can be established to meet management's profit expectations:

$$\text{Price} = \frac{\dfrac{\$1{,}000{,}000}{500{,}000} + \dfrac{(\$50{,}000 + \$40{,}000)}{500{,}000 \times .40}}{1 - .175} = \$2.9697$$

Desired profit = .05 × $1,000,000 = $50,000

Loss on fixed-price payers = .4 × $1,000,000 × .10 = $40,000

Proportion of charge payers = (100,000 + 70,000 + 30,000)/500,000 = .40

$$\text{Proportion of charge payers for which revenue is not collected} = \frac{30{,}000 + .05 \times 100{,}000}{100{,}000 + 70{,}000 + 30{,}000} = .175$$

Medicare inpatient (.4 × $1,000,000 × .9)	$ 360,000
Medicare outpatient (.1 × $1,000,000)	100,000
Medicaid (.1 × $1,000,000)	100,000
Blue Cross (100,000 × $2.9697 × .95)	282,121
Commercial insurance and HMO (70,000 × $2.9697)	207,879
Bad debt and charity	0
Total revenue	$1,050,000
Less expenses	1,000,000
Budget profit	$ 50,000

8. Cash realized from patient sources could be expressed as follows:

Cash flow = Net patient revenue + Beginning patient accounts receivable
         − Ending patient account receivables

9. Zero-base budgeting starts from a zero base. That is, all expenditures must be justified in the budgeting review. Conventional budgeting looks primarily at expenditures that are above prior levels.

10. The volume of actual cases treated (discharges or admissions) and outpatient activity are the key variables that affect departmental volumes. For example, laboratory tests are usually related to discharges and outpatient visits. Patient days are derived from discharges by assuming an average length of stay. Refinements in forecasting can be achieved by projecting case mix. Finally, more or fewer ancillary services per discharge may be required, depending on the type of case.

Chapter 11

Cost Variance Analysis

Cost variance analysis is of great potential importance to the health care industry. Successful utilization of cost variance analysis requires the existence of a sound system of standard setting, or budgeting, and a related system of cost accounting. Perhaps the major factor impeding the widespread adoption of more effective cost variance analysis in the health care industry has been the lack of interaction between it and our systems of cost accounting.

Cost accounting systems usually serve two basic informational needs. First, they supply data essential for product/service costing. Second, they provide information for managerial cost control activity. This second role is the major topic of this chapter.

COST CONTROL

The following conceptual model is used to discuss the major alternatives to cost control in organizations:

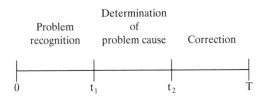

315

In general, there are three distinct time phases in an out-of-control situation:

1. recognition of problem (0 to t_1)
2. determination of problem cause (t_1 to t_2)
3. correction of problem (t_2 to T)

The unit of time used in the above representation may be minutes, hours, days, weeks, or even months. The important point is that, the longer the problem remains uncorrected (0 to T), the greater the cost to the organization.

The term *efficiency cost* is sometimes used to describe the total cost incurred by an organization as a result of an out-of-control situation. Efficiency cost may be represented as follows:

$$\text{Efficiency cost} = T \times R \times P$$

where

T = total time units that the problem remains uncorrected
R = loss or cost per time unit
P = probability that the problem occurrence is correctable

The objective of management should be to minimize the efficiency cost in any given situation. In the accomplishment of this objective, two major alternatives are available to management: (1) the preventive approach and (2) the detection-correction (DC) approach.

In the preventive approach, management attempts to minimize the efficiency cost by minimizing the probability that a problem will occur (P). One of the major methods for reducing the value of P centers on staffing. Management attempts not only to hire the most competent individuals available but also to provide them with relevant training programs and materials to ensure consistently high levels of performance. The nature of the reward structure, both monetary and nonmonetary, also enters into this management strategy. The preventive approach is obviously employed by most organizations, but the emphasis on it is usually greater in small organizations. In these organizations, the control span is usually smaller and the evaluation of individual performance is more direct.

The DC approach seeks to minimize efficiency cost by minimizing the time that a problem remains uncorrected (T). This method is directly related to the effectiveness of variance analysis. Effective variance analysis should result in a reduction of both the recognition of problem phase (0 to t_1) and the determination of cause phase (t_1 to t_2). The actual correction phase (t_2 to T) rests primarily on the effective motivation of management.

The development of cost variance analysis systems to reduce the recognition and determination phases usually involves the expenditure of funds. Prudent management dictates that the marginal expenditures of funds for system improvements be evaluated by their expected reductions in efficiency cost. For example, the frequency of reporting could be altered to reduce the problem recognition phase, or the number of cost areas reported could be increased to improve both recognition and determination times. However, these improvements are likely to result in increased cost and may not be justified. Areas of relatively small dollar expenditure or largely uncontrolled costs thus are not prime candidates for major system improvements.

INVESTIGATION OF VARIANCES

In the DC approach to cost control, cost variances are the clues that both signal that a potential problem exists and suggest a possible cause. These variances are usually an integral part of any management-by-exception plan of operations. A decision to investigate a given variance is not an automatic occurrence. It involves some financial commitment by the organization and thus should be weighed carefully against the expected benefits. Unfortunately, management rarely knows whether any given variance is due to a random or noncontrollable cause or to an underlying problem that is correctable or controllable.

Many organizations have developed rules by which to determine what variances will be investigated. Common examples of such rules are to investigate

- all variances that exceed an absolute dollar size (for example, $500)
- all variances that exceed budgeted or standard values by some fixed percentage (for example, 10 percent)
- all variances that have been unfavorable for a defined number of periods (for example, three periods)
- some combination of the above

Actual specification of criteria values in the above rules is highly dependent on management judgment and experience. A variance of $1,000 may be considered normal in some circumstances and abnormal in others.

At some point, management may wish to determine whether the historical criteria values should be changed. In that case, some method of testing whether the historical values are acceptable or not acceptable must be developed. In general, there are two possible theories that may be used to develop this information, (1) classical statistical theory and (2) decision theory.

Classical Statistical Theory

One of the most commonly employed means to determine which cost variances to investigate is the control chart. The control chart is often used to monitor a physical process by comparing output observations with predetermined tolerance limits. If actual observations fall between predetermined upper and lower control limits on the chart, the process is assumed to be in control.

Control charts can be established for determining when a cost variance should be investigated. The major assumption underlying the traditional development of control charts is that observed cost variances are distributed in accordance with a normal probability distribution. In a normal distribution, it can be anticipated that approximately 68.3 percent of the observations will fall within one standard deviation (σ) of the mean $(\bar{x})$, 95.5 percent will fall within two standard deviations $(\bar{x} \pm 2\sigma)$, and 99.7 percent will fall within three standard deviations $(\bar{x} \pm 3\sigma)$.

The control limits for any given variance will then be set at

$$\bar{x} \pm K\sigma$$

If the costs of investigation are high relative to the benefits in a given situation, then K may be set to a high value (for example, 3.0). This will ensure that few investigations will be made and that some out-of-control situations may continue. Conversely, if benefits are high relative to the costs of investigation, then lower values of K may be selected that will ensure that more investigations will be performed and that some individuals in out-of-control situations will be investigated.

To develop the control chart, the underlying distribution must be specified. An assumption that the distribution is normal means that the analyst must define both the mean ($\bar{x}$) and the standard deviation (σ). In most situations, this specification will result from an analysis of prior observations. To illustrate this process, assume that the following pattern of labor variances occurred during the 13 biweekly pay periods:

Pay Period	Variances (x_i)
1	800
2	400
3	− 500
4	− 100
5	200
6	− 700
7	500
8	− 300
9	− 200
10	300
11	200
12	− 200
13	− 400
	0

The mean ($\bar{x}$) of these observations is calculated as follows:

$$\bar{x} = \frac{\Sigma x_i}{n} = \frac{0}{13} = 0$$

An estimate of the standard deviation (s) is calculated as follows:

$$s = \sqrt{\frac{\Sigma(x_i - \bar{x})^2}{n - 1}} = \$437.80$$

If the labor cost variances in this example are expected to follow a normal distribution in the future with $\bar{x} = 0$ and $\sigma = \$437.80$, control limits for investigation at the 95 percent level could be defined by multiplying the estimated standard deviation by 2. The following control chart would result:

$\bar{x} + 2\sigma = 875.60$

$\bar{x} = 0$

$\bar{x} - 2\sigma = -875.60$

Any observation falling within the control limits would not be investigated, whereas variances falling outside the established limits would be investigated.

The major deficiency in the classical statistical approach is that it does not relate the expected costs of investigation and benefits with the probability that the variance signals are out of control. The control chart can signal when a situation is likely to be out of control, but it cannot directly evaluate whether an investigation is warranted.

Decision Theory

Decision theory provides a framework for directly integrating the probability of the system's being out of control and the costs and benefits of investigation into a definite decision rule. Central to this approach is the payoff table, which specifically considers costs and benefits. An example of a payoff table is presented below:

	State	
Action	In Control	Out of Control
Investigate	I	I + C
Do not investigate	O	L

where

I = cost of investigation
C = cost of correcting an out-of-control situation
L = cost of letting an out-of-control situation continue
      (expected loss)

The payoff table is a conceptualization of the actual decision evaluation process. It can be applied in any cost variance situation. The objective is to minimize the actual cost for a given situation. To accomplish this, estimates of the probabilities for the two states, in control and out-of-control, are required.

Assume that P denotes the probability that the system is in control and that $(1 - P)$ represents the probability that the system is out of control.

The expected cost of the two courses of action can be defined as follows:

Expected cost of investigating	$= (P \times I) + (1 - P)(I + C)$
	$= I + (1 - P)C$
Expected cost of not investigating	$= (P \times O) + (1 - P)L = (1 - P)L$

By setting the two expected costs equal to each other, we can determine the value of P to which the decision maker is indifferent. This break-even probability would be calculated as follows:

$$P^* = 1 - \frac{I}{L - C}$$

Evaluation of this formula provides a nice summarization of earlier comments concerning the costs and benefits of investigating variances. In situations of high investigation costs (I) and low net benefits (L − C), the critical value of P (P*) becomes quite low. This, of course, means that, in order to justify an investigation, the probability that the system is actually in control (P) must be very low, or, alternatively, the probability that the system is actually out of control (1 − P) must be quite large.

To employ the decision theory model just described, the analyst must have estimates of I, C, L, and P. In most situations, there is a reasonable expectation that I and C will be relatively constant. These costs are usually directly related to the labor involved in the analysis. L, however, usually varies, depending on the size of the cost variance. In short, the loss depends on the proportion of the variance to be saved in future periods and the number of periods over which the loss is expected to occur if the situation is not corrected.

The value of P is in many respects the most difficult of the parameter values to specify. Either objective or subjective approaches may be used. An objective method may be used to develop an estimated probability distribution for the system. If the underlying distribution is assumed to be normal, estimating the mean and standard deviation from prior observations will enable the analyst to specify the distribution from this estimated distribution. The probability that any given system is under control (P) can then be defined.

Subjective estimates of P are possible on both an a priori basis and an ex post facto basis. A subjective normalized distribution of variances can be built in advance as a basis for the estimate. The analyst might ask department managers between which two values they would expect 50 percent of actual observations to fall. If the budget cost for labor in a department is $4,000 per pay period, the department manager might specify that 50 percent of the time the manager would expect actual observations to fall between $3,700 and $4,300. Using this information, a normalized distribution could be defined as follows:

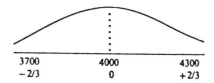

| 3700 | 4000 | 4300 |
| -2/3 | 0 | +2/3 |

Subjective estimates of P may also be made after the fact and then related directly to the actual size of the cost variance. This assessment can then be related to a table of critical values of P necessary for an investigation decision of a given variance. This permits analysts to employ directly sensitivity analysis in their decisions. For example, assume that I is $100 and that C is $200. Assume further that L is equal to two times the absolute size of the variance. The following table of critical values of P could then be defined:

Critical Value of P(P*)	Size of Variance
0.50	$200
0.75	300
0.83	400
0.88	500
0.90	600

This table is relatively straightforward. As the dollar size of the variance increases, the probability that the system is under control must increase to justify a "do not investigate" decision. For example, if a $600 variance occurred, the analyst must believe that there is at least a 90 percent probability that the system is under control.

VARIANCE ANALYSIS CALCULATIONS

Variance analysis is simply an examination of the deviation of an actual observation from a standard. For the purposes of this chapter, two types of standards for comparative purposes are used, (1) prior-period values and (2) departmental values. In each case, the objective of cost variance analysis is to explain why actual costs are different, either from budgeted values or from prior-period actual values. This objective is a very important element in the cost control process in the organization.

Prior-Period Comparisons

Relevant Factors

An evaluation of the difference between current levels of cost and prior costs should suggest to management which factors have contributed to the change. In general, three major factors influence costs: (1) input prices, (2) productivity of inputs, and (3) output levels.

Input prices usually may be expected to increase over time. It is important, however, from management's perspective to evaluate what portion, if any, of that increase was controllable or avoidable. Rapidly increasing prices for some commodities may signal opportunities for resource substitutions, for example, by switching to a less expensive mix of labor or substituting one supply item for another. Measuring productivity has in fact become increasingly important in the health care industry as a result of the emphasis on cost containment. One of the major difficulties in evaluating productivity, however, has been the changing nature of health care services. Comparison of productivity within a hospital for two time periods requires that the services in each period be identical. For example, a comparison of full-time equivalents (FTEs) per patient day in 1993 with FTEs per patient day of care in 1990 is meaningless unless a patient day of care in 1993 is identical to a patient day of care in 1990. Finally, changes in output levels also influence the level of costs. This influence may occur in two ways. First, the absolute level of output provided may affect the quantity of resources necessary to produce the output level. Second, service intensity may affect resource requirements. Any increase in the number of services required per unit of output will directly affect costs. For example, a change in the number of laboratory procedures performed per patient day of care will probably affect the total cost per patient day of care.

This discussion can be summarized in the following cost function:

$$\text{Total cost} = P \times \frac{I}{X} \times \frac{X}{Q} \times Q$$

where:

$$P = \text{input prices}$$
$$I = \text{physical quantities of inputs}$$
$$X = \text{services required per unit of output}$$
$$Q = \text{output level}$$

In the above cost equation, P represents the effect of input prices, I/X represents the effect of productivity, X/Q represents the effect of service intensity, and Q represents the influence of output. Changes in cost can result from changes in any one of these four terms.

Macroanalysis

There are many occasions when it is important to discover and communicate the causes for cost increases at the organizationwide level, whether that organization is a hospital, nursing home, or surgicenter. For example, your board may want to know why your total costs have jumped 60 percent in the last three years. A very useful framework can be developed to provide answers to questions such as this, provided that some critical pieces of information can be defined.

- There must be one measure of activity or output for the entire organization. This might be an adjusted discharge, patient day, visit, or other measure.
- It must be possible to define a measure of activity for each department within the organization and to define a cost per unit for that measure. It may not be necessary to define an output unit for indirect departments—those departments that do not directly provide a product or service to the patient—provided that the costs of the indirect departments have been allocated to the direct departments.

We will now develop a model and example for a hospital to illustrate the use of this macroanalysis. First, we will assume that our measure of activity is an adjusted discharge. The term *adjusted* simply reflects that outpatient activity has been recognized. This recognition may have come about through a simple ratio of inpatient revenue to total patient revenue at the organizationwide level or at the individual departmental level.

The general cost per discharge (CPD) can be defined in the following equation:

$$CPD^t = C^t \times Q^t$$

where:

C^t = Cost (direct and indirect) per unit of output in each department
Q^t = Units of output in each department required per adjusted discharge

The following example is now presented to help clarify the concepts presented above. The data set below represent cost and volume information for the year 1993. These data are compared with cost and volume data two years ago, in 1991.

1993 Cost Summary
11,600 Discharges

Department	Volume	Cost (000s)	Cost/ Unit (C^t)	Units/ Discharge (X^t)
Intensive care unit	5,600	$ 4,000	$714.29	.4828
Routine nursing	71,400	22,000	308.12	6.1552
Operating room	20,000	10,000	500.00	1.7241
Laboratory	70,000	6,000	85.71	6.0345
Radiology	28,000	8,000	285.71	2.4138
		$50,000		

CPD = $50,000,000/11,600 = $4,310.34

1991 Cost Summary
12,000 Discharges

Department	Volume	Cost (000s)	Cost/ Unit (C^t)	Units/ Discharge (X^t)
Intensive care unit	4,800	$ 2,700	$562.50	.4000
Routine nursing	79,200	20,000	252.52	6.6000
Operating room	18,000	8,500	472.22	1.5000
Laboratory	60,00	4,500	75.00	5.0000
Radiology	24,000	3,600	150.00	2.0000
		$39,300		

CPD = $39,300,000/12,000 = $3,275.00

In this example the CPD increased 31.6 percent from 1991 to 1993. Causes for the increase could be partitioned into two possible areas:

1. *Intensity of service*—More units of intermediate services are required per discharge, such as laboratory tests and days in intensive care unit.
2. *Cost*—Cost increases could have resulted from higher prices paid for inputs such as wages and salaries, changes in the nature of the service

provided (such as a change in the proportion of routine chest x-rays to computed tomography scans), or a change in efficiency of production.

Two indices can be defined that capture the impact of each of these two areas:

$$\frac{CDP^t}{CPD^o} = \frac{C^t X^t}{C^o X^o} = HCI \times HII$$

The hospital cost index (HCI) is defined as

$$HCI = \frac{C^t X^o}{C^o X^o}$$

The HCI measures the change in cost attributed to both price increases and productivity changes. The other index, the hospital intensity index (HII) is defined as:

$$HII = \frac{C^o X^t}{C^o X^o}$$

The HII measures the change in cost due to changes in service intensity.

Using this framework in our example data would yield the following values:

$$HCI = \frac{\begin{array}{c}(\$714.29 \times .4000) + (\$308.12 \times 6.6000) + (\$500.00 \times 1.5000) \\ (\$85.71 \times 5.0000) + (\$285.71 \times 2.0000)\end{array}}{\begin{array}{c}(\$562.50 \times .4000) + (\$252.52 \times 6.6000) + (\$472.22 \times 1.5000) \\ (\$75.00 \times 5.0000) + (\$150.00 \times 2.0000)\end{array}}$$

$$= \frac{\$4,069}{\$3,275} = 1.242$$

$$HII = \frac{\begin{array}{c}(\$562.50 \times .4828) + (\$252.52 \times 6.1552) + (\$472.22 \times 1.7241) \\ (\$75.00 \times 6.0345) + (\$150.00 \times 2.4138)\end{array}}{\begin{array}{c}(\$562.50 \times .4000) + (\$252.52 \times 6.6000) + (\$472.22 \times 1.5000) \\ (\$75.00 \times 5.0000) + (\$150.00 \times 2.0000)\end{array}}$$

$$= \frac{\$3,455}{\$3,275} = 1.055$$

The above calculations show that the increase in CPD from 1991 to 1993 could be broken down as follows:

Percentage increase due to cost increases	24.2%
Percentage increase due to intensity	5.5
Joint cost and intensity	1.9
Total increase	31.6%

For those who wish to break down further the causes for the increase in CPD during the two-year period, some individual departmental analysis could be done. For example, in 1993 the average laboratory CPD was $517.22 ($85.71 × 6.0345), compared with $375.00 ($75.00 × 5.000) in 1991. This represents a 37.9 percent increase and could be broken down into cost and intensity factors also. The next section addresses the issue of departmental analysis of cost variances.

Departmental Analysis of Variance

The preceding indices are very useful for analyzing cost changes at the total facility level. In such situations, a measure of output for the facility as a whole—such as patient days, admissions, discharges, visits, or enrollees—would be used. However, although this type of analysis may be very useful, it is also often desirable to analyze the reasons for cost changes at the departmental level. In general, the primary reason for a cost change at the departmental level between two time periods can be stated as a function of three factors:

1. changes in input prices
2. changes in input productivity (efficiency)
3. changes in departmental volume

The following variances can be calculated to compute the effects of these three factors:

$$\text{Price variance} = (\text{Present price} - \text{Old price}) \times \text{Present quantity}$$
$$\text{Efficiency variance} = (\text{Present quantity} - \text{Expected quantity at old productivity}) \times \text{Old price}$$
$$\text{Volume variance} = (\text{Present volume} - \text{Old volume}) \times \text{Old cost per unit}$$

These formulas may be applied to the following laundry example. It is assumed that the laundry has only two inputs: soap and labor.

	1993	1996
Pounds of laundry	140,000	180,000
Units of soap	1,400	1,800
Soap units per pound of laundry	.01	.01
Price per soap unit	$ 40.00	$ 50.00
Productive hours worked	19,600	27,000
Productive hours per pound of laundry	.14	.15
Wage rate per productive hour	5.25	6.00
Total cost	$158,900	$252,000
Cost per pound	$ 1.135	$ 1.40
Patient days	70,000	80,000

Price variances

   Soap = ($50.00 − $40.00) × 1,800 = $18,000 (Unfavorable)
   Labor = ($6.00 − $5.25) × 27,000 = $20,250 (Unfavorable)

Efficiency variances

   Soap = (1,800 − [.01 × 180,000]) × $40.00 = 0
   Labor = (27,000 − [.14 × 180,000]) × $5.25 = $9,450 (Unfavorable)

Volume variances

   Volume variance = (180,000 − 140,000) × $1.135 = 45,400 (Unfavorable)

With these calculations, the following table can be generated to summarize the factors that created cost changes in the laundry department:

Causes of Laundry Department
Cost Change—1993 to 1996

	Dollars	% Change
Increase in wages	$20,250	21.8
Increase in soap price	18,000	19.3
Decline in labor efficiency	9,450	10.1
Increase in volume	45,400	48.8
Total change in cost	$93,100	

The table indicates that increased volume was the largest source of the total change in cost. It is often useful to factor this volume variance into two areas:

   Intensity = (Change in volume due to intensity difference) × Old cost per unit
   Pure volume = (Change in volume due to change in overall service) × Old cost per unit

Here, the intensity variance represents the change in volume due to increased intensity of service. For example, assume that, in 1996, 2.25 pounds of laundry were provided per patient day. The corresponding value for 1993 was 2.00 pounds per patient day. Also assume that total patient days were 70,000 in 1993 and 80,000 in 1996. The two volume variances would be:

$$\text{Intensity variance} = (\,[2.25 - 2.00] \times 80,000) \times \$1.135 = \$22,700$$
$$\text{Pure volume} = 2.00 \times (80,000 - 70,000) \times \$1.135 = \$22,700$$

The system of cost variance analysis described above should be a useful framework in which to discuss factors causing changes in departmental costs. Aggregation of some resource categories will probably be both necessary and desirable. There would be little point in calculating price and efficiency variances for each of a hundred or more supply items. Only major supply categories should be examined. The supply items that are aggregated together could not be broken down in terms of individual price and efficiency variances because there would be no common input quantity measure. For example, the addition of numbers of pencils, sheets of paper, and boxes of paper clips would not produce a comparable unit of measure. For these smaller areas of supply or material costs, a simple change in cost per unit of departmental output may be just as informative as detailed price and efficiency variances.

VARIANCE ANALYSIS IN BUDGETARY SETTINGS

A final area in which variance analysis can be applied is in the operation of a formalized budgeting system. The presentation that follows assumes a budgeting system that is based on a flexible model. This means the management must have identified in the budgetary process those elements of cost that are presumed to be fixed and those that are presumed to be variable. Although relatively few health care organizations employ flexible budgeting models at the present time, a trend toward their adoption is clearly visible. In this context, the variance analysis models examined here may be applied in any budgetary situation, fixed or flexible.

The cost equation for any given department may be represented as follows:

$$\text{Cost} = F + (V \times Q)$$

where

$$F = \text{fixed costs}$$
$$V = \text{variable costs per unit of output}$$
$$Q = \text{output in units}$$

The fixed and variable cost coefficients are the sum of many individual resource quantity and unit price products. These terms can be represented as follows:

$$F = I_f \times P_f$$
$$V = I_v \times P_v$$

where

I_f = physical units of fixed resources
P_f = price per unit of fixed resources
I_v = physical units of variable resources per unit of output
P_v = price per unit of variable resources

In most budgeting situations, there are three levels of output or volume that are critical in cost variance analysis. The first is the actual level of volume produced in the budget reporting period. This level of activity is critical because, if management has established a set of expectations concerning how costs should behave, given changes in volume from budgeted levels, an adjustment to budgeted cost can be made.

The second critical level is that of budgeted or expected volume. It is on this expected volume level that management establishes its commitments for resources, and therefore incurs cost. An unjustified faith in volume forecasts can lock management into a very sizable fixed-cost position, especially with respect to labor costs.

The third critical level is that of standard volume. Standard volume is equal to actual volume, unless there is some indication that not all of the output was necessary. For example, a utilization review committee may determine that a certain number of patient days were medically unnecessary or that some surgical procedures were not warranted. Alternatively, in some indirect departments, such as maintenance, it may be important to identify the difference between actual and standard, or necessary, output.

The cost effect of these output decisions needs to be isolated and control directed at the individual(s) responsible.

The expected level of costs to be incurred at each of the three levels of volume (actual, budgeted, and standard) may be expressed as follows:

$$FB^a = F + (V \times Q^a)$$
$$FB^b = F + (V \times Q^b)$$
$$FB^s = F + (V \times Q^s)$$

where

FB^a = flexible budget at actual output level
FB^b = flexible budget at budgeted output level
FB^s = flexible budget at standard output level
Q^a = actual output
Q^b = budgeted output
Q^s = standard output

The major categories of variances can now be defined to explain the difference between actual cost (AC) and applied cost ($Q^s \times FB^b/Q^b$):

Variance Name	Definition	Cause
Spending	$(AC - FB^a)$	Price and efficiency
Utilization	$(Q^a - Q^s) \times (FB^b/Q^b)$	Excessive services
Volume	$(Q^b - Q^a) \times F/Q^b$	Difference from budgeted volume

For control purposes, it is important to break down the spending variance further into individual resource categories, and also to isolate the change due to price and efficiency factors. This will not only better isolate control for budget deviations but also improve the problem definition and determination phase times discussed earlier in the DC approach to cost control. The spending variances are broken down as follows:

$$\text{Efficiency} = (I^a - I^b)P^b$$
$$\text{Price} = (P^a - P^b)I^a$$

where

I^a = actual physical units of resource
I^b = budgeted physical units of resource
P^a = actual price per unit of resource
P^b = budgeted price per unit of resource

With this background, we must now relate the structure we developed for standard costing in Chapter 9 to our analyses of budgetary variances. Two sets of standards are involved: (1) standard cost profiles (SCPs) and (2) standard treatment protocols (STPs). SCPs are developed at the departmental level. They reflect the quantity of resources that should be used and the prices that should be paid for those resources to produce a specific departmental output unit, defined as a service unit (SU). Below is an SCP for a nursing unit, with the SU defined as a patient day:

Standard Cost Profile
Nursing Unit No. 6
Patient Day = Service Unit
Expected Patient Days = 630

Resource	Quantity Variable	Quantity Fixed	Unit Cost	Variable Cost	Average Fixed Cost	Average Total Cost
Head nurse	0.00	.30	$15.00	$ 0.00	$ 4.50	$ 4.50
RN	2.00	1.00	12.00	24.00	12.00	36.00
LPN	2.00	0.00	8.00	16.00	0.00	16.00
Aides	3.00	1.00	5.00	15.00	5.00	20.00
Supplies	2.00	0.00	2.20	4.40	0.00	4.40
Totals				$59.40	$21.50	$80.90

Using this table, a standard variance analysis could be performed for any time period. For example, the following data reflect actual experience in the most recent month:

Actual Months Cost
Nursing Unit No. 6
Actual Patient Days = 600

Resource	Quantity Used	Unit Cost	Total Cost
Head nurse	180	$15.50	$ 2,790.00
RN	1,800	12.50	22,500.00
LPN	1,200	8.10	9,720.00
Aides	2,400	4.80	11,520.00
Supplies	1,300	2.40	3,120.00
Total			$49,650.00

In this example, the nursing unit would have incurred actual expenditures of $49,650 during the month. It would have charged to the treated patient its standard cost times the number of patient days:

$$\text{Costs charged to patients} = \$48,540 = \$80.90 \times 600$$

The total variance to be accounted for would be the difference, or $1,110.00, which is an unfavorable variance. The individual variances that constitute this total are shown in the following calculations:

1. Spending variances
   - Efficiency variances ($[I^a - I^b]P^b$)
     a. Head nurse = $(180 - 189) \times \$15.00 = \$135.00$ (Favorable)
     b. RN = $(1,800 - 1,830) \times \$12.00 = \$360.00$ (Favorable)
     c. LPN = $(1,200 - 1,200) \times \$8.00 = 0$
     d. Aides = $(2,400 - 2,430) \times \$5.00 = \$150.00$ (Favorable)
     e. Supplies = $(1,300 - 1,200) \times \$2.20 = \$220.00$ (Unfavorable)
   - Price variances ($[P^a - P^b]I^a$)
     a. Head nurse = $(\$15.50 - \$15.00) \times 180 = \$90.00$ (Unfavorable)
     b. RN = $(\$12.50 - \$12.00) \times 1,800 = \$900.00$ (Unfavorable)
     c. LPN = $(\$8.10 - \$8.00) \times 1,200 = \$120.00$ (Unfavorable)
     d. Aides = $(\$4.80 - \$5.00) \times 2,400 = \$480.00$ (Favorable)
     e. Supplies = $(\$2.40 - \$2.20) \times 1,300 = \$260.00$ (Unfavorable)
   L2. Volume variance ($[Q^b - Q^a][F/Q^b]$)
   - Volume variance = $(630 - 600) \times \$21.50 = \$645.00$ (Unfavorable)

Totaling up the above individual variances validates the accuracy of our calculations:

Price—Head nurse	$ 90.00 (Unfavorable)
Price—RN	900.00 (Unfavorable)
Price—LPN	120.00 (Unfavorable)
Price—Aides	480.00 (Favorable)
Price—Supplies	260.00 (Unfavorable)
Efficiency—Head nurse	135.00 (Favorable)
Efficiency—RN	360.00 (Favorable)
Efficiency—LPN	0.00
Efficiency—Aides	150.00 (Favorable)
Efficiency—Supplies	220.00 (Unfavorable)
Volume	645.00 (Unfavorable)
Total	$1,110.00 (Unfavorable)

A few additional words about the calculation of the efficiency variances may be in order. The formula states that the difference between actual quantity (I^a) and budgeted quantity (I^b) is multiplied by budgeted price (P^b). The most difficult calculation is that for budgeted quantity. It represents the quantity of resource that should have been used at the actual level of output, or the sum of the budgeted fixed requirement plus the variable requirement at actual output (600 patient days). The following table shows the calculation of fixed and variable requirements for the individual resource categories:

1	2	3	4	5	6
		Budgeted		Budgeted	
	Average	Fixed	Average	Variable	Total
	Fixed	Requirement	Variable	Requirement	Requirements
Resource	Require-	(Col. 2 ×	Require-	(Col. 4 ×	(Col. 3 +
Category	ment/Unit	630)	ment/Unit	600)	Col. 5)
Head					
nurse	.30	189	0.00	0	189
RN	1.00	630	2.00	1,200	1,830
LPN	0.00	0	2.00	1,200	1,200
Aides	1.00	630	3.00	1,800	2,430
Supplies	0.00	0	2.00	1,200	1,200

The calculation for volume variance may also require some further explanation. This variance is simply the product of the difference between budgeted and actual volume $(Q^a - Q^b)$ and the average fixed cost budgeted (F/Q^b). The average fixed cost, as calculated in the standard cost profile, amounted to $21.50. You will notice that, in our example, volume variance is unfavorable because actual volume of patient days (600) was less than budgeted patient days (630). Because actual volume was less than that budgeted, the average fixed cost per unit will rise. The reverse situation would have existed if actual volume had exceeded budgeted volume. In that situation, the volume variance would have been favorable.

The third type of variance, utilization variance, results from a difference between actual volume and standard volume, or the quantity of volume actually needed. The measure of standard volume is generated from the STPs, which define how much output or how many SUs are required per treated patient type.

Let us generate a hypothetical set of data to apply to our nursing unit example. Assume that the patients treated in nursing unit no. 6 are all in diagnosis-related group (DRG) #209 (Major Joint Procedures) and are all associated with one physician, Dr. Mallard. Our STP for DRG #209 calls for a 14-day length of stay. A review of Dr. Mallard's patient records reveals that only 560 patient days of care should have been used (40 cases at 14 days per case). Dr. Mallard had 20 patients with lengths of stay greater than 14 days. These 20 patients accounted for an excess of 80 patient days. Dr. Mallard also had 10 patients with shorter lengths of stay. These patients offset 40 days of the 80-day surplus. Thus, while 600 patient days of care were provided, only 560 should have been used. This creates an unfavorable utilization variance, calculated as the product of budgeted cost per unit and the difference between actual and standard volume. In our example of nursing unit no. 6, the utilization variance would be

$$\text{Utilization variance} = (600 - 560) \times \$80.90 = \$3,236.00 \ (\text{Unfavorable})$$

This variance is not charged to the nursing department. It is charged to the manager of patient treatment, in this case Dr. Mallard.

The following schematic depicts the flow of costs and the variances associated with each account:

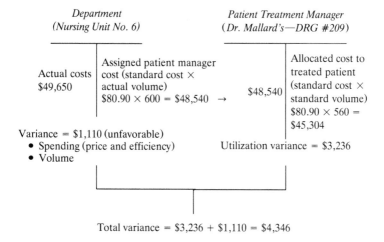

This delineation of variances represents a very powerful analytical tool for analyzing cost variances from budgeted cost levels. The existence of a flexible budget model is not a prerequisite to its employment. The only real prerequisite is that major resource cost categories be separated into price and utilization components. Since effective cost control appears to be predicated on a separate analysis of price and utilization decisions, this does not seem too difficult a task, in view of the potential payoff. Finally, it should be noted that there is no requirement for a formalization of these variances into the budget reporting models. They can be calculated on an ad hoc basis to investigate and explain large cost variances.

SUMMARY

In general, within the framework for cost control, two approaches are possible: (1) preventive and (2) DC. The DC approach is usually based on some system of variance analysis. From a decision-theory perspective, the investigation of a variance is based on the cost of investigation, the probability that a correctable problem exists, the potential loss if the problem is not corrected, and the costs of problem correction. It may not always be possible to develop truly objective measures for these values, but sensitivity analysis may offer a useful aid in such situations.

ASSIGNMENTS

1. Two general approaches to internal control are preventive and detection. Preventive approaches stress the elimination of problems, whereas detection approaches stress the early recognition and correction of problems. What sorts of things could you do if you used a preventive approach to reduce costs?

2. What is a coefficient of variation, and how can that information be used in budgeting?

3. Which would you investigate first—a budget variance that is 1.0 standard deviation away from the expected value or one that is 1.5 standard deviations away from the value? Why?

4. When is the utilization of a flexible budget likely to be most effective?

5. Standard cost accounting systems often separate variance into price and efficiency components. Why?

6. Utilization of a multivariable flexible budget may reduce the time involved in investigating variances. Why might this be true?

7. Ned Zechman is the dietary manager of a large convalescent center. He is disturbed by variances, all highly unfavorable, in his food budget for the past three months. Ned has been reducing both the quantity and quality of delivered meals, but to date there has been no reflection of this in his monthly budget variance report. A recent organizational change brought in Pat Schumaker, who is now responsible for all purchasing activity, including dietary. All purchased food costs are charged to dietary at the time of purchase. What do you think might explain Ned's problem, and how would you determine the cause?

8. Assume that the budgeted cost for a department is $10,000 and the amount represented by the standard deviation is $500. The decision to investigate a variance requires a comparison of expected benefits with expected costs. Suppose an unfavorable variance of $1,000 is observed. The normal distribution indicates the probability of observing this variance is .0228 if the system is in control. Furthermore, assume that the benefits would be 50 percent of the variance and that investigation costs are $200. Should this variance

be investigated? Assume that the variance is still $1,000, but it is favorable. Should it still be investigated?

9. Departmental costs may be out of control if either the variance is outside specified limits or the number of successive observations, above or below expected costs, is excessive. The binomial distribution can be used as a basis for determining what is or is not excessive. If we assume that the probability of being either above or below budgeted costs is .50, then the probability of n successive observations of actual costs being greater than budgeted costs is $.50^n$. What is the probability of observing six successive periods in which actual costs are greater then budgeted costs?

10. You are evaluating the performance of the radiology department manager. The SU or output for this department is the number of x-rays. A static budget was prepared at the start of the year. You are now examining that budget in relation to actual experience. The relevant data are as follows:

	Actual	Original Budget	Variance	
Volume of x-rays	100,000	120,000	20,000	(Unfavorable)
Variable costs	$1,200,000	$1,320,000	$120,000	(Favorable)
Fixed costs	600,000	600,000	—	
Total costs	$1,800,000	$1,920,000	$120,000	(Favorable)

The department manager is pleased because he has a favorable $120,000 cost variance. Evaluate the effectiveness claims of the manager, using the budgetary variance model described in the chapter.

11. The following data were assembled for a laundry department during the period 1994–1995:

	1994	*1995*
Weighted patient days	24,140	24,539
Pounds of laundry	333,225	328,624
Pounds per day	13.80385	13.39191
Number of FTEs	3.0	3.0
FTEs per pound	.00000900292	.00000912897
Average salary	$7,260.67	$7,873.00
Salary cost per pound	$.065367	$.071872
Supply units	3,332	3,286
Supply units per pound	.01	.01
Cost per supply unit	$2.6946	$3.1848
Total cost	$30,761	$34,085
Cost per pound	$.092313	$.10372

Break down the total change in cost ($3,324) into the variance categories described in the chapter, that, is, price, efficiency, intensity volume, and pure volume variances.

12. John Jones, CEO at Valley Hospital, is concerned by the rapid increase in cost per case during the last five years at his hospital. Five years ago his average cost per case was

$9,295; it is now $14,355. Using the data below, help John understand what factors have fueled the increase in costs during the last five years.

	Total Cost	Present Volume	Average Cost
DRG #106	$150,000	10	$15,000
DRG #107	200,000	20	10,000
DRG #103	95,000	1	95,000
	$445,000	31	$14,355

	Total Cost	Five Years Ago Volume	Average Cost
DRG #106	$114,750	9	$12,750
DRG #107	192,000	24	8,000
DRG #103	0	0	0
	$306,750	33	$9,295

SOLUTIONS AND ANSWERS

1. The following are some of the things you could do, using a preventive approach: improve employee training, increase inspection of material, improve equipment maintenance, and increase supervision.

2. The coefficient of variation is the ratio of the standard deviation to the mean. A large value implies great variability in the results. In a budgeting context, operations with large prior coefficients of variation typically require a more sophisticated budget model, such as a flexible budget, to account for deviations from average performance.

3. The budget variance that is 1.5 standard deviations from expected performance is more likely to be controllable and should be investigated first. However, adjustments for the relative differences in investigation costs and variance size should be considered.

4. A flexible budget is likely to be most effective when costs in a department are not fixed and are expected to vary with changes in output or other variables.

5. Standard cost accounting systems separate variances into price and efficiency components because, in many situations, one person does not have decision responsibility for both purchases and usage. Even in situations where one person does have responsibility for both components, the separation is useful because it provides information for focused management correction.

6. To the extent that a multivariable budget model reflects cost behavior more accurately, it may provide a better indication of when actual costs are out of control. This may reduce the number of times needless investigations or justification efforts are conducted.

7. Prices paid for food may have increased significantly either because of recent changes in food prices or because of ineptness or fraud on the part of Mr. Schumaker. An audit of purchasing costs should be initiated, especially if other departments in the center have similar problems.

8. The following calculations should be made as a basis for deciding whether an investigation should be conducted:

Expected benefits = .5 × $1,000 × (1 − .0228)* = $488.60
Expected costs = $200
*(1 − .0228) = Probability that the variance is not a random occurrence

Yes, the variance should be investigated, since the expected benefits are greater than the expected costs. Even if the variance is favorable, it should be investigated, because it may indicate that the budget is not accurate. A reduction of the budget may promote a future reduction in costs.

9. The probability of observing six successive periods in which actual costs are greater than budgeted costs is $.50^6 = .0156$.

10. In your evaluation, you can calculate spending and volume variances for the radiology department. The total variance would be calculated as

Actual cost less assigned cost,

$$\text{or } \$1,800,000 - \left(100,000 \times \frac{\$1,920,000}{\$120,000}\right) = \$200,000 \text{ (Unfavorable)}$$

The radiology department has an unfavorable variance of $200,000, as opposed to a favorable variance of $120,000. The $200,000 unfavorable variance can be broken into spending and volume variances:

Spending variance =
$1,800,000 − $600,000 − ($11 × $100,000) = $100,000 (Unfavorable)

$$\text{Volume variance} = (120,000 - 100,000) \times \frac{\$600,000}{120,000} = \$100,000 \text{ (Unfavorable)}$$

The department manager may not be responsible for the volume variance, but the unfavorable spending variance of $100,000 should be analyzed to see what caused it. More detail would permit further breakdowns by price and efficiency variances.

11. The causes of the change in cost and the resulting variances for the laundry department are as follows:

Labor price	1,837	(Unfavorable)	55.26%
Supply price	1,611	(Unfavorable)	48.47
Labor efficiency	301	(Unfavorable)	9.06
Pure volume	508	(Unfavorable)	15.28
Intensity volume	933	(Favorable)	(28.07)
	3,324	100.00%	

Labor price = ($7,873.00 − $7,260.67) × 3.0 = $1,837 (Unfavorable)
Supply price = ($3.1848 − $2.6946) × 3,286 = $1,611 (Unfavorable)
Labor efficiency = (3.0 − .00000900292 × 328,624) × $7,260.67 = $301 (Unfavorable)
Pure volume = (13.80385 × [24,539 − 24,140]) × $.092313 = 508 (Unfavorable)
Intensity volume = ([13.39191 − 13.80385] × 24,539) × $.092313 = $933 (Favorable)

Labor price = ($7,873.00 − $7,260.67) × 3.0 = $1,837 (Unfavorable)
Supply price = ($3.1848 − $2.6946) × 3,286 = $1,611 (Unfavorable)
Labor efficiency = (3.0 − .00000900292 × 328,624) × $7,260.67 = $301 (Unfavorable)
Pure volume = (13.80385 × [24,539 − 24,140]) × $.092313 = 508 (Unfavorable)
Intensity volume = ([13.39191 − 13.80385] × 24,539) × $.092313 = $933 (Favorable)

12. The primary cause for the increase in cost has been the start up of a new DRG category that is very expensive to produce. This case illustrates the importance of case-mix and severity-adjusting cost data. The table below breaks the variances into price/cost and volume variances.

| | Variance Analysis by DRG | | |
	Cost	Volume	New
DRG #106	$22,500	$12,750	0
DRG #107	40,000	(32,000)	0
DRG #103	0		95,000
	$62,500	($19,250)	$95,000

Chapter 12

Financial Mathematics

In this chapter, we examine the concepts and methods of discounting sums of money received at various points in time through the use of compound interest formulas and tables. This material is of special importance in the context of the next two chapters on capital budgeting (Chapter 13) and capital financing (Chapter 14). The present abbreviated discussion of financial mathematics is intended as a review for those who have had prior exposure; if this material is new, some background reading may be necessary.

The two major questions in the financial decision-making process of any business are: (1) Where shall we invest our funds? and (2) How shall we finance our investment needs? Investment decisions involve the expenditure of funds today in the expectation of realizing returns in future periods. Financing decisions involve the receipt of funds today in return for a promise to make payments in the future. The evaluation of the relative attractiveness of alternative investment and financing opportunities is a major task of management. Differences in the timing of either receipts or payments can have a significant impact on the ultimate decision to invest or finance in a certain way. A payment that is made or received in the first year has a greater value than an identical payment made or received in the tenth year. The concept underlying this point is often referred to as the time value of money. A time value for money simply assigns a cost or interest rate for money.

Money or funds can be thought of as a commodity, like any other commodity that can be bought or sold. The price for the commodity called money is often stated as an interest rate, for example, 10 percent per year. An interest rate of 10 percent per year implies exchange rates between money at different time periods. When the interest rate is 10 percent, a dollar received one year from today is worth only .9091 of a dollar received today, and a dollar received ten years from today is worth only .3855 of a dollar today. Compound interest rate tables are merely values that provide relative weighting for money received or paid in different time periods at specified prices or interest rates. With these relative weightings, money received or paid can be added or subtracted to produce some logical meaningful result. The major purpose of compound interest tables is to permit addition and subtraction of money paid or received in different time periods. The resulting sums of individual yearly or period values are usually expressed in dollars at one of two time points: (1) present value and (2) future value.

The compound interest tables we shall use in this chapter are categorized as either present value or future value tables. The present value tables provide the relative weights that should be used to restate money of future time periods back to the present. Future value tables provide the relative weighting for restating money of one time period to some designated future time period.

SINGLE-SUM PROBLEMS

Future Value—Single Sum

There are a number of situations in which a business would be interested in the future value of a single sum. For example, a nursing home may want to invest $100,000 today in a fund to be used in two years for replacement. It would like to know what sum of money would be available two years from now.

This type of problem is easily solved, using the values presented in Table 12-1. The first step in solving the problem is to set up a time graph. This involves the four variables that make up any simple compound interest problem:

1. number of time periods in which the compounding takes place (n)
2. present value of future sum (p)
3. future value of present sum (f)
4. interest rate per time period (i)

If you know the values of any three of these variables, you can solve for the fourth. The time graph is a simple device that helps you to conceptualize the problem and identify the known values to permit solution. In the above nursing home investment example, a 10 percent interest rate per

Table 12–1 Future Value of $1.00 Received in n Periods

Period	2%	4%	5%	6%	8%	10%
1	1.0200	1.0400	1.0500	1.0600	1.0800	1.1000
2	1.0404	1.0816	1.1025	1.1236	1.1664	1.2100
3	1.0612	1.1249	1.1576	1.1910	1.2597	1.3310
4	1.0824	1.1699	1.2155	1.2625	1.3605	1.4641
5	1.1041	1.2167	1.2763	1.3382	1.4693	1.6105
6	1.1262	1.2653	1.3401	1.4185	1.5869	1.7716
7	1.1487	1.3159	1.4071	1.5036	1.7138	1.9488
8	1.1717	1.3686	1.4775	1.5938	1.8509	2.1436
9	1.1951	1.4233	1.5513	1.6895	1.9990	2.3589
10	1.2190	1.4802	1.6289	1.7908	2.1589	2.5938
11	1.2434	1.5395	1.7103	1.8983	2.3316	2.8532
12	1.2682	1.6010	1.7959	2.0122	2.5182	3.1385
13	1.2936	1.6651	1.8856	2.1329	2.7196	3.4524
14	1.3195	1.7317	1.9799	2.2609	2.9372	3.7976
15	1.3459	1.8009	2.0709	2.3966	3.1722	4.1774
16	1.3728	1.8730	2.1829	2.5404	3.4259	4.5951
17	1.4002	1.9479	2.2920	2.6928	3.7000	5.0545
18	1.4282	2.0258	2.4066	2.8543	3.9960	5.5600
19	1.4568	2.1068	2.5270	3.0256	4.3157	6.1160
20	1.4859	2.1911	2.6533	3.2071	4.6610	6.7275
30	1.8114	3.2434	4.3219	5.7435	10.0627	17.4495
40	2.2080	4.8010	7.0400	10.2857	21.7245	45.2597

period would be reflected in the following time graph:

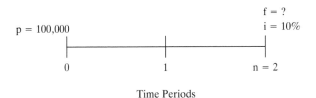

Time Periods

The value 0 on this time graph represents the present time, whereas the values 1 and 2 represent year 1 and year 2. In the nursing home example, we know three of the four variables and can therefore solve the problem through substitution in the following formula:

$$f = p \times f(i, n)$$

The factor f(i, n) is the future value of $1.00 invested today for n periods at i rate of interest per period. These value can be found in Table 12–1, using the above generic formula. The following calculation can then be made to solve the problem:

$$f = \$100,00 \times f(10\%, 2) \text{ or}$$

$$f = \$100,000 \times 1.210 \text{ or}$$

$$f = \$121,000$$

In some situations it may be the interest rate that we wish to determine. Assume that we can invest $8,576 today in a discounted note that will pay us $10,000 two years from today. The following time graph summarizes the problem:

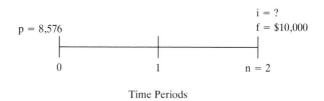

Time Periods

The following calculation can then be made to solve the problem:

$$\$10,000 = \$8,576 \times f(i, 2) \text{ or}$$

$$f(i, 2) = 1.166$$

A check of the values in Table 12–1 indicates that the interest rate would be 8 percent (f[8%, 2] = 1.166). If the above value had not matched exactly a figure in the table, some interpolation would have been required.

A microcomputer or a calculator with a financial mathematics function could also be used to solve the above types of problems. It is still useful, however, to set up a time graph to conceptualize the problem before entering numbers into the calculator or computer.

Present Value—Single Sum

In some situations, it is the present value of a future sum that is of interest. This type of problem is similar to those we examined with regard to the future value of a single sum. In fact, the same table of values could be used, except that now we would use division rather than multiplication.

The general equation used to solve present value—single sum problems is

$$p = f \times p(i, n)$$

The factor $p(i, n)$ represents the present value of $1.00 received in n periods at an interest rate of i. Values for $p(i, n)$ can be found in Table 12–2.

Assume that your HMO has a $100,000 debt service obligation due in two years. You are interested in learning how much money must be set aside today to meet the obligation if the expected yield on the investment is 12 percent. The relevant time graph would be

and the calculation to solve the problem would be

$$p = f \times p(i, n) \text{ or}$$

$$p = \$100,000 \times p(12\%, 2) \text{ or}$$

$$p = \$100,000 \times .797 \text{ or}$$

$$p = \$79,700$$

It is important to note that the values of Table 12–1 and Table 12–2 are reciprocals of each other. That is

$$f(i, n) = 1/p(i, n)$$

In effect, this means that only one of the two tables is necessary to solve either a present value or future value problem involving a single sum.

ANNUITY PROBLEMS

Future Value

In many business situations, there is more than one payment or receipt. In the case of multiple payments or receipts, when each payment or receipt is constant per time period, we have an annuity situation. The time

Table 12-2 Present Value of $1.00 Due in n Periods

Period	4%	6%	8%	10%	12%	14%	16%	18%	20%	22%	24%	26%	28%	30%	40%
1	0.962	0.943	0.926	0.909	0.893	0.877	0.862	0.847	0.833	0.820	0.806	0.794	0.781	0.769	0.714
2	0.925	0.890	0.857	0.826	0.797	0.769	0.743	0.718	0.694	0.672	0.650	0.630	0.610	0.592	0.510
3	0.889	0.840	0.794	0.751	0.712	0.675	0.641	0.609	0.579	0.551	0.524	0.500	0.477	0.455	0.364
4	0.855	0.792	0.735	0.683	0.636	0.592	0.552	0.516	0.482	0.451	0.423	0.397	0.373	0.350	0.260
5	0.822	0.747	0.681	0.621	0.567	0.519	0.476	0.437	0.402	0.370	0.341	0.315	0.291	0.269	0.186
6	0.790	0.705	0.630	0.564	0.507	0.456	0.410	0.370	0.335	0.303	0.275	0.250	0.227	0.207	0.133
7	0.760	0.665	0.583	0.513	0.452	0.400	0.354	0.314	0.279	0.249	0.222	0.198	0.178	0.159	0.095
8	0.731	0.627	0.540	0.467	0.404	0.351	0.305	0.266	0.233	0.204	0.179	0.157	0.139	0.123	0.068
9	0.703	0.592	0.500	0.424	0.361	0.308	0.263	0.225	0.194	0.167	0.144	0.125	0.108	0.094	0.048
10	0.676	0.558	0.463	0.386	0.322	0.270	0.227	0.191	0.162	0.137	0.116	0.099	0.085	0.073	0.035
11	0.650	0.527	0.429	0.350	0.287	0.237	0.195	0.162	0.135	0.112	0.094	0.079	0.066	0.056	0.025
12	0.625	0.497	0.397	0.319	0.257	0.208	0.168	0.137	0.112	0.092	0.076	0.062	0.052	0.043	0.018
13	0.601	0.469	0.368	0.290	0.229	0.182	0.145	0.116	0.093	0.075	0.061	0.050	0.040	0.033	0.013
14	0.577	0.442	0.340	0.263	0.205	0.160	0.125	0.099	0.078	0.062	0.049	0.039	0.032	0.025	0.009
15	0.555	0.417	0.315	0.239	0.183	0.140	0.108	0.084	0.065	0.051	0.040	0.031	0.025	0.020	0.006

n															
16	*0.534*	*0.394*	*0.292*	*0.218*	*0.163*	*0.123*	*0.093*	*0.071*	*0.054*	*0.042*	*0.032*	*0.025*	*0.019*	*0.015*	*0.005*
17	*0.513*	*0.371*	*0.270*	*0.198*	*0.146*	*0.108*	*0.080*	*0.060*	*0.045*	*0.034*	*0.026*	*0.020*	*0.015*	*0.012*	*0.003*
18	*0.494*	*0.350*	*0.250*	*0.180*	*0.130*	*0.095*	*0.069*	*0.051*	*0.038*	*0.028*	*0.021*	*0.016*	*0.012*	*0.009*	*0.002*
19	*0.475*	*0.331*	*0.232*	*0.164*	*0.116*	*0.083*	*0.060*	*0.043*	*0.031*	*0.023*	*0.017*	*0.012*	*0.009*	*0.007*	*0.002*
20	*0.456*	*0.312*	*0.215*	*0.149*	*0.104*	*0.073*	*0.051*	*0.037*	*0.026*	*0.019*	*0.014*	*0.010*	*0.007*	*0.005*	*0.001*
21	*0.439*	*0.294*	*0.199*	*0.135*	*0.093*	*0.064*	*0.044*	*0.031*	*0.022*	*0.015*	*0.011*	*0.008*	*0.006*	*0.004*	*0.001*
22	*0.422*	*0.278*	*0.184*	*0.123*	*0.083*	*0.056*	*0.038*	*0.026*	*0.018*	*0.013*	*0.009*	*0.006*	*0.004*	*0.003*	*0.001*
23	*0.406*	*0.262*	*0.170*	*0.112*	*0.074*	*0.049*	*0.033*	*0.022*	*0.015*	*0.010*	*0.007*	*0.005*	*0.003*	*0.002*	
24	*0.390*	*0.247*	*0.158*	*0.102*	*0.066*	*0.043*	*0.028*	*0.019*	*0.013*	*0.008*	*0.006*	*0.004*	*0.003*	*0.002*	
25	*0.375*	*0.233*	*0.146*	*0.092*	*0.059*	*0.038*	*0.024*	*0.016*	*0.010*	*0.007*	*0.005*	*0.003*	*0.002*	*0.001*	
26	*0.361*	*0.220*	*0.135*	*0.084*	*0.053*	*0.033*	*0.021*	*0.014*	*0.009*	*0.006*	*0.004*	*0.002*	*0.002*	*0.001*	
27	*0.347*	*0.207*	*0.125*	*0.076*	*0.047*	*0.029*	*0.018*	*0.011*	*0.007*	*0.005*	*0.003*	*0.002*	*0.001*	*0.001*	
28	*0.333*	*0.196*	*0.116*	*0.069*	*0.042*	*0.026*	*0.016*	*0.010*	*0.006*	*0.004*	*0.002*	*0.002*	*0.001*	*0.001*	
29	*0.321*	*0.185*	*0.107*	*0.063*	*0.037*	*0.022*	*0.014*	*0.008*	*0.005*	*0.003*	*0.002*	*0.001*	*0.001*	*0.001*	
30	*0.308*	*0.174*	*0.099*	*0.057*	*0.033*	*0.020*	*0.012*	*0.007*	*0.004*	*0.003*	*0.002*	*0.001*	*0.001*	*0.001*	
40	*0.208*	*0.097*	*0.046*	*0.022*	*0.011*	*0.005*	*0.003*	*0.001*	*0.001*						

graph for an annuity looks like this:

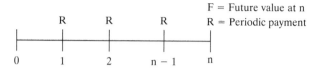

In this graph, F represents the future value of the invested annuity deposits at the end of period n. The values for R represent the periodic deposits that are constant for each time period. It should be emphasized that the deposits are made at the end of each time period. Such a system of deposits is often described as an ordinary annuity. The values presented in Tables 12–3 and 12–4 assume an ordinary annuity situation in which deposits or receipts occur at the end of the period.

The basic equation for a future value annuity is

$$F = R \times F(i, n)$$

Table 12–3 Future Value of $1.00 Received Each Period for n Periods

Period	2%	4%	5%	6%	8%	10%
1	1.0000	1.0000	1.0000	1.0000	1.0000	1.0000
2	2.0200	2.0400	2.0500	2.0600	2.0800	2.1000
3	3.0604	3.1216	3.1525	3.1836	3.2464	3.3100
4	4.1216	4.2465	4.3101	4.3746	4.5061	4.6410
5	5.2040	5.4163	5.5256	5.6371	5.8666	6.1051
6	6.3081	6.6330	6.8019	6.9753	7.3359	7.7156
7	7.4343	7.8983	8.1420	8.3938	8.9228	9.4872
8	8.5830	9.2142	9.5491	9.8975	10.6366	11.4360
9	9.7546	10.5828	11.0266	11.4913	12.4876	13.5796
10	10.9497	12.0061	12.5779	13.1808	14.4866	15.9376
11	12.1687	13.4864	14.2068	14.9716	16.6455	18.5314
12	13.4121	15.0258	15.9171	16.8699	18.9771	21.3846
13	14.6803	16.6268	17.7130	18.8821	21.4953	24.5231
14	15.9739	18.2919	19.5986	21.0151	24.2149	27.9755
15	17.2934	20.0236	21.5786	23.2760	27.1521	31.7731
16	18.6393	21.8245	23.6575	25.6725	30.3243	35.9503
17	20.0121	23.6975	25.8404	28.2129	33.7502	40.5456
18	21.4123	25.6454	28.1324	30.9057	37.4502	45.6001
19	22.8406	27.6712	30.5390	33.7600	41.4463	51.1601
20	24.2974	29.7781	33.0660	36.7856	45.7620	57.2761
30	40.5681	56.0849	66.4388	79.0582	113.2832	164.4962
40	60.4020	95.0255	120.7998	154.7620	259.0565	442.5974

Table 12–4 Present Value of $1.00 Received Each Period for n Periods

Period	4%	6%	8%	10%	12%	14%	16%	18%	20%	22%	24%	25%	26%	28%	30%	40%
1	0.962	0.943	0.926	0.909	0.893	0.877	0.862	0.847	0.833	0.820	0.806	0.800	0.794	0.781	0.769	0.714
2	1.886	1.833	1.783	1.736	1.690	1.647	1.605	1.566	1.528	1.492	1.457	1.440	1.424	1.392	1.361	1.224
3	2.775	2.673	2.577	2.487	2.402	2.322	2.246	2.174	2.106	2.042	1.981	1.952	1.868	1.816	1.816	1.589
4	3.630	3.465	3.312	3.170	3.037	2.914	2.798	2.690	2.589	2.494	2.404	2.362	2.320	2.241	2.166	1.849
5	4.452	4.212	3.993	3.791	3.605	3.433	3.274	3.127	2.991	2.864	2.745	2.689	2.635	2.532	2.436	2.035
6	5.242	4.917	4.623	4.355	4.111	3.889	3.685	3.498	3.326	3.167	3.020	2.951	2.885	2.759	2.643	2.168
7	6.002	5.582	5.206	4.868	4.564	4.288	4.039	3.812	3.605	3.416	3.242	3.161	3.083	2.937	2.802	2.263
8	6.733	6.210	5.747	5.335	4.968	4.639	4.344	4.078	3.837	3.619	3.421	3.329	3.241	3.076	2.925	2.331
9	7.435	6.802	6.247	5.759	5.328	4.946	4.607	4.303	4.031	3.786	3.566	3.463	3.366	3.184	3.019	2.379
10	8.111	7.360	6.710	6.145	5.650	5.216	4.833	4.494	4.192	3.923	3.682	3.571	3.465	3.269	3.092	2.414
11	8.760	7.887	7.139	6.495	5.988	5.453	5.029	4.656	4.327	4.035	3.776	3.656	3.544	3.335	3.147	2.438
12	9.385	8.384	7.536	6.814	6.194	5.660	5.197	4.793	4.439	4.127	3.851	3.725	3.606	3.387	3.190	2.456
13	9.986	8.853	7.904	7.103	6.424	5.842	5.342	4.910	4.533	4.203	3.912	3.780	3.656	3.427	3.223	2.468
14	10.563	9.295	8.244	7.367	6.628	6.002	5.468	5.008	4.611	4.265	3.962	3.824	3.695	3.459	3.249	2.477
15	11.118	9.712	8.559	7.606	6.811	6.142	5.575	5.092	4.675	4.315	4.001	3.859	3.726	3.483	3.268	2.484

continues

Table 12–4 continued

Period	4%	6%	8%	10%	12%	14%	16%	18%	20%	22%	24%	25%	26%	28%	30%	40%
16	11.652	10.106	8.851	7.824	6.974	6.265	5.669	5.162	4.730	4.357	4.033	3.887	3.751	3.503	3.283	2.489
17	12.166	10.477	9.122	8.022	7.120	6.373	5.749	5.222	4.775	4.391	4.059	3.910	3.771	3.518	3.295	2.492
18	12.659	10.828	9.372	8.201	7.250	6.467	5.818	5.273	4.812	4.419	4.080	3.928	3.786	3.529	3.304	2.494
19	13.134	11.158	9.604	8.365	7.366	6.550	5.877	5.316	4.844	4.442	4.097	3.942	3.799	3.539	3.311	2.496
20	13.590	11.470	9.818	8.514	7.469	6.623	5.929	5.353	4.870	4.460	4.110	3.954	3.808	3.546	3.316	2.497
21	14.029	11.764	10.017	8.649	7.562	6.687	5.973	5.384	4.891	4.476	4.121	3.963	3.816	3.551	3.320	2.498
22	14.451	12.042	10.201	8.772	7.645	6.743	6.011	5.410	4.909	4.488	4.130	3.970	3.822	3.556	3.323	2.498
23	14.857	12.303	10.371	8.883	7.718	6.792	6.044	5.432	4.925	4.499	4.137	3.976	3.827	3.559	3.325	2.499
24	15.247	12.550	10.529	8.985	7.784	6.835	6.073	5.451	4.937	4.507	4.143	3.981	3.831	3.562	3.327	2.499
25	15.622	12.783	10.675	9.077	7.843	6.873	6.097	5.467	4.948	4.514	4.147	3.985	3.834	3.564	3.329	2.499
26	15.983	13.003	10.810	9.161	7.896	6.906	6.118	5.480	4.956	4.520	4.151	3.988	3.837	3.566	3.330	2.500
27	16.330	13.211	10.935	9.237	7.943	6.935	6.136	5.492	4.964	4.525	4.154	3.990	3.839	3.567	3.331	2.500
28	16.663	13.406	11.051	9.307	7.984	6.961	6.152	5.502	4.970	4.528	4.157	3.992	3.840	3.568	3.331	2.500
29	16.984	13.591	11.158	9.370	8.022	6.983	6.166	5.510	4.975	4.531	4.159	3.994	3.841	3.569	3.332	2.500
30	17.292	13.765	11.258	9.427	8.055	7.003	6.177	5.517	4.979	4.534	4.160	3.995	3.842	3.569	3.332	2.500
40	19.793	15.046	11.925	9.779	8.244	7.105	6.234	5.548	4.997	4.544	4.166	3.999	3.846	3.571	3.333	2.500

The factor F(i, n) represents the future value of $1.00 invested each period for n periods at i rate of interest. Values for F(i, n) can be found in Table 12–3. Again, if three of the four variables (F, R, i, and n) in the above equation are known, the equation can be solved to determine the fourth. Thus, if we know F, i, and n, we can solve for R.

Assume that a hospital wants to know the future value in three years of $50,000 annual deposits in a trust fund for professional malpractice insurance if the fund earns 8 percent per year. The time graph for this problem would be

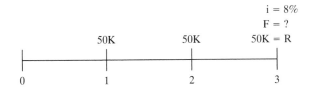

The calculation to solve the problem would be

$$F = R \times F(i, n) \text{ or}$$

$$F = \$50,000 \times F(8\%, 3) \text{ or}$$

$$F = \$50,000 \times 3.2464 \text{ or}$$

$$F = \$162,320$$

The values in Table 12–3 could also be determined through simple addition of the values for a single sum in Table 12–1. This can be seen easily by a further examination of our hospital example. The following table summarizes the relevant data:

Year	Future Value Factor (8%)	Future Value	Year Invested 1	2	3
1	1.1664	$ 58,320	$50,000		
2	1.0800	54,000		$50,000	
3	1.0000	50,000			$50,000
Total	3.2464	$162,320			

Notice that the future value total in the table above is identical to that in the earlier annuity formula. Also note that the summation of the individual future value factors yields the value of the annuity factor

(3.2464). In general, a future value annuity factor can be expressed as follows:

$$F(i, n) = f(i, 1) + f(i, 2) + \ldots + f(i, n - 1) + 1.0$$

In many situations, a financial mathematics problem may be part annuity and part single sum. In such cases, the use of a time graph will help you spot this duality and solve the problem correctly. Assume that a hospital has a sinking fund payment requirement for the last 10 years of a bond's life. At the end of that period of time, there must be $45 million available to retire the debt. The hospital has created a $5 million fund today, 20 years before debt retirement, to offset part of the future sinking fund requirement. If the investment yield is expected to be 10 percent per year, what annual deposit must be made to the sinking fund? The following time graph summarizes the problem:

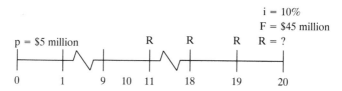

The first step is to determine the future value of the $5 million deposit:

$$f = \$5,000,000 \times f(10\%, 20) \text{ or}$$

$$f = \$5,000,000 \times 6.7275 \text{ or}$$

$$f = \$33,637,500$$

This means that the amount of money that must be generated by the ten sinking fund deposits must equal $11,362,500. The following calculation provides the solution:

$$F - f = R \times F(i, n) \text{ or}$$

$$\$11,362,500 = R \times F(10\%, 10) \text{ or}$$

$$\$11,362,500 = R \times 15.9376 \text{ or}$$

$$R = \$712,937$$

Present Value

In determining the present value of an annuity, the procedure is analogous to that used to determine the future value of an annuity, except that our attention is now on present value rather than future value. The following time graph represents the typical present value annuity problem:

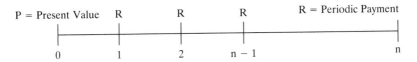

As noted earlier, this is an ordinary annuity situation because the payments are at the end of the period. The basic equation used to solve a present value annuity problem is

$$P = R \times P(i, n)$$

The factor $P(i, n)$ represents the present value of $1.00 received at the end of each period for n periods when i is the rate of interest. Values for $P(i, n)$ are found in Table 12−4.

Assume that a hospital is considering buying an older hospital and consolidating its operations in another nearby facility. An actuary has estimated that pension payments of $100,000 per year for the next four years will be required to satisfy the obligation to vested employees. The hospital wants to know what the present value of this obligation is so that it can be subtracted from the negotiated purchase price. The obligation's discount rate is assumed to be 12 percent. Here is the time graph for the problem:

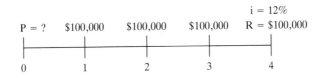

The calculation to solve the problem is

$$P = \$100,000 \times P(12\%, 4) \text{ or}$$

$$P = \$100,000 \times 3.037$$

$$P = \$303,700$$

Present value annuity problems can be thought of as a series of individual single-sum problems. The present value annuity factor $P(i, n)$ is the sum of the individual single-sum values of Table 12−2. The data below summarize this calculation in our hospital example:

Year	Present Value Factor (12%)	Present Value	Year of Payment			
			1	2	3	4
1	.893	$ 89,300	$100,000			
2	.797	79,700		$100,000		
3	.712	71,200			$100,000	
4	.636	63,600				$100,000
Total	3.038	$303,800				

The small differences between the annuity values and the single-sum values in the above table are due to rounding errors.

The present value annuity factor [P(i, n)] can be expressed as follows:

$$P(i, n) = p(i, 1) + p(i, 2) + \ldots + p(i, n)$$

In most business situations, ordinary annuity problems do not arise. A classic exception to the ordinary annuity situation is a lease with front-end payments. Assume that a clinic wants to lease a computer for the next five years with quarterly payments of $1,000 due at the beginning of each quarter. If the clinic's discount rate is 16 percent per annum, what is the present value of the lease liability? The relevant time graph is presented below:

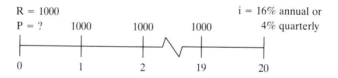

The above graph tells us that the clinic has a 19-period ordinary annuity with each period three months. The effective interest rate for each quarter is 4 percent. The present value of the first payment is $1,000, since it occurs at the start of the first quarter. The following calculation provides the solution to the problem:

$$P = \$1,000 + \$1,000 \times P(4\%, 19) \text{ or}$$

$$P = \$1,000 + \$1,000 \times 13.134 \text{ or}$$

$$P = \$14,134$$

SUMMARY

In the area of financial mathematics, compound interest rate tables provide us with values with which we can weight money flows that are received or paid in different time periods. The relative weighting assigned to each period's money flow is a function of the price of money or the interest rate. The relative weightings permit us to add or subtract money flows from different time periods and produce a meaningful measure. The value of money is usually expressed in terms of present value or value at some future specified date.

ASSIGNMENTS

1. Steven Hudson has agreed to settle a debt of $100,000 by paying $14,903 per year for ten years. What effective rate of interest is Steven paying under this agreement?

2. Findling Hospital is planning a major expansion project. The construction cost of the project is to be paid from the proceeds of serial notes. The notes are of equal amounts and include a provision for interest at an annual rate of 8 percent payable semiannually over the next 10 years. It is expected that receipts from the hospital will provide for the repayment of principal and interest on the notes. Allan Klein, controller of the hospital, has estimated that the cash flow available for repayment of principal and interest will be $450,000 per year. The construction project is expected to cost $3,420,000. Can the hospital meet the peak debt service with existing cash flows?

3. Jerry Scott has just accepted a position with a state agency that has a retirement pension plan calling for joint contributions by the employee and the employer. Jerry is now 10 years from retirement age of 65 and expects to contribute $400 per year to the plan, which would make him eligible for payments of $1,000 per year for the remainder of his life, starting in 10 years. Since this retirement plan is optional, Jerry is considering the alternative of investing annually an amount equal to his $400 per year contribution. If Jerry can assume that his investments would earn 8 percent annually, and that his life expectancy is 80 years, should he invest in his own plan or should he make contributions to his employer's fund?

4. Meany Hospital wishes to provide for the retirement of an obligation of $10,000,000 that becomes due July 1, 2005. The hospital plans to deposit $500,000 in a special fund each July 1 for eight years, starting July 1, 1997. In addition, the hospital wishes to deposit on July 1, 1997, an amount that, with accumulated interest at 10 percent compounded annually, will bring the total value of the fund to the required $10,000,000 at the end of 2005. What dollar amount should the hospital deposit?

5. Jim Hubert, an investment banker with The Ohio Company, is arranging a financing package with Bill Andrews, president of Liebish Hospital. The financing package calls for $20 million in bonds to be repaid in 20 years. A decision must be made regarding the amount that must be deposited on an annual basis in a sinking fund. It is estimated that the sinking fund will earn interest at the rate of 8 percent compounded annually. What dollar amount must be set aside annually in the sinking fund to meet the $20 million repayment in the 20th year?

6. General Hospital is evaluating a zero-interest capital financing alternative. General would borrow $100,000,000 and receive $62,100,000 in cash. The $100,000,000 note would carry no interest payment but would be due at the end of the fifth year. The lendor would require an annual sinking fund payment over the next five years to meet the maturity value of $100,000,000. If the fund is scheduled to earn interest at the rate of 6 percent annually, what amount must be deposited annually?

7. ABC Hospital is embarking on a major renovation program. The total cost of construction will be $50,000,000. Payments will be $10,000,000 at the end of year 1, $30,000,000 at the end of year 2, and $10,000,000 at the end of year 3. ABC wants to set aside sufficient funds today to meet the expected construction draws. If the fund can be expected to earn 8 percent per annum, what amount should be set aside?

8. If you issue $100,000 of 10 percent bonds with interest payable semiannually over the next five years, what is the market value of the bonds if the required market rate of interest is 12% annually? Assume that no payment of principal is made until maturity.

9. You have agreed to buy an adjacent medical office building with quarterly payments of $100,000 for the next six years. Payments are due at the beginning of each quarter. If the cost of money to you is 16% per annum, would you pay $1,200,000 in cash today to the present owners?

10. You plan to invest $1 million per year for the next three years to meet future professional liability payments. If the fund earns interest at a rate of 10 percent per annum, how large will the balance be in five years? Assume that no payments for claims are made until then.

SOLUTIONS AND ANSWERS

1. The following graph and calculations show the effective rate of interest Steven is paying:

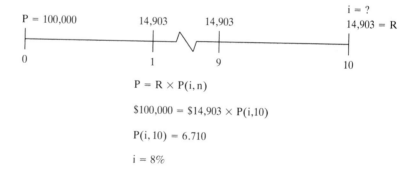

$$P = R \times P(i, n)$$

$$\$100,000 = \$14,903 \times P(i,10)$$

$$P(i, 10) = 6.710$$

$$i = 8\%$$

2. In this hospital expansion project, it is necessary to recognize that debt service will be at the maximum or peak in the first year. This is the pattern that results with a serial note. Thus:

Debt principal payment = $3,420,000/20 = $171,000

Interest in first six months = .04 × $3,420,000 = $136,800

Interest in second six months = .04 × ($3,420,000 − $171,000) = $129,960

Total first-year debt service = $171,000 + $136,800 + $171,000 + $129,960
                                      = $608,760

Thus, Findling Hospital's project cannot be financed with the existing cash flow of $450,000.

3. The following graph and calculations are relevant to Jerry's retirement fund decision:

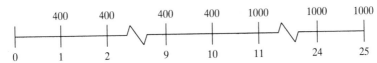

Calculation of the value of the state agency's payments at Year 10:

$$P = \$1,000 \times P(8\%, 15)$$

$$P = \$1,000 \times 8.559$$

$$P = \$8,559$$

Calculation of the value of Jerry's deposits at Year 10:

$$F = \$400 \times F(8\%, 10)$$

$$F = \$400 \times 14.4866$$

$$F = \$5,795$$

Thus, Jerry is better off with the state agency's retirement plan. His deposits of $400 would not provide a fund large enough to give him $1,000 a year for 15 years.

4. The relevant calculations for Meany Hospital are as follows:

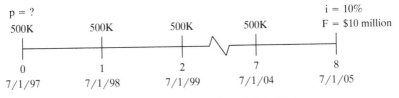

Calculation of the value of annual deposits at July 1, 1995:

$$F = \$500,000 \times f(10\%, 8)$$

$$+ [\$500,000 \times F(10\%, 7)]f(10\%, 1)$$

$$F = \$500,000 \times 2.1436 + (\$500,000 \times 9.4872) \times 1.10$$

$$F = \$1,071,800 + \$5,217,960 = \$6,289,760$$

Calculation of the required deposit at July 1, 1997.

Required amount at July 1, 2005, must equal $10,000,000 − $6,289,760, or $3,710,240

$$P = \$3,710,240 \times p(10\%, 8) = \text{required deposit at July 1, 1997}$$

$$P = \$3,710,240 \times .467$$

$$P = \$1,732,682 = \text{deposit required at July 1, 1997}$$

5. The following graph and calculations show the dollar amount that must be set aside annually in the sinking fund to meet the $20-million repayment in the 20th year:

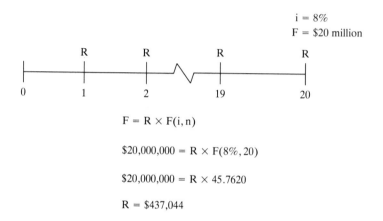

$$i = 8\%$$
$$F = \$20 \text{ million}$$

$$F = R \times F(i, n)$$

$$\$20,000,000 = R \times F(8\%, 20)$$

$$\$20,000,000 = R \times 45.7620$$

$$R = \$437,044$$

6. The following graph and calculations show the amount that General Hospital will have to deposit in the sinking fund each year:

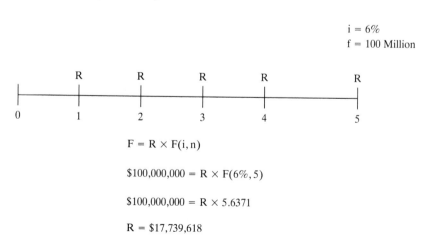

$$i = 6\%$$
$$f = 100 \text{ Million}$$

$$F = R \times F(i, n)$$

$$\$100,000,000 = R \times F(6\%, 5)$$

$$\$100,000,000 = R \times 5.6371$$

$$R = \$17,739,618$$

7. The following graph and calculations show the amount that ABC Hospital must set aside to meet expected construction draws:

i = 8%

P = ?

$10 Million $30 Million $10 Million

1   2   3

$$P = \$10,000,000 \times P(8\%, 1) + \$30,000,000 \times P(8\%, 2) + \$10,000,000 \times P(8\%, 3)$$

$$P = \$10,000,000 \times .926 + \$30,000,000 \times .857 + \$10,000,000 \times .794$$

$$P = \$42,910,000$$

8. The market value of the bonds may be calculated as follows:

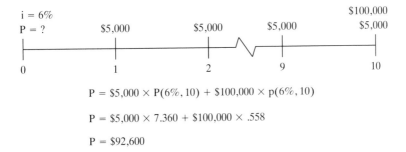

i = 6%

P = ?

$5,000 $5,000 $5,000 $100,000 / $5,000

0   1   2   9   10

$$P = \$5,000 \times P(6\%, 10) + \$100,000 \times p(6\%, 10)$$

$$P = \$5,000 \times 7.360 + \$100,000 \times .558$$

$$P = \$92,600$$

9. To determine whether you should pay $1,200,000 in cash today to the present owners, the following graph and calculations are relevant:

i = 4%

P = ?

$100,000 $100,000 $100,000 $100,000

0   1   2   23   24

$$P = \$100,000 + \$100,000 \times P(4\%, 23)$$

$$P = \$100,000 + \$100,000 \times 14.857$$

$$P = \$1,585,700$$

Yes, you should make the $1,200,000 cash payment to the present owners. The present value of an outright purchase price of $1,200,000 is less than the present value of the installment sale arrangement.

10. The following graph and calculations show the amount of the fund balance in five years:

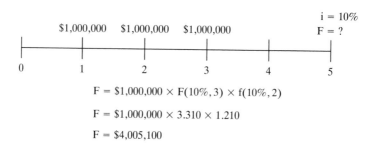

$$F = \$1,000,000 \times F(10\%, 3) \times f(10\%, 2)$$

$$F = \$1,000,000 \times 3.310 \times 1.210$$

$$F = \$4,005,100$$

Chapter 13

Capital Project Analysis

Capital project analysis falls in the programming phase of the management control process. Whereas zero-base budgeting or zero-base review can be thought of as the programming phase of management control concerned with old or existing programs, capital project analysis is the phase primarily concerned with new programs. Here, it is broadly defined to include the selection of investment projects.

Capital project analysis is an ongoing activity, but it is not usually summarized annually in the budget. The capital budget is the yearly estimate of resources that will be expended for new programs during the coming year. Capital budgeting may be thought of as less comprehensive and shorter term than capital project analysis.

PARTICIPANTS IN THE ANALYTICAL PROCESS

The capital decision-making process in the health care industry is complex for several reasons. First, the stated goals and objectives of a health care facility are likely to be more complex and less quantifiable than those of a for-profit firm in which profit is the major, if not exclusive, goal. Second, the number of individuals involved in the process, either directly or indirectly, is likely to be greater in the health care industry than in most other industries. Figure 13-1 illustrates the relationships of various parties involved in the capital decision-making process of a health care facility.

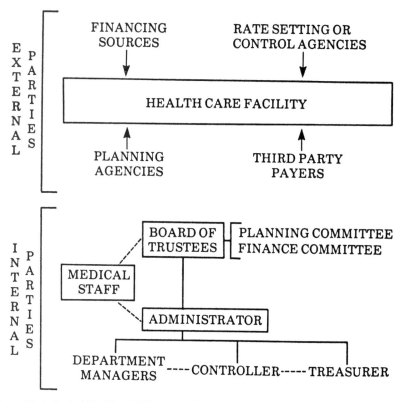

Figure 13-1 Capital Decision-Making Participants

External Participants

Financing Sources

The availability of external funding for many new programs is an important variable in the capital decision-making process. A variety of individual organizations are involved in the credit determination process, including investment bankers, bond rating agencies, bankers, and feasibility consultants. Many of these entities and their roles are discussed in Chapter 14. At this juncture, it is important to recognize that, collectively, these entities may influence the amount of money that can be borrowed and the terms of the borrowing, and this can affect the nature and size of capital projects undertaken by a given health care facility.

Rate-Setting and Rate Control Agencies

Many states have agencies that set and control the rates that hospitals and other health care facilities can charge for services. The influence exerted by rate-setting or rate control organizations on capital decision making is indirect but still extremely important. Control of rates can limit both short-term and long-term profitability. This control can reduce a health care facility's ability to repay indebtedness and thus limit its access to the capital markets. More directly, rate-setting organizations can limit the amount of money available for financing capital projects by reducing the amount of profits that may be retained. One of the major effects of rate control is to reduce significantly the level of capital expenditures by hospitals.

Third-Party Payers

Like rate-setting and rate control agencies, third-party payers can indirectly influence the capital decision-making process. Through their reimbursement provisions, third-party payers can affect both capital expenditure levels and sources of financing. For example, many individuals feel that third-party cost reimbursement provides a strong incentive for increased capital spending: in most situations, such cost reimbursement provides for the reimbursement of depreciation and interest expense, which may then be used to repay financial requirements associated with any indebtedness. As a result, the risk associated with hospital indebtedness is reduced. In the past, third-party cost reimbursement favorably affected the availability of credit. Conversely, recent departures from cost reimbursement have had an adverse impact on credit availability.

Planning Agencies

In many states, state approval of capital expenditures is still required. In some areas, planning agencies at the local level initially review certificate of need applications. Their recommendations are then passed on to the state authority responsible for final approval or disapproval. An unfavorable decision by the state can be appealed in court.

Internal Participants

Board of Trustees

Ultimately, the board of trustees is responsible for the capital expenditure and capital financing program of the health care facility. However, in most situations, the board delegates this authority to management and special board committees. The board's major function should be to establish clearly defined goals and objectives. The statement of goals and objectives is a prerequisite to the programming phase of management control, which includes capital expenditure analysis. Without a clear statement of goals and objectives, capital expenditure programs cannot be adequately defined and analyzed.

Another role of the governing board should be to approve a preliminary five-year capital expenditure program. This capital expenditure program should link back to the strategic financial plan discussed in Chapter 7. The list of capital expenditures should be generated by management and should reflect not just a wish list of capital expenditures that would be nice to make, but should represent management's best guess concerning what future capital expenditures will be essential in order to meet and maintain the organization's mission.

Planning Committee

Many health care facility boards of trustees have established planning committees whose primary function is to define, analyze, and propose programs to help the organization attain its goals and objectives. These committees are specialized groups, within the board of trustees, that are directly involved in capital expenditure analysis.

Finance Committee

Some boards of trustees have also established finance committees that have authority in several key financial functional areas, including budgeting and capital financing. In the latter two areas, a finance committee may be involved with translating programs, perhaps identified by the planning committee, into financing requirements. These requirements may be operational or capital. The ensuring of adequate financing to meet program requirements is the finance committee's major responsibility. Many of the finance committee's budgetary functions are delegated to the controller; many of its capital financing functions are delegated to the treasurer.

Administration

The administration is responsible on a day-to-day basis for implementing approved capital expenditure programs and developing related financing plans. The administration must develop an organizational system that responds to the requests of department managers and medical staff for capital expenditures. Much of the authority vested in the administrator's position is delegated by the board of trustees. The administration may also seek board approval for its own programs.

Department Managers

Department managers make most of the internal requests for capital expenditure approval. In many health care facilities, formal systems for approving capital expenditures have been developed to receive, process, and answer departmental requests. The allocation of a limited capital budget to competing departmental areas is a difficult task for management. Careful definition of the criteria for capital decision making can help make this problem less political and more objective.

Medical Staff

Medical staff demands for capital expenditures are a problem unique to the health care industry. Medical staff members, in most situations, are not employees of the health care facility but rather use it to treat their private patients. Because of their ability to change a facility's use patterns dramatically and thus affect financial solvency, administrators listen to, and frequently honor, their wishes. Health care facilities are thus faced with strong pressure from individuals who have little financial interest in the organization and whose financial interest may in fact be contrary to that of the health care facility.

Controller

The controller facilitates approval of capital expenditure. The controller is usually responsible for developing capital expenditure request forms and for assisting department managers in preparing their capital expenditure proposals. The controller usually serves as an analyst, assisting the administrator in allocating the budget to competing departmental areas. In many small health care facilities, the controller's function may be merged with that of the treasurer.

Treasurer

The treasurer is responsible for obtaining funds for both short- and long-term programs. The treasurer may work with the finance committee to negotiate for funds necessary to implement approved programs.

CLASSIFICATION OF CAPITAL EXPENDITURES

A capital expenditure is a commitment of resources that is expected to provide benefits over a reasonably long period of time, at least two or more years. Any system of management control must take into account the various types of capital expenditures. Different types raise different problems; they may require specific individuals to evaluate them or special methods of evaluation.

The more important classifications of capital expenditures are

- time period over which the investment occurs
- types of resources invested
- dollar amounts of capital expenditures
- types of benefits received

Time Period of Investment

Determining the amount of resources committed to a capital project depends heavily on the definition of the time period. For example, how would you determine the capital expenditures needed by a project that had a very low initial investment cost but a significant investment cost in future years? Should just the initial capital expenditure be considered, or should total expenditures over the life of the project be considered? If the latter is the answer, is it appropriate just to add the total expenditures together, or should expenditures made in later years be weighted to reflect their lower present value? If so, at what discount rate? These are not simple questions to answer, but they are very important in evaluating capital projects.

A classic example of this type of problem in the health care industry is the initiation of programs that have been funded by grants. In many such situations, there appears to be little or no investment of capital expenditure, since the amounts are funded almost totally through the grant. The programs thus appear to be highly desirable. However, if there is a formal or informal commitment to continue the programs for a longer period of time, capital expenditures and additional operating funds for later periods may be required. In such cases, it is imperative that the grant-funded projects be classified separately and their long-run capital cost requirements be identified. The health care facility may very well not have a sufficient capital base to finance a program's continuation. Thus, granting agencies should assess the health care facility's financial capability to continue funded programs after the grant period expires.

Types of Resources Invested

When discussing capital expenditures, many individuals are apt to limit their attention just to the expenditure or resources invested in capital assets, that is, tangible fixed assets. This narrow focus has several shortcomings, however, and may result in ineffective capital expenditure decisions.

First, focusing on tangible fixed assets implies ownership; yet many health care facilities lease a significant percentage of their fixed assets, especially in the major movable equipment area. If a lease is not construed to be a capital expenditure, it may escape the normal review and approval system. Lease payments should be considered as a capital expenditure. Furthermore, the contractual provisions of the lease should be considered in determining the total expenditure amount. Weight should be given to future payments or to the alternative purchase price of the asset.

Second, the capital costs of a capital expenditure are only one part of total cost; indeed, in the labor-intensive health care industry, capital costs may be just the tip of the iceberg. All of the operating costs associated with beginning and continuing a capital project should be considered. Programs with very low capital investment costs may not look as good when their operating costs are considered.

Life cycle costing is a method for estimating the cost of a capital project that reflects total costs, both operating and capital, over the project's estimated useful life. The life cycle cost of all contemplated programs should be considered; failure to do this can cause errors in the capital decision-making process, especially in the selection of alternative programs. Consider, for example, two alternative renal dialysis projects; both may have the same capacity, but one may have a significantly greater investment cost because it uses equipment requiring less monitoring and lower operating costs. Failure to consider the operating cost differences between these two projects may bias the decision in favor of the project with lower capital expenditures, and result in higher expenses in the long run.

Amounts of Expenditures

Different systems of control and evaluation are required for different-sized projects. It would not be economical to spend $500 in administrative time evaluating the purchase of a $100 calculator. Nor would it be wise to spend only $500 to evaluate a $25 million building program. Obviously, control over capital expenditures should be conditioned by the total amount involved; and, if appropriate, the amount should be based on the total life cycle cost.

Control of capital expenditures in most organizations, including health care facilities, typically follows one of three patterns:

1. approval required for all capital expenditures
2. approval required for all capital expenditures above a pre-established limit
3. no approval required for individual capital expenditure projects below a total budgeted amount

Retaining final approval of all capital expenditures lets management exert maximum control over the resource-spending area. However, the cost of management time to develop and review expenditure proposals is high. In most organizations of any size, management review of all capital expenditure requests is not productive. However, some review is needed, so a limit must be established. For example, a given responsibility center or department need not submit any justification for individual capital expenditure projects requiring less than $500 in investment cost. In such cases, there is usually some formal or informal limitation on the total dollar size of the capital budget that will be available for small-dollar capital expenditures. This prevents responsibility center managers from making excessive investments in capital expenditures that have no formalized reviewing system.

Another form of management control over capital expenditures is an absolute dollar limit; that is, any responsibility center manager may spend up to an authorized capital budget on any items in question. The real negotiation involves determining the size of the capital budget that will be available for individual departments. However, this system, although least costly in terms of review time, does not ensure that the capital expenditures actually made are necessarily in the best interests of the organization.

Types of Benefits

Depending on the types of benefits envisioned for a capital expenditure, different systems of management control and evaluation may be necessary. For example, investment in a medical office building brings different benefits than investment in an alcoholic rehabilitation unit. Such differences make it inappropriate to rely exclusively on any one method of evaluating projects. This is important: *traditional methods of evaluating capital budgeting may not be appropriate in the health care industry.* Traditional methods evaluate only the financial aspects of a capital expenditure.

However, projects in the health care industry may produce benefits that are far more important than a reduction in cost or an increase in profit.

The major categories of investment in which benefits may be differentially evaluated are:

- operational continuance
- financial
- other

The first category of investment produces benefits that permit continued operations of the facility along present lines. Here, the governing board or management must usually make two decisions: (1) Are continued operations in the present form desirable? (In most cases the answer is yes.) (2) Which alternative investment project can achieve continued operations in the most desirable way (for example, with lowest cost, patient safety, and so on)? A classic example of this type of investment is one based on a licensure requirement for installation of a sprinkler system in a nursing home. Failure to make the investment may result in discontinuance of operations.

The second category of investment provides benefits that are largely financial, in terms of either reduced cost or increased profits to the organization. Many individuals may believe that these two are identical, that is, that reduced costs imply increased profits. However, as we will see, this may not be true if cost reimbursement for either operating or capital costs is present. The important point to remember is that, if the major benefits are financial, traditional capital budgeting methods may be more appropriate.

The third category of investments is a catch-all category. Investments here would range from projects that activate major new medical areas (such as outpatient or mental health services) to projects that improve employee working conditions (such as employee gymnasiums). In this category, benefits may be harder to quantify and evaluate. Traditional capital budgeting methods may thus be appropriate only in the selection of least costly ways to provide designated services.

THE CAPITAL PROJECT DECISION-MAKING PROCESS

Making decisions on which capital projects will be undertaken is not an easy task. In many respects, this may represent the most difficult and important management decision area. The allocation of limited resources to specific project areas will directly affect the efficiency and effectiveness, and ultimately the continued viability, of the organization.

For our purposes we can divide the capital decision-making process into four inter-related activities or stages:

1. generation of project information
2. evaluation of projects
3. decisions about which projects to fund
4. project implementation and reporting

Generation of Project Information

In this stage of the decision-making process, information is gathered that can later be analyzed and evaluated. This is an extremely important stage because inadequate or inaccurate information can lead to bad decision making. Specifically, there are six major categories of information that should be included in most capital expenditure proposals:

1. alternatives available
2. resources available
3. cost data
4. benefit data
5. prior performance
6. risk projection

Alternatives Available

A major deficiency in many capital expenditure decisions is the failure to consider possible alternatives. Too many times, capital expenditures are presented on a "take it or leave it" basis; yet there usually are alternatives. For example, different manufacturers might be selected, different methods of financing could be used, or different boundaries in the scope of the project could be defined.

Resources Available

Capital expenditure decisions are not made in a vacuum. In most situations, there are constraints on the amount of available funding. This is the whole rationale behind capital expenditure decision making: scarce resources must be allocated among a virtually unlimited number of investment opportunities. There is little question about the necessity of information concerning the availability of funding at the top level of management.

However, there is some question about its importance at the departmental level. On one hand, a budgetary constraint may temper requests for capital expenditures. On the other hand, it may encourage a department manager to submit only those projects that are in the department's best interests. These may, in fact, conflict with the broader goals and objectives of the organization as a whole.

Cost Data

It goes without saying that cost information is an important variable in the decision-making process. In all cases, the life cycle costs of a project should be presented. Limiting cost information just to capital costs can be counterproductive.

Benefit Data

We can divide benefit data into two categories: quantitative and nonquantitative. It is believed by some that many of the benefit data in the health care industry are nonquantitative. To a large extent, quantitative data are viewed as synonymous with financial data. And since financial criteria are sometimes viewed as less important in the nonprofit health care industry, the assumption is that quantitative data are also less important. This is not true. Quantitative data can and should be used. Effective management control is predicated on the use of numbers that relate to the organization's stated goals and objectives. It may not be easy to develop quantitative estimates of benefits, but it is not impossible. For example, assume that a hospital in an urban area opens a clinic in a medically underserved area. One of the stated goals for the clinic is the reduction of unnecessary use of the hospital's emergency room for nonurgent care. A realistic and quantifiable benefit of this project should be a numerical reduction in the use of the hospital's emergency room for nonurgent care by individuals from the clinic area. However, no quantitative assessments are either projected or reported; the only quantitative statistics used are those of a financial nature. The management control process in this situation is less valuable than it should have been.

Prior Performance

Information on prior operating results of projects proposed by responsibility center managers can be useful. A comparison of prior actual results with forecast results can give a decision maker some idea of the manager's reliability in forecasting. In too many cases, project planners are likely to overstate a project's benefits if the project interests them. Review of prior performance can help a manager evaluate the accuracy of the projections.

It is generally acknowledged that most people requesting capital expenditure approval for their projects will overstate benefits (revenues) and understate costs. This type of behavior is not necessarily intentional, but may reflect sincere faith and interest in the project. Individuals reviewing proposals must recognize this inherent bias and also recognize that not all individuals make the same magnitude of errors in forecasts.

Risk Projection

Nothing is certain in this world except death and taxes, especially when evaluating capital expenditure projects. It is important to ask "what-if" questions. For example, how would costs and benefits change if volume changed? Volume of service is a key variable in most capital expenditure forecasts, and its effects should be understood. In some situations requiring projections for the highest, the lowest, and the most likely, projections of volume can help answer the questions. The same types of calculations can be made for other key factors, such as prices of key inputs and technological changes. This is an important area to understand because some capital expenditure projects are inherently more risky than others. Specifically, programs with extremely high proportions of fixed or sunk costs are far more sensitive to changes in volume than those with low percentages of fixed or sunk costs.

Evaluation of Projects

Although financial criteria are clearly not the only factors that should be evaluated in capital expenditure decisions, there are few, if any, capital expenditure decisions that can omit financial considerations. Our focus is on two prime financial criteria: solvency and cost.

Solvency

A project that cannot show a positive rate of return in the long run should be questioned. If implemented, such a program will need to be subsidized by some other existing program area. For example, should a hospital subsidize an outpatient clinic? If so, to what extent? This is the kind of policy and *financial* question the governing board of the organization needs to determine. The fairness of some patients subsidizing other patients is one of the basic qualitative issues in capital project analysis. Operation of an insolvent program can eventually threaten the solvency of the entire organization. Thus, organizations that plan to subsidize insolvent programs must be in good financial condition. And assessment of financial condition can only be done after the organization's financial statements are examined.

Cost

Cost is the second important financial concern. An organization needs to select the projects that contribute most to the attainment of its objectives, given resource constraints. This type of analysis is often called *cost benefit analysis*. Benefits differ from project to project. In evaluating alternative programs, decision makers must weight those benefits according to their own preferences and then compare them with cost.

There is a second dimension to the cost criterion. All projects that are eventually selected should cost the least to provide the service. This type of evaluation is sometimes called *cost effectiveness analysis*. Least cost should be defined as the present value of both operating and capital costs (methods for determining this are discussed later in the chapter).

Decisions about Which Projects To Fund

At this juncture of the capital expenditure decision-making process, it is time to make the decisions. In front of the decision makers are lists of possible projects that may be funded. Each project should represent the lowest cost of providing the desired service or output. In addition, various benefit data on each project should be described. These data should be consistent with the criteria that the decision makers used in their capital expenditure decision making.

To illustrate this process, assume that the members of the governing board are deciding on how many, if any, of three proposed programs they will fund in the coming year. The three programs are a burn care unit, a hemodialysis unit, and a commercial laboratory. Assume further that the members have decided that there are only four criteria of importance to them:

1. solvency
2. incremental management time required
3. public image
4. medical staff approval

Since none of the three projects clearly dominates, it is not clear which, if any, should be funded. Thus, the decision makers must weight the criteria according to their own preferences and determine the overall ranking of the three projects. For example, one manager might weight solvency and management time very highly, relative to public image and the medical staff, and thus select the commercial laboratory project. Another manager might weight medical staff and public image more heavily and thus select the hemodialysis or burn care unit project.

In this example, the three projects can be ranked in terms of their relative standing on each of the four criteria:

	Project		
Criterion	Hemodialysis Unit	Burn Care Unit	Commercial Laboratory
Solvency	2	3	1
Management time	2	3	1
Public image	2	1	3
Medical staff	1	2	3

Project Implementation and Reporting

Most capital expenditure control systems are concerned primarily, if not exclusively, with analysis and evaluation prior to selection. However, a very real concern should be focused on whether the projected benefits are actually being realized as forecast. Without this feedback on the actual results of prior investments, the capital expenditure control system's feedback loop is not complete.

Here are some of the specific advantages of establishing a capital expenditure review program:

- Capital expenditure review could highlight differences between planned versus actual performance that may permit corrective action. If actual performance is never evaluated, corrective action may not be taken. This could mean that the projected benefits might never be realized.

- Use of a review process may result in more accurate estimates. If individuals realize that they will be held responsible for their estimates, they may tend to be more careful with their projections. This will ensure greater accuracy in forecast results.
- Forecasts by individuals with a continuous record of biased forecasts can be adjusted to reflect that bias. This should result in a better forecast of actual results.

JUSTIFICATION OF CAPITAL EXPENDITURES

In most health care organizations, there is a very formalized process for approval of a capital expenditure. Usually, this approval process is initiated by a department or responsibility center manager through the completion of a capital expenditure approval form. An example of a completed capital expenditure approval form is shown in Exhibit 13–1. Both the approval form and the approval process may vary across health care organizations, depending on the nature of the management control process in each case.

Exhibit 13–1 Completed Capital Expenditure Approval Form

APPRAISAL SHEET FOR
CAPITAL EXPENDITURE PROPOSALS

Department and #   Surgery #818

Date of request for purchase   1/7/93

Summary description of item or package of items (attach original request for purchase)

IABP Model 10 with cardiac output computer and recorder (Intra Aortic Balloon Pump)

Total capital expenditure, including training, renovation, and purchase of equipment (attach list) — $19,500

Undepreciated value of equipment being replaced — 0

　Total cost of implementation — $19,500

Appraisal Instructions

　Level I—Complete a Level I assessment for:
　　1　a new item having a total capital expenditure exceeding $2,000, or
　　2.　a replacement item having a total capital expenditure exceeding $20,000, or
　　3.　a proposed capital expenditure requiring an evaluation before a purchase (or lease) decision may be made.

Exhibit 13–1 continued

Level II—Complete both a Level I and a Level II assessment for any proposed capital expenditure that:
1. exceeds $100,000, or
2. initiates or modifies the scope or type of health services rendered in the community and may require a certificate of need, or
3. requires a more extensive evaluation than offered by a Level I review.

Appraisal Outcome	By (initials)	Date	Priority Status
Request denied	_____	_____	_____
Request accepted & pending	_____	_____	_____
Request approved	_____	_____	_____

I. Level I Review—Complete the following assessment for any proposed capital expenditure requiring either a Level I or Level II review.

A. Need
   1. Indicate whether the proposed capital expenditure contributes *directly* to the achievement of any of the following management goals (check those that apply)
      - _____ Revenue
      - _____ Hospital improvement study
      - _____ Productivity
      - ____X____ Quality assurance
      - _____ Employee development
      - _____ Management services consultant package
      - _____ Other goal (specify) _____

   2. Indicate whether the proposed capital expenditure contributes *directly* to the achievement of any of the following hospital goals (check one or more goals)
      - ____X____ Patient care
      - _____ Medical and allied health education
      - ____X____ Community service
      - _____ Cost containment
      - ____X____ The leadership role
      - _____ Clinical research

   3. Provide the following information on historical and projected utilization of items for the provision of patient care services. (See the Finance Department for assistance in completing this section.)

      a. For replacement items only:

         (1) Identify units of service, if any, provided through the utilization of existing equipment; the actual volume of services provided during the most recent year for which statistics are available; the current patient charge, if any, for these services; and the annual revenue realized.

Exhibit 13-1 continued

	Unit of Service	Historical Annual Volume	Patient Charge	Annual Revenue
1.				
2.				
3.				
4.				
Total		Units	$	

(2) Serial # of item _____

(3) Fixed asset tag # _____

    b. For both new and replacement items:

        (1) Identify the units of service, if any, to be offered through acquisition of the proposed item and the estimated volume of services to be provided annually. If known, provide the proposed patient charge per unit of service.

	Unit of Service	Estimated Annual Volume	Proposed Patient Charge
1.	Ped. open heart	161	$459.16(Avg)
2.			
3.			
4.			

        (2) Identify any other services whose volume of utilization will be affected through acquisition of the proposed item.

        (3) Percentage of charge patients for department (from cost report) __93.1__

        (4) Estimated useful life of equipment: _____10_____ years.

    4. Document the reasons justifying the acquisition of the proposed capital expenditure, particularly as they relate to the achievement of hospital, departmental, and management goals and objectives.
We presently borrow General Hospital's Balloon Pumps 3 or 4 times per month. This is a life-saving device. Without it, some patients cannot survive open-heart surgery.

B. Economic feasibility
    1. Estimate any change in the annual operating costs associated with acquisition of this proposed capital expenditure. (See the Finance Department for assistance in completing this section.)

Exhibit 13–1 continued

	Change in Annual Operating Cost
Personal	
Employee Benefits @23%	
Physician Cost	
Materials and Supplies	
Maintenance Contracts	
Insurance	
Other Depreciation	$1,950
Total Change in Annual Operating Cost	$1,950

Provide documentation in support of the above estimates.

2. Financial analysis (to be completed by Finance):

Estimated Cost to Purchase
IAPB Model 10 with Cardiac Output Computer

Cash Expenditure	Cost Reimbursement @ 26%	Net Cash (Disbursed) Received	Present Value @6%
$(19,500)	$ 507	$(18,993)	$(17,918)
	507	507	451
	507	507	426
	507	507	402
	507	507	379
	507	507	357
	507	507	337
	507	507	318
	507	507	300
	507	507	283
$(19,500)	$5,070	$(14,430)	$(14,665)
Total present value (cost)			$(14,665)

3. Space analysis:
   a. Change in the number of square feet of space required for item: N/A
   b. Is existing department space available for the item?

(Circle one)   (Yes)   No
If not, document plan for acquiring additional space.

C. Acceptability
   1. Physician impact of the capital expenditure decision:
      a. What is the *scope* of any physician attitude change? (check one)
         _____ 1 No change. (skip to Section C-2)
         ___X___ 2 One or two physicians will be affected.
         _____ 3 The majority of the physicians in a hospital service will be
                      affected.

Exhibit 13–1 continued

    b. What is the *intensity* of the effect on physician attitude? (check two answers—one for acceptance and one for nonacceptance)

Not accepted:

    _____ 4 The physicians affected will move their practices to other hospitals.

    ____X____ 3 The physicians affected will tend to reduce their practices at the hospital.

    _____ 2 The physicians affected, at the very least, will be disgruntled and will tend to discuss in the community and with other physicians the lack of the expenditure or project.

    _____ 1 The physicians will be aware of the lack of support for the project and will be less likely to believe that the hospital is maintaining a proper level of patient care.

    _____ 0 No effect.

Accepted:

    _____ 0 No effect.

    _____ 1 The physicians affected will be aware of the expenditure or project and will be satisfied that the hospital is maintaining a high level of patient care.

    ____X____ 2 The physicians affected will be very impressed and will tend to discuss the expenditure or project favorably in the community and with other physicians.

    _____ 3 The physicians affected will tend to increase their practices moderately in the hospital.

    _____ 4 The physician affected will move their practices to the hospital.

2. Employee impact of the capital expenditure decision:

    What is the effect on the attitude of hospital employees?

    (Check two answers—one for acceptance and one for nonacceptance.)

Not accepted:

    _____ 4 Major and widespread negative impact on employee morale and attitude toward the hospital.

    _____ 3 Widespread disappointment with the hospital and some general negative effect on the hospital's image among employees.

    ____X____ 2 Negative reaction from a limited group of employees (one or two departments).

    _____ 1 Limited reaction from a few employees.

    _____ 0 No effect.

Accepted:

    _____ 0 No effect.

    _____ 1 Limited reaction from a few employees.

    ____X____ 2 Positive reaction from a limited group of employees (one or two departments).

    _____ 3 Positive impact on nearly all employees.

    _____ 4 Major and widespread impact with long-term effect on employee attitude toward the hospital.

Exhibit 13–1 continued

3. Community impact of the capital expenditure decision:
What is the expected community impact?
(Check the answers below which best describe the expected community impact; check one for acceptance and one for nonacceptance.)
Not accepted:

_____ 4 Intense and widespread negative reaction in the community will result in a severe blow to the hospital's image.

____X____ 3 A widespread negative effect on the hospital's general image and reputation will result.

_____ 1 The attitudes of relatively few people will be negatively affected.

_____ 0 No effect.

Accepted:

_____ 0 No effect.

_____ 1 Relatively few people will be positively affected.

_____ 2 Certain groups in the community will be favorably impressed.

____X____ 3 A widespread positive effect on the hospital's image and reputation will result.

_____ 4 Significant and widespread positive community reaction will contribute significantly to the hospital's general image and reputation.

APPRAISAL SCORE SHEET FOR
CAPITAL EXPENDITURE PROPOSALS

	Assigned Value	Raw Score	Priority Instructions	Priority Score
A. Need evaluation				
1. If proposal directly contributes to one or more management goals (I-A-1)	+1	+1		
2. If proposal directly contributes to one or more hospital goals (I-A-2)	+1	+1		
(For Level II reviews only)				
3. Performance expectations (II-A-4)				
If negative or questionable	−1			
If positive	+1			

Exhibit 13–1 continued

	Assigned Value	Raw Score	Priority Instructions	Priority Score
4. If certificate-of-need approval is necessary, but unlikely (II-A-5)	−3	—	Enter positive raw score as	—
Subtotal, need raw score		2	priority score.	2
B. Economic Evaluation				
1. If annual operating costs (including depreciation) are reduced (I-B-1-a)	+1			
2. Return on investment (I-B-2-a)				
If greater than 7.5%	+2			
If positive	0			
If negative	−2	−2		
3. If significant additional space is required (I-B-3)	−1			
(For Level II reviews only)				
4. If external financing is required (II-B-1)	−1	—	Enter positive raw score as	—
Subtotal, economic raw score		−2	priority score.	
C. Acceptability Evaluation				
1. Physician attitude			If scope score is greater than 2,	
a. Scope (enter score for response to question I-C-1-A)	1 to 3	1	enter raw score in priority score column.	
b. Intensity (add responses to question I-C-1-b)	0 to 8	5	If raw score exceeds 4, the excess is priority score.	1

Exhibit 13–1 continued

	Assigned Value	Raw Score	Priority Instructions	Priority Score
2. Employee attitude (add responses to question I-C-2)	0 to 8	4	If raw score exceeds 4, the excess is priority score.	
3. Community attitude (add responses to question I-C-3)	0 to 8	6	If raw score exceeds 4, the excess is priority score.	2
Subtotal, acceptability raw score		16		3
Total Raw Score		16	Total priority score	5

Note: A capital expenditure proposal may be approved, disapproved, or deferred on the basis of an appraisal of the raw scores for need, economy, and acceptability, considered either independently or together. An approved capital expenditure proposal is ranked according to its priority score for future appropriation of capital expenditure funds.

The approval form in Exhibit 13–1 is in fact more comprehensive than that used in most health care organizations. Thus, it provides a detailed summary of the key aspects involved in capital expenditure approval:

- amount and type of expenditure
- attainment of key decision criteria
- detailed financial analysis

In most firms, small capital expenditures are usually not subjected to detailed analysis and do not require justification. For example, capital expenditures under $2,000 are not reviewed according to the instructions in Exhibit 13–1. This does not mean that a department has an unlimited capital expenditures budget if it spends less than $2,000 per item; the department is most likely subject to some overall level for small capital expenditures. For example, a department such as physical therapy might have an $8,000 limit on small capital expenditure items. No justification for capital expenditure items under $2,000 would be required if the aggregate limit of $8,000 is not violated.

Special recognition is also often given to replacement items. In the example in Exhibit 13-1, a replacement expenditure below $20,000 is not subject to review. The rationale for this higher limit relates to the operational continuance of capital expenditures. Replacement expenditures are often viewed as essential to the continuation of existing operations. They are therefore not as closely evaluated as are expenditures for new pieces of equipment.

In any decision-making process, it is important to define carefully the criteria that will be used in the selection process. The example in Exhibit 13-1 has three categories of criteria:

1. need (management goals, hospital goals)
2. economic feasibility
3. acceptability (physicians, employees, community)

Most capital expenditure forms would probably ask for data in the area of economic or financial feasibility. Exhibit 13-1 provides data in other areas as well, and also includes a means for scoring the project. For the specific project being appraised, a raw score of 16 and a priority score of 5 resulted. Different values could be obtained by changing the form's measures and their relative weightings.

The important point to recognize is that project selection usually involves the consideration of criteria other than financial. Failure to collect data on the attainment of those additional criteria for specific projects will often lead to more subjectivity in the process. Without such relevant data, individuals may make inferences that are not legitimate.

A key aspect of the capital expenditure approval process is the financial or economic feasibility of the project. In most capital expenditure forms, there is some summary statistic that measures the project's overall financial performance. In general, such measures are usually categorized as either (1) discounted cash flow methods or (2) nondiscounted cash flow methods. In the present discussion, we shall not be concerned with nondiscounted cash flow methods because they are usually regarded as less sophisticated than discounted cash flow methods.

DISCOUNTED CASH FLOW METHODS

In this section, we examine three discounted cash flow (DCF) methods that are relatively easy to understand and use:

1. net present value
2. profitability index
3. equivalent annual cost

Before examining these three methods, a word of caution is in order: In our view, the calculation of specific DCF measures is an important, but not a critical, phase of capital expenditure review. We strongly believe that the most important phase in the capital expenditure review process is the generation of quality project information. Specifically, the set of alternatives being considered must include the best ones; it does a firm little good to select the best five projects from a list of ten inferior ones. Beyond that, the validity of the forecasted data is critical; small changes in projected volumes, rates, or costs can have profound effects on cash flow. Determination of possible changes in both of these parameters is far more important than discussions about the appropriate discount rate or cost of capital.

Each of the above three DCF methods is based on a time value concept of money. Each is useful in evaluating a specific type of capital expenditure or capital financing alternative. Specifically, their areas of application are

Method of Evaluation	Area of Application
Net present value	Capital financing alternatives
Profitability index	Capital expenditures with financial benefits
Equivalent annual cost	Capital expenditures with nonfinancial benefits

Net Present Value

A net present value (NPV) analysis is a very useful way to analyze alternative methods of capital financing. In most situations, the objective in such a situation is clear: the commodity being dealt with is money, and it is management's goal to minimize the cost of financing operations. (We will consider shortly how this goal may conflict with solvency when the effects of cost reimbursement are considered.)

NPV equals discounted cash inflows less discounted cash outflows. In a comparison of two alternative financing packages, the one with the highest NPV should be selected.

For example, assume that an asset can be financed with a four-year annual $1,000 lease payment or can be purchased outright for $2,800. Assume further that the discount rate is 10 percent, which may reflect either the borrowing cost or the investment rate, depending on which alternative is relevant. (We will discuss the issue of an appropriate discount rate shortly.) The present value cost of the lease is $3,169. This amount is greater than the present value cost of the purchase, $2,800.

With no consideration given to cost reimbursement, the purchase alternative is the lowest cost alternative method of financing.

However, for accuracy, the effects of cost reimbursement should be considered. Reimbursement of costs would mean that the facility would be entitled to reimbursement for depreciation if the asset were purchased, or entitled to the rent payment if the asset were leased. (Some third-party cost payers limit reimbursement on leases to depreciation and interest if the lease is treated as an installment purchase.) Assuming that straight-line depreciation is used and that 20 percent of capital expenses are reimbursed by third-party cost payers, the present value of the reimbursed cash inflow (using the discount factors from Table 12–4) would be as follows:

		Annual Reimbursement	Discount Factor	% of Cost Reimbursement	
Present value of reimbursed depreciation	=	$\dfrac{\$2,800}{4}$	× 3.170 ×	.20	= $444
Present values of reimbursed lease payments	=	$1,000	× 3.170 ×	.20	= $634

If the asset were purchased, the organization would pay out $2,800 immediately. For each of the next four years, it would be reimbursed for the noncash expense item of depreciation in the amount of $700 per year ($2,800/4). However, since only 20 percent of the patients are capital cost payers, only $140 per year would be received (.20 × $700). If the asset were leased, the organization would be permitted reimbursement of the lease payment in the amount of $1,000 per year. However, since only 20 percent of the patients are capital cost payers, only $200 (.20 × $1000) would be paid.

The NPV of the above two financing methods for considering cost reimbursement would be as follows:

		Present Value of Reimbursement (Cash Inflows)	Present Value of Payments (Cash Outflows)	NPV
NPV of purchase	=	$444	− $2,800	= − $2,356
NPV of lease	=	$634	− $3,170	= − $2,536

In this example, it is clear that the best method of financing is outright purchase. By purchasing the asset, annual expenses will be $700 in depreciation, compared with $1,000 per year with the leasing plan. In addition, purchasing is also a lower NPV cost plan. Relative ratings with respect to NPV could change quickly, however, given higher percentages of capital cost reimbursement. To see the impact of cost reimbursement on NPV, assume that 80 percent of capital costs will be reimbursed. When this change is reflected in the above calculations, leasing's NPV (− $633) is lower than purchasing's NPV (− $1,025).

Profitability Index

The profitability index method of capital project evaluation is of primary importance in cases where the benefits of the projects are mostly financial, for example, a capital project that saves costs or expands revenue with a primary purpose of increased profits. In these situations, there is usually a constraint on the availability of funding. Thus, those projects with the highest rate of return per dollar of capital investment are the best candidates for selection. The profitability index attempts to compare rates of return. The numerator is the NPV of the project, and the denominator is the investment cost:

$$\text{Profitability index} = \frac{\text{NPV}}{\text{Investment cost}}$$

To illustrate the use of this measure, let us assume that a hospital is considering an investment in a laundry shared with a group of neighboring hospitals. The initial investment cost is $10,000 for the purchase of new equipment and delivery trucks. Savings in operating costs are estimated to be $2,000 per year for the entire ten-year life of the project. If the discount rate is assumed to be 10 percent, the following calculations could be made, ignoring the effect of cost reimbursement and using the discount factors of Table 12–4.

Present value of operating savings = $2,000 × 6.145 = $12,290

NPV = $12,290 − $10,000 = $2,290

$$\text{Profitability index} = \frac{\$2,290}{\$10,000} = .229$$

Values for profitability indices that are greater than zero imply that the project is earning at a rate greater than the discount rate. Given no funding constraints, all projects with profitability indices greater than zero should be funded. However, in most situations funding constraints do exist, and only a portion of those projects with profitability indices greater than zero are actually accepted.

The above calculations give no consideration to the effects of cost reimbursement. If we assume that 80 percent of the facility's capital expenses are reimbursed and 20 percent of its operating expenses are reimbursed, then the following additional calculations must be made:

$$\text{Present value of reimbursed depreciation} = \frac{\$10,000}{10} \times 6.145 \times .80 = \$4,916$$

$$\text{Present value of lost reimbursement from operating savings} = \$2,000 \times 6.145 \times .20$$

$$= \$2,458$$

$$\text{NPV} = \$2,290 + \$4,916 - \$2,458 = \$4,748$$

$$\text{Profitability index} = \frac{\$4,748}{\$10,000} = .4748$$

The above calculations require some clarification. We are adjusting the initially calculated NPV of $2,290 to reflect the effects of cost reimbursement. Depreciation is the first item to be considered. Since 80 percent of the facility's patients are on capital cost reimbursement formulas, it can expect to receive 80 percent of the annual depreciation charge of $1,000 ($10,000/10) or $800 per year as a reimbursement cash flow. The present value of this stream, $4,916, is added to the initial net present value of $2,290.

The second item to be considered is the operating savings. If the investment is undertaken, the facility can anticipate a yearly savings of $2,000 for the next ten years. However, that savings will reduce its reimbursable costs by $2,000 annually, which means that 20 percent of that amount, or $400, will be lost annually in reimbursement. The present value of that loss for the ten years is $2,458, which is subtracted from the initial NPV. The effect of cost reimbursement thus reduces increased costs associated with new programs, but it also reduces the cost savings associated with new programs.

The preceding example illustrates an important financial concept discussed in Chapter 2. Because some third-party payers still reimburse actual capital costs, a strong financial incentive exists for investment in projects that reduce operating costs. In the above example, the laundry facility's profitability index increased from .229 to .4748 when the effects of capital and operating cost reimbursement were considered.

Equivalent Annual Cost

Equivalent annual cost is of primary value in the selection of capital projects for which alternatives exist. Usually these are capital expenditure projects that are classified as operational continuance or other. (The profitability index measure just discussed is used for projects in which the benefits are primarily financial in nature.)

Equivalent annual cost is the expected average cost, considering both capital and operating cost, over the life of the project. It is calculated by dividing the sum of the present value of operating costs over the life of the project and the present value of the investment cost by the discount factor for an annualized stream of equal payments (as derived from Table 12–4):

$$\text{Equivalent annual cost} = \frac{\text{Present value of operating cost} + \text{Present value of investment cost}}{\text{Present value of annuity}}$$

To illustrate use of this measure, assume that an extended care facility must invest in a sprinkler system to maintain its license. After investigation, two alternatives are identified. One sprinkler system would require a $5,000 investment and an annual maintenance cost of $500 in each year of its estimated 10-year life. An alternative sprinkler system can be purchased for $10,000 and would require only $200 in maintenance cost each year of its estimated 20-year life. Ignoring cost reimbursement and assuming a discount factor of 10 percent, the following calculations can be made:

Equivalent annual cost of $5,000 sprinkler system:

Present value of operating costs = $500 × 6.145 = $3,073

Present value of investment = $5,000

$$\text{Equivalent annual cost} = \frac{\$3,073 + \$5,000}{6.145} = \$1,314$$

Equivalent annual cost of $10,000 sprinkler system:

Present value of operating costs = $200 × 8.514 = $1,703

Present value of investment = $10,000

$$\text{Equivalent annual cost} = \frac{\$1,703 + \$10,000}{8.541} = \$1,375$$

From this analysis, it can be seen that the $5,000 sprinkler system would produce the lowest equivalent annual cost, $1,314 per year, compared with the $1,375 equivalent annual cost of the $10,000 system.

Two points should be made with respect to this analysis. First, the equivalent annual cost method permits comparison of two alternative projects with different lives. In this case, a 10-year life project was compared with a project with a 20-year life. There is an assumption here that the technology will not change and that in ten years the relevant alternatives will still be the two systems being analyzed. However, in situations of estimated rapid technological changes, some subjective weight should be given to projects of shorter duration. In the above example, this is no problem, since the project with the shorter life also has the lowest equivalent annual cost.

Second, equivalent annual cost is not identical to the reported or accounting cost. The annual reported accounting cost for the two alternatives would be the annual depreciation expenses plus the maintenance cost. Thus

$$\text{Accounting expense per year (\$5,000 sprinkler system)} = \frac{\$5,000}{10} + \$500 = \$1,000$$

$$\text{Accounting expense per year (\$10,000 sprinkler system)} = \frac{\$10,000}{20} + \$200 = \$700$$

Reliance on information like the above that does not incorporate the time value concept of money can produce misleading results, as it does in the above example. The second alternative is not the lowest cost alternative when the cost of capital is included. In this case, the savings of $5,000 in investment cost between the two systems can be used either to generate additional investment income or to reduce outstanding indebtedness. It is assumed that the appropriate discount rate for each of these two alternatives would be 10 percent.

Once again, the effects of cost reimbursement should be considered. In our example, we assume that 50 percent of the extended care facility's capital costs will be reimbursed and 10 percent of its operating costs will be reimbursed. The following adjustments result:

Equivalent annual cost of $5,000 sprinkler system:

$$\text{Present value of reimbursed operating costs} = \$500 \times 6.145 \times .10 = \$307.25$$

$$\text{Present value of reimbursed depreciation} = \frac{\$5,000}{10} \times 6.145 \times .50 = \$1,536.25$$

$$\text{Equivalent annual cost} = \$1,314 - \frac{(\$307.25 + \$1,536.25)}{6.145} = \$1,014$$

Equivalent annual cost of $10,000 sprinkler system:

Present value of reimbursed operating costs = $200 × 8.514 × .10 = $170.25

$$\text{Present value of reimbursed depreciation} = \frac{\$10,000}{20} \times 8.514 \times .5 = \$2,128.50$$

$$\text{Equivalent annual cost} = \$1,375 - \frac{(\$170.25 + \$2,128.50)}{8.514} = \$1,105$$

Again, some clarification of the calculations may be useful. To reflect the effect of cost reimbursement, consideration must be given to the reimbursement of reported expenses for the two alternative sprinkler systems. The reported expense items for both sprinkler systems are depreciation and maintenance cost, which is referred to as an operating cost. Depreciation for the $5,000 sprinkler system will be $500 per year ($500/10), and 50 percent of this amount ($250) will be reimbursed each year. The present value of the reimbursed depreciation ($250 × 6.145) is $1,536.25. Using the same procedure, the present value of reimbursed depreciation for the $10,000 sprinkler system is $2,128.50 ($250 × 8.514). In a similar fashion, the maintenance costs for the two sprinkler systems will also be reimbursed. For the $5,000 system, the annual $500 maintenance cost will yield $50 in new reimbursement (.10 × $500) per year. The present value of this reimbursement inflow is $307.25. Using the same calculations for the $10,000 sprinkler system yields a present value of $170.25. The present values of both reimbursed depreciation and maintenance costs are then annualized and subtracted from the initially calculated equivalent annual cost to derive new equivalent annual costs that reflect cost reimbursement effects.

In this case, cost reimbursement did not change the decision. The lower-cost sprinkler system, after consideration of the effects of reimbursement, is still the best alternative. In fact, the relative difference has increased.

SELECTION OF THE DISCOUNT RATE

In the three DCF methods just discussed, to specify the discount rate we simply selected a number arbitrarily for each of our examples. In an actual case, however, the question of how to select the appropriate discount rate requires careful attention.

Before discussing methods of determining the appropriate discount rate, it may be useful to evaluate the role of the discount rate in project selection. A natural question at this point is, would an alternative discount rate affect the list of capital projects selected? For example, if we used a discount rate of 10 percent and later learned that 12 percent should have been used, would our list of approved projects change? The answer is maybe. In some cases, alternative values for the discount rate would alter the relative ranking and therefore the desirability of particular projects.

Again, we believe that the definition of the discount rate is an important issue, but not a critical one—especially for health care organizations. This is true for several reasons. First, in the case of health care organizations, the financial criterion is not likely to be the only criterion. Other areas—such as need, quality of care, and teaching—may also be important. Second, a change in the relative ranking of projects is much more likely to result from an accurate forecast of cash flows than it is from an alternative discount rate. Efforts to improve forecasting would appear to be far more important than esoteric discussions over the relevancy of cost-of-capital alternatives.

In this context, we can examine three primary methods for defining a discount rate or the cost of capital for use in a DCF analysis:

1. cost of specific financing source
2. yield achievable on other investments
3. weighted cost of capital

The cost of a specific financing source is sometimes used as the discount rate. Usually, the identified financing source is debt. For example, if a hospital can borrow money at 8 percent in the bond market, that rate would become its cost of capital or discount rate.

Another alternative is to use the yield rate possible on other investments. In many cases, this rate might be equal to the investment yield possible in the firm's security portfolio. For example, if the firm currently earned 10 percent on its security investments, than 10 percent would be its discount rate. This method, based on an opportunity cost concept, is relatively easy to understand.

The last alternative is to use the weighted cost of capital. This is the most widely discussed and used method of defining the discount rate. In its simplest form, it is calculated as

$$\text{Cost of capital} = (\% \text{ Debt} \times \text{Cost of debt}) + (\% \text{ Equity} \times \text{Cost of equity})$$

The advantage of this method is that it clearly represents the cost of capital to the firm. A major problem with its use, however, is the definition of the cost of equity capital. This is an especially difficult problem for nonprofit firms. How do you define the cost of equity capital? Detailed exploration of this issue and other aspects of discount rate selection are beyond the scope of the present discussion.

Readers who are interested in examining these topics in greater depth are referred to any good introductory finance textbook.

VALUATION

It is becoming an almost everyday occurrence to read about one health care entity's buying or acquiring another related health care business. Hospitals buy other hospitals, nursing homes, physician practices, durable medical equipment firms, and other types of businesses. Nursing homes buy other nursing homes, home health firms, and other businesses. Although there are many tasks that need to be accomplished in any business acquisition, one of the most difficult and most important is valuation. Exactly what is the value of the business being acquired?

Valuation is really a subset of capital expenditure analysis. The business being acquired can be thought of as a capital expenditure that needs to be evaluated just as any other capital expenditure made in the organization. Nonfinancial criteria should be considered, and the contribution that the acquired business will make toward the acquiring firm's mission must be addressed.

Valuation of a business is not a scientific process that results in one objective measure of value. Different measures of value result for three reasons:

1. Different methods of valuation are used to determine value.
2. Different expectations regarding future performance of the acquired business are assumed.
3. Different values may be assigned by different prospective buyers.

Alternative Valuation Methods

In general, three major methods of valuation are often cited:

1. asset based
2. comparable sales
3. income/cash flow

Asset-based approaches to valuation rely on the availability of objective measures for the assets being acquired. Usually three alternative asset-based valuation approaches are identified. One approach is simply to take the tangible book value of the acquired firm's assets. While this method is very objective, there is great doubt about the relevance of the resulting value. For example, consider a computed tomography (CT) scanner that was acquired two years ago at a cost of $700,000 that now has a book value of $500,000, which reflects two years of depreciation. The $500,000 value is most likely not a good measure of the value of this asset to an acquiring firm.

A second asset-based method would be to use the replacement cost of the assets. For example, assume that the CT scanner in the example above now has a current replacement cost of $1,400,000. Recognizing two years' worth of depreciation would produce an adjusted replacement cost of $1,000,000:

Current replacement cost	$1,400,000
– Allowance for depreciation	400,000
Estimated replacement cost	$1,000,000

This estimate of value would be useful for a firm that anticipated using the CT scanner in the future. Replacement cost is often associated with a "going concern" basis of operation. The acquired firm will continue to operate pretty much as it currently does and therefore the existing capital assets will be needed.

The third asset-based approach assumes that the assets are not really needed and will be sold. For example, the CT scanner referenced above will be sold in a secondhand market for $600,000. This value is often associated with liquidation.

Comparable sales methods are widely employed in real estate valuation. Real estate appraisers will look at properties similar to the one being valued that have sold in that location during a recent time interval. This method of valuation is not often used for health care businesses because there are not enough comparable sales to make the valuation meaningful. Common rules of thumb based on sales around the country are sometimes used. For example, nursing homes may sell in a range of $15,000 to $45,000 per bed depending on the payer mix and the present age of the facility. Although these numbers are widely known, they usually are not the basis for valuation; instead they represent ranges that can be compared with the final valuation study.

The most common methods of valuing health care firms are usually based on some projections of income or cash flow. The three most common methods are

1. Direct capitalization
2. Price earnings multiple
3. Discounted cash flow

In direct capitalization, a projected value for cash flow is determined. That number is then divided by some discount rate. The discount rate ideally represents the acquiring firm's cost of capital, but it is often adjusted up or down to reflect the riskiness of the business being acquired. For example, if a durable medical equipment (DME) firm was thought to have cash flow of $100,000 per year for the foreseeable future and the purchasing firm's cost of capital was 12.0 percent, the value of the DME firm would be

$$\text{Value of DME firm} = \frac{\$100,000}{.12} = \$833,333$$

To reflect greater risk in the business, the discount rate could be increased to 20 percent. This increase would effectively reduce the value to $500,000. A preferable way to reflect risk rather than adjust the discount rate would be to conduct a sensitivity analysis on the forecast of cash flows. It is highly desirable to have at least three scenarios forecast: most likely, pessimistic, and optimistic.

A price earnings approach is very similar to direct capitalization, except it uses earnings rather than cash flow to discount, and multiplication rather than division is used. Assume that the DME firm above had earnings—not cash flow—of $125,000. If the purchasing firm applied a price/earnings ratio of 8 to the earnings, the value would be

$$\text{Value of DME firm} = \$125,000 \times 8.0 = \$1,000,000$$

DCF methods are most commonly used in most health care firm valuations. The typical approach will estimate cash flows for each of the next five years. These cash flows are then discounted to reflect the present value of the firm. The last remaining requirement is to estimate what the value of the acquired firm will be at the end of year 5, or whenever annual cash flows are no longer estimated. Generically, the value of a firm would be stated as follows:

Value = Present value of estimated future cash flows
+ Present value of residual value

To illustrate this method, assume that the DME firm described earlier is projected to generate $100,000 per year in annual cash flow for each of the next five years. Thereafter, the firm will continue to generate $100,000 of cash flow for as far as can be forecast into the future. If a discount rate of 12 percent is used, the value should be $833,333, the same value that resulted in direct capitalization:

Present Value of Cash Flows	Amount	Present Value Factor	Present Value
1st year	$100,000	.893	$ 89,300
2nd year	100,000	.797	79,700
3rd year	100,000	.712	71,200
4th year	100,000	.636	63,600
5th year	100,000	.567	56,700
Present value of residual value			
Cash flows after year 5	833,333	.567	472,500
Total value			$833,000

The residual value is derived by using the direct capitalization method on the projected cash flows that are forecast to occur for every year past year 5. The present value factors were taken from Table 12–2.

Use of the direct capitalization method on cash flows is not the only way to construct a residual value. In some cases an estimate of the resale value of the firm might be used. Other methods might also be used in certain situations. One point, however, is important: the residual value may be very uncertain and as a result some alternative scenarios should be tested. One value should never be accepted. Alternative valuations under different assumptions should be sought.

Valuation Concepts

Before concluding our discussion of valuation, there are several concepts that are important to a fuller understanding of valuation. Great emphasis has been placed on cash flow, but what exactly is cash flow for valuation purposes?

Cash flow is usually defined more broadly than net income plus depreciation for valuation purposes. Often the term *free cash flow* is used. Free cash flow is defined as follows:

Net income + Depreciation + Interest − Capital

Expenditures − Working capital expenditures

Most analysts think of depreciation plus net income as cash flow. Interest is added back in the above concept of free cash flow to recognize that the business may be financed in a manner different from its present form. If a business was purchased and the existing debt of that business was assumed by the purchaser, then interest should not be subtracted. Capital expenditures are subtracted to recognize that businesses need to renovate and replace their physical assets if they are to stay in business, and this in fact represents a reduction of available cash flow. In the same manner, expenditures for working capital also represent a drain on available funds, or free cash flow. A buildup in accounts receivable means that not all of the firm's net income is available.

It is also important to understand the term *goodwill*. Goodwill is defined as the price or value paid for a business less the fair market value of the tangible assets acquired. For example, assume that a hospital paid $4,000,000 for a 100-bed nursing home. All of the tangible assets of the nursing home would be appraised at fair market value. A piece of land on the nursing home's books may have a recorded cost of $100,000, but its current market value might be $800,000. The fair market value of the land would be $800,000. Alternatively, some equipment items might be written down below their cost because they are no longer of value.

Goodwill is an intangible asset that will be amortized over future years. For example, assume that the fair market value of the acquired assets in the nursing home were $3,000,000. The amount of goodwill would be $1,000,000 and would be written off as a cost of operation in the future. Goodwill plus fair market value will equal the price paid for the business.

SUMMARY

The capital decision-making process in the health care industry is very complex, involving a great many independent decision makers. In this chapter, we examined the process and focused on methods for evaluating capital projects. Although capital expenditure decisions in the health care industry are not usually decided exclusively on the basis of financial criteria, most health care decision makers regard financial factors as important elements in the process. In that context, the three DCF methods we have examined can serve as useful tools in capital project analysis for health care facilities.

ASSIGNMENTS

1. A health care firm's investment of $1,000 in a piece of equipment will reduce labor costs by $400 per year for the next five years. Eighty percent of all patients seen by the firm have a third-party payer arrangement that pays for capital costs on a retrospective basis. Ten percent of all patients reimburse for actual operating costs. What is the annual cash flow of the investment? Assume a five-year life and straight-line depreciation.

2. A hospital has just experienced a breakdown of one of its boilers. The boiler must be replaced very quickly if the hospital is to continue operations. Should this investment be subjected to any analysis?

3. Few firms ever track the actual results achieved from a specific capital investment against projected results. What are the likely effects of such a management policy?

4. Santa Cruz Community Hospital is considering investing $90,000 in new laundry equipment to replace its present equipment, which is completely depreciated and outmoded. An alternative to this investment is a long-term contract with a local firm to perform the hospital's laundry service. It is expected that the hospital would save $20,000 per year in operating costs if the laundry service were performed internally. Both the expected life and the depreciable life of the projected equipment are six years. Salvage value of the present equipment is expected to be zero.

   Assuming that Santa Cruz Community Hospital can borrow or invest money at 8 percent, calculate the payback, the NPV, and the profitability index. Ignore any reimbursement effects.

5. Frances Gebauer, president of Lucas Valley Hospital System, is investigating the purchase of 36 TV sets for rental purposes. The sets have an expected life of two years and cost $500 apiece. The possible rental income flows are:

Year 1		Year 2	
Rental Income	*Conditional Probability*	*Rental Income*	*Conditional Probability*
$12,000	.40	$4,000	.40
		7,000	.60
$15,000	.60	6,000	.30
		8,000	.70

   If funds cost Lucas Valley 10 percent, calculate the expected NPV of this project.

6. Mr. Dobbs, administrator at Innovative Hospital, is considering opening a new health screening department in the hospital. However, he is terribly concerned about the financial consequences of this action, since his board has indicated that, because the current financial position of the hospital is not good, the project must pay for itself.

Mr. Dobbs is thus especially interested in the establishment of a rate for the service and has called on you for your expert financial advice. He has prepared the following cost and utilization data for your review:

Year	Variable Cost	Fixed Costs*	Patients Screened
1	$ 96,000	$120,000	2,400
2	144,000	135,000	3,600
3	192,000	150,000	4,800
4	192,000	150,000	4,800
5	192,000	150,000	4,800

*Includes depreciation of equipment costing $350,000 over a five-year life, assuming straight-line depreciation.

Mr. Dobbs is aware of the rapid pace of technological change and anticipates that the current equipment, costing $350,000, will need to be replaced at the end of year 5 for $500,000. He is not concerned about price inflation for his other operating costs because he believes that the increased costs can be recovered by increased charges. However, he is concerned about establishing a current charge for the new service that will generate a fund of sufficient size to meet the year 5 replacement cost. Mr. Dobbs believes that any invested funds will earn interest at a rate of 8 percent compounded annually. Assume that all payments and receipts are made at year end.

What rate would you recommend charging for the new health screening service? Assume this rate to be effective for the entire five-year period.

7. Two hospitals are considering merging their laundry departments and constructing a new facility to take care of their future laundry requirements. Some relevant cost data are presented below:

	Hospital A	Hospital B	Merged C
Variable cost/pound	.030	.032	.024
Pounds of laundry	300,000	700,000	1,000,000
Fixed costs/year			
Depreciation (lease)	$ 1,000	$ 5,000	$ 8,000
Maintenance	1,400	2,500	3,000
Administrative salaries	8,000	16,000	20,000
Transportation	0	0	3,000
Total fixed cost	$10,400	$23,500	$34,000

The new laundry facility will cost approximately $40,000 to construct and will be located between the two hospitals in a leased building. Average life of the equipment is assumed to be eight years, which generates a $5,000 yearly depreciation charge. Lease payment is fixed at $3,000 per year for the next eight years. Financing for the project will be generated from available funds in each institution: $12,000 from hospital A and $28,000 from hospital B. Expenses will be shared using the same ratios (30 and 70 percent). Both hospitals employ a discount factor of 10 percent on their cost reduction investment projects.

Given this information, do you think the merger would be beneficial to both individual hospitals? What other information would you like to have to help you evaluate this investment project?

8. In the preceding laundry merger problem, assume that hospital B would expect to replace its present equipment with new equipment in two years at a cost of $64,000. The equipment would have an eight-year life. Ignoring cost reimbursement considerations, does the merger make economic sense for hospital B under these conditions?

9. Scioto Valley Convalescent Center is considering buying a $25,000 computer to improve its medical record and accounting functions. It is estimated that, with the computer, operating costs will be reduced by $7,000 per year. The computer has an estimated five-year life with an estimated $5,000 salvage value. What is this investment's profitability index if the discount rate is 8 percent? Ignore reimbursement considerations.

10. In problem 9, assume that capital costs are reimbursed 80 percent and there is no reimbursement based on operating costs. Further assume that Scioto Valley is a tax-paying entity with a marginal tax rate of 40 percent. What is the profitability index for this project now?

11. You have been asked to provide an estimate of the value for a nursing home that your client is interested in buying. Financial data and projections are presented below:

	Year 1	*Year 2*	*Year 3*	*Year 4*	*Year 5*
Net income	$2,000	$2,200	$2,400	$2,700	$3,000
+ Depreciation	1,400	$1,500	1,700	2,000	2,200
− Working capital	500	600	700	800	1,000
− Capital expenditures	4,000	4,000	5,000	300	300
Free cash flow	($1,100)	($ 900)	($1,600)	$3,600	$3,900

Use an assumed discount rate of 10 percent to value the firm, and assume that the fifth-year cash flow will carry into the future. After you have completed your valuation, what additional information or steps would you suggest to the client?

SOLUTIONS AND ANSWERS

1. The cash flow of the equipment investment by the health care firm may be calculated as follows:

Cash flow = Annual depreciation × Proportion of capital cost payers

+ (Annual operating savings × [1 − Proportion of operating cost payers])

= $200 × .80 + ($400[1 − .10])

= $160 + $360 = $520

2. The investment in a new boiler would have benefits for the hospital in the area of operational continuance. Failure to make the needed investment would mean discontinued service. In this case, less analysis is needed, but care should still be exercised in identifying alternatives. The lowest-cost alternative to meet the need should be selected.

3. If it does not compare actual with projected results, management may lose some of the benefits that were originally expected to be realized with its investment. If the control loop is not closed, management will not know, and therefore cannot correct for, deviations from forecasted results. It is also possible that some department managers will overstate benefits for their favorite capital projects and that such actions will not be perceived as having any adverse consequences, since no comparison of forecast with actual results was made.

4. The following calculations show the payback, the NPV, and the profitability index for the laundry service investment:

$$\text{Payback} = \frac{\text{Investment cost}}{\text{Annual cash flow}} = \frac{\$90,000}{\$20,000} = 4.5 \text{ years}$$

$$
\begin{aligned}
\text{Net present value} \quad &= \text{Present value of cash inflows} - \text{Investment cost} \\
&= \$20,000 \times P(8\%, 6) - \$90,000 \\
&= \$20,000 \times 4.623 - \$90,000 = \$2,460
\end{aligned}
$$

$$\text{Profitability index} = \frac{\text{Net present value}}{\text{Investment cost}} = \frac{\$2,460}{\$90,000} = .0273$$

5. The NPV of Lucas Valley's TV purchase project is shown in the following data:

Item	Amount	Year	Probability	Expected Value	Present Value Factor	Expected Present Value
Rental income	$12,000	1	.40	$4,800	.909	$4,363.20
Rental income	15,000	1	.60	9,000	.909	8,181.00
Rental income	4,000	2	.16	640	.826	528.64
Rental income	7,000	2	.24	1,680	.826	1,387.68
Rental income	6,000	2	.18	1,080	.826	892.08
Rental income	8,000	2	.42	3,360	.826	2,775.36
TV cost	(18,000)	0	1.00	(18,000)	1.000	(18,000.00)
Expected NPV						$ 127.96

6. The first step in determining the rate that Mr. Dobbs should charge for the new health screening service is to calculate the present value of the cash flow requirements that need to be covered by the charge for the service:

Item	Amount	Year	Present value Factor (8%)	Present Value
Costs less depreciation	$146,000	1	.926	$ 135,196
Costs less depreciation	209,000	2	.857	179,113
Costs less depreciation	272,000	3	.794	215,968
Costs less depreciation	272,000	4	.735	199,920
Costs less depreciation	272,000	5	.681	185,232
Replacement	500,000	5	.681	340,500
				$1,255,929

The second step is to define the rate that will generate the required present value as calculated above. If we define r as the required rate per screening, the following calculation can be made:

$$\$1,255,929 = (2,400 \times r \times p[8\%, 1]) + (3,600 \times r \times p[8\%, 2])$$
$$+ (4,800 \times r \times p[8\%, 3]) + (4,800 \times r \times p[8\%, 4])$$
$$+ (4,800 \times r \times p[8\%, 5])$$

$$\$1,255,929 = (2,400r[.926]) + (3,600r[.857]) + (4,800r[.794])$$
$$+ (4,800r[.735]) + (4,800r[.681])$$

$$\$1,255,929 = 15,915.6r$$

$$r = \frac{\$1,255,929}{15,915}$$

$$r = \$78.91$$

7. The relevant data and calculations in the laundry service merger between hospital A and hospital B are presented below:

	Hospital A	Hospital B
Cash outflow—unmerged		
Variable costs	$ 9,000	$22,400
Maintenance	1,400	2,500
Salaries	8,000	16,000
Total	$18,400	$40,900
Cash outflow—merged		
Variable costs	$ 7,200	$16,800
Lease	900	2,100
Maintenance	900	2,100
Salaries	6,000	14,000
Transportation	900	2,100
	$15,900	$37,100
Net savings	$ 2,500	$ 3,800

Hospital A:

Present value of savings = $2,500 × P(10%, 8) = $2,500 × 5.335 = $13,337.50

$$\text{Profitability index} = \frac{\$1,337.50}{\$12,000.00} = .111$$

Hospital B:

Present value of savings = $3,800 × P(10%, 8) = $3,800 × 5.335 = $20,273

$$\text{Profitability index} = \frac{-7,727}{28,000} = -.276$$

Thus, given present data, the merger would be beneficial to hospital A but not to hospital B. A key piece of additional data that is needed is the replacement cost of the existing equipment. If hospital B would need to acquire new equipment in the near future, the merger might also be favorable to it. The effects of cost reimbursement should also be considered.

8. The laundry merger project in these new circumstances would require use of the equivalent annual cost method. The merged alternative would have an eight-year life, whereas the unmerged alternative would have a ten-year life cycle.

Merged:

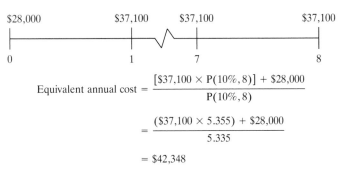

$$\text{Equivalent annual cost} = \frac{[\$37,100 \times P(10\%, 8)] + \$28,000}{P(10\%, 8)}$$

$$= \frac{(\$37,100 \times 5.355) + \$28,000}{5.335}$$

$$= \$42,348$$

Unmerged:

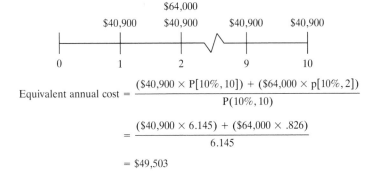

$$\text{Equivalent annual cost} = \frac{(\$40,900 \times P[10\%, 10]) + (\$64,000 \times p[10\%, 2])}{P(10\%, 10)}$$

$$= \frac{(\$40,900 \times 6.145) + (\$64,000 \times .826)}{6.145}$$

$$= \$49,503$$

The merger alternative is now more desirable for hospital B because it has a lower equivalent annual cost compared with the nonmerger alternative.

9. The profitability index for the computer investment by Scioto Valley Convalescent Center is calculated as follows:

$$\text{Present value of cash inflows} = (\$7,000 \times P[8\%,5]) + (\$5,000 \times p[8\%,5])$$

$$= (\$7,000 \times 3.993) + (\$5,000 \times .681)$$

$$= \$31,356$$

$$\text{Profitability index} = \frac{\$31,356 - \$25,000}{\$25,000} = .254$$

10. The calculation of the profitability index for the computer investment in these new circumstances is now:

Calculation of present value of cash inflows:

Operating savings	
$7,000 \times (1 - .40) \times 3.993 =$	$16,770.60
Reimbursed depreciation	
$4,000 \times .80 \times (1 - .40) \times 3.993 =$	7,666.56
Depreciation tax shelter effect	
$4,000 \times .40 \times 3.993 =$	6,388.80
Salvage value	
$5,000 \times .681 =$	3,405.00
Total present value	$34,230.96

$$\text{Profitability index} = \frac{\$34,230.96 - \$25,000}{\$25,000} = .369$$

11. Using the values from Table 12–2, the following estimate of value would result:

Present Value of Cash Flows	Amount	Present Value Factor	Present Value
1st year	$(1,100)	.909	$(1,000)
2nd year	(900)	.826	(743)
3rd year	(1,600)	.751	(1,202)
4th year	3,600	.683	2,459
5th year	3,900	.621	2,422
Present value of residual value			
Cash flows after year 5	39,000	.621	24,220
Total value			$26,156

A sensitivity analysis should be performed, especially on cash flows in year 5. Most of the total value is attributed to the residual value of the firm at the end of year 5. Even small changes in this value will have a very dramatic impact on the value.

Chapter 14

Capital Formation

In this chapter, we shall examine the concepts and principles of capital formation in the health care industry. Few areas are more important to the financial well-being of a health care firm. A firm that cannot obtain the amounts of capital specified in its strategic financial plan will not be able to achieve its long-run objectives. Indeed, if the firm finds it difficult to acquire capital in any amount at a reasonable cost, its future survival may be questionable. Successful firms have the capability to provide capital financing when needed and at a cost that is reasonable.

Three key questions are relevant to our discussion of capital formation in the health care industry. First, how much capital is needed? Ideally, the firm should have defined its capital needs in its strategic financial plan. Capital needs should include working capital requirements and replacement reserves, as well as the funding needs for buildings and equipment.

Second, what sources of capital financing are available? At the time of this writing, the future availability of tax-exempt financing is unclear. Tax-exempt financing has been the largest source of capital for the hospital industry for the last 20 years. If it were eliminated, a major shift in financing patterns would take place. The exact direction of this shift is unclear at this time, although it would seem that taxable sources of debt would have to be substituted for tax-exempt sources.

Third, how are the costs of capital financing provided for in third-party payment plans? This area is critical to the discussion of capital financing and selection of capital financing alternatives. At the time of this writing, Medicare and Medicaid provide for the payment of actual capital costs, such as interest expense. It is expected, however, that this situation will change and that cost reimbursement of capital costs will be replaced by some scheme of prospective prices.

Table 14–1 presents a summary of investment and financing patterns in the hospital industry for the period 1986 to 1990. In general, we can classify the sources of financing into the following two categories: (1) equity and (2) debt. In the hospital industry, approximately 50 percent of total assets are financed with equity and 50 percent are financed with debt. However, financing patterns may vary somewhat in different sectors of the health care industry. For example, many long-term care facilities have much higher proportions of debt. Debt financing in such facilities may run as high as 90 percent.

EQUITY FINANCING

In general there are only two ways in which a firm can generate new equity capital: (1) profit retention and (2) contributions. We have already stressed in past chapters the importance of earning adequate

Table 14–1 Percentage Balance Sheet for U.S. Hospitals, 1986–1990

	1986	1987	1988	1989	1990
Assets					
Cash and marketable securities	6.8%	6.2%	6.0%	5.7%	6.1%
Net accounts receivable	14.9%	15.4%	16.5%	17.1%	16.9%
Inventory	1.1%	1.1%	1.2%	1.2%	1.2%
Other current assets	1.9%	2.2%	2.2%	2.1%	2.3%
Total current assets	24.6%	25.0%	25.9%	26.1%	26.4%
Other investments	13.9%	13.8%	13.8%	14.1%	14.7%
Net fixed assets	50.0%	49.6%	49.3%	48.3%	47.5%
Other assets	11.5%	11.7%	11.0%	11.5%	11.4%
	100.0%	100.0%	100.0%	100.0%	100.0%
Liabilities and fund balance					
Current liabilities	12.3%	12.8%	13.2%	13.4%	13.7%
Long-term debt	36.6%	36.0%	35.6%	35.8%	35.1%
Other liabilities	2.2%	2.3%	2.2%	2.8%	3.0%
Fund balance	48.9%	48.9%	49.0%	48.0%	48.2%
	100.0%	100.0%	100.0%	100.0%	100.0%

Source: Adapted from data taken from the Healthcare Financial Management Association.

levels of profit. Hence, our discussion at this point is focused primarily on contributions. A contribution may be given to a firm for a variety of reasons. Normally, in tax-exempt health care firms, a contribution is given with no thought of a future return. The donor may derive some immediate or deferred tax benefit, but there is no expectation of a financial return to be paid by the health care entity. In contrast, contributions are given to a taxable health care entity in the expectation of a future financial return. The contribution may be in the form of a stock purchase or a limited partnership unit. It is important to note that this form of contribution may also be available to tax-exempt entities through a corporate restructuring arrangement. We will discuss this point in more detail shortly.

Philanthropy is definitely not dead in our nation. In 1990, approximately 2 percent of our nation's gross national product, or $122.5 billion, was in the form of philanthropic gifts. Tables 14–2 and 14–3 provide data showing the sources and the distribution of giving for the period 1985 to 1990. These data present an encouraging picture. Total giving was up almost 53 percent over the five-year period 1985 to 1990. That is a promising growth rate in almost anyone's book. Individuals were clearly

Table 14–2 Sources of Giving

	1985 Dollars Billions	%	1990 Dollars Billions	%
Individuals	$65.9	82.3%	$101.8	83.0%
Bequests	$4.8	6.0%	$7.8	6.4%
Foundations	$4.9	6.1%	$7.1	5.8%
Corporations	$4.5	5.6%	$5.9	4.8%
Total	$80.1	100.0%	$122.6	100.0%

Table 14–3 Distribution of Giving

	1985 Dollars Billions	%	1990 Dollars Billions	%
Religion	$38.2	47.7%	$65.8	53.7%
Education	$8.2	10.2%	$12.4	10.1%
Health	$7.7	9.6%	$9.9	8.1%
Human services	$8.5	10.6%	$11.8	9.6%
Arts and culture	$5.1	6.4%	$7.9	6.4%
Other	$12.4	15.5%	$14.8	12.1%
Total	$80.1	100.0%	$122.6	100.0%

the largest source of giving, representing well over 80 percent of total giving.

To be successful, an equity financing program should have the following key elements:

- A *"case statement."* This document should carefully and persuasively define why you need money.
- A *designated development officer.* This individual may not be full-time, but duties and expectations should be precisely defined. Incentives for development officers should be related to expectations for giving.
- *Trustee and medical staff involvement.* People give to people, not to organizations.
- *Prospect lists.* You should know who in the community are prime prospects for giving.
- *Programs for giving.* This is critical. You should have a variety of methods and means to encourage giving. For example, you may have a number of deferred giving plans, such as unitrusts, annuity trusts, or pooled-income funds. Your development officer should be familiar with these methods.
- *Goals.* You need to define realistic targets for long-range planning.

There are many ways to encourage individuals to give to charitable tax-exempt health care firms. Many large firms employ full-time development staff. These individuals can do much to increase charitable giving.

One of the most promising areas of philanthropic giving is in deferred gift arrangements. In a deferred giving plan, a taxpayer donor may get an immediate tax benefit in return for a later gift to the tax-exempt firm. An interesting recent example of deferred giving is the case of a hospital in California that initiated a provocative new fund-raising effort, called the home value program (HVP). HVP is designed for senior citizens, aged 70 or above, who own mortgage-free homes. The homeowners sign a revocable agreement that, on their death, transfers title to their homes to the hospital. In return, they receive from the hospital a monthly payment that is based on a loan. In concept, HVP is very similar to the reverse annuity mortgages that are being used in some banking circles. An HVP program is also being used to finance long-term care for individual patients in nursing homes and home health agencies. It is especially useful for the elderly who have no means of supporting themselves other than the equity built up in their homes.

The following case illustrates the mechanics of HVP. Assume that Mrs. Jones, aged 70, has a mortgage-free home with a market value of $100,000. The hospital, or its foundation, executes a loan of $50,000 at 12 percent interest that will pay Mrs. Jones $717 per month for ten years. Mrs. Jones signs a revocable agreement.

How does the hospital benefit? First, for a $50,000 loan, the hospital receives title to property that is valued at $100,000. Second, the hospital benefits from any appreciation on the property. In ten years, if the annual appreciation rate is 5 percent, Mrs. Jone's $100,000 home will be worth $163,000. Third, the hospital establishes a relationship with Mrs. Jones that may lead to other donations.

How does Mrs. Jones benefit? First, the monthly payment is considered tax-free income. Second, there is no risk to Mrs. Jones since the agreement is revocable and can be rescinded with payment of the loan plus a penalty. Third, HVP provides Mrs. Jones with a tangible way of supporting the hospital. The last factor is the key to the ultimate success of the program.

An HVP, or some adaptation of it, can provide a significant return to a hospital. However, some forethought is required. For one thing, working capital obviously is necessary. Payments to homeowners will precede any recovery through sale of the donated homes. Also, a significant amount of legal, accounting, and actuarial consulting is essential. Finally, such a program should not be perceived as a pure donation program. It is intended to be a method of investment diversification, albeit one with unusually high returns. Thus, a program such as HVP can provide an excellent vehicle for long-term equity capital growth.

Both taxable and tax-exempt health care providers have shown great interest in the issuance of equity to investors. For taxable health care firms, this interest is not new; for most such firms, the issuance of equity has been a major source of financing over the years. Most taxable health care firms began with a small amount of venture capital. They were able to use that original funding to develop a successful track record of operations. Based on that record of success, an initial public offering of stock was made. The resulting funds were then used to expand operations, part of which was fueled by leveraging funds acquired in the initial public offering.

The technique of expanding operations quickly through the issuance of equity and then leveraging that equity has been used extensively in the tax-exempt sector. The following data illustrate the growth potential of a taxable entity:

Organizational Type	Historical Net Income	Equity Issue (Stock)	Debt Addition	Possible Total Capital
Tax-exempt	$1.0	.0	$ 2.0	$ 3.0
Taxable	$ .7	$14.0	$28.0	$42.7

These data indicate that a taxable entity could raise approximately 14 times the amount of total capital that a tax-exempt entity could. Let us examine these data and their related assumptions more closely to understand clearly the underlying process behind capital formation. It is assumed that some business unit or firm has generated $1.0 million in before-tax income. If the firm were a taxable entity, it would be required to pay approximately 30 percent of this income as tax. However, the taxable firm could issue stock, limited partnership units, or some other type of equity security. Furthermore, it is assumed that a price-to-earnings multiple of 20 is in effect. This means that the taxable firm could raise $14.0 million in equity based on its net income of $700,000. Both the tax-exempt and the taxable firms could issue debt based on their equity positions. We have assumed that a leverage ratio of 2 to 1 exists; that is, the firms could borrow $2.00 for every $1.00 of equity. The taxable firm could issue $28.0 million in debt, whereas the tax-exempt firm would be limited to $2.0 million in debt. Total capital, both debt and equity, would be $3.0 million for the tax-exempt firm and $42.7 million for the taxable firm.

In the preceding example, some of the assumptions might be changed, but the relative growth potential would remain the same. In this situation, is there any way that a tax-exempt firm can take advantage of this growth potential? The answer is yes: a tax-exempt firm could change its status to taxable. This is not an easy thing to do, but it is not impossible. Several large HMOs started out as tax-exempt firms but changed their ownership status to maximize their growth potential.

An easier alternative method is to restructure the firm. Figure 14–1 presents a generic structure that is used by many tax-exempt health care firms to create an equity capital formation alternative. This structure involves the creation of taxable entities that can issue equity securities directly to investors. In the parent holding company model in Figure 14–1, there are several taxable entities that could issue equity to investors and help generate capital for the entire consolidated structure.

An actual case example may help to illustrate the potential for capital formation created by restructuring a tax-exempt health care firm. ABC hospital needed to replace its computed tomography (CT) scanner with a new one. The estimated cost of the new scanner was $1,160,000. The hospital did not wish to use any of its debt capacity in this project. The solution was to create a limited partnership/joint venture with its physicians. A new entity was created, called ABC Scanner, which was a limited partnership. The ABC Properties Company, which was a subsidiary of the

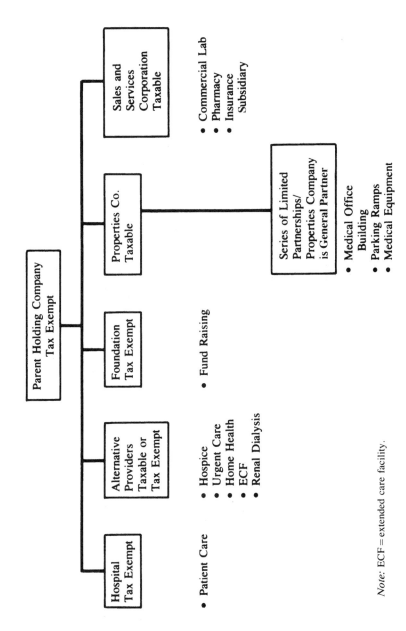

Note: ECF = extended care facility.

Figure 14–1 A Parent Holding Company

hospital's parent holding company, was the general partner. A bank loan of $1,180,000 was obtained; the loan was guaranteed by the limited partners (30 limited partners) and the general partner. The source and use-of-funds statement for the new structure is presented below:

Sources of Funds		
Bank loan		$1,180,00
Guaranteed by:		
General partner	$295,000	
Limited partners (@ $29,500)	885,000	
General partner's cash contribution		50,000
Limited partner's cash contribution (@ $5,000)		150,000
Total sources		$1,380,000
Uses of Funds		
Purchase and installation of CT scanner		$1,160,000
Leasehold (suite) improvements		95,000
Loan placement fee		35,400
Legal and other organizational expenses		15,000
Reserve for working capital		74,600
Total uses		$1,380,000

This statement documents the capability of the new structure to enhance ABC hospital's capital position with little funding commitment from the hospital. The general partner, a member of the restructured health care entity, has contributed only $50,000 of cash and guaranteed $295,000 in loans. For this rather modest level of commitment, total funding of $1,380,000 was made available.

LONG-TERM DEBT FINANCING

An examination of the specific sources of long-term debt financing in the health care industry can be a very complex and confusing process. Part of the problem stems from the use of jargon by those involved. Unless one is familiar with this jargon, meaningful communication with financing people may be difficult. Before describing the alternatives for long-term debt financing in the health care industry, we should note five key characteristics of financing that greatly affect the relative desirability of alternative sources of financing. As we describe these characteristics, we shall introduce some new terminology that will facilitate later discussion.

The five key characteristics are

1. cost
2. control
3. risk
4. availability
5. adequacy

Cost

The most important characteristic that affects the cost of alternative debt financing is interest rates. The fixed return of a long-term debt instrument is often called the *coupon rate*. For example, a 9.8 percent hospital revenue bond indicates that the issuer will pay the investor $98 annually for every $1,000 of principal. Sometimes the term *basis point* is used to describe differences in coupon rates. A basis point is $\frac{1}{100}$ of 1 percent. For example, the difference between a coupon rate of 9.80 percent and 9.65 percent would be 15 basis points.

Although interest is the primary measure of financing cost, it is not the only aspect of cost that should be considered. Issuance costs can be sizable in some types of financing. Issuance costs are simply those expenditures that are essential to consummate the financing. There is a great difference in the amount of issuance costs for *publicly placed* and *privately placed* issues. A privately placed issue is one that is not sold to the general market but rather is purchased directly by only a few major buyers. In a publicly placed issue, there are a number of costs that must be incurred in order legally to sell the securities to the general public. There are printing costs associated with producing the official statements that will be sent to prospective clients. There are costs for attorneys and accountants who must certify various aspects of the issue, such as its financial feasibility and its tax-exempt status. Finally, there is the *underwriters spread* that is charged by the investment banking firm that arranges the sale of the securities. When aggregated, issuance costs can sometimes amount to as much as 5 percent of the total issue. This means that an issuer must borrow $100 to get $95.

Another large cost of financing is *reserve requirements*. Some types of financing require the creation of fund balances in escrow accounts under the custody of the *bond trustee*. The bond trustee is designated by the issuer to represent the interests of the bondholders. The obligations of the trustee are defined in the Trust Indenture Act of 1939, which is administered by the Securities and Exchange Commission. There are two primary categories of reserve requirements. The first is the *debt service reserve*. This fund represents a cushion for the investors if the issuer gets into some type of fiscal crisis. It is usually set equal to one year's worth of principal and interest payments. The second category of reserve requirement is the *depreciation reserve*. This fund is sometimes set up to equal the cumulative difference between debt principal repayment and depreciation expense on the financial assets. Usually the amount of depreciation expense is greatest in the early years after a major construction program has been completed, when debt principal may be at its lowest level. Since reimbursed depreciation may represent the primary source of debt principal payment, there is a need to accumulate these funds to ensure their availability in later years, when the amount of debt principal payment exceeds depreciation. Figure 14–2 presents a graphic display of this relationship.

Control

Ideally, when issuing debt financing, the issuer would like to have little or no interference by the investors in management. It is usually not possible to avoid such interference, however. The investors will often specify some conditions or restraints that they would like to see included in the bond contract. Such conditions or restrictions are often known as *covenants*. These are spelled out in great detail in the *indenture*, which is the written contract between the investors and the issuing company.

One category of restrictive covenants concerns specific financial performance indicators. For example, most indentures define values for the firm's debt service coverage ratio and its current ratio. If actual values for these indicators are below the defined values, the bond trustee may take certain actions. The trustee may assume a position on the board of trustees, replace current management, or require the entire outstanding principal to be paid immediately.

Another category of covenants concerns future financing. A section in the indenture referred to as *additional parity financing* defines the conditions that must be satisfied before the firm can issue any additional debt. The most important condition is usually prior and projected debt service coverage.

There is a trend developing in the issuance of tax-exempt bonds to replace the projected debt service coverage provision with a stated level of debt to equity. For example, the initial bond placement may specify that

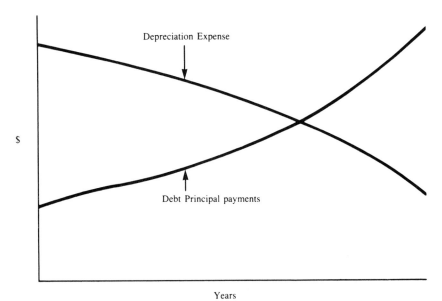

Figure 14–2 Depreciation Reserve Requirement: Relationship between Depreciation Expense and Debt Principal Payments

---

new financing can be issued if long-term debt does not equal a multiple of 1.5 times present equity or fund balance. This would permit large health care systems more flexibility in issuing future debt and is more closely akin to provisions that exist in the corporate taxable debt markets.

Risk

From the issuer's perspective, flexibility in repayment terms is highly desirable. An issuer with flexible repayment terms can alter payments to meet the issuer's current cash flow. The investor, on the other hand, wants some protection that the principal will be repaid in accordance with some pre-established plan.

One of the most important indenture elements is the *prepayment provision*. This provision specifies the point in time at which the debt can be retired, and the penalty that will be imposed for an early retirement. For example, the indenture may prohibit the issuer from prepaying the debt for the first ten years of issue life. Thereafter, the debt may be repaid, but only if there is a *call premium*. The call premium is some percentage of the par or face value of the bonds. Thus, a call premium of 5 percent would mean that a $50 premium would be paid for each $1,000 of bonds. The issuer would like to have the option of retiring outstanding debt at any point with no call premium. However, investors do not usually permit this in debt that has a fixed interest rate.

Another aspect of risk relates to the debt principal amortization pattern. Most debt retirement plans can be categorized as *level debt service* or *level debt principal*. In a level debt service plan, the amount of interest and principal that is repaid each year remains fairly constant. This is the type of repayment that is usually associated with home mortgages. In the early years, the amount of interest is far greater than the debt principal. Over time, this pattern changes and the amount of principal repaid each year begins to exceed the interest payment. Figure 14−3 presents a graphic view of this relationship. Level debt principal means that equal amount of debt principal is repaid each year. In this pattern of debt retirement, the total debt service payment falls over time. Figure 14−4 shows this relationship.

Many financing plans approximate a level debt service plan. This pattern of debt amortization extends the debt retirement life and may benefit the issuer. The benefit is predicated on three factors:

1. the ability of the issuer to earn a return greater than the interest rate on the debt
2. the presence of reimbursement for capital costs
3. the availability of tax-exempt financing

To illustrate the desirability of principal repayment delay, we will examine a simple case. Let us assume that we have two alternative financing plans. One plan will permit us to borrow $10 million for five years with no payment of principal until the fifth year. We will be required to pay 10 percent per year as our interest payment for each of the five years. The second financing plan will permit us to borrow the same $10 million for five years; however, there will be an annual payment of principal equal to $2 million per year. The interest rate on this financing plan will be 8 percent per year, which is below the interest rate in the first plan. Let us further assume that 80 percent of our interest expense will be repaid by our third-party payers, who still pay us for the actual costs of capital incurred. Finally, let us assume that any differences in cash flow between the two plans could be invested at 10 percent. Table 14−4 provides a comparison of the net present values for these two financing plans. The values indicate that the higher-interest balloon payment plan is the lower cost source of financing. This is a direct result of the large

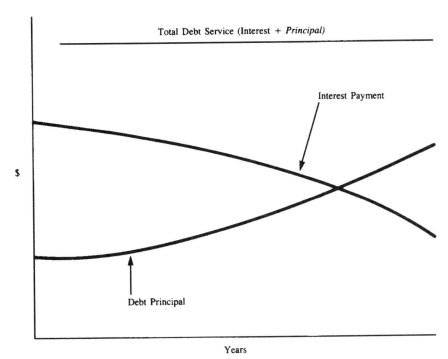

Figure 14-3 Level Debt Service: Relationship between Interest Payment and Debt Principal

percentage (80 percent) of capital cost payment. An 80 percent capital cost payment means that the effective interest rate is (1 − .80) times the interest rate. This means that the effective interest rate for the balloon plan would be 2.0 percent, and the corresponding value for the equal principal plan would be 1.6 percent. The difference in interest rates has decreased from 2.0 percent to .4 percent. An investment yield of 10 percent means that we can make money from delaying principal payment. In short, our cost is less than our return. It is only natural to want to retain money as long as possible.

Availability

Once a health care firm has decided that it needs debt financing, it usually wants to obtain the funds as quickly as possible. A delay can have

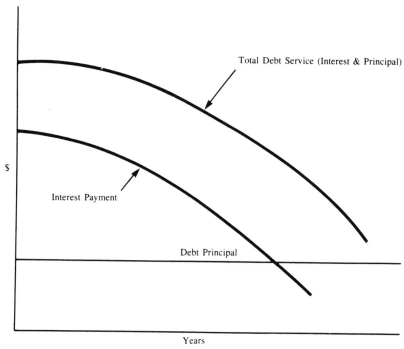

Figure 14–4 Level Debt Principal: Relationship between Interest Payment and Total Debt Service

rather severe consequences. A delay could postpone the start of a construction program. This might increase the cost of the total program because of normal inflation in construction costs. A delay could also result in an unexpected increase in interest rates. Although privately placed issues can usually be arranged more quickly than publicly placed issues, there is usually a higher interest rate associated with privately placed issues. However, the difference in interest rates may more than offset the costs of delay.

Adequacy

A key requirement of any proposed plan of financing is that it cover all the associated costs. One of the key areas of adequacy is that of refinancing costs. In many situations, a new program of construction that requires

Table 14–4 Cost of Alternative Debt Amortization Plans

Item	Amount before Reimbursement Effect	Amount after Reimbursement Effect	Years	Present Value Factor (10%)	Present Value
		Equal Principal Payment—8%			
Principal	$2,000,000	$2,000,000	1–5	3.791	$7,582,000
Interest	800,000	160,000	1	.909	145,440
Interest	640,000	128,000	2	.826	105,728
Interest	480,000	96,000	3	.751	72,096
Interest	320,000	64,000	4	.683	43,712
Interest	160,000	32,000	5	.621	19,872
Net present value cost					$7,968,848
		Balloon Principal—10%			
Interest	$ 1,000,000	$ 200,000	1–5	3.791	$ 758,200
Principal	10,000,000	10,000,000	5	.621	6,210,000
Net present value cost					$6,968,200

new financing may not be possible unless existing financing can be retired or refinanced. Not all types of financing permit the issuer to include the costs of refinancing in the amount borrowed.

Funding during construction is another important area of financing. Some types of financing do not permit the issuer to borrow during the construction period. A loan will be made only after the construction has been completed and the new assets are available for operations. In this situation, the issuer must arrange for a separate source of funding to finance the construction. Permanent financing must then be arranged on completion of the construction program.

Interest incurred during construction can be rather sizable. For example, a $50 million construction program might incur $10 to $15 million in interest during the construction period. It is thus important to have a source of financing that also permits the issuer to borrow to cover interest costs.

Last, the percentage of financing available varies across financing plans. Some plans permit up to 100 percent of the cost, whereas others may limit the amount to 70 or 80 percent. Depending on the availability of other funds, these limitations may pose real problems in some situations.

ALTERNATIVE DEBT FINANCING SOURCES

Sources

At present time, there are four major alternative sources of long-term debt available to health care facilities:

1. tax-exempt revenue bonds
2. Federal Housing Administration (FHA)-insured mortgages
3. public taxable bonds
4. conventional mortgage financing

Table 14–5 compares these four sources of financing with respect to the factors that affect capital financing desirability.

Tax Exempt Revenue Bonds

Tax-exempt revenue bonds permit the interest earned on them to be exempt from federal income taxation. The primary security for such loans is usually a pledge of the revenues of the facility seeking the loan, plus a first mortgage on the assets of the facility. If the tax revenue of a government entity is also pledged, the bonds are referred to as "general obligation bonds." Because of the income tax exemption, the interest rates on a tax-exempt bond are usually $1\frac{1}{2}$ to 2 percent lower than other sources of financing.

Most tax-exempt revenue bonds are issued by a state or local authority. The health care facility then enters into a lease arrangement with the authority. Title to the assets remains with the authority until the indebtedness is repaid.

Legislation has been issued by Congress that has begun to limit both the total amount of tax-exempt revenue bonds that can be issued and the purpose for which the financing can be used. For example, a hospital can no longer issue tax-exempt revenue bonds to finance the construction of a medical office building.

FHA-Insured Mortgages

FHA-insured mortgages are sponsored by the Federal Housing Administration, but initial processing begins in the Department of Health and Human Services. Through the FHA program, the government provides mortgage insurance for both proprietary and nonproprietary hospitals. This guarantee reduces the risk of a loan to investors and thus lowers the

Table 14–5 Comparative Analysis: Long-Term Debt Alternatives for Hospitals

Program Characteristics	Conventional Mortgage	Taxable Bonds	Tax-Exempt Bonds	FHA-Insured Mortgage (GNMA Guarantee)
Security	First mortgage given to lender; pledge of gross revenues (substantially all hospital assets pledged)	First mortgage given to trustee bank for benefit of bondholder; pledge of gross revenue (substantially all assets pledged)	First mortgage given to trustee bank for benefit of bondholders; pledge of gross revenue (substantially all assets pledged)	First mortgage given to FHA-approved mortgagee for benefit of HUD; pledge of gross revenue (substantially all assets pledged)
Timing for alternative	1–6 months	4–8 months	3–6 months	6–12 months
Percentage financing available	Usually 70–75% of eligible assets available to be pledged (as determined by appraisal)	Up to 100%, limited by available cash flow and available assets in some cases	Up to 100%, subject to available cash flow	
Construction financing	Normally required	Optional	Not required	Not required
Financing costs	Covers all costs of assets, excluding some movable equipment	Covers all costs	Covers all costs	Covers all costs, including startup costs
Term of financing	15–20 years	15–20 years (occasionally with balloon payment based on longer amortization)	30–35 years common	25 years subsequent to construction completion
Front end fees	1–2% commitment fee subject to amount financed; other fees $5–$25,000	1% underwriting (private placement) or 2–4% underwriting (public offering); other expenses approximately $\frac{1}{2}$ of 1% plus feasibility study	1% underwriting (private placement) or 2–3.5% underwriting (public offering); other expenses approximate $\frac{1}{2}$ of 1% plus feasibility study	1% placement fee, 0.8% filing fee, 0.5% insurance (FHA) fee, 0.25% GNMA fee

continues

Table 14–5 continued

Program Characteristics	Conventional Mortgage	Taxable Bonds	Tax-Exempt Bonds	FHA-Insured Mortgage (GNMA Guarantee)
Continuing annual fee	$\frac{1}{8}$ of 1% servicing if multiple lenders	Trustee fees (nominal)	Trustee fees (nominal)	0.5% FHA insurance fee; 0.25% GNMA fee
Prepayment provisions	Normally 10-year, no prepayment; 5% penalty descending thereafter	Normally 5-year and prepayment; no penalty unless refinancing	10-year, no prepayment; 3% penalty descending thereafter	15% of loan may be prepaid each year; 3% penalty over 15%, declining by $\frac{1}{8}$ of 1% each year
Required reserves	Usually none; depreciation reserve optional	None	Debt service reserve equal to one year's P & I; depreciation reserve equal to deficiency amount	Usually none
Restriction on leasing	Yes; subject to cash flow levels by covenant	None	None	None
Additional parity financing	Yes; normally subject to lender approval	Yes; subject to approval of underwriter or to provisions of financing agreement; normally required coverage of 110–150%	Yes; subject to meeting coverage requirement of 110–150% on both historical and pro forma basis	Yes; only with FHA-compatible program
Payment	Monthly	Semiannually	Quarterly/semiannually	Monthly
Reporting	Lender(s) only	Lender(s) or bond trustee and underwriter as appropriate, and rating agencies	Bond trustee, underwriter, and rating agencies as appropriate	HUD and mortgagee

interest rate that a hospital must pay. However, obtaining the appropriate approvals can often be a time-consuming process.

Public Taxable Bonds

Public taxable bonds are issued in much the same way as tax-exempt revenue bonds, except that there is no issuing authority and no interest income tax exemption. An investment banking firm usually underwrites the loan and markets the issue to individual investors. Interest rates are thus higher on this type of financing than they are on a tax-exempt issue.

Conventional Mortgage Financing

Conventional mortgage financing is usually privately placed with a bank, pension fund, savings and loan institution, life insurance company, or real estate investment trust. This source of financing can be arranged quickly, but, compared with other alternatives, it does not provide as large a percentage of the total financing requirements for large projects. Thus, greater amounts of equity must be contributed.

Parties Involved

Figure 14–5 is a schematic representation of the parties involved and their relationships in issuing a public tax-exempt revenue bond. This schematic could also be used to illustrate the process of issuing a public taxable bond. The only change would be the deletion of the issuing authority and addition of a line showing the direct issuance of the bonds by the health care facility. The specific parties in a bond financing include the following:

- issuing authority
- investment banker
- health care facility
- market
- trustee bank
- feasibility consultant
- legal counsel
- bond-rating agency

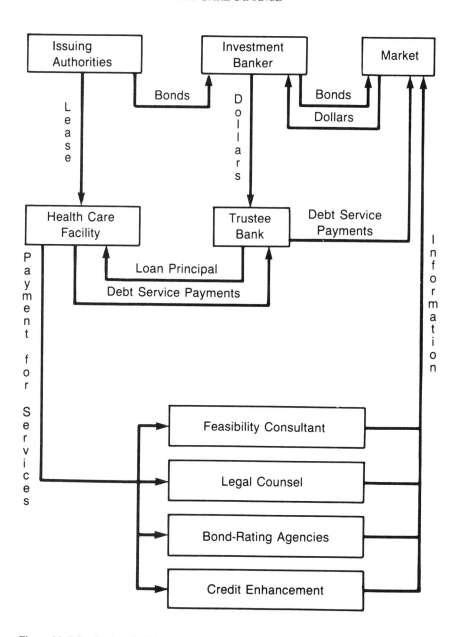

Figure 14–5 Parties Involved in a Public Tax-Exempt Revenue Bond Issue

Issuing Authority

The issuing authority is involved only in tax-exempt financing. In most cases, the issuing authority is some state or local governmental authority, which may be specially created for the sole purpose of issuing revenue bonds. The issuing authority serves as a conduit between the health care facility and the investment banker. In a public taxable issue or in a situation in which tax-exempt revenue bonds are issued directly by the health care facility, the role of the issuing authority may be eliminated.

Investment Banker

In public or private issues, investment bankers have a dual role. First, they serve as advisors to the health care facility that is issuing the bonds. In many circumstances, they are the focal point for coordinating the services of the feasibility consultant, the legal counsel, and the bond-rating agencies. Their advice can be extremely important in obtaining timely funding under favorable conditions. Second, investment bankers serve as brokers between the market and the issuer of the bond. If investment bankers underwrite the issue, it means that they technically buy the entire issue and are at risk for the sale of the bonds to individual investors. If investment bankers place the issue on a *best efforts basis*, they do not purchase the issue, and any unsold bonds become the property of the issuer.

Health Care Facility

The health care facility is the ultimate beneficiary of the bond issue. The health care facility is also responsible for repayment of the loan principal. The financial condition of the health care facility and its ability to repay the indebtedness are thus the central concerns of the investor. To provide evidence of its financial condition and the risk of the investment to the market, the health care facility usually employs independent consultants who assess various aspects of the facility. Such consultants include the feasibility consultant, the legal counsel, and the bond-rating agencies.

Market

For any given bond issue, the market may consist of a large number of individual investors, or it may consist of a small number of large institutional investors. In any case, the market purchases the bonds of the issuer with the expectation of some stated rate of return. The market also wants assurances that the bonds will be repaid on a timely basis and that there is not an unreasonable amount of risk.

Trustee Bank

A trustee bank serves as the market's agent once the bonds are sold. Typically, the trustee bank is a commercial bank—in some cases the same bank at which the health care facility has its accounts. The trustee bank may receive the proceeds from the sale of the bond issue and deliver the monies directly to the hospital or to the contractor, as required. The trustee bank also receives the debt service payments from the health care facility and distributes these to the market or investors. It may retire outstanding bonds according to a prearranged schedule of retirement and hold additional reserve requirements deposited by the health care facility. Finally, the trustee bank ensures that the health care facility is adhering to the provisions of the bond contract or indenture, such as those concerning adequate debt service coverage and working capital positions.

Feasibility Consultant

The feasibility consultant is usually an independent certified public accountant who may or may not be the health care facility's outside auditor. The feasibility consultant's primary function is to assess the financial feasibility of the project and the ability of the health care facility to meet the associated indebtedness. Financial projections are usually made for a five-year period. These projections provide a basis for the investor and the bond-rating agency to assess the risk of default.

Legal Counsel

Legal counsel is needed for several reasons. First, in a tax-exempt revenue bond issue, the market is concerned with the legality of the tax exemption. If the interest payments are not determined to be tax-exempt by the Internal Revenue Service, the investors will suffer a significant loss. Second, legal opinion is necessary to ensure that the security pledged by the health care facility, whether it be revenue or assets, is legal and enforceable.

Bond-Rating Agencies

Moody's and Standard & Poor's are the two primary bond-rating agencies, although other smaller ones exist. Their function is to assess the relative risk associated with a given bond issue. The two agencies have developed detailed coding systems to assess risk (see Table 14–6). The resulting bond rating has important implications. First, there is a definite correlation between the interest rate that an issuer must pay and the bond rating associated with the issue. Generally speaking, the higher the bond

Table 14-6 Bond Ratings

Classification	Moody's	Standard & Poor's
Investment grade	Aaa	AAA
	Aa	AA
	Al	A +
	A	A
	Baa1	BBB +
	Baa	BBB
Not Investment grade	Ba	BB
	B	B
	Caa	CCC
	Ca	CC
	C	C

rating, the lower the interest rate. Thus, a bond rated AAA by Standard & Poor's would be likely to have a much lower rate of interest than one rated BBB. Second, issues rated below BBB by Standard & Poor's or Baa by Moody's are not classified as investment grade. Many institutional investors are prohibited from investing in bonds that carry a rating lower than investment grade. Thus, the market for such issues is likely to be thin.

Credit Enhancement

Credit enhancement is a term that has only recently come into use in the health care financing field. A credit enhancement device is simply a mechanism by which the risk of default can be shifted from the issuer to a third party. Thus, the FHA-insured mortgage program provides a form of credit enhancement.

Aside from the FHA program, two basic types of credit enhancement are commonly used. The first type is municipal bond insurance. Municipal bond insurance is a surety bond that ensures that the debt service will be repaid. When municipal bond insurance is used, the credit rating for the issue becomes the credit rating of the insurance firm that is writing the insurance. In most cases, this means that the bond rating would be AAA or Aaa. Table 14-7 presents a summary of the major firms that currently provide municipal bond insurance and gives some idea of the relative cost of such insurance.

The second form of credit enhancement is a letter of credit. A letter of credit, usually issued by a commercial bank, provides a formal assurance that a specified sum of money will be available over some defined time

Table 14–7 Municipal Bond Insurers

Insurer	Types of Issues	Rating	Premiums	Principal and Interest Insured (Billions)	
				All Types	Health Care
AMBAC Indemnity (212-248-3307)	New-issue GOs, tax and revenue anticipation note	AAA Aaa	.33–.94%	$ 86.2	$12.9
MBIA (914-765-3893)	New-issue GOs, utility issues, commercial paper, hospital goods	AAA Aaa	.30–90%	$157.7	$32.1
FGIC (212-607-3009)	New issues, GOs, revenue bonds, and unit investment trusts	AAA Aaa	NA	$ 92.6	NA
Capital Guarantee (415-995-8012)	New issues, GOs and revenue bonds	AAA NR	.20–2.00%	$ 9.0	$ .56
FSA (212-826-0100)	New issues, GOs, revenue bonds, and municipal utilities	AAA Aaa	NA	$ 21.6	$ .67

Source: Prepared by James LeBuhn, Ziegler Securities, Chicago, Illinois.

period. Usually the time period matches the maturity of the debt, and the amount provided in the letter of credit corresponds to the amount of indebtedness. As with bond insurance, the credit rating of the bank would be substituted for the credit rating of the issuer. In most situations, this would mean an automatic AAA or Aaa rating. The bank requires a fee for providing the letter of credit, and the issuer must determine whether the cost of the letter of credit exceeds any possible savings in reduced interest expense that would result from an improved bond rating.

NEW DEVELOPMENTS

Four recent modifications in the traditional sources of long-term debt should be noted at this juncture:

1. variable rate financing
2. pooled or shared financing
3. zero-coupon/original issue discount bonds
4. interest rate swaps

Variable Rate Financing

Recently, in the health care sector as well as in other industries, there has been a shift to the use of variable rate financing. In variable rate financing, the outstanding debt principal is fixed, but the interest rate on the principal is variable. This contrasts with the traditional situation in which the interest rate is fixed for the life of the bonds. Variable rate financing requires that the interest rate be adjusted periodically—weekly in some cases—to a current market index.

A feature that is often associated with variable rate financing is the use of a tender option or put. A tender option or put permits investors to redeem their bonds at some predetermined interval—perhaps daily—at the face value. In reality, this type of financing is short-term, not long-term. As a result, the interest rate may be significantly below a comparable long-term rate at the initiation of the financing. Many firms—not just health care firms—have opted to use variable rate financing to achieve a lower cost of financing. Sometimes this strategy is referred to as "moving down the yield curve." Figure 14-6 shows a typical upward-sloping yield curve.

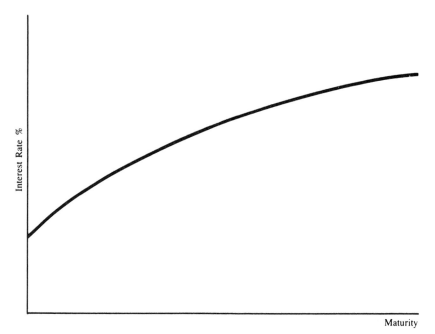

Figure 14–6 The Yield Curve

Pooled Financing

In the health care sector, there has been increasing interest in developing financing packages that encompass more than one entity. The major rationale for this interest lies in the relationship between size and cost of debt; larger organizations are better able to obtain debt capital and to realize lower costs of financing.

In general, there are three ways in which pooled or shared arrangements have been created in the health care sector. The first is through the use of master indenture financing by health care systems. In such cases, master indenture financing means that the debt is guaranteed by all the members who are a part of the master indenture. For example, a system of ten hospitals could finance through some master indenture arrangement in which all ten hospitals, or some subset of the ten hospitals, would be a party to the financing.

A second alternative is the use of pooled equipment financing programs. These programs are often sponsored by the state hospital association or some regional association. Individual hospitals are a party to the financing and can obtain funds from the pool. The interest rate is usually much lower because the risk is spread across several hospitals.

The third alternative is an arrangement similar to the above except that the sponsor is different. Here, the pooled approach is used either for equipment needs or, in some cases, for major building programs. The issuer and sponsor of the pool is not the state or regional association, however, but some voluntary association of health care entities. The Voluntary Hospitals of America have created such pooled financings for their members, and other associations are rapidly developing similar financing programs for their members.

Zero-Coupon/Original Issue Discount Bonds

Bonds that are issued at a deep discount have a coupon rate of interest that is below the rate required by the market for that type of security. In a zero-coupon situation, there is no interest paid, thus the term *zero coupon*. Certain investors see advantages in purchasing zero-coupon bonds to meet their portfolio needs. There may also be advantages for the issuer. The major advantage for the issuer is in the delay of interest payments. This can conserve needed cash flow and may match the cash needs of the issuer. There is also the possibility that the after-reimbursement cost of the debt will be below the investment yield.

It is important to note that, in most zero-coupon situations, there is a periodic payment to a sinking fund. The sinking fund is an account under the control of the bond trustee, and the proceeds of the fund are used to retire the bonds at maturity.

The mechanics of a zero-coupon situation may be seen in the following case example. Assume that General Hospital issues $100,000,000 in zero-coupon five-year bonds. General would receive $62,100,000 from the market if the current market rate of interest is 10 percent. Although no interest is paid, each year an amount is recorded for interest expense. This amount is an amortization of the difference between the face value of the bonds ($100,000,000) and the actual cash received ($62,100,000). Thus, during the five-year period, $37,900,000 will be recognized as interest expense. General will also be required to make semiannual payments of $7,586,793 to a sinking fund. This fund is assumed to earn interest at 12 percent annually or 6 percent semiannually. Assume also that equal amounts of the total discount will be recognized as interest expense each year. This would amount to $7,580,000. The calculation in Table 14–8 shows the net present value cost of this financing, assuming that 50

Table 14–8 Net Present Value of Zero-Coupon Financing

Item	Amount before Reimbursement	Amount after Reimbursement	Years (Periods)	Present Value Factor (12%)	Present Value
Sinking fund	$7,586,793	$7,586,793	1–10*	7.360*	$55,838,800
Interest expense (amortization)	(7,580,000)	(3,790,000)	1–5	3.605	(13,662,950)
		Net present value cost			$42,175,850

*Ten semiannual payments; the present value factor is for ten periods at 6%.

percent of capital costs are reimbursed and that the appropriate discount rate for the hospital is its investment yield of 12 percent.

The net present value cost of General's financing is $42,175,850, which is significantly less than the $62,100,000 that the hospital will receive. The sinking fund is not recognized as a capital expense item, which explains why the before- and after-reimbursement amounts are the same. The annual amortization of the discount, which is recognized by third-party payers as a reimbursable capital item, reduces the cost of the financing significantly. In some cases, this pattern of amortization may not be permitted by the payers. Instead, the payer may require a type of payment called *effective yield*. This type of payment requires that the same total amount of interest expense be recorded over the five years ($37,900,000), but the amounts in the earlier years would be less. This would reduce the present value of the benefit somewhat.

Interest Rate Swaps

A number of hospitals and other health care providers have begun to use interest rate swaps. Interest rate swaps may enable firms to deal with the volatility in the financial markets and obtain lower-cost financing that better meets their needs. To understand an interest rate swap, three questions must be answered:

1. What is an interest rate swap?
2. Why are interest rate swaps beneficial? For every winner, won't there be a loser?
3. How can a swap arrangement be analyzed?

An interest rate swap is merely an exchange of interest rate payments between two firms, with a bank usually acting as a broker. For example, a firm that has issued fixed-rate debt may wish to make floating-rate payments. If a firm with floating-rate payments can be found that would like to substitute fixed-rate payments, a swap may be arranged. It is also possible to swap two different types of floating-rate debt. In a swap, only the coupon payments are exchanged, not the principal. Payments are also conditional. One party can break the deal at any time.

The basic nature of the swap is fairly easy to understand. The aspect that is often puzzling is, how could both parties benefit from the swap? Many people believe that the only party that truly benefits is the broker.

The rationale for swaps is purely and simply a function of a supposed market imperfection. This means that one borrower has a better relative position in one maturity market than another. This difference is often ascribed to differential information and institutional restrictions that lead to differences in transaction costs. Because of these imperfections the opportunity for financial arbitrage occurs.

To understand this concept more fully, let us assume that hospital A and hospital B face the following interest rates:

Type of Debt	Hospital A	Hospital B	Rate Differential
Fixed	7.15%	8.10%	95 bps
Floating	Variable + 25 bps*	Variable + 40 bps	15 bps

*bps = Basis point (1/100 of 1 percent)

In the above example, hospital A has a better relative position in both markets, fixed and floating. The differential, however, is much larger in the fixed-market rate (95 bps) than in the floating-rate market (15 bps). The net differential is 80 bps (95 − 15). This difference implies that there is a swap opportunity present and that the total advantage is 80 bps. It is this 80 bps differential that will be split among hospital A, hospital B, and the broker.

Assume now that both hospitals issue $50 million of debt. Hospital A issues fixed-rate debt and hospital B issues floating-rate debt. A broker could put these two hospitals together, and the following set of payments might result:

Payments	Hospital A	Hospital B	Broker
To bondholders	715 bps	Variable + 40 bps	0
To broker	Variable + 15 bps	750 bps	(Variable + 765 bps)
From broker to A	(740 bps)	0	740 bps
From broker to B	0	(Variable + 10 bps)	Variable + 10 bps
Net payment	Variable − 10 bps	780 bps	15 bps
Advantage	35 bps	30 bps	15 bps

The above data show that all parties have realized some financial advantage as a result of the swap. Hospital A has reduced its floating rate to variable minus 10 basis points from variable plus 25 basis points. This is a savings of 35 basis points from its initial position. Hospital B has also gained. It now has fixed-rate debt at 7.80 percent, which is 30 basis points under its projected rate of 8.10 percent. Of course, the broker has kept 15 basis points for the time and effort required to bring the parties together.

This is the way in which a swap is supposed to work. Everyone has benefited. It is not always true, however, that every party will benefit, and each swap opportunity must be carefully analyzed to ensure that benefits will be realized.

EARLY RETIREMENT OF DEBT

In many cases, an issuer would like to retire an existing debt issue prior to its maturity. There are a variety of reasons for wanting to do this. One important reason is that it permits the issuer to take advantage of a reduction in interest rates. An issue may have been marketed several years ago when interest rates were 10 percent, and rates may now have dropped to 7 percent. If the present lower interest rate could be substituted for the original rate, a major improvement in net income could result. Other reasons for wishing to retire an existing indebtedness might be that it would enable the issuer to avoid onerous covenants in the existing indenture or to take advantage of changes in bond ratings or changes in policy regarding tax-exempt financing. Whatever the reason, most health care issues in fact do not remain outstanding for their full life cycles; most are retired early.

Two common ways of retiring an issue early are (1) refinancing and (2) refunding. In a refinancing, the issuer buys back the outstanding bonds from the investors. This can be accomplished in either of two ways. In the first way, the issuer may have the option of an early call. If the outstanding bonds are callable, the issuer would notify the present bondholders that the bonds are being called and should be tendered for payment. The principal or face value would then be paid, along with any call premium plus accrued interest. A second way to effect a refinancing would be for the issuer to buy back the bonds in open market transactions or to send a letter to existing bondholders, offering to buy the bonds at some stated price.

Early retirement of existing bonds can also be accomplished through refunding. In a refunding, the outstanding bonds are not acquired by the issuer, and the present bondholders continue to maintain their investment. Although the refunding does not actually retire the bonds, they are not shown on the issuer's financial statements, and the covenants present in the indenture are now voided. The process of voiding existing indenture covenants and removing the bonds from the issuer's financial statements is called *defeasance*. In effect, defeasance in a refunding involves the deposit of a sum of money with the bond trustee, which is then used to buy specially designated securities of the federal government. With these securities, there is a guarantee that all future interest and principal payments can be met from the proceeds controlled by the bond trustee.

Here is a simple example to illustrate the refunding process: On January 1, 1993, $1 million of 15 percent level-debt service bonds are issued. The bonds have a five-year life. The earliest call date is January 1, 1995. No call premium is involved. On January 1, 1994, interest rates have dropped to 7 percent, and management advance-refunds the January 1, 1993, issue. In this example, the original January 1, 1993, issue would have the following debt service schedule:

Date	Interest	Principal	Total Debt Service	Ending Debt Principal
Jan. 1, 1992	$150,000	$148,320	$298,320	$851,680
Jan. 1, 1993	127,750	170,570	298,320	681,110
Jan. 1, 1994	102,170	196,150	298,320	484,960
Jan. 1, 1995	72,740	225,580	298,320	259,380
Jan. 1, 1996	38,940	259,380	298,320	0

To retire or advance-refund the issue on January 1, 1994, management must place on deposit with a trustee a sum of money that will guarantee payment of the following amounts on January 1, 1995 (the earliest call date):

Interest due Jan. 1, 1995	$127,750
Debt principal due Jan. 1, 1995	170,570
Ending debt principal on Jan. 1, 1995	681,110
	$979,430

If management borrows all the funds necessary to meet the $979,430 payment on January 1, 1995, how much must it borrow on January 1, 1994? Ignoring placement fees and other debt issuance costs, the hospital would borrow $915,360. Why $915,360? It is assumed that the hospital will be able to invest the proceeds at 7 percent, the effective interest rate on January 1, 1994. In tax-exempt issues, an arbitrage restriction limits investment yields for all practical purposes to the interest rate of the refunding issue.

Is there any real savings in debt service costs? Yes; the following new issue schedule shows annual savings of $28,080 ($298,320 − $270,240) for the next four years:

Date	Interest	Principal	Total Debt Service	Ending Debt	Savings in Debt Service
Jan. 1, 1995	$64,080	$206,160	$270,240	$709,200	$28,080
Jan. 1, 1996	49,640	220,600	270,240	488,600	28,080
Jan. 1, 1997	34,200	236,040	270,240	252,560	28,080
Jan. 1, 1998	17,680	252,560	270,240	0	28,080

Thus far, the refinancing looks good. However, there is an accounting loss that must be recorded. At the end of the first year (January 1, 1994), the value for the old debt, $851,680, will be removed from the balance sheet. But the defeased debt will be replaced by $915,360 of new debt, and this will reduce income in that year by $63,680 ($915,360 − $851,680). This will be treated as an extraordinary loss in the period in which refunding takes place.

A real world case may make the magnitude of these numbers more apparent. A hospital recently refunded $65 million of two-year-old debt with $79 million of new debt at a lower effective interest rate. Estimated savings in debt service over the life of the issue were $22 million, but there was an accounting loss of approximately $13 million in the initial year. More important, this loss reduced the hospital's ratio of equity to assets from 26 percent to 16 percent. This is a rather sizable reduction that could have some impact on future credit availability. Many lenders establish target equity-to-debt ratios beyond which they will not lend funds at reasonable interest rates.

In sum, refunding to take advantage of reduced interest rates usually makes a lot of economic sense. But the presence of an accounting loss should be considered, especially in light of its potential impact on future credit availability.

SUMMARY

The major sources of capital financing available to health care firms may be categorized as (1) equity and (2) debt. Equity has become an important source of capital, even for traditional tax-exempt health care firms. Corporate restructuring can greatly facilitate the process of accessing equity capital. However, long-term debt will probably continue to represent the major source of capital for most health care firms. Evaluation of alternative sources of long-term debt requires more than a simple comparison of interest rates. The impact of other factors should also be carefully reviewed to determine the overall attractiveness of alternative financing packages.

ASSIGNMENTS

1. Explain the term *defeasance*. What does it mean?

2. Assuming a normal or typical yield curve (that is, upward sloping), discuss the advantages and disadvantages of borrowing money for a major construction program with three-year term financing.

3. When is a master trust indenture used, and what is its value?

4. Under what circumstances might your hospital be interested in issuing zero-coupon bonds?

5. In an advance refunding of debt, accounting gains or losses usually occur. Under what conditions could there be an accounting gain?

6. United Hospital has received a leasing proposal from Leasing, Inc., for a Siemens cardiac catheterization unit. The terms are

- five-year lease
- annual payments of $200,000 payable one year in advance
- payment of property tax estimated to be $23,000 annually
- renewal at end of year 5 at fair market value

Alternatively, United can buy the catheterization unit for $725,000. United must debt-finance this equipment. It anticipates a bank loan with an initial down payment of $125,000 and a three-year term loan at 16 percent with equal principal payments. The residual value of the equipment at year 5 is estimated to be $225,000. The lease is treated as an operating lease. Depreciation is calculated on a straight-line basis. Assuming a discount rate of 14 percent, what financing option should United select? Assume that there is no reimbursement of capital costs.

7. Nutty Hospital wishes to advance-refund its existing 15 percent long-term debt. The present $30,000,000 is not callable until five years from today. The payout on the issue over the next five years is as follows:

	Interest	Principal	Total
End of year 1	$4,500,000	$1,000,000	$5,500,000
End of year 2	4,350,000	1,000,000	5,350,000
End of year 3	4,200,000	1,000,000	5,200,000
End of year 4	4,050,000	1,000,000	5,050,000
End of year 5	3,900,000	1,000,000	4,900,000

At the end of the fifth year, the debt ($25,000,000 outstanding balance at that time) may be called with a 10 percent penalty. If present interest rates are 10 percent and the investment rate on the funds to be received from the new issue cannot exceed 10 percent, what amount must Nutty Hospital borrow today? Assume that underwriting fees and other issuance costs will be 5 percent of the issue and that all debt service on the old issue must be met from the proceeds of the refunding issue and related investment income.

8. You have the option of leasing an asset for $100,000 per year, with payments to be made at the end of each year of use. This is a noncancelable lease. Alternatively, you may buy the asset for $248,700. For reimbursement purposes, the lease must be capitalized. If the asset is purchased, it will be debt-financed with $210,000 of three-year serial notes (that is, $70,000 of principal will be repaid each year). The effective interest rate on this loan will be 8 percent. Assume that the asset has an allowable useful life of three years with no estimated salvage value.

Assignment:
• Determine the amount of expense that would be reported in each of the three years under the two financing plans.

• Assuming that 80 percent of all reported capital expenses are reimbursed and that the discount rate is 6 percent, determine the present value of the asset in these two methods of financing.

9. Happy Valley is considering moving from its present location into a new 200-bed facility. The estimated construction cost for the new facility is $40 million. The hospital has no internal funds and is considering a 20-year mortgage with interest scheduled to be 8 percent. The issue will be repaid over 20 years with equal annual principal payments of $2.0 million. Interest expense would decline each year by $160,000.

The cost of the plant and fixed equipment would be 80 percent of the total cost or $32.0 million and the movable equipment would be $8.0 million. The movable equipment would need to be replaced in ten years, and it is estimated that the replacement cost would be $17,271,200 (inflation is assumed to be 8 percent per year). The plant and fixed equipment would need to be replaced in 30 years at a cost of $322,006,400 (inflation again assumed to be 8 percent per year). All costs reflect only the investment required to provide inpatient services. A separate analysis will be done for outpatient services.

Happy Valley anticipates that its operation will generate about 9,700 discharges per year. The hospital anticipates that its operating costs, excluding capital costs, will be $4,000 per discharge, or $38,800,000 in the first full year of operation.

The payer mix at Happy Valley is expected to be 60 percent Medicare and Medicaid on the inpatient side. These payers will pay approximately $4,400 per discharge. This payment reflects both operating and capital cost payments. Approximately 10 percent of Happy Valley's operating and capital costs will be paid by payers who reimburse the hospital on a cost-related basis for both capital and operating costs. The remaining 30 percent of Happy Valley's business will be charge based, but it is expected that discounts to commercial insurers and bad debt and charity write-offs will average 30 percent.

Assignment:
Assuming that Happy Valley wishes to break even on a cash flow basis in the first year of operation, what charge per discharge must be set? If the hospital wanted to include an element in its rate structure to reflect replacement cost of the building and movable equipment, what additional amount would that be? Assume that 50 percent of the movable equipment cost would be debt financed and 80 percent of the building and fixed equipment would be debt financed. Also assume that the hospital can earn 10 percent on any invested money.

10. Mayberry Hospital is considering a joint venture relationship with your physicians to acquire a full-body CT scanner. Projected revenues and expenses for the scanner are presented below:

	Year 1	Year 2	Year 3	Year 4	Year 5
Revenues	$521,000	$531,000	$542,000	$533,000	$564,000
Less bad debts and discounts	52,100	53,100	54,200	53,300	56,400
Net revenues	468,900	477,900	487,800	479,700	507,600
Expenses					
Wages and employee benefits	60,000	63,000	66,150	69,458	72,930
Maintenance	55,000	57,750	60,638	63,669	66,853
Supplies	20,000	21,000	22,050	23,153	24,310
Rent	18,000	18,900	19,845	20,837	21,879
Administrative	10,000	10,500	11,025	11,576	12,155
Utilities	5,000	5,250	5,513	5,788	6,078
Insurance	5,000	5,250	5,513	5,788	6,078
Taxes	10,000	10,000	10,000	10,000	10,000
Depreciation	94,050	137,940	131,670	131,670	131,670
Interest	40,620	33,384	25,271	16,176	5,977
Total expenses	317,670	362,974	357,675	358,115	357,930
Net income before tax or interest	$151,230	$114,926	$130,125	$121,585	149,670

The scanner is expected to cost $627,000 and have a useful life of five years. Two possible financing plans have been proposed. The first plan would be a limited partnership arrangement. There would be 34 shares; 33 would be sold to investors for $19,000 apiece. The 34th would be retained by the hospital for its development effort. In the second financing plan, a $380,000 level debt service plan with a five-year maturity and interest at 10 percent would be arranged. The remainder of the funding would be generated through the sale of 33 limited partnership shares at $7,500 per share. Again, a 34th share would be issued to the hospital for its development efforts. Assuming that a 30 percent marginal tax rate will exist, project cash flow per partnership unit under each financing alternative for each of the five years.

SOLUTIONS AND ANSWERS

1. Defeasance means that, on final payment of all interest and principal, the rights of the bond trustee cease to exist; that is, they are defeased. The security covenants in an indenture may also be satisfied through the creation of a trust (escrow) in which sufficient monies are held to guarantee payment at some future date. Defeasance means that the issue defeased is no longer an obligation of the issuer and can be removed from the issuer's books.

2. The typical, upward-sloping yield curve implies that a 3-year interest rate will probably be much lower than a 20- to 25-year rate. Therefore, cost will be lower with a 3-year construction loan. At the end of the third year, however, permanent financing must be sought; and there is no guarantee that interest rates will not have increased during the period or that financing will be available at the end of the third year.

3. A master trust indenture usually pledges the assets and revenues of several firms in a combined financing package. It is often used by health care systems to gain better access to capital and lower interest rates.

4. Zero-coupon bonds are especially desirable if the issuer's effective interest rate on the bonds is well below the yield or discount rate of the issuer. In a zero-coupon bond issue, the postponement of interest payment maximizes the possibility for additional arbitrage, that is, for investing at a yield greater than the cost of funds.

5. Accounting gains usually take place when the advance-refunding issue has a higher rate of interest than the refunded issue. Accounting losses often occur when the reverse is true.

6. United Hospital's financing options for the cardiac catheterization unit are detailed below:

Item	Amount before Reimbursement	Amount after Reimbursement	Years	Present Value Factor (14%)	Present Value
Lease					
Rent	$200,000	$200,000	0	1.000	$200,000
Rent	200,000	200,000	1–4	2.914	582,800
Property tax*	23,000	23,000	1–5	3.433	78,959
		Net present value cost of lease			$861,759

Item	Amount before Reimbursement	Amount after Reimbursement	Years	Present Value Factor (14%)	Present Value
Purchase					
Down payment	$125,000	$125,000	0	1.000	$125,000
Principal	200,000	200,000	1–3	2.322	464,400
Interest	96,000	96,000	1	.877	84,192
Interest	64,000	64,000	2	.769	49,216
Interest	32,000	32,000	3	.675	21,600
Salvage	(225,000)	(225,000)	5	.519	(116,775)
		Net present value of purchase			$627,633

*Property tax would be passed on to the lessee. There is no property tax purchase because the hospital is a tax exempt firm.

From the above data, it can be seen that purchase of the catheterization unit would produce a lower net present value cost, compared with a lease.

7. Nutty Hospital's present borrowing needs are detailed below:

Item	Amount Required	Years	Present Value Factor (10%)	Present Value
Debt service—Year 1	$ 5,500,000	1	.909	$ 4,999,500
Debt service—Year 2	5,350,000	2	.826	4,419,100
Debt service—Year 3	5,200,000	3	.751	3,905,200
Debt service—Year 4	5,050,000	4	.683	3,449,150
Debt service—Year 5	4,900,000	5	.621	3,042,900
Principal at Year 5	25,000,000	5	.621	15,525,000
Call premium	2,500,000	5	.621	1,552,500
		Net present value		$36,893,350

$$\text{Amount borrowed} = \frac{\$36,893,350}{.95} = \$38,835,105$$

8. The following data show the comparative expense and present values for leasing versus debt financing the asset over the three-year period:

• Expenses for Lease

$$\text{Interest rate} = 10\%$$

$$\$248,700 = \$100,000 \times P\,(i,3)$$

$$P\,(i,3) = 2.487$$

- Interest expense per year

Year	Beginning Principal	Interest (at 10%)	Reduction in Principal	Total
1	$248,700	$24,870	$ 75,130	$100,000
2	173,570	17,357	82,643	100,000
3	90,927	9,073*	90,927	100,000
		$51,300	$248,700	$300,000

*Last year's interest is derived by subtracting the principal payment of $90,927 from the total payment of $100,000.

- Depreciation expense per year: $248,700/3 = $82,900
- Expenses for debt financing

Interest expense per year

Year	Interest
1	.08 × 210,000 = $16,800
2	.08 × 140,000 = 11,200
3	.08 × 70,000 = 5,600

Depreciation expense per year: $82,900

- Comparison of expenses

	Lease Alternative			Debt Alternative		
Year	Interest	Depreciation	Total	Interest	Depreciation	Total
1	$24,870	$ 82,900	$107,770	$16,800	$ 82,900	$ 99,700
2	17,357	82,900	100,257	11,200	82,900	94,100
3	9,073	82,900	91,973	5,600	82,900	88,500
Totals	$51,300	$248,700	$300,000	$33,600	$248,700	$282,300

- Comparison of cash flows—present value basis

Item	Amount before Reimbursement	Amount after Reimbursement	Years	Present Value Factor (6%)	Present Value
Lease financing					
Rentals	$100,000	$100,000	1–3	2.673	$267,300
Depreciation	(82,900)	(66,320)	1–3	2.673	(177,273)
Interest*	(24,870)	(19,896)	1	.943	(18,762)
Interest*	(17,357)	(13,886)	2	.890	(12,358)
Interest*	(9,073)	(7,258)	3	.840	(6,097)
		Net present value cost of lease			$ 52,810

Item	Amount before Reimbursement	Amount after Reimbursement	Years	Present Value Factor (6%)	Present Value
Debt financing					
Down payment	$38,700	38,700	0	1.000	$ 38,700
Principal payment	70,000	70,000	1–3	2.673	187,110
Depreciation	(82,900)	(66,320)	1–3	2.673	(177,273)
Interest	16,800	3,360	1	.943	3,168
Interest	11,200	2,240	2	.890	1,993
Interest	5,600	1,120	3	.840	941
		Net present value cost of debt			$ 54,639

*Interest is shown as a reduction of cost because the lease payment reflects the interest paid to the lessor. The interest deduction recognizes third party payments for interest expense.

9. The following chart reflects the required charge that Happy Valley must set to break even on a cash flow basis and the additional charge required to cover the funded depreciation requirement necessary for eventual replacement:

Cash expenditures	
Principal payment	$ 2,000,000
Interest payment	3,200,000
Operating costs	38,800,000
Total cash costs	$44,000,000
Reimbursement	
Medicare and Medicaid ($4,400 × 5,820)	$25,608,000
Reimbursed interest (.10 × $3,200,000)	320,000
Reimbursed operating costs (.10 × 38,800,000)	3,880,000
Reimbursed equipment depreciation (.1 × $8,000,000/10)	80,000
Reimbursed building depreciation (.1 × $32,000,000/30)	106,667
Total payments	$29,994,667
Required charge to cover cash expenditures	
Cash expenditures remaining after reimbursement	$14,005,333
Number of charge-paying discharges	2,910
Required charge without discount	$4,813.83
Required charge with discount	$6,875.47
Required additional amounts for funded depreciation to meet replacement needs	
Annual deposit for movable equipment	$ 541,838
[.5 × $17,271,200/F (10%, 10 years)]	
Annual deposit for building	391,506
[.2 × $322,006,400/F (10%, 30 years)]	
Total Deposit Required	$ 933,344

Number of charge-paying discharges		2,910
Required charge without discount	$	320.74
Required charge with discount	$	458.20

10. The following data show the projected cash flow per partnership unit under the two financing alternatives.

	Years				
	1	*2*	*3*	*4*	*5*
Alternative 1—no debt					
Income before tax					
and interest	$151,230	$114,926	$130,125	$121,585	$149,670
Less income tax	45,369	34,478	39,038	36,476	44,901
Income after tax	$105,861	$ 80,448	$ 91,088	$ 85,110	$104,769
Add depreciation	94,050	137,940	131,670	131,670	131,670
Cash flow	$199,911	$218,388	$222,758	$216,780	$236,439
Cash flow per share	$ 5,880	$ 6,423	$ 6,552	$ 6,376	$ 6,954
Percentage return	30.9%	33.8%	34.5%	33.6%	36.6%
Alternative 2—debt financing					
Income before tax					
and interest	$151,230	$114,926	$130,125	$121,585	$149,670
Less interest	38,000	31,776	24,930	17,400	9,116
Taxable income	113,230	83,150	105,195	104,185	140,554
Less income tax	33,969	24,945	31,559	31,256	42,166
Income after tax	$ 79,261	$ 58,205	$ 73,637	$ 72,930	$ 98,388
Add depreciation	94,050	137,940	131,670	131,670	131,670
Less principal	62,237	68,461	75,307	82,837	91,158
Cash flow	$111,074	$127,684	$130,000	$121,763	$138,900
Cash flow per share	$ 3,267	$ 3,755	$ 3,824	$ 3,581	$ 4,085
Percentage return	43.6%	50.1%	51.0%	47.8%	54.5%

Chapter 15

Working Capital
and Cash Management

Few topics in finance are more important than cash and investment management. Cash is the lifeblood of a business operation. A firm that controls its access to cash and the generation of cash will usually survive and thrive. A firm that ignores or manages its cash position poorly may fail. Experience has shown that more firms fail for a lack of ready cash than for any other reason—even firms with sound profitability. It is extremely important, therefore, to recognize and appreciate that profit and cash management are not the same thing.

It would seem logical to expect that great volumes of literature would be devoted to such an important topic as cash and investment management. Unfortunately, this is not the case. Although a major portion of a financial manager's time is devoted to working capital problems, relatively little space is devoted to them in most financial management textbooks. A typical text often contains only several chapters that deal with working capital management and perhaps a single chapter that discusses cash management.

Cash management is probably more important in the health care industry than in many other industries, but often it is less understood. Health care financial executives frequently advance through the accounting route. While finance texts provide little coverage to cash management, accounting texts provide almost no coverage. Health care financial executives traditionally think cash management in terms of receivables control. They often believe that better cash management will result if accounts

---

Source: Adapted from *Cash and Investment Management for the Health Care Industry* by A. G. Seidner and W.O. Cleverley, pp. 1–19, Aspen Publishers, Inc., © 1990.

receivable can be reduced or the collection cycle shortened. Although accounts receivable management in health care organizations is clearly important, limiting attention to this one area is myopic. Good cash management should focus not only on the acceleration of receivables, but also on the complete cash conversion cycle. Reduction of the cash conversion cycle, along with the related investment of surplus funds, should be the critical objective of financial managers.

Many hospitals and health care firms often are willing to let their banks handle most of their cash management decisions. Although this strategy is acceptable in some situations, it may produce less than optimal performance. Risks are sometimes unnecessarily increased or yields on investments sacrificed. Real or perceived conflicts of interest also exist when the bank is represented on the hospital's governing board.

Why is cash and investment management of importance to health care executives? Hospitals have very large sums of investable funds compared with firms of similar size in other industries. For example, in 1990 the average hospital maintained a $16.7 million investment, or 20.8 percent of its total assets, in short-term cash, marketable securities, or other investments (see Table 14–1). Hospitals and other health care firms are also more likely to have greater investment management needs than other industries for several reasons:

- Most hospitals are voluntary, not-for-profit firms and must set aside funds for replacement of plants and equipment. Investor-owned firms can rely on the issuance of new stockholders' equity to finance some of their replacement needs.
- Hospitals are increasingly beginning to self-insure all or a portion of their professional liability risk. This requires that rather sizable investment pools be available to meet estimated actuarial needs.
- Many hospitals receive gifts and endowments. Although these sums may not be large for individual hospitals, they can provide additional sources of investment.
- Many hospitals also have rather sizable funding requirements for defined-benefit pension plans and debt service requirements associated with the issuance of bonds. These funds are usually held by a trustee.

With greater investments in the hospital industry, one should expect to find greater levels of investment income. For the average hospital in 1990, approximately 40 percent of total net income was derived from nonoperating revenue sources. Much of this nonoperating revenue is clearly related to investment income.

CASH AND INVESTMENT MANAGEMENT STRUCTURE

Effective cash management is often related to the cash conversion cycle, as depicted in Figure 15–1. In its simplest form, the cash conversion cycle represents the time that it takes a firm to go from an outlay of cash to purchase the needed factors of production, such as labor and supplies, to the actual collection of cash for the produced product or service, such as a completed treatment for a given patient. Usually the objectives in cash management are to minimize the collection period and to maximize the payment period. Trade-offs often exist; for example, accelerating collection of receivables may result in lost sales, and delaying payments to vendors could result in increased prices.

The primary tool used in cash planning is the cash budget. (Cash budgeting is discussed more fully in Chapter 16.) Cash balances are affected by changes in working capital over time. Working capital may be defined as the difference between current assets and current liabilities. The following items are usually included in these two categories:

1. current assets
   - cash and investment
   - accounts receivable
   - inventories
   - other current assets
2. current liabilities
   - accounts payable
   - accrued salaries and wages
   - accrued expenses
   - notes payable
   - current position of long-term debt

The cash budget focuses on four major activities that affect working capital:

1. purchasing of resources
2. production/sale of service
3. billing
4. collection

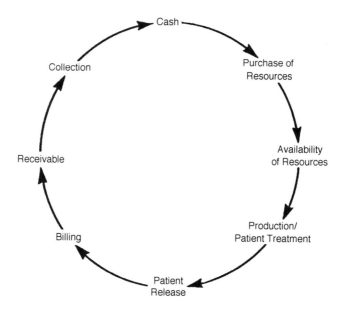

Figure 15–1 Cash Conversion Cycle

These activities represent time intervals in the cash conversion cycle. The purchasing of resources relates to the acquisition of supplies and labor, such as the level of inventory necessary to maintain realistic production schedules and the staff required to ensure adequate provision of services. Production and sale are virtually the same in the health care industry; there is no inventory of products or services. However, there is a delay between the production of service and final delivery. A patient may be in the hospital for 10 to 15 days before discharge, which could be regarded as the final point of sale. Billing represents the interval between the release or discharge of a patient and the generation of a bill. Collection represents the time interval between the generation of a bill to the actual collection of the cash from the patient or the patient's third-party payer.

Estimating these four time intervals is critical to cash budgeting and, therefore cash planning. For example, the average collection period will dramatically influence the need for cash assets. In periods when sales are expected to increase, a long collection period will require the hospital to finance a larger amount of working capital in the form of increased receivables. The hospital must pay for its factors of production (i.e., supplies and labor) at the beginning of the cycle and wait to receive payment from its customers at the end of the cycle.

The above example also illustrates why a focus on a static measure of liquidity, such as a current ratio, sometimes can be deceiving. A rapid buildup in sales results in a large increase in accounts receivable, which increases the current ratio. Liquidity position, however, might not be improved in this case. The speed with which these receivables can be turned into cash is also an extremely important measure of liquidity.

The major purpose of a cash budget, an example of which is shown in Table 15-1, is to prepare an accurate estimate of future cash flows. With this estimate, the firm can arrange for short-term financing from a bank through a line of credit if it projects a period of cash deficiency, or it can invest surplus funds. Since yields are usually higher on longer-term investments, an investment for a six-month term is likely to result in greater income than an investment broken down into two three-month cycles. The cash budget, then, is the key document in terms of providing information regarding short-term investment and short-term financing decisions. A key factor in these projections is the desired level of cash balances that the firm would like to maintain. Firms that set low cash requirement levels are assuming more risks.

The entire cash management process can be broken down into five sequential steps.

1. Understand and manage the cash conversion cycle. In most situations, the objective is to minimize the required investment in working capital, where working capital is defined as current assets less current liabilities.
2. Develop a sound cash budget that accurately projects cash inflows and cash outflows during the planning horizon.
3. Establish the firm's minimum required cash balance. This level should be set in a manner consistent with the firm's overall risk assumption posture.
4. Arrange for working capital loans during those periods when the cash budget indicates short-term financing will be needed.
5. Invest cash surpluses in a way that will maximize the expected yield to the firm, subject to a prudent assumption of risk.

MANAGEMENT OF WORKING CAPITAL

The management of working capital items is related to short-term bank financing and investment of cash surpluses, which are discussed in subsequent sections of this chapter. The balance sheet for ABC Medical Center in Table 15-2 presents a useful way to examine the relevant items of working capital management. As examples, the following two categories

Table 15–1 Sample Cash Budget

| | First Quarter | | | Second Quarter | Third Quarter | Fourth Quarter |
	January	February	March			
Receipts from operations	$300,000	$310,000	$320,000	$1,000,000	$1,100,000	$1,100,000
Disbursements from operations	280,000	280,000	300,000	940,000	1,000,000	1,000,000
Cash available from operations	$ 20,000	$ 30,000	$ 20,000	$ 60,000	$ 100,000	$ 100,000
Other receipts						
Increase in mortgage payable		20,000		500,000		
Sale of fixed assets						
Unrestricted income—endowment			40,000	40,000	40,000	40,000
Total other receipts	0	$ 20,000	$ 40,000	$ 540,000	$ 40,000	$ 40,000
Other disbursements						
Mortgage payments			150,000		150,000	
Fixed-asset purchase				$ 480,000		
Funded depreciation			30,000	130,000	30,000	30,000
Total other disbursements	0	0	180,000	610,000	180,000	30,000
Net cash gain (loss)	$ 20,000	$ 50,000	$(120,000)	$ (10,000)	$ (40,000)	$ 110,000
Beginning cash balance	100,000	120,000	170,000	50,000	40,000	0
Cumulative cash	$120,000	$170,000	$ 50,000	$ 40,000	$ 0	$ 110,000
Desired level of cash	100,000	100,000	100,000	100,000	100,000	100,000
Cash above minimum needs (financing needs)	$ 20,000	$ 70,000	$ (50,000)	$ (60,000)	$ (100,000)	$ 10,000

Table 15-2 ABC Medical Center—Consolidated Balance Sheets, June 30, 1992 and 1991

	Assets	
	1992	1991
Current assets		
Cash	$ 1,216,980	$ 362,422
Investments	4,042,407	4,597,806
Patient accounts receivable (1992, $7,356,120; 1991, $6,253,629), less allowance for uncollectables	5,892,339	5,143,471
Other receivables		
Medicare	2,672,612	2,113,655
Miscellaneous	213,726	164,631
Inventories	1,302,598	1,174,295
Prepaid expenses	1,021,972	249,455
Current portion of deferred receivable from Medicare	454,404	502,904
Assets held by trustee	180,000	247,181
Total current assets	$16,997,038	$14,555,840
Other assets		
Investments	$ 10,642,621	$10,983,125
Accounts receivable—affiliated companies	4,510,105	2,036,436
Note receivable—affiliated company	700,000	700,000
Assets held by trustee		
Temporary cash account	—	59,643
Construction fund	2,717,846	4,018,948
Sinking fund	6,751,942	6,112,530
Interest receivable	118,142	94,231
Self-insurance funds	10,942,749	7,875,602
Unamortized debt issuance expenses	934,535	954,078
Investment in ABC insurance, Ltd.	209,655	—
Deferred receivables from Medicare	2,620,162	3,074,567
Prepaid pension cost	840,499	—
Unamortized past service cost	1,784,160	—
Total other assets	$ 42,772,416	$35,909,160
Property, plant, and equipment		
Land	$ 1,654,394	$ 1,649,912
Buildings	36,505,277	34,504,398
Improvements to land and leaseholds	1,272,205	1,263,959
Fixed equipment	8,812,615	8,713,615
Movable equipment	20,290,037	15,461,276
Capitalized leases	2,998,295	3,293,693

continues

Table 15–2 continued

	Assets	
	1992	1991
Total property, plant, and equipment	$ 71,532,823	$64,886,853
Less allowance for depreciation	27,763,195	22,037,503
	$ 43,769,628	$42,849,350
Construction and other work in progress	4,396,463	3,869,866
	$ 48,166,091	$46,719,216
Total assets	$107,935,545	$97,184,216

	Liabilities fund balances	
	1992	1991
Current liabilities		
Accounts payable trade	$ 2,297,672	$ 2,531,257
Accrued salaries and wages	1,366,777	1,035,496
Accrued liability for compensated absences	1,232,586	1,119,800
Accrued Medicare liability	317,302	1,881,895
Accrued indigent care assessment	1,170,001	1,061,742
Other accrued liabilities	611,230	444,916
Current portion of long-term debt	1,528,910	1,442,420
Total current liabilities	$ 8,524,478	$ 9,517,526
Other liabilities		
Accounts payable—affiliated companies	$ 1,993,815	—
Self-insurance liabilities	8,904,000	$ 7,048,000
	$ 10,897,815	$ 7,048,000
Long-term debt, less current maturities		
Series B bonds, less unamortized discount		
(1991, $1,144,348; 1986, $1,186,425)	$ 45,745,652	$46,063,575
Notes payable	3,902,113	1,888,504
Capital leases payable	127,535	595,407
	$ 49,775,300	$48,547,486
Fund balance		
Unrestricted		
Operations	$ 29,909,968	$24,781,866
Board designated	8,259,181	6,792,182
	38,169,149	31,574,048
Restricted	568,803	497,156
	$ 38,737,952	$32,071,204
	$107,935,545	$97,184,216

are discussed: (1) receivables and (2) accounts payable and accrued salaries and wages.

Receivables

Industry experience suggests that receivables constitute the most critical, but not exclusive, area of importance in cash management. In general, accounts receivable usually represent about 60 to 70 percent of a hospital's total investment in current assets. ABC Medical Center has $8,778,677 of receivables, or 51.6 percent of its total current assets, in 1992. This value is below the range cited above, largely because ABC Medical Center has a relatively low value for days in accounts receivable (50.3 days). This situation, of course, is favorable and is an objective of most financial managers. In general, the following three objectives are usually associated with accounts receivable management:

1. minimize lost charges.
2. minimize write-offs for uncollectable accounts
3. minimize the accounts receivable collection cycle

All three objectives are important, but our attention will be directed at the third, minimizing the collection cycle. Figure 15-2 provides a schematic that predicts intervals involved in the entire accounts receivable cycle. The following intervals usually exist in the hospital inpatient accounts receivable collection cycle:

- admission to discharge
- discharge to bill completion
- bill completion to receipt by payer
- receipt by payer to mailing of payment
- mailing of payment to receipt by hospital
- receipt by hospital to deposit in bank

The schematic in Figure 15-2 also provides the estimated time that could be involved in each interval, but these numbers vary widely among hospitals and payer categories within hospitals. They are intended only to

Figure 15–2 Accounts Receivable Collection Cycle in Days

---

show the relative importance of each interval in the overall accounts receivable collection cycle. The total number of days represented in Figure 15–2 is 66, which is reasonably close to the national average of 71 days during 1990.

Admission to Discharge (Seven Days)

Shortening this interval is not the critical objective from an accounts receivable perspective. This does not imply, however, that a reduction in length of stay is not an objective, because clearly it is. With fixed prices per case, reduced length of stay is particularly desirable from a cost management viewpoint.

In terms of managing the accounts receivable cycle, the real solution appears to be what takes place during this interval to expedite later collection. The following specific suggestions are provided:

- Determine whether interim billings are possible for patients with a long length of stay. Some third-party payers permit interim billings if the length of stay exceeds a specified time interval. Often this is 21 days. Although there may be relatively few patients in this category, it is important to recognize that the absolute value of accounts receivable represented by these patients can be quite large.

- Use advance deposits for nonemergent admissions. If insurance coverage can be verified, estimates of the total deductible and copayment amounts can be made. They can be requested from the patient prior to or at admission. In situations where this is not possible, a financing plan should be developed jointly between the hospital and the patient. Many patients appreciate being told before the fact what their insurance will pay and what their individual liability is likely to be.

- Obtain required insurance and eligibility information prior to admission for nonemergent patients. For emergency admissions, obtain the same data during the hospital stay. This will permit the preparation of a bill at, or shortly after, discharge.

Discharge to Bill Completion (15 Days)

Ideally this interval should be reduced as much as possible. Although this may be an objective, there are clearly some cost/benefit trade-offs to be evaluated. For example, speeding up the processing of bills is desirable only if the cost involved does not exceed the benefits of more rapid bill preparation. Basic suggestions include the following:

- Implement more timely billing and remove bottlenecks. Usually bills are not prepared at discharge so that late charges can be posted. If there is a constant delay in certain ancillary departments, corrective steps should be taken to improve posting. A holding period in excess of two to three days is probably not reasonable.
- Develop educational programs to show the effects of delays in completion of medical charts by physicians. Quite often, the major reason for delay in billing is an incomplete medical chart. Physicians must be informed of the effect these delays have on the hospital. Some hospitals have suspended admitting privileges of physicians who are constantly delinquent. Although this strategy may not be useful in many hospitals, it is worth considering in some situations.

Bill Completion to Receipt by Payer (Four Days)

The estimated four-day length of this time interval is directly related to mail time. Several steps may be useful in shortening this interval:

- Deliver bills to the post office as soon as they are prepared for mailing. Bills may be stacked in nice, neat piles and left on a desk for one or more days before being mailed.
- Consider electronic invoicing for large payers where this alternative is available. This cuts mail time to zero, and it may reduce the accounts receivable cycle for these payers by as much as four days.
- Try to settle all outpatient accounts at the point of discharge or departure. Each outpatient should be presented with a bill at the point of departure, and payment should be requested at this time.
- Submit a bill for any deductible and copayment amounts for hospital inpatients at the point of discharge. Settlement should take place at this point if the patient has been advised previously of the total amount due.

Receipt by Payer to Mailing of Payment (35 Days)

This interval varies greatly by type of payer. Some self-pay patients may have outstanding accounts for more than a year. Insurance companies may take an inordinate amount of time to settle bills because of disputes over coverage or reasonableness. Steps to be considered include the following:

- Selling some accounts receivable. Until recently hospitals could not legally sell Medicare accounts, but this is no longer true. More and more hospitals are considering selling accounts receivable because the rates of interest charged for these loans are relatively low. On a taxable basis, the interest rate will be slightly below prime for these asset-backed transactions.

- Using discounts for prompt payment. Many businesses have long provided discounts as financial incentives for early payment. This strategy may be used for self-pay portions of hospital bills and also for insurance payers. Sufficiently large discounts can also greatly reduce collection costs and write-offs. How large an inducement should be offered? This decision, of course, is firm-specific, but a 5 percent reduction for payment at discharge does not seem excessive.

- Setting up a system to respond quickly to third-party requests for additional data. Third-party payers often delay payment until requested information has been received and reviewed. At a minimum, a log should be maintained that shows dates of requests and dates of responses.

- Claiming all bad debts on the Medicare deductible and copayment portion of hospital bills. Medicare is liable for payment of bad debts experienced in these areas. It is important, however, to document reasonable collection efforts on the part of the hospital before Medicare liability for payment can be assured.

- Using frequent telephone follow-up to detect problems or concern with bills. In many situations self-pay hospital bills are not paid because there is a disagreement over the amount of the bill. This type of dispute can be avoided through prompt contact by a nonthreatening hospital employee who inquires about the patient's health and the amount of the bill. Sometimes this may be better handled by an independent party. When this approach has been used, reductions in bad debt write-offs have been very large.

Payment Mailed to Receipt by Hospital (Four Days)

Mail time is the cause for this four-day interval. These delays cannot be prevented for most small, personal accounts. In the case of a government or large insurance payer, a courier service can be used. Checks are picked up as they become available. For large out-of-town payers, a special courier arrangement can be used or direct deposits to an area bank initiated. Relatively large sums of money must be involved for these strategies to be cost effective.

Receipt by Hospital to Deposit in Bank (One or More Days)

Perhaps the only effective way this interval can be shortened is through the use of a lockbox arrangement in which payments go directly to a post office box that is cleaned at least once a day by bank employees. Bank employees deposit all payments, usually photocopy the checks, and send the copies—along with any enclosures—to the hospital for proper crediting. There is usually a cost for this service. The hospital must determine whether improvement in the cash flow, plus potential reduction in clerical costs, is worth the fee charged.

Accounts Payable and Accrued Salaries and Wages

Accounts payable and accrued salaries and wages represent spontaneous sources of financing. This means that these amounts are not usually negotiated but vary directly with the level of operations. Table 15–2 shows that ABC Medical Center had $2,297,672 in accounts payable trade and $1,366,777 in accrued salaries and wages in 1992. In addition, $1,993,815 of accounts payable from affiliated companies also existed. These amounts are not small and represent a sizable proportion of ABC's total financing.

Managing accounts payable and accrued salaries is similar to the management of accounts receivable, except in a reverse direction. Instead of acceleration, most financial managers would like to slow payment to these accounts. A number of approaches, as discussed in the literature, attempt to do this. Several relevant approaches for a free-standing hospital are as follows:

- Delay payment of an account payable until the actual due date. A number of hospitals often process invoices on receipt and initiate payment even when the invoices are not due for several weeks or several months. For example, many invoices for subscriptions to journals are sent out three to five months prior to their due dates. There is no reason to pay these invoices until they are actually due.
- Stretch accounts payable. This technique has been described frequently in the literature and is familiar to most individuals. Stretching

accounts payable simply means delaying payment until some point after the due date. Although this technique is often used, the ethics of the method are clearly debatable. In addition, delays may cause a hospital's credit rating to deteriorate. Vendors eventually will be unwilling to grant credit, or they may alter payment terms.

- Change the frequency of payroll. Although not a popular decision with employees, lengthening the payroll period can provide a significant amount of additional financing that is virtually free. For example, ABC Medical Center has an estimated weekly payroll of approximately $1,150,000. If ABC changes its payroll period from a weekly to a biweekly basis, it can create an additional source of financing equal to one week's payroll, or $1,150,000. Investing that money at 8 percent provides $92,000 in annual investment income. Fewer payroll periods may also reduce bookkeeping costs.

- Use banks in distant cities to pay vendors and employees. This method may delay check clearing and create a day or two of float. Float is defined as the difference between the bank balance and the checkbook balance. It also may be a questionable practice, depending on applicable state laws.

- Schedule deposits to checking accounts to match expected disbursements on a daily basis. A daily cash report can be prepared for each account, using information obtained daily through a telephone call to the bank or electronic access to the account. The report can thus reconcile data on beginning cash balances and disbursements expected to be made that day. Separate accounts for payroll are often maintained to recognize the predictability of check clearing. For example, payroll checks issued on a Friday may have a highly predictable pattern of check clearing. Knowledge of this distribution enables the treasurer to minimize the amount of funds needed in the account on any given day to meet actual disbursements and thus maximize the amount of invested funds.

SHORT-TERM BANK FINANCING

Many health care firms may experience a short-term need for funds during their operating cycles. The need for funds may have resulted from a predictable seasonality in the receipt and disbursement of cash or it may represent an unexpected business event, such as a strike. Commercial banks are the predominant sources of short-term loans, but other sources are also available. Several common arrangements used by health care firms to arrange for short-term loans include those discussed below.

Single-Payment Loan

The single-payment loan is the simplest credit arrangement and is usually given for a specific purpose, such as the purchase of inventory. The note can be either on a discount or an add-on basis. In the discount arrangement, the interest is computed and deducted from the face value of the note. The actual proceeds of the loan, then, would be in an amount less than the face of the note. In an add-on note, the interest is added to the final payment of the loan. In this arrangement, the borrower receives the full value of the loan at loan origination.

Line of Credit

A line of credit is an agreement that permits a firm to borrow up to a specified limit during a defined loan period. For example, a commercial bank may grant a $2 million line of credit to a hospital during a specific year. In that year, the hospital could borrow up to $2 million from the bank with presumably little or no additional paper work required. Lines of credit are either committed or uncommitted. In an uncommitted line, there is no formal or binding agreement on the part of the bank to loan money. If conditions change, the bank could decide not to loan any funds at all. In a committed line of credit, there is a written agreement that conveys the terms and conditions of the line of credit. The bank is legally required to lend money under the line as long as the terms and conditions have been met by the borrower. To cover the costs and risks incurred by the commercial bank in a committed line of credit, the bank charges a commitment fee. The fee is usually based on either the total credit line or the unused portion of the line.

Revolving Credit Agreements

A revolving credit is similar to a line of credit except that it is usually for a period of time greater than one year. Revolving credit agreements may be in effect for two to three years. Most revolving credit agreements are renegotiated prior to maturity. If the renegotiation occurs more than one year prior to maturity, a revolving credit agreement loan may be stated as a long-term debt and never appear as a current liability on a firm's balance sheet. Terms of revolving credit agreements are similar to those of lines of credit. Interest rates are usually variable and based on the prime rate or other money market rates.

Term Loans

Term loans are made for a specific period of time, usually ranging between two and seven years. The loans usually require periodic installment payments of the principal. This type of loan is frequently used to finance a tangible asset that will produce income in future periods, such as a computed tomography scanner. The asset acquired with the loan proceeds may be pledged as collateral for the loan.

Letters of Credit

Letters of credit are used by some hospitals as a method of bond insurance. A letter of credit is simply a letter from a bank stating that a loan will be made if certain conditions are met. In hospital bond financing, a letter of credit from a bank guarantees payment of the loan if the hospital defaults.

INVESTMENT OF CASH SURPLUSES

The term *surplus* is confusing, even among financial executives. For the purpose of this discussion, cash surplus is defined as money exceeding a minimum balance that the firm prefers to keep on hand to meet immediate operating expenses and to meet minor contingencies, plus any compensating balance required at its banks.

The balance sheet for ABC Medical Center shown in Table 15-2 lists a cash balance of $1,216,980 plus $4,042,407 in short-term investments as of June 30, 1992. These are the funds that are most often referred to as surplus cash when discussing short-term investment strategy. It is important to note that ABC Medical Center has significant investments in other areas. Most hospitals follow this procedure. For example, ABC Medical Center, as of June 30, 1992, has $10,642,621 in an investments account under the "Other assets" section of the balance sheet. These funds are probably designated for the eventual replacement of the hospital plant. In addition, sizable balances of funds are maintained with a trustee. For example, there is $2,717,846 in the construction fund account, $6,751,942 in the sinking fund account, $118,142 in the interest receivable account, and $10,942,749 in the self-insurance fund account. Most hospitals and health care firms maintain similar fund balances. It is critical for management to make investments that will meet the objectives of each specific fund and maximize the potential yield to the firm.

Often a portion of a firm's investment funds is restricted to money market investments. The term *money market* refers to the market for short-term securities, including U.S. Treasury bills, negotiable certificates of deposit, bankers' acceptances, commercial paper, and repurchase agreements. Maturities for money market investments can range from one day to one year. Funds invested in money market securities usually serve two roles. They represent (1) a liquidity reserve that can be used if the firm experiences a need for these funds and (2) a temporary investment of surplus funds that can result in the earning of a return.

If the funds are invested for periods of time longer than one year (for example, the investment of a replacement reserve fund), higher yields often result. These longer-term maturity investments may not be referred to as money market securities.

In evaluating alternative investment strategies, there are usually five basic criteria that should be reviewed. These are

1. price stability
2. safety of principal
3. marketability
4. maturity
5. yield

Price Stability

The importance of price stability, especially for money market investments, cannot be overemphasized. If a firm has a sudden need for cash, most major money market investments can be sold without any serious capital losses. Generally, U.S. Treasury bills are the most creditworthy money market investments, followed closely by other U.S. Treasury obligations and federal agency issues. Investment in securities with long-term maturities are subject to risk if interest rates rise. This explains why money market investments are usually restricted to maturities of less than one year.

Safety of Principal

Financial managers expect that the principal of their investment is generally not at risk. Treasury and federal agency obligations have little risk of principal loss through default. Bank securities (such as negotiable certificates of deposit and bankers' acceptances) and corporate obligations (such as commercial paper) are different matters. There may be a loss of principal through default, and care should be exercised in choosing these instruments. Information on banks is available in Polk's *World Bank Directory* and Moody's *Bank and Finance Manual.* There is no reason why a firm should not review the creditworthiness of its banks as carefully as banks review the financial position of loan applicants. It should be noted, however, that erosion of principal can occur through increases in money market interest rates, and these increases will subsequently have an impact on fixed-rate securities.

Marketability

Marketability varies among money market instruments. The term refers to the ability to sell a security quickly and with little price concession prior to maturity. In general, an active secondary trading market must exist to ensure the presence of marketability. Most major money market instruments do have active secondary markets, especially obligations of the U.S. Treasury. Some commercial paper, especially that of industrial firms, may be difficult to redeem prior to maturity.

Maturity

There is a clear relationship between the yield of a security and its maturity that can be summarized in a yield curve. Table 15–3 shows a set

Table 15–3 Yield to Maturity for Treasury Bills, July 6, 1989

Days to Maturity	Annualized Yield (%)
7	4.41
14	4.53
21	4.92
28	4.76
35	5.02
42	5.02
49	5.05
56	5.15
63	5.18
70	5.21

of values for Treasury bills on July 6, 1989. Some firms employ a strategy of investment described as "riding the yield curve." This strategy relies on the existence of an upward-sloping yield curve. Investments are made in longer-term securities that are sold prior to maturity.

Yield

Yield is a measure of the investment's return and is an important consideration. Yield is usually affected by maturity, expected default risk of principal, marketability, and price stability. In addition, taxability is often an issue. A tax-exempt health care firm has no incentive to invest in securities that are exempt from federal income taxes.

SUMMARY

Working capital management is concerned with decisions that have an impact on operating cash flows of the firm. Ideally, the objective of most working capital management systems is to accelerate the collection of cash from customers and to slow down the payment to suppliers and employees. Investment management is very important in many health care firms because of the relative size of their investment portfolios. Hospitals, for example, generate about 40 percent of their total net income from nonoperating sources, largely investment income. With so much at stake, health care firms need to improve performance in the cash and investment management area.

ASSIGNMENTS

1. Data from Table 15–2 indicate that $8,778,677 of accounts receivable were present at the end of 1992. If this value represented 50 days of average net patient revenue, and the hospital believed that this value could be reduced to 40 days, what dollar amount of new cash flow would be generated? If these funds were invested at 8.5 percent, how much additional investment income would result per year?

2. Alpha Home Health Inc. has received an invoice for medical supplies for $5,000 with terms of a 2 percent discount if paid within ten days. The invoice is due on the 30th day. What is the annual effective cost of interest on this invoice? If the 2 percent discount could still be taken even though the invoice was not paid until the 20th day, what would the effective interest rate be?

3. Pauly Hospital has been thinking about changing its payroll period from biweekly to monthly. Pauly currently has 600 employees with an annual payroll of $18,000,000. If Pauly could earn 9.5 percent on invested funds, what amount of new investment income could be

generated on an annual basis? If the cost of writing a payroll check is $1.50, what additional amount could be saved on an annual basis from switching to a monthly payroll period?

SOLUTIONS AND ANSWERS

1. The amount of new cash flow would be $1,755,735:

$$[(\$8,778,677)/50] \times [50 - 40]$$

The amount of additional investment income per year would be $149,238 (.085 × $1,755,735).

2. The 2 percent discount would be realized for making payment 20 days before required. The annual interest cost would be approximately 36 percent:

$$2.0\% \times [360 \text{ days}/20 \text{ days}] = 36.0\%$$

The new effective rate would be 18.0 percent if payment was delayed until the 20th day.

3. There are two ways to estimate the annual savings. The easiest method would be to multiply the difference in average wages payable by 9.5 percent:

$$\left[\frac{(18,000,000/12)}{2} - \frac{(18,000,000/26)}{2} \right] \times .095$$

$$= \$38,365$$

Alternatively, the difference in average payable amount per day can be calculated and multiplied times the average daily interest rate (.095/360), which is shown below:

Day	Average Payable Balance Monthly	Biweekly	Amount Invested	Investment Income
1	$49,315	$49,315	$0	$ 0.00
2	98,630	98,630	0	0.00
3	147,945	147,945	0	0.00
4	197,260	197,260	0	0.00
5	246,575	246,575	0	0.00
6	295,890	295,890	0	0.00
7	345,205	345,205	0	0.00
8	394,521	394,521	0	0.00
9	443,836	443,836	0	0.00
10	493,151	493,151	0	0.00
11	542,466	542,466	0	0.00
12	591,781	591,781	0	0.00
13	641,096	641,096	0	0.00
14	690,411	690,411	0	0.00
15	739,726	49,315	690,411	182.19
16	789,041	98,630	690,411	183.19
17	838,356	147,945	690,411	182.19

| | Average Payable Balance | | Amount | Investment |
Day	Monthly	Biweekly	Invested	Income
18	887,671	197,260	690,411	183.19
19	936,986	246,575	690,411	182.19
20	986,301	295,890	690,411	182.19
21	1,035,616	345,205	690,411	182.19
22	1,084,932	394,521	690,411	182.19
23	1,134,247	443,836	690,411	182.19
24	1,183,562	493,151	690,411	182.19
25	1,232,877	542,466	690,411	182.19
26	1,282,192	591,781	690,411	182.19
27	1,331,507	641,096	690,411	182.19
28	1,380,822	690,411	690,411	182.19
29	1,430,137	49,315	1,380,822	364.38
30	1,479,452	98,630	1,380,822	364.38
Monthly total				$3,279.45

Assuming that the above pattern holds, the annual return would be $39,353—12 times the monthly return. The savings from reduced checks would be $12,600 = [600 (26−12) × $1.50].

Chapter 16

Developing the Cash Budget

Chapter 15 stressed the importance of developing a sound cash budget that accurately projects cash inflows and cash outflows in the cash management process. Cash budgets embody the key source of information that permits management to determine the short-term needs for cash in the firm. When a cash budget is modified to include the effects of alternative outcomes, financial executives can better assess the issue of liquidity risk and make decisions that will reduce the probability of a liquidity crisis. These decisions fall into one of three categories:

1. Increase the level of cash and investment reserves.
2. Restructure the maturity of existing debt.
3. Arrange a line of credit with a bank.

DETERMINING REQUIRED CASH AND INVESTMENT RESERVES

Historically, the finance literature has identified three major reasons for holding cash balances:

1. transactional
2. precautionary
3. speculative

The transactional motive relates to the need to hold cash balances to allow routine expenditures for such things as payroll, supplies, and capital investment. The precautionary motive revolves around the concept of risk.

Most firms do not know with certainty what their actual disbursements and receipts will be during any interval of time. To avoid this risk, many firms add some cushion to their cash balances so that they can meet unexpected contingencies. The speculative motive represents the desire by management to have access to cash in order to take advantage of special investment opportunities that promise unusually high returns.

In the health care sector, which comprises many voluntary firms, there is another major need for holding cash and investment reserves—replacing fixed assets. Voluntary health care providers are not in a position to raise new equity from the stock market, and therefore they must set aside cash to meet normal replacement needs. Failure to set aside adequate levels of replacement reserves ultimately will result in excessive levels of debt financing and/or closure.

Firms differ with respect to their needs for cash to meet transactions and in their precautionary motives. Firms that have greater instability in cash flows need to carry more liquid assets to reduce the risk of cash insolvency. Access to short-term lines of credit may also be important in determining required cash position. Although these factors and others may affect the level of cash carried to meet transactional and precautionary motives, there are some reasonable and generally accepted norms. For example, the average days' cash on hand for both the hospital industry and the Standard & Poor's 400 industrials generally runs between 15 and 20 days. (See Chapter 6 for a further discussion of this indicator.) For most health care providers, a sum of 20 days' cash on hand seems like a reasonable target.

Some funds should also be set aside to meet replacement needs in the future. As a general rule of thumb, most voluntary health care firms should try to have the following amount of cash available for replacement needs:

$$(100\% - \text{Desired debt policy }\%) \times \text{Replacement cost need}$$

The firm's desired debt policy represents the expected overall percentage of future capital needs that will be financed with debt. This represents the target for all capital expenditures, not just major renovation projects. For many voluntary hospitals, this percentage appears to be about 50. Hospitals may finance major renovation projects with 80 to 90 percent debt, but then they will use 80 to 90 percent equity on smaller routine replacement projects, such as capital equipment. The replacement cost need is equal to the amount of accumulated depreciation that would currently exist if the fixed assets were stated in current replacement cost dollars rather than historical acquisition dollars. Table 16–1 illustrates this concept.

Table 16–1 Estimating Replacement Cost Need

	Acquisition Cost	*Replacement Cost*
Gross property, plant and equipment	$24,000,000	$42,000,000
Less accumulated depreciation	8,000,000	14,000,000
Net property, plant and equipment	$16,000,000	$28,000,000

The replacement cost need in Table 16–1 would be $14,000,000. The firm has a plant base that would require $42,000,000 to replace in today's market, but it has already used up one-third of that plant base because one-third of the historical cost has depreciated to date. If the firm's board had established a debt policy of 50 percent, the firm would need $7,000,000 worth of investments to meet this debt target. A firm with a target debt policy of 50 percent would require a replacement viability ratio of 1.0. (See Chapter 6 for a discussion of this indicator.)

Table 16–2 illustrates how a firm might calculate its desired cash and investment position. In the example in Table 16–2 there is a surplus of short-term cash because the firm has 30.5 days' cash on hand when its required target is only 20.0. The firm, however, is deficient in the area of replacement reserves because its replacement viability ratio is only .68 and the target ratio is 1.00. Overall, the firm has a total cash deficiency of $2,836,000.

There are several other areas in which a firm must maintain cash and liquid asset investment that result from legal or regulatory requirements. For example, hospitals that self-insure their professional liability are usually required to maintain stipulated levels of funds with a trustee,

Table 16–2 Calculation of Required Cash and Investment Position

	Short-Term Cash	*Replacement Reserves*	*Total*
Present balance	$4,200,000	$ 9,100,000	$13,300,000
Present ratio*	30.5	.68	
Desired target ratio	20.0	1.00	
Multiplier (Desired/present)	20.0/30.5	1.00/.68	
Required position	$2,754,000	$13,382,000	$16,136,000
Surplus (deficiency)	($1,446,000)	($ 4,282,000)	($ 2,836,000)

*Days' cash on hand ratio is the short-term ratio used, and replacement viability ratio is the replacement reserve ratio used.

usually a bank. In a similar manner, funding for pension or retirement programs also requires cash and investment balances to be set aside. Finally, most long-term tax-exempt lenders require borrowers to maintain reserves of cash and investments to meet several stipulated purposes, such as debt service reserve.

SOURCES AND USES OF CASH

In its most basic form, a cash budget is a statement that projects how the firm's cash balance position will change between two points in time. Changes to cash position are categorized as either sources of cash flow (sometimes called *receipts*) or uses of cash flow (sometimes called *disbursements*). Sources of cash include

- collection of accounts receivable
- cash sales
- investment income
- sale of assets
- financings
- capital contributions

Uses of cash include

- payments to employees
- payments to suppliers
- payments to lenders for interest and principal
- purchase of fixed assets
- investments

It is important to note that the definition of *income* and the definition of *cash flows* are not the same. This means that the amount reported for revenues in any given time period most likely will not equal the actual amount of cash realized. The only exception would be a case in which all revenues were produced by cash sales. In most health care settings there is a lag between the recording of revenue and the collection of the resulting account receivable. In the same manner, expenses reported for wages and salaries and supplies may not actually equal the amount of cash expended within the time period. As the time period expands, say from a month to a year, the differences between revenues and expenses and receipts and disbursements begin to narrow. If one expanded the time period from one year to twenty years the difference between cash flows and income would be very minimal. Unfortunately, most financial managers are interested in cash flows over much shorter periods of time. Many firms have cash budgets defined on at least a monthly basis, and some have biweekly or weekly cash budgets.

When cash flows are extremely volatile but reasonably forecastable, cash budgets for shorter terms are desirable. If cash flows are reasonably stable, a cash budget on a quarterly basis may be appropriate. Although most firms develop cash budgets on a monthly basis, it is very common for these budgets to be revised on a periodic basis because original budget assumptions often prove inaccurate.

The primary factor affecting the validity of the cash budget is the accuracy of the forecasts for individual cash flow categories. The greater the degree of possible variation between actual and forecasted cash flow, the higher the liquidity need of the firm. Firms that cannot predict cash flow with much certainty should increase their cash balances or negotiate lines of credit to escape the possibility of severe cash insolvency problems.

PREPARING THE CASH BUDGET

The single most important area in cash budgeting is the revenue forecast. The revenue for health care providers will be a function of two factors: (1) volumes by product line and (2) expected prices by payer category.

Most firms use a variety of methods to estimate volumes of services during the cash budget period. As discussed in Chapter 10 and shown in Figure 16–1, the revenue budget is critically related to the statistics budget. In general there are two major categories of methods used to develop estimates of volumes: (1) subjective forecasts and (2) statistical forecasts.

In reality most forecasts probably combine elements of both subjective and statistical methods. Subjective forecasts are often referred to as "seat of the pants" methods, and other less flattering names. Subjective forecasts do, however, have a place in the estimation of product line volumes. The critical factor in the reliability of a subjective forecast is the wisdom and understanding of the forecaster. In cases where future volumes are likely to deviate from historical patterns, subjective forecasts may be the most reliable method of forecasting. Surveying medical staff members regarding their expected admissions during the next year is a form of subjective forecasting, but one that may be extremely reliable.

Statistical forecasts run the gamut from major econometric studies to simple time series techniques. Whatever the method, there is an underly-

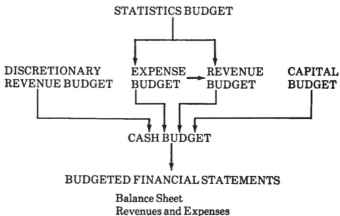

Figure 16–1 Integration of the Budgetary Process

ing assumption surrounding a statistical forecast that says the future can be predicted based on some mathematical model extrapolated from the past. If the relationships or model on which the forecasts are based have changed, future forecasts can be misleading.

In some cases predicting prices for the firm's products and services may be almost as difficult as projecting volumes. Health care firms are price takers in most situations. This means that they rely on someone else to establish prices for their services. Medicare and Medicaid are two organizations that set prices and exert tremendous influence on a major portion of the total revenue budget. One would think that prices would be established far enough in advance by these payers so that forecasting prices would be a simple matter. Unfortunately, sometimes interim prices stay interim for longer than expected, and promised increases just never materialize. Although the differences between expected and actual prices may be relatively small, the sheer volume of the Medicare and Medicaid book of business is so large that small swings in prices have a major impact on net cash flows. Most health care providers operate with relatively small margins—somewhere between 1 and 3 percent. When Medicare and Medicaid account for 50 percent or more of a firm's total business, a small forecast error of 1 or 2 percent in the final prices to be paid by Medicare and Medicaid can have a disastrous impact on final operating margins.

Health care firms also increasingly are being asked to discount more and more of their business to other major groups such as HMOs, preferred provider organizations, commercial insurers, and self-insured employers. This makes projecting actual realized net prices more and more difficult.

Projecting revenues does not equate to projecting cash flows. Collections will lag the actual booking of revenues by some time period. One common way to develop forecasts of patient receipts is through the use of "decay curves." These curves relate future collections to past billings. Figure 16–2 depicts a decay curve with the following pattern of collections:

1. The first 15 percent of any month's revenue is collected in the first month.
2. The next 30 percent of any month's revenue is collected in the second month.
3. The next 25 percent of any month's revenue is collected in the third month.
4. The next 20 percent of any month's revenue is collected in the fourth month.
5. The next 5 percent of any month's revenue is collected in the fifth month.
6. The remaining 5 percent of any month's revenue is written off and not collected.

Table 16–3 presents a cash receipts summary for the first six months of the year. The collection pattern reflected in the decay curve of Figure 16–2 can be seen in Table 16–3. For example, of the $2,000,000 of January revenue, 15 percent ($300,000) is collected in January, 30 percent ($600,000) is collected in February, 25 percent ($500,000) is collected in March, 20 percent ($400,000) is collected in April, 5 percent ($100,000) is collected in May, and the remaining 5 percent ($100,000) is written off and not collected. The revenues in the following months reflect the same collection pattern. Although cash receipts and revenues are most often correlated, it is not always true that the months producing the highest revenue will be the months with the highest cash collection. For many hospitals, the highest cash collection month is often one to two months after the highest revenue month.

Changes in collection patterns of major third-party payers can have a significant effect on cash flows and should be reflected immediately in revised cash budgets. For example, if Medicaid decides to delay the payment of patient bills by 60 days to conserve cash, the cash budget must be revised to reflect this new payment pattern. Increasing values for deductibles and copayments under many health care insurance plans may also delay collection patterns and increase eventual write-offs because the self-pay portion of the total health care bill may not be paid by the patient.

Additional cash receipts may come from sources other than revenue collection. Investment income and sale of assets are identified as the only

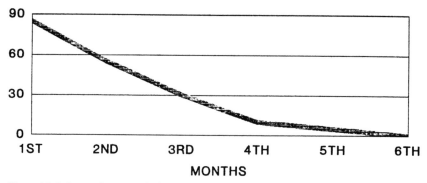

Figure 16-2 Decay Curve Analysis: Percentage Uncollected by Month after Billing

Table 16-3 Cash Receipts Summary (in thousands)

		January	February	March	April	May	June
Beginning accounts							
receivable revenue	$3,600	$1,600	$1,000	$500	$100		
January	2,000	300	600	500	400	100	0
February	2,100	0	315	630	525	420	105
March	2,000	0	0	300	600	500	400
April	1,900	0	0	0	285	570	475
May	1,800	0	0	0	0	270	540
June	1,800	0	0	0	0	0	270
Subtotal		$1,900	$1,915	$1,930	$1,910	$1,860	$1,790
Other cash							
investment income		20	20	50	20	20	50
Sale of assets		0	0	25	0	0	0
Subtotal		$ 20	$ 20	$ 75	$ 20	$ 20	$ 50
Estimated cash							
receipts		$1,920	$1,935	$2,005	$1,930	$1,880	$1,840

other sources in Table 16-3, but other sources may also exist. Contributions, sale of stock, and the issuance of new debt are also possibilities.

After forecasting cash receipts, a schedule of expected cash disbursements is necessary before the cash budget is complete. The two largest categories in most health care firms are labor and supplies. Labor costs or payroll most often represents about 60 percent of a hospital's total expenses. The expense budget will identify expected labor or payroll expenses by month, but payroll expenses do not translate into cash disbursements. Most health care firms have the majority of their payroll on a biweekly basis, which necessitates some accruals. For example, labor expense in January might be $1,200,000, but actual payroll might be $1,650,000 because there were three biweekly payroll periods. (There are 26 biweekly payroll periods in a year. Every month will have at least two payroll periods, but two months will have three.) Conversely, in other months during which only two biweekly pay periods were present, actual payroll expense might be less than budgeted labor expense.

Payroll expense must also be adjusted for withholding and other deductions. For example, the January payroll of $1,650,000 might be broken down as follows:

Total Payroll	$1,650,000
Less	
Income taxes	330,000
Social security	126,000
Other deductions	85,000
Net payroll	$1,109,000

The above figure for net payroll—$1,109,000—does not include additional payroll taxes, such as workers' compensation, unemployment, and the employer's share of social security. Other fringe benefits such as pension and health insurance also are not included.

As with payroll, the expense budget will include a value for supplies expense, but that value will not equal the actual disbursement for supplies. Table 16–4 presents a schedule of expected cash disbursements.

The only remaining task is to combine the cash receipts summary and the cash disbursements summary to create the cash budget. Before doing so, a desired level of cash balances must be defined. For this example, it will be assumed that a short-term cash balance of $1,300,000 is required to

---

Table 16–4 Cash Disbursements Summary (in thousands)

	January	February	March	April	May	June
Salary and wages	$1,190	$ 900	$ 980	$ 880	$ 850	$ 840
Fringe benefits	155	130	135	125	115	110
Purchases	315	385	405	390	385	385
Other disbursements	185	205	225	190	210	250
Capital expenditures	25	15	100	350	45	60
Debt service	0	0	300	0	0	300
Estimated disbursement	$1,870	$1,635	$2,145	$1,935	$1,605	$1,945

Table 16-5 Cash Budget Summary (in thousands)

	January	February	March	April	May	June
Beginning cash balance	$1,350	$1,400	$1,700	$1,560	$1,555	$1,830
Add receipts	1,920	1,935	2,005	1,930	1,880	1,840
Less disbursements	1,870	1,635	2,145	1,935	1,605	1,945
Cash flow	50	300	(140)	(5)	275	(105)
Ending cash balance	$1,400	$1,700	$1,560	$1,555	$1,830	$1,725

meet the firm's transactional and precautionary motives. If the firm cannot maintain this balance it must make a decision whether it will transfer funds from its replacement reserves or whether it will borrow short-term through a line of credit arrangement.

Table 16-5 combines the cash receipts and cash disbursements summaries to produce the cash budget. The cash budget shows that in some months the firm will experience negative cash flows. However, there is no month in this initial six-month forecast that will fall below the required cash balance of $1,300,000. If the forecast proves to be accurate, the firm will not need to arrange any short-term financing, nor will it need to transfer any replacement reserves. In fact, it could transfer some of the short-term cash balances that are above the required minimal balance of $1,300,000 to replacement reserves. The firm could transfer all of the $50,000 in cash flow that occurs in January to replacement reserves, but only $160,000 of the $300,000 net cash flow in February could be transferred to replacement reserves. Because the months of March and April have negative cash flows, some of the February surplus ($140,000) will be needed to meet the deficits in March and April.

By examining the pattern of expected cash flows, the treasurer of the firm can better decide the duration and maturity of possible investments. Usually, longer-term securities will yield higher returns. Therefore, if the funds are not expected to be needed for six months, the firm would be better off to invest in a six-month Treasury bill than a 30-day Treasury bill.

SUMMARY

Cash budgets are critical pieces of information that financial executives in all health care firms need to prepare and monitor very closely. The forecast of cash flows should help management determine whether additional financing will be needed and in what amounts and for what duration of time. The information will also permit the short-term investment of surplus funds so that yields on those investments might be improved.

Cash budgets are forecasts, and there is no guarantee that the results forecast will be achieved. It is important for management to test the sensitivity of the forecasts to alternative scenarios, such as slowdowns in collections or declines in revenues.

ASSIGNMENTS

1. Morgan Village is a voluntary, nonprofit, continuing care retirement center. At the present time it has $1,200,000 set aside for replacement and renovation. If its replacement viability ratio is presently .35 and it would like a target replacement viability ratio of .75, how much additional funding must it set aside for replacement purposes?

2. Huntley Hospital must maintain $3.3 million in a debt service reserve fund maintained by the bond trustee. The board members would like to count this balance when determining the amount of cash that they should carry for meeting normal transactions needs. Is this reasonable?

3. Dean Nursing Home has a payer mix of approximately 60 percent Medicaid and 40 percent private pay. The state Medicaid program has recently experienced major funding problems, and the frequency of payment for Medicaid beneficiaries is unclear for the next year. How might this information affect Dean's cash management?

4. Prepare a cash budget for Aztec Home Health Agency for the months of May, June, and July. The firm wishes to maintain a $200,000 minimum cash balance during the period, and it presently has a $220,000 balance. Revenues are presented below:

January	$ 500,000
February	500,000
March	600,000
April	600,000
May	700,000
June	800,000
July	1,000,000
August	1,000,000

The firm collects 30 percent of its revenue in the month billed, 30 percent in the next month, and 25 percent in the following month. The firm fails to collect 15 percent of its revenue because of either bad debt or contractual allowances. Expense budget relationships are presented below:

Payroll = $50,000 per month plus .50 × Revenues
Supplies = .10 × Revenues
Rent = $50,000 per month
Debt service = $150,000 in July
Capital expenditures = $75,000 in June

Payroll expense is paid 80 percent in the month incurred and 20 percent in the following month. Supplies expense is paid in the following month. All other items are paid in the month reported. Determine during which months Aztec will be able to invest surplus funds and during which months it might need to borrow.

SOLUTIONS AND ANSWERS

1. The total amount of required replacement reserves should be $(.75/.35) \times \$1,200,000$, or $2,571,428. Morgan Village therefore set aside $1,371,428.

2. No. The debt service reserve fund is not under the control of Huntley Hospital management and could not be used to meet normal transactional needs for cash such as payroll and purchases.

3. Because cash flows are likely to be more volatile next year, Dean should consider enhancing its liquidity position. This might be accomplished by increasing the amount of short-term cash reserves or negotiating a line of credit.

4. Surplus funds will be available during May and June, but a loan will need to be obtained during July, as the following cash budget shows:

	May	June	July
Receipts			
March revenue	150,000	0	0
April revenue	180,000	150,000	0
May revenue	210,000	210,000	175,000
June revenue	0	240,000	240,000
July revenue	0	0	300,000
Total receipts	540,000	600,000	715,000
Disbursements			
Payroll			
April	70,000	0	0
May	320,000	80,000	0
June	0	360,000	90,000
July	0	0	440,000
Total payroll	390,000	440,000	530,000
Supplies	60,000	70,000	80,000
Rent	50,000	50,000	50,000
Debt service	0	0	150,000
Capital expenditures	0	75,000	0
Total Disbursements	500,000	635,000	810,000
Net cash flow	40,000	(35,000)	(95,000)
Beginning balance	220,000	260,000	225,000
Ending cash	260,000	225,000	130,000
Less required minimum amount	200,000	200,000	200,000
to invest (borrow)	60,000	25,000	(70,000)

Index